The Walls
Came Tumbling
Down

The Walls Came Tumbling Down

The Collapse of Communism in Eastern Europe

Gale Stokes

New York   Oxford
OXFORD UNIVERSITY PRESS
1993

Oxford University Press

Oxford   New York   Toronto
Delhi   Bombay   Calcutta   Madras   Karachi
Kuala Lumpur   Singapore   Hong Kong   Tokyo
Nairobi   Dar es Salaam   Cape Town
Melbourne   Auckland   Madrid

and associated companies in
Berlin   Ibadan

Published by Oxford University Press, Inc.
200 Madison Avenue, New York, New York 10016

Oxford is a registered trademark of Oxford University Press

Library of Congress Cataloging-in-Publication Data
Stokes, Gale, 1933–
The walls came tumbling down :
the collapse of communism in Eastern Europe /
Gale Stokes.
p.   cm.   Includes index.
ISBN 0-19-506644-8 (cloth). — ISBN 0-19-506645-6 (pbk.)
1. Europe, Eastern—History—1945–
I. Title.   DJK50.S75   1993   940'.09717—dc20   92-44862

4 6 8 9 7 5 3

Printed in the United States of America
on acid-free paper

For Roberta, John, and Karen

Preface

The term *Eastern Europe* as used in this book refers to the five countries of east central Europe and of southeastern Europe that were formerly part of the Soviet bloc, plus the German Democratic Republic and Yugoslavia. Albania is not discussed. The book is based in part on interviews conducted with a number of persons who experienced the events of the past twenty years. A few interviews were conducted in the United States, but most were done in Eastern Europe early in 1992. During these interviews, which usually lasted from one to two hours, I took notes by hand. Within a few hours of each interview I transcribed the handwritten notes into my note-book computer, and when I returned to the United States I printed them out. When a citation in the text is made to "interview," with no further identification, it refers to one of these interviews, the printed notes of which are in my possession.

Throughout the book citations are made to *Keesing's*, with a page number. This refers to *Keesing's Record of World Events*, or its predecessor, which is a consecutively paginated publication dating from 1931. The abbreviation RFE refers to the various publications of Radio Free Europe, such as a Situation Report (SR). JPRS refers to the publications of the Joint Publication Report Service. FBIS refers to the daily reports published by the Federal Broadcast Information Service. Materials cited from all three of these extremely useful sources can be located by the data given in the footnotes referring to them. Abbreviations for organizations and their original titles can be found in the index.

The book was written over a two-year period. I spent the first year (1990–1991) at the Woodrow Wilson International Center for Scholars, where access to the Library of Congress and contact with many knowl-edgeable scholars were of enormous help to me. I would especially like to thank John Lampe, director of the East European Program of the Center for his professional and particularly for his personal counsel; Sam Wells for assigning me such a nice office; and Dean Anderson for being such a good listener. The second year (1991–1992) was made possible by a grant from the National Council for Soviet and East European Research, which permitted me to spend five months as a guest of the Institute for Sino-Soviet Studies of George Washington University (now the Institute for European, Russian, and Eurasian Studies). I do not think I could have completed this book in its final form without access to this organization's unparalleled collection of materials, which is unusually accessible to scholars. In particular, I would like to thank James R. Millar, director of the institute, for being such an accommodating and friendly host.

During the last six months of the two-year period, Allen J. Matusow, dean of humanities at Rice University, provided me with relief from my teaching duties. I would like to thank both him and the university for the extremely generous way they have supported this project. My grant from the National Council also provided the funds with which I took a seven-week trip through all six countries discussed in this book during February and March 1992. The impressions and interviews that this trip provided were very important in shaping the final version. Naturally, errors and infelicities remain my responsibility. I would appreciate hearing from readers who notice factual or other errors.

During the course of working on this book various assistants have provided valuable aid in finding materials, photocopying, and the like, and I would like to thank them very much for their invaluable help. They are Zlatko Kovac, Susan Lusi, and Mark Teel. At Rice University I would like to thank Cathy Monholland, whose meticulous editing saved me many and varied errors. I am also grateful to Nancy Lane of Oxford University Press for having confidence in this project.

It is not possible to thank all of the approximately eighty persons who were kind enough to meet with me on my trip through Eastern Europe, but I would like to give special thanks to my main hosts in several cities: Jiří Zlatuška in Brno; Miroslav Hroch in Prague; Włodek Wesełowski in Warsaw; Mária Kovács in Budapest; Kurt Treptow in Cluj; Mihai Ionescu and Harry Bucur in Bucharest; Ivanka Nedeva and Ivan Ilchev in Sofia; Miodrag Perišić, Andrej Mitrović, and Ljubinka Trgovčević in Belgrade; and Vid Pečjak in Ljubljana. I thank you all, and I hope to see each of you again soon.

At many points in the writing of this book my wife Roberta also might have said, "I hope to see you again soon," since we spent five months apart while I was at George Washington and two more apart while I was traveling in Eastern Europe. I do not think either of us liked this much, but at least I had my project to keep me company. I have been blessed by her love and her understanding many times and in many ways, and the period over which this book was written was not the least of those. Some things in life we can choose, others are blind luck. Finding Roberta, or somehow being in the right place to be found some thirty-five years ago, was certainly the luckiest thing that ever happened to me.

Houston   G. S.
February 1993

Contents

The Walls
Came Tumbling
Down

Introduction

Students who graduate from college after the turn of the millennium will almost certainly look back on the two great movements of the twentieth century, fascism and communism, with the same sort of incomprehension that students of earlier generations looked back on the religious wars of the sixteenth and seventeenth centuries. How was it possible that two movements whose claims seem so implausible, almost even comical—only a few months after the collapse of the Communist regimes in Eastern Europe the main reaction of visitors viewing historical displays from the Communist era was laughter[1]—should have not only attracted millions of enthusiastic followers but, on the basis of what their adherents considered high principle, sent millions of people to anguished deaths? Attuned to a world in which diversity is not only the order of the day but intellectually the only respectable theoretical position, students will need substantial imaginative powers to recreate the mindset in which claims to absolute truth justified dictators in dominating not only their neighbors but their own people as well.

The young people of the next century will need to make this imaginative effort in good measure because of events that took place in Eastern Europe in 1989, when suddenly and—all hindsight to the contrary—quite unexpectedly the hitherto subjugated and passive peoples of Eastern Europe appeared in the streets and threw off the hollow regimes that had ruled them for forty years. In the space of a few months the nations of Eastern Europe, which since 1948 had been considered simply adjuncts of the Soviet system—a bloc of subservient satellites tied by iron apron strings to the motherland of revolution—showed themselves to be full participants in the drama of European transformation, or at least expectant participants. Economically devastated by forty years of mismanagement, the East Europeans proved to be considerably less politically devastated by forty years of living a lie. Within a few months most of the East European countries established new, non-Communist governments that superficially looked a good deal like democratic systems elsewhere in Europe, began or promised economic reforms, and repudiated the Communist parties that had seemed all powerful only one or two years earlier. How could this have happened with such speed and thoroughness that the old regimes already have receded into the mists of a futile and lost past?

The answer given in this book concentrates on the decay and collapse of communism in Eastern Europe since 1968, the year when an invasion of Czechoslovakia by Soviet-led forces ended any realistic hopes that the system of central planning and totalitarian political aspiration could reform itself. But the historical setting in which the decline of "real existing socialism," as East European communism styled itself in the 1980s, took place is a very broad one. The collapse of communism in Eastern Europe was a significant milestone in the history of the fundamental transformation human societies have undergone over the past few hundred years. Even though this process has no generally accepted name—the industrial revolution, the great transformation, the energy revolution, the great transition, and many others have been proposed—it is clear that something quite remarkable has occurred. Devices that convert chemical energy into useful work through electricity and internal combustion engines dominate the daily life of the industrialized world. Information systems, beginning with printing by movable type, moving on to the newspaper and the telegraph, and today characterized by television and the computer, daily place enormous amounts of data into the hands of billions of people. Transportation systems, limited two hundred years ago to the speed of the horse, now routinely move large numbers of people and goods at high speeds hundreds, even thousands, of miles in a single day. In the industrialized world most human beings no longer live in rural areas as they did for ten thousand years after the invention of agriculture but in huge urban agglomerations, often covered with foul-smelling air. Gender relations, family linkages, work habits, ways of dying, care of the sick—in short, every aspect of life—has changed, often dramatically, in the last few hundred years.

These entirely new social and economic conditions made the political structures societies had found useful for hundreds or even thousands of years obsolete. In the twentieth century, for example, kings, for tens of generations the vital linchpins of European societies, became merely sentimental icons of national tradition, figures out of living wax museums, while the proud title "emperor" dropped almost completely out of use, retaining nothing of its grandeur except the musty odor of a distant past. Since about the eighteenth century first Western societies and then societies throughout the world have had to find new political devices to cope with new situations. In the twentieth century Europeans have tried three extensive experiments in new forms of political and economic organization in their efforts to meet the challenge of the great transformation. I call these three experiments, all first broached in the eighteenth century, the antirational, the hyperrational, and the pluralist genres of political and economic solutions.

By calling the fascist and Nazi experiments of the period between the two world wars antirationalist I mean to suggest that the leaders of these movements of rage and rejection craved the technological power put into their hands by the industrial revolution, but at the same time they dis- avowed the rationalizing intellectual and social concomitants of the Enlightenment and the French Revolution. As Joseph Goebbels put it in 1933, "The year 1789 is hereby eradicated from history."[2] The Nazis believed, as Schelling did, that the universe held "a primal, nonrational force that can be grasped only by the intuitive power of men of imaginative genius."[3] Nazism and fascism rejected reason for power, individuality for *sacro egoismo,* virtue for vainglory, transparency for obscurantism, consti- tutions for the *Führerprinzip,* humanitarianism for racial fanaticism, objec- tivity for prejudice, and, in the end, the guillotine for the gas chamber. The horrible end of Nazism in the holocaust of World War II clearly dem- onstrated the bankruptcy of the antirational experiment.

I call the second major twentieth-century effort to organize the great transformation hyperrational not because the policies of Communist states were instrumentally suited to their goal of liberating mankind, because they were not, and not because the effort was rational in the economic sense, because the centrally planned economies were economically irratio- nal, but because Communists based their pretensions to power on their claim that they could transform the world through understanding it ratio- nally. If the Nazis rejected reason in favor of blood, the Communists ele- vated Descartes's assertion that through reason we humans could "render ourselves the masters and possessors of nature" to a transcendent law of society that justified a totalitarian regime.[4] Communists believed they had a right to direct all aspects of society because they had a correct, or "sci- entific," understanding of the laws of human development, which they were putting to use to conquer nature and to create a truly human society. If 1945 proved the antirationalist genre of solutions inadequate to the twentieth century, 1989 was the year that the hyperrationalist genre proved wanting as well.[5]

The pedigree of the third genre of solutions, pluralism, is not as clear or as easily traced as the ones that led to Nazism or Stalinism because by definition pluralism is so multifaceted. Pluralism comprises a set of inter- acting and more or less balanced institutions that permit change to occur. Pluralism is not a system so much as it is a process regulated by elections, parliaments, relatively open public media, free association, and mixed forms of property ownership. The pluralist political systems established by the second half of the twentieth century in Western Europe and North

America are characterized by representative democracy, a politics of accommodation in which interests contend openly in the public sphere, political parties that compete in contested elections, government that is responsible in some way to the people, an electorate that eventually takes in all adults, and legal protection of civil rights. To the extent that these societies base themselves on the insight that political structures must be constructed to encompass human frailties rather than to eradicate them, one may speak of them as constituting a genre of solutions to the problems posed by the great transformation of the past few centuries.

The most dynamic sphere in which pluralist political structures have permitted process to occur is the economic. Underlying the flexible nature of pluralist economies is a confidence that in the end market mechanisms are the best regulators of production and distribution. But within that general rubric the variety of types of mixed economies is enormous: French indicative planning and ownership of large enterprises, Swedish socialism, German codetermination, American mixed economy, and Japanese cooperative structures. These societies demonstrated their flexibility with particular clarity in the 1970s and 1980s, when the socialist economies were collapsing. The multiplication of computers, accelerated by the inventions and financial success of thousands of individual innovators, completely transformed the way world business was conducted but did not threaten the political stability of any pluralist society.

Of the three main genres of political and economic experimentation, only pluralism has proven minimally adequate to the social and technological demands of the twentieth century. A glance at the problems facing most people in the Third World and many people in the First World suggests that many issues remain on the agenda of pluralist societies. But the pluralist genre has been far less costly in human suffering than the other two genres, each of which contributed tens of millions of violent deaths to the slaughter bench of history, and pluralism has proven able to contain and even to encourage economic growth. This does not mean that no one will ever propose a fascist solution or a Communist one again. It may be that in some places, possibly even in Eastern Europe, such proposals will even be tried. But it does mean that fascism and communism will never be able to generate the same kind of enthusiastic hopefulness among broad strata of society that was their hallmark at the peak of their twentieth-century successes. The great message of the twentieth century is not positive but negative: we have not learned what works so much as what does not work. But at least pluralism can still look forward. The failures of 1945 and 1989 mean that from now on the other two genres will always be backward-looking dead ends.

One of the fields on which both these failed experiments were tried was Eastern Europe, and it is in Eastern Europe that the heirs of fascism and communism are embarked on a new experiment: creating the pluralistic societies that the pressures of the other two experiments made impossible earlier. Under the best of circumstances, the brand new East European states issuing from World War I would have found it difficult to achieve stability and democracy. But given the faulty international settlements of the Great War, strong feelings of national pride, a worldwide economic depression, and the re-emergence of a strong Germany under aggressive leadership, it is no wonder that the first approximations of democracy and parliamentary government in these countries wilted, with only Czechoslovakia able to preserve some measure of democratic rule until Hitler partitioned it in 1939. Buffeted by powerful forces outside of their control, some East European intellectuals in the 1930s imagined that it might be possible to find an indigenous route toward modernity that was neither capitalist nor collectivist, a third way in which cottage industries of small, local producers would replace urban agglomerations of industrial workers or huge collectivized farms. But these daydreams failed just as completely as their more realistic-seeming fascist counterparts in the debacle of World War II.

The East European nations entered this devastating war among the poorest in Europe. Only the Czech lands had achieved a developed level of agricultural and industrial production. Poland's industrial base of 1938 was statistically only slightly behind that of Italy, but it, like the other East European economies, was pervaded by cartels, monopolies, state ownership, and state controls that "bore only passing resemblance to the classical model of competitive capitalism."[6] And the poverty was frightening. In the poorer parts of Croatia, for example, more than half the population had no sanitary facilities at all, not even an outdoor privy—they just relieved themselves in the woods.[7] Even without the destruction of the war, therefore, all the East European peoples would have entered the postwar period bereft of much usable political experience and burdened with the difficult tasks of economic reorganization and development.

The desire for a new start, for a real change, for something different from the tired solutions of the 1930s, therefore, was strong in Eastern Europe after the war. Charles Gati has suggested that in Hungary approximately half the voters in 1945 favored a revolutionary change of some kind, although not necessarily a Communist one, and in Poland sentiment was similar.[8] Prior to the Communist seizure of power in 1948, all legal parties in Czechoslovakia, not just the Communists, were committed to a policy of nationalization, which was essentially completed before the Communist coup of 1948.[9] In Bulgaria, which had been a German ally, postwar revulsion at Nazi war crimes and a tradition of pro-Russian sentiment helped pave the way for acceptance of the new Communist regime.[10] "It is true that the Communist party dictatorship was brought to the small East European countries by the victorious troops of Stalin," said Gáspár Miklós Tamás, "but we should admit that we were ready for it."[11]

For many East Europeans, the only way to attack the unprecedented problems of rebuilding and modernization seemed to be for the state to take over direction of the economy. Even in Western Europe state intervention greatly increased after World War II, and of course the Soviet economy was directed entirely from the center. Some economic theorists in the late 1940s disputed the assertions of the Austrian economists Ludwig von Mises and Friedrich A. von Hayek that the lack of competitive prices doomed any scheme of centralized planning to failure. The Polish economist Oskar Lange argued that it would be quite possible for a central planning board, through a rigorous process of trial and error, to achieve prices that "would, or at least could, work *much better* in a socialist economy than . . . in a competitive market."[12] Lange believed that centralized planning could create an economy that was as harmonious and efficient as capitalism but that would have the added advantage of being directed toward socially beneficial ends rather than being left alone to create waste, inefficiency, and hardship.[13] As American economist Abram Bergson wrote in 1948: "By now it seems generally agreed [that von Mises's argument] is without much force."[14]

In addition to the practical need for increased governmental intrusion into postwar economies and the presumed theoretical possibilities of centralized planning, the Soviet Union's victory over Nazi Germany, a country most observers had seen in 1939 and 1940 as an industrial giant, suggested that the Soviet system had considerable real-world vigor. The brutality of Stalin's policies in Eastern Europe, coupled with their long-term failure, have made it difficult for us to recall that in 1945 it was quite possible for honest and intelligent people to believe that the great caesura provided by World War II gave Eastern Europe a historically unique moment at which to ameliorate the failures and injustices of capitalism by adopting Soviet-style socialism.

Of course East Europeans did not voluntarily adopt socialism after carefully weighing its possible advantages and pitfalls. Stalin imposed the hyperrationalist vision on Eastern Europe by force. This accounts in good measure for the thoroughness with which Eastern Europe changed in less than a decade from the end of World War II until Stalin's death. No democracy could have created such havoc in such a short time. The new East European regimes swept aside private property, wiped out the middle class, collectivized agriculture, brought millions of country people to work in the city, dramatically increased the number of working women, brought entirely new people to power, reorganized and repopulated all levels of government, created new systems of education and scholarship, eliminated freedom of expression, turned East European trade away from its natural partnership with Western Europe toward the Soviet Union, propagated a new public ethic, built a strong military, and, in general, seized control of all aspects of public life. Joseph Rothschild has summed up the principles of mature Stalinism that provided the impetus for these changes:

> Mature Stalinism was characterized by the enforced imitation of Soviet political, administrative, and cultural institutions; absolute obedience to Soviet directive and even hints; administrative supervision by Soviet personnel; bureaucratic arbitrariness; police terror uncontrolled even by the local party; economic deprivation while pursuing overambitious industrial investment pro-

grams and undercapitalized agricultural collectivization drives . . . ; colonial-like foreign-trade dependence on the Soviet Union; isolation from the non-Communist world and to some extent even from other people's democracies; synthetic Russomania; a mindless cult of Stalin adulation; and resultant widespread social anomie, intellectual stagnation, and ideological sterility.[15]

East European history from World War II until 1989 can be characterized as a sudden, spasmodic moment of imposition of those principles of mature Stalinism followed by thirty-five years of adjustment, tinkering, reform, backsliding, and frustration. In broadest terms this history can be divided into halves, the period before the invasion of Czechoslovakia in 1968, when it still seemed possible that socialism could work, and the period after 1968, when almost everyone realized it could not. This book is about the second period, the era of disillusion and dissolution, not the first period, the era of the illusion that socialism provided solutions.

In the 1950s, dramatic confrontations marked the thaw that followed Stalin's death—workers' riots in Eastern Germany in 1953; similar riots in Poland in 1956 that led to the assumption of power by Władysław Gomułka as a nationally oriented leader; and the Hungarian Revolution of 1956, which was put down with great force by the Red Army. Nevertheless, the Communist regimes of Eastern Europe entered the 1960s with great confidence, particularly in the economic prospects of their socialist commonwealth. In 1961 a Soviet party congress declared that the Soviet Union had achieved socialism and was now building the material bases of communism, which would be achieved by 1980. The Czechoslovaks added the word "socialist" to the country's name (Czechoslovak Socialist Republic) and stated confidently that Czechoslovakia was well on its way to creating a "mature socialist society."[16] Most extreme, perhaps, was a confidential (that is, not propaganda) memorandum of autumn 1961 in which the Hungarian National Planning Office envisioned growth by 1980 that would "not merely exempt our people wholly from problems of livelihood but allow the attainment of consumption targets . . . sufficient to satisfy the harmonious physical and intellectual needs of man." The Central Committee agreed, adding that "the proposed levels of consumption will arrive at a standard of *saturation* on a society-wide scale."[17]

This high level of confidence did not reflect the actual state of the centrally planned economies. Among the many reasons they never functioned well, one of the most important is that planners set prices administratively rather than through market mechanisms. Since this produced prices that bore little relationship to costs of production, supplies of raw materials, or demand, the centrally planned economies became very inefficient. Planners tried to correct the overinvestment, the losses, and the shoddy quality that were the indicators of this inefficiency by subsidizing food production and heavy industry and by trying to make the plan more scientific, but both of these remedies actually exacerbated their problems.

Soviet-style economies pursued what they called the *extensive strategy* of economic development. This strategy sought to create economic growth by adding inputs, such as raw materials and particularly labor. One of the main thrusts of the economic policies of the pre-1968 period was to build heavy industrial plants that would give employment to formerly underemployed peasants and women, thereby increasing their productivity and creating growth. As implemented by Stalin, the extensive strategy of growth forced the East European economies to turn away from participation in the world economy and orient themselves toward the Soviet Union and the other socialist countries of Eastern Europe. The entire strategy was put into effect by means of rigid centralized planning that was consistent with the hyperrationalist belief that only the party leaders at the center had a true understanding of the laws of social development.

During the 1950s, the extensive strategy implemented by central planning produced excellent overall rates of growth.[18] But during the 1960s, the centrally planned economies encountered their first indications of an intractable problem. Since most of the underemployed peasants and eligible women by that time had entered the workforce, it was no longer possible to grow by adding more labor. The only other possibility was to create growth by adding technological improvements to increase the productivity of the workforce. But this possibility, called the *intensive strategy* of development, meant importing new technology and then exporting products into the world market to pay for it, which in turn meant adopting world prices and generally turning toward market mechanisms. Adopting this strategy would threaten the self-contained structure of the socialist economic system and undermine the ability of the party to rule society directly.

In the 1960s, as economic problems multiplied, professional economists in Eastern Europe began to challenge some of the basic assumptions that underlay the Stalinist strategy. Hungary was the country in which reforms based on these ideas went the furthest. Hungarian economists had started theoretical work as soon as Stalin died and even after the revolution of 1956 produced sophisticated studies of price formation and other technical problems.[19] In 1963 a study group headed by Rezső Nyers, a member of the Central Committee, produced a comprehensive assessment of the Hungarian economy, and by the end of 1965 the Central Committee committed itself to real reform based on the idea that Hungary could only advance economically if it reentered the world market. Once Hungary's top leadership agreed that economic reforms were the order of the day, they initiated a comprehensive preparatory process involving tens of thousands of people. After several years of planning, the New Economic Mechanism (NEM) took effect January 1, 1968.[20]

Economists in other countries, such as Branko Horvat in Yugoslavia and Włodzimierz Brus in Poland, developed theoretical notions using a Marxist vocabulary that made some of the principles of the market more palatable to state planners, but the place where reform seemed to have the best chance, outside of Hungary, was in Czechoslovakia. Just as in other countries, a debate began there as early as 1961, although at first it remained confined to party circles.[21] The best known reform advocate was Ota Šik, director of the Economics Institute of the Academy of Sciences and a Central Committee member, whose book *Plan and Market under Socialism,* published in 1967, provides a convenient guide to the thinking of Czech reform advocates.[22] Šik's basic idea was not to abandon central planning but to make it responsible only for the general direction of the economy while leaving the detailed management to individual firms. In 1965 the Central Committee, having been convinced by a report prepared the previous year by Šik's group that change was needed, introduced some indicative planning, began tentatively to deregulate prices, and consolidated industries into large trusts.[23]

These efforts at economic reform came to an end in 1968 when political events (to be discussed in the next chapter) led to the crushing of the "Prague Spring" by an invasion of Soviet and Warsaw Pact troops. The invasion of Czechoslovakia and the subsequent enunciation of the Brezhnev Doctrine, which stated that the Soviet Union would aid any previously established socialist regime to stay in power, marked the end of the era when serious people could hope that it would be possible to change the socialist system from within, either economically or politically. By giving notice that it would not tolerate any fundamental deviations from a neo-Stalinist model of socialism nor permit any meddling with its East European sphere of hegemony, the Soviet Union chilled the new winds that had been blowing through Eastern Europe.

This not only called forth a resigned sort of political apathy, but it also killed any chance that socialism would be able to repair its economies. Leonid Brezhnev tried a few marketizing reforms briefly in the Soviet Union, but the relative openness they implied struck at the heart of the hyperrationalist principle that the party, as the bearer of the true view of history, was the only agent that had the right to direct society. Confronted with the necessity of adopting the intensive strategy and entering the world market, the Soviets chose instead to stick with the increasingly obsolete extensive strategy. This seemed a safe and comfortable thing to do, but in fact it doomed the East European economies to eventual collapse at the very moment that the environment of world trade was changing decisively. The Soviet-imposed policy of inward-looking mutual trade conducted by central planning agencies isolated the East Europeans from the stimulus of the rapidly changing world economy and thus hindered them from making the only structural improvement that held long-term promise— increased productivity. When Brezhnev and his counterparts in Eastern Europe made their decision that the economic and political reforms proposed in Czechoslovakia in 1968 were too dangerous for socialism, they signed the death warrant of the system they thought they were saving.

1

The New Opposition: Antipolitics and Solidarity

The suppression of the Prague Spring was an extremely depressing moment for Socialists on both side of the Iron Curtain. Socialism has "sustained so many blows," a group of leftist scholars gathered at Reading University in England in the summer of 1973 complained, that "the idea itself seems to be dying in socialist countries."[1] The Soviet invasion had made it bitterly clear to these scholars that socialism sustained itself east of the Elbe River not because of the purity of its aims, the clarity of its analysis, or the humanity of its methods but by coercion, compulsion, duress, and violence. The impact among intellectuals in Eastern Europe was even more dramatic. "The fun was definitely over," said Václav Havel.[2] But unlike their colleagues in the West, many of the East Europeans abandoned socialism altogether. After Stalin's death in 1953 some intellectuals had begun to criticize their regimes, but almost always using Marxist categories and rhetoric. After 1968, with some exceptions in Hungary and East Germany, that vocabulary disappeared among oppositionists. At the same time a new phenomenon appeared in Poland—the independent workers' movement called "Solidarity." The appearance of nonsocialist opposition and the emergence of Solidarity were basic ingredients in the creation of a new pluralism in Eastern Europe.

The Disappointments of 1968

During the 1960s most oppositionists retained a commitment to the ideals of socialism, however they understood them, and voiced their opposition in Marxist terms. Just as East European economists at that time still believed it possible to reform the centrally planned economies by creating "social" rather than "state" property, by introducing workers' self-management, or by increasing enterprise autonomy, so many critics of the Stalinist political system maintained their belief in revolutionary socialism. A striking example was the *Open Letter to the Party* written in 1965 by two Warsaw University graduate students. Jacek Kuroń and Karol Modzelewski conceded that after the war Poland needed rapid industrialization and that this constituted a bona fide policy aim of the new government, but they argued that by vesting all power to accomplish this goal in the hands of the central bureaucracy the party had created a new class whose industrialization policies benefited no element in society except itself. Yugoslav Milovan Djilas had been among the first to invoke the term *new class* to describe the *apparat* that ran Communist systems.[3] In 1956 Djilas correctly foresaw that when the day came for that class to leave the historical scene, "there will be less sorrow over its passing than there was for any other class before it."[4] But Kuroń and Modzelewski went further— they called for bringing that day closer through a revolution that would rid society of the parasitic class of bureaucrats and would create a true workers' democracy. Even though the two authors did not publish this essay, did not lecture on it, and did not agitate on its behalf, they were convicted of advocating the overthrow of the Polish state and spent three years in prison.[5]

Another, more sophisticated example of principled criticism of socialism by Socialists was the work of the philosophers who surrounded the Yugoslav journal *Praxis*.[6] In place of the mechanical and formulaic dialectical materialism drawn from Marx's mature text *Capital,* the *Praxis* philosophers cultivated a philosophy of authentic action, genuine needs, and transformative growth inspired by Marx's youthful work, *The Economic and Philosophical Manuscripts of 1844.* "The basic purpose of critical inquiry," one of the leading *Praxis* authors said, "is the discovery of those specific social institutions and structures that cripple human beings, arrest their development and impose on them patterns of simple, easily predictable, dull, stereotyped behavior."[7] It did not take a particularly acute League of Yugoslav Communists to grasp which institution in Yugoslav society the *Praxis* philosophers considered dull and stereotyped. Nevertheless, the *Praxis* group dominated Yugoslav philosophical thought in the reformist 1960s and through its journal had a significant impact on Marxist thought throughout Europe.[8]

This style of opposition reached its peak in 1968, when events in three East European countries showed its limitations. The most famous but not the most productive of these events was the Prague Spring itself. During the 1960s Czechoslovakia experienced a cultural revival that was not associated with Marxism at all. Novels such as Ludvík Vaculík's *The Axe* and Milan Kundera's *The Joke* matched the vibrancy of Czech theater, particularly the plays of Václav Havel, while a new wave of Czech films impressed

critics throughout the world. In 1965 a group of writers not associated
with the Communist party were even able to establish an independent
literary journal, *Tvář* (Face), the first of its kind, and in 1967 several writers
spoke out boldly at the annual meeting of the writers union. On that
occasion Kundera criticized those "who live only in the immediate present,
unaware of historical continuity and without culture," because such people
"are capable of transforming their country into a desert without history,
without memory, without echoes, and without beauty."[9]

Tvář was able to publish for a short time and writers were able to
struggle to get the speeches from the 1967 conference into print because
the party contained a group of reform-minded people, "antidogmatists"
Havel called them, who, while retaining their confidence in socialism,
believed the system could be softened and made to work in a more democratic way. In October 1967 one of these persons, Alexander Dubček,
raised a question in an otherwise routine meeting of the Central Committee that set the events of the next year in motion.[10] Dubček, a Slovak
who had grown up in the Soviet Union, had already been among those
suggesting that the economic reforms then under consideration would
harm Slovakia, which contained many of the country's least efficient factories.[11] At the fateful October meeting he made the suggestion, radical
for its time, that party functions be separated from those of the state as a
way of increasing Slovakia's room for maneuver. To the surprise of most
of the leadership Dubček's intervention led to an unprecedented and bitter
internal debate over a number of issues, especially economic reform, the
outcome of which, early in 1968, was the resignation of the Stalinist head
of the party, Antonín Novotný, and his replacement, after lengthy negotiations, by Dubček.

The loosening up of censorship under Dubček and the adoption of
the party's "Action Program" of April 1968 produced enormous ferment
in Czechoslovak society. Characteristically, however, almost no one was
prepared to call for the abandonment of socialism. Even one of the most
radical and, to the Soviets at least, most disturbing proposals, Václav Havel's suggestion to create "a dignified counterpart of the Communist
party," was couched in terms of democratic socialism.[12] Havel and others
who stood outside the system did not believe in socialism particularly, but
they did not reject the goals of social justice either. Given the power of
the Communist party in Czechoslovakia and the overhanging presence of
the Soviet Union, dreams of anything other than a reformed socialism were
unrealistic, if not downright suicidal. The crushing blow to all who hoped
to keep reform within bounds and thereby humanize the Stalinist system
came on August 21, 1968, when the armies of the Warsaw Pact countries
invaded Czechoslovakia and, within a few months, installed a new leadership under Gustav Husák.

Two other countries in Eastern Europe had their 1968s, as indeed did
France in a different way. In Yugoslavia, students occupied Belgrade University in June, creating a small-scale version of the massive student dem-

onstrations that had taken place in Paris in May.[13] After several days of disciplined and principled confrontation in which the students demanded improvements in the curriculum, better job prospects, and a more open party life, party leader Josip Broz Tito calmed the situation with a speech in which he admitted the justice of many of the students' complaints and promised to take them into account. Many students greeted Tito's intervention with great enthusiasm—"Tito is with us!" they exulted—but as the summer wore on most realized that their hopes had been misplaced. Party cadres purged reformist elements, the student newspaper continued to find itself in hot water, and no substantive reforms of student life took place.[14] Since the Belgrade students had stuck closely to the etiquette of party forms during their protest, their disenchantment when they returned in the fall was that much greater. The Belgrade student revolt remained a high point in that generation's collective memory—it was "the moment I became an adult," one participant recalled.[15] But the disillusionment, which extended as well to some party members who had felt Yugoslav socialism was different from that of its repressive neighbors, did not create an antipolitical reaction. Instead, Yugoslav estrangement found its outlet in nationalism, a subject that will be discussed separately in Chapter 7.

Student rebellion in Poland in the first three months of 1968 was angrier and more violent than in Belgrade. For students slowly becoming disillusioned with Marxism, the arrest of Kuroń and Modzelewski in 1965 was simply the most egregious affront in a long series of harassments by the authorities. The students' efforts reached a climax early in January 1968. At that time Warsaw theater audiences had taken to applauding a production of Adam Mickiewicz's nineteenth-century play *Forefathers* whenever lines came up that were critical of Russia, such as "Moscow sends only rogues to Poland." This show of hostility to what Poles considered almost an occupying power caused the regime so much embarrassment that it decided to close the production. The students seized the opportunity to turn the final performance into an antigovernment demonstration, to which the regime responded by arresting some thirty-five student leaders.

As their riposte, the students of Warsaw University came out on strike. In Paris the massive student strikes of May 1968 led within one year to the fall of Charles de Gaulle, while in Belgrade Tito found a way to calm the students with false promises. Władysław Gomułka was neither as honorable as de Gaulle nor as clever as Tito. His police moved in, clubbing and beating students on university grounds that had hitherto been considered inviolable. Gomułka closed down the faculties of economics, philosophy, sociology, and psychology; expelled student leaders; and dismissed six professors, including Włodzimierz Brus, the philosopher Leszek Kołakowski, and Zygmunt Bauman, one of Poland's most promising sociologists.

The ugliest feature of these "March Days," as they became known to Poles, was the vicious campaign of anti-Semitism that accompanied it. The regime extended its attacks on student leaders, some of whom had Jewish family backgrounds, to the relatively small remaining population of Polish Jews that had survived the Holocaust. Merely to be of Jewish origin was sufficient to merit prosecution as an element hostile to the Polish state. By the end of 1968 most of the thirty to forty thousand Jews remaining in Poland had been forced to emigrate.

For the Polish intelligentsia, the March Days were as wrenching a turning point as the Prague Spring was for the Czechs and Slovaks. Before 1968 the regime had nourished hopes that the system could still be reformed by maintaining what David Ost calls a "coquettish" social democratic relationship with the intelligentsia.[16] Adam Michnik even claimed that the students he led were only trying to be true Communists according to the definition he had learned from his Boy Scout leader (who was Jacek Kuroń!).[17] But the removal of the final veil covering the regime's mindless face destroyed any hope of reform based on the ideals of 1956. The jail sentences that many of the students suffered were no less than they expected, but the primitiveness of the regime's anti-Semitism produced a shock of revulsion that no amount of later equivocation could erase. Equally depressing was the paucity of support the students and their professors received from the working class of Poland, whom the most active among the intelligentsia still considered the only sound basis for a lasting and stable society. No groundswell of strikes and protests emerged in the factories to overwhelm the repressive measures, and the regime had little difficulty finding workers to demonstrate against the students.[18]

Gierek's Poland

The relative apathy among the Polish working class in 1968 did not mean that it was satisfied with Gomułka. Quite the contrary. The workers' turn for outrage came in December 1970, when, without prior preparation or announcement, the government announced a significant rise in the price of basic foodstuffs. From the technical point of view there is little question that the highly subsidized food prices needed adjustment. But as Polish regimes continually found almost from the moment they began the Stalinist policy of subsidizing food prices, nothing was more difficult than taking away a perquisite that the public had come to perceive as one of the few benefits of socialism: low prices for basic needs. It is almost as if the population had worked out an arrangement with the party: you subsidize housing, medical care, and food, and we will not complain about the arbitrary way you run society.

On the first working day after the announcement, three thousand workers in the Gdańsk shipyard demonstrated before party headquarters, and in the next few days strikes and demonstrations quickly spread to other industrial cities along the Baltic coast.[19] The rigid Gomułka refused any concessions to what his prime minister called "scum, adventurers, anarchist hooligans, criminal elements, enemies of socialism, and enemies of

Poland.''[20] Gomułka hectored his politburo into authorizing the use of the military, and eventually a massive force consisting of perhaps thirty-five thousand troops with tanks and armored vehicles took up positions in the main port cities on the Baltic. On December 15 police in Gdańsk opened fire on workers, and in the ensuing melee the party headquarters building burned down. Troops and police fired on workers in Gdańsk, Gdynia, and Szczecin also, eventually killing 44 and wounding 1,164 persons.[21] Thoroughly panicked by what appeared to be a workers' revolution and assisted by apparent Soviet indifference to Gomułka's fate, party leaders hastily chose a new chief, Edward Gierek. But the damage had been done.[22]

On December 18, workers in the Warski Shipyard in Szczecin and the repair shipyard in nearby Gryfino, who were surrounded by troops that confined them to their factories, elected strike committees and agreed on a common set of twenty-one demands. The first of these was that ''independent trade unions dependent on the working class'' take the place of the party-dominated Central Trade Union Council. Thus appeared for the first time the principle that became the backbone of Solidarity's program in 1980 and 1981 and was the basis of its resistance throughout the remainder of the 1980s. That same evening delegates from ten striking factories in and near Szczecin formed the Citywide Strike Committee, the forerunner of Solidarity's Interfactory Strike Committee of ten years later. Within a few days ninety-four nearby striking workplaces signified their adherence to the committee. Despite these propitious beginnings and the rediscovery by the Szczecin workers of the efficacy of the occupation, or sit-in, strike, within two days the two main leaders of the Warski workers, both of them party members, agreed to a settlement, betting mistakenly that the party would make good on its promises of reform. The strikes fizzled out, but an important milestone had been passed: self-activated workers had demanded the right to conduct their own union affairs and had momentarily found strategies—the occupation strike and the interfactory strike committee—that would work in the future.

Resentments boiled over again in Szczecin January 1971, when the government faked a television report that showed workers there vigorously supporting new party leader Gierek and agreeing ''voluntarily'' to work an extra Sunday. Suddenly the Baltic coast was on strike again. On January 24 Gierek, alarmed by renewed rejection of his regime, undertook an unprecedented gesture. He made surprise appearances at the Warski Shipyard in Szczecin and the Lenin Shipyard in Gdańsk. In lengthy confrontations that were broadcast live, Gierek appealed to huge crowds of gathered workers on the basis of their solidarity as working-class people. He himself had worked for twenty-two years in coal mines and similar positions in France and Belgium, and he knew what the workers wanted and needed. ''I say to you: Help us, help me.... I am only a worker like you.... But now, and I tell you this in all solemnity as a Pole and as a Communist, the fate of our nation and the cause of socialism are in the balance."[23] "We will help! We will help!" rolled back the roar of the people crowded in the square in Gdańsk, where only a month before their compatriots had been shot by Gierek's predecessor. Frustrated and angry, the workers were at the same time impressed that Gierek had actually come to talk with them personally, and they believed him when he said he would see to their needs. Shortly thereafter he started to make good on his word by restoring 1965 prices, by rescinding an unpopular system of incentive bonuses based on piecework, and by raising wages and pension payments for many workers. "Consumption must become the engine of growth," said one of the theorists of the government's new policy.[24]

Gierek naturally assumed that what the workers wanted was to have a sausage stuffed in their mouths, as one observer crudely put it.[25] He tried to oblige them, almost literally. The Soviet Union helped immediately with a $100 million advance to buy meat abroad. In 1971 government procurement agencies raised prices paid for slaughter cattle and agreed to buy all the cattle farmers could produce. In 1972 Gierek dropped compulsory crop deliveries, lowered peasant taxes, extended national health care to peasants, and granted legal ownership rights to almost one million peasants with unsettled claims.[26] Of the more than $20 billion Poland borrowed abroad in the 1970s, $6 billion went for the importation of foodstuffs, a high proportion of which was grain that went into the production of meat.[27] Between 1969 and 1979 these policies pushed meat consumption up 40 percent to a level equal to that of Italy and Great Britain.[28]

But Gierek gained no political benefit from this success. He increased the meat supply, but he increased wages too. Real per capita income rose at an average rate of 7.7 percent from 1971 through 1975.[29] More meat appeared in state stores at low prices, but more money chased it, so that meat remained scarce and lines at butcher shops were common. Since the Poles are great meat eaters, or, to put it more formally, since the elasticity of demand for meat in Poland is very high, the government could never produce or import enough meat to meet the demand generated by higher wages. The public sense, therefore, was simply continuing shortage.

Increasing consumption was only one aspect of Gierek's overall plan. In return for more meat he wanted more work, or at least more effective work. But for the workers to become more efficient Poland needed better technology, which meant importing it from the West. This is what Gierek decided to do, although he had no intention of adopting the full schedule of reforms that a real turn toward the intensive strategy of development would entail. The imported technology would be financed with foreign loans, which in theory would be retired once appropriate capital investments had enabled Polish industries to modernize and to produce competitive exportable products. By chance, loans for this purpose became widely available after the oil crisis of 1973, as international banks sought to recycle a massive supply of newly generated petrodollars. Poland seemed a relatively attractive economy in which to place hard currency loans because it exported coal, a reliable, low-tech natural resource whose value had increased because of the energy crisis.

At the beginning of Gierek's regime hopes for positive economic results temporarily rose. Known himself as technically competent and with a good reputation for administration, Gierek assembled a team of technicians rather than a team of party bureaucrats and began "building a New Poland," as they put it. In actuality the specialists proved no more able than their predecessors to resist the pressures of industrial and regional lobbies, in good measure because they themselves were drawn from those lobbies, as was Gierek himself. More concerned perhaps with their industrial clients than with the balance of the economy as a whole, they accelerated investment to almost 30 percent of the gross national product by 1975, 50 percent higher than in the pre-1970 period.[30] This produced the inflationary pressures characteristic of such a policy but without creating either new productive capacity or more efficient old capacity. Both domestically generated investment and the huge foreign loans disappeared into the clunky heavy industries that had always gobbled them up, such as the steel works at Katowice, and into poorly conceived new projects based on expensive Western license agreements. An ill-fated agreement between the Ursus tractor factory and the international firm of Massey-Ferguson-Perkins, for example, produced little increase in farm productivity but saddled Poland with a large hard currency debt incurred for purchasing the license.[31]

The Ursus fiasco was repeated dozens of times in dozens of ways. Polish managers were at least one technological generation out of date; marketing skills were rusty or nonexistent; and, despite exhortations from above, the planning bureaucracies continued to favor the noncompetitive heavy industries that gave meaning to their positions. Large-scale graft and corruption—ranging from cooked books and skim-offs to luxury summer homes in Switzerland—only confirmed the total incompetence of the team Gierek had claimed would give Poland its new start. By 1980 imports had exceeded exports for nine straight years, external debt had risen to $23 billion and was increasing at a rate of about 10 percent per year. This enormous expenditure of borrowed money produced only a small growth in efficiency and productivity in the first half of the decade, and in 1975 productivity began a steadily accelerating decline.[32]

In the face of these problems Gierek continued to maintain his policy of increasing wages for active workers (he did not increase them for pensioners and students) and keeping food prices low. "The price policy will be subordinated to the main aim of increasing the real incomes of the working people," Gierek said in 1973.[33] Such a combination of increased wages and stagnating economic efficiency could not last. In effect Gierek was simply passing along the vast amounts of money he was borrowing abroad to the workers in the form of higher wages (and to the bureaucracy in the form of graft). By the time Western banks finally caught on to this gigantic Ponzi scheme, as they did in the late 1970s, Poland's economy was in deep trouble.

Bad as it was, Gierek's inability to use the infusion of foreign capital effectively was not his most fundamental mistake. He based his entire policy of consumerism and intensive development on a misperception of what the workers actually wanted. Yes, they wanted sausage, and it was imperative to do what was possible to provide it. But they also wanted dignity, self-respect, autonomy, and acceptance. "Even if people never speak of it," Václav Havel said in a famous open letter to Czechoslovak party leader Gustav Husák in 1975, they "have a very acute appreciation of the price they have paid for outward peace and quiet: the permanent *humiliation of their human dignity*."[34] "It was not the compulsion, the use of force so much," said one participant in the strikes in Szczecin in 1970 and 1971, "but the moral element, the element of honor [that motivated us]." Polish workers wanted no more than what all conscious people in the postindustrial age want: to be autonomous actors in their own lives. Despite their shouts of "we will help" and Gierek's apparent commitment to help them, in fact the workers in this workers' state regarded the regime as false, restrictive, humiliating, and oppressive—as "Lackeys of Moscow!" as one of the first wall slogans to appear in Gdańsk in 1970 put it.[35]

The leaders of Communist parties throughout Eastern Europe who attempted what in Hungary was called "goulash communism" were constantly surprised by this feeling, but they should not have been. The workers' feelings were simply a mirror image of the party's own condescension toward the working class. No Leninist really believed workers could understand their own interests. Left to their own devices, they would be co-opted into the capitalist system by offers of higher wages and other benefits, thereby sacrificing for temporary and passing gains the transcendental success to be won by revolution. This supposed weakness was precisely the one Gierek hoped to exploit. He assumed that in order to swallow more sausage, Polish workers would continue to swallow the humiliation of being treated as dependents. In one way this was an advance over Stalinist strategies, which gave workers neither sausage nor dignity. But by suggesting that sausage really was the important thing, and not socialism, Gierek tacitly admitted that the idea of a vanguard party leading the country to socialism was just what the opposition said it was: "a dead creature, an empty gesture, an official ritual."[36]

For all this, no regime could abandon the hyperrationalist ideology of the all-knowing vanguard party. Quite the contrary: it constituted the sole justification for the system through which the party ruled. In Gierek's case, as long as he could contrive to keep the standard of living on the rise he could hope to hold back the tide of resentments many members of society felt at their lack of control over their lives. But as soon as the bribery faltered, as it was bound to given the inefficiencies of the central planning system, the emptiness of the reservoir of belief would be revealed: As philosopher Leszek Kołakowski put it in 1971, "the dead and by now also grotesque creature called Marxism-Leninism still hangs at the necks of the rulers like a hopeless tumor."[37]

The Antipoliticians

Kołakowski's graphic remark came in an article entitled "Hope and Hopelessness," published in 1971 in *Kultura,* a distinguished Polish émigré journal published in Paris. His title expressed the grave moral problem East Europeans faced after the depressing events of 1968. After the invasion of Czechoslovakia, Soviet leader Leonid Brezhnev asserted that "the triumph of the socialist system in a country can be regarded as final" and pledged to use "the armed might of the socialist commonwealth" to make sure it remained so.[38] How could one live a genuinely conscious life knowing that there was no hope of resisting the overwhelming power of the Soviet Union, which stood prepared to sustain an emotionally and intellectually barren despotism in Eastern Europe indefinitely? As Jacek Kuroń put it much later, "What is to be done when nothing can be done?"[39] The post-1968 depression in Eastern Europe was severe, but in a way it was a blessing, because by asking, as a Hungarian philosopher did at the end of the 1970s, "What can we do at the place where we live, which we are most familiar with, where we can best grasp the situation?" many East Europeans began to find the road that led them finally from Stalinism to pluralism.[40] No longer harboring any illusions about socialism, they were free to think freshly. The first step was simply to admit that in traditional political terms the situation was hopeless. In his essay Kołakowski listed the reasons why this was so. Democratization of socialist regimes was impossible, he said, since every democratizing reform appropriates some aspect of the total control the regime enjoys and will not relinquish. Freedom of information was also unthinkable in the East European socialist system, as was any extension of rights. Even though the governing apparatus will inevitably suffer moral and mental decline, Kołakowski predicted that it would remain aggressive and attempt to destroy all forms of social life not directly related to itself. A "technocratic" revolution, such as Gierek claimed to be instituting in Poland, was therefore impossible, Kołakowski argued, since it implied a progressive abandonment by the regime of its authority.

In this bleak situation, was there any space for hope? For Kołakowski, the very necessity of regimes to concentrate power hinted at a potential weakness. The conflicts of interest that inevitably occur among the leadership ("life sows confusion in their council chambers," is the way Havel put it), are hidden behind an ideological screen.[41] This will complete the work of depriving the system of its small remaining meaning and is therefore a cause for hope that the system is not as eternal and all-powerful as it presents itself as being.

But for Kołakowski true hope did not lie in the working out of the inevitable historical process of the system's division and decline. That kind of thinking was the underlying mistake of hyperrationalism. Hope lay with the power of individuals to think that honesty is possible. Accepting the principle that the system is utterly unreformable makes "every act of cowardice, passivity and cooperation with evil" possible. Instead, Kołakowski argued, we must move beyond mere acceptance to live an ethical life in which we are not silent in the face of knavery, servile to those in authority, or accepting of the petty gifts of our oppressors.

Hope, that is, lay in living an ethical life, not in forming a political opposition, because the very act of forming an opposition based on a particular political program ran the risk of simply substituting one form of utopianism for another. "By using force to storm the existing Bastilles we shall unwittingly build new ones," Adam Michnik wrote.[42] Václav Havel felt that it was depraved to oppose the posttotalitarian system with an approach in "which people are first organized in one way or another (by someone who always knows best 'what the people need') so they may then allegedly be liberated."[43] "My greatest nightmare," György Konrád said, "is to have to tell millions of people what to do next."[44] These men rejected the entire hyperrationalist premise of modern politics—that all social life is essentially political—in favor of its opposite, an ethic of antipolitics. Having accepted the hopelessness of changing the false but powerful political structures they confronted, the antipoliticians focused on the interior ethical world of the individual as the space in which change could occur. "Power can enlarge or reduce the sphere of our free expression, but it can not make us free men," wrote Michnik. "Our freedom begins with ourselves."[45] Living the truth might have an impact in the traditional world of politics someday, or it might not, but in any event it would at least be a true and authentic way to live in a world of lies.

For an antipolitician like Havel even the term *hope* needed a redefinition. It was not the optimism that a better future was in store, nor a prognostication of some saving event, he argued, but an orientation of the spirit, "the certainty that something makes sense."[46] The fact that we are surrounded by lies, Havel believed, does not excuse us from doing our best to live in the truth. And this sphere, the realm of the ethical, is where real life resides. The alienation one feels in the totalitarian state is possible precisely because there actually is something in human beings to alienate. "Under the orderly surface of the life of lies, therefore, there slumbers the hidden sphere of life in its real aims. . . . The singular, explosive, incalculable political power of living within the truth resides in the fact that living openly within the truth has an ally, invisible to be sure, but omnipresent: this hidden sphere."[47] The ability to find this sphere of the authentic and to live according to it was what Havel called "the power of the powerless."

At the Fourth Congress of Czechoslovak Writers, held in the summer of 1967, Ludvík Vaculík, speaking as a "citizen of a state which I will never abandon, but in which I cannot contentedly live," called upon the writers to "make speeches as if we were grown up and legally independent."[48] In the 1970s, living "as if" emerged as a numerically minuscule but ideologically devastating threat to the Communist regimes of Eastern Europe. As long as some shred of belief in reform existed and traditional political ideologies motivated the opposition, regimes knew what to do. They co-opted those whom they could convince reform was possible and isolated the rest. But when people in different walks of life began "living in truth," regimes found themselves contesting a space they could not enter. A Polish writer, Konstanty Gebert, put it this way: "A small, portable barricade between me and silence, submission, humiliation, shame. Impregnable for tanks, uncircumventable. As long as I man it, there is, around me, a small area of freedom."[49] Immune from corruption by the sphere of lies, living the truth was a subversive, implacable, and unreachable opponent. "Is not *honesty*," asked the Romanian writer Norman Manea, "in the final analysis the mortal enemy of totalitarianism?"[50] During the 1970s the most powerful answer to the question of how to live in a hopeless situation proved to be classically simple and impossibly difficult: live honestly—undertake that " 'hopeless enterprise' which stands at the beginning of most good things."[51]

Helsinki and Charter 77

Not everyone agreed that living in truth was a practical strategy. For example, the brilliant Czech novelist and former Communist Milan Kundera believed it was not only idealistic but even stupid to confront an immutable regime with meaningless small deeds, such as passing around carbon copies of manifestos. His solution to hopelessness was to abandon any form of hope and emigrate to France. In a sense this was a victory for the government, since Kundera, while denying the regime's moral legitimacy, at the same time left it in command of a terrain of its own choosing. The anti-politicians who remained found a remarkably clear and powerful strategy to contest that terrain, a strategy that had already been tried in the Soviet Union in the 1960s. They simply demanded that regimes follow their own laws on human rights, which of course was the last thing that regimes intent on retaining social control were willing to do.[52] For more than a century Marxists had occupied the moral high ground in politics by claiming to be the true opponents of repression. When the antipoliticians began to show the hollowness of that pretension with their simple but effective strategy of living in truth, they began to edge the Communists off that high ground and to assume the moral leadership of their societies. This process, more than any single political, economic, or military event, is what doomed the Communist regimes of Eastern Europe.

A major stimulus for pushing this moral struggle beyond the interior world of the individual was the signing of the Helsinki Agreements of 1975.[53] These agreements concluded a two-year series of negotiations concerning peace and security in Europe that had become possible in the early 1970s, when West Germany changed its long-standing policy of hostility toward East Germany. Ever since the creation of two Germanies after

World War II the Soviet Union had advocated an international conference to regularize the status of East Germany and to confirm the western border of Poland, but under Konrad Adenauer West Germany had refused to deal with East Germany at all. As soon as a new West German chancellor, Willy Brandt, announced a policy of reconciliation with East Germany in 1969 *(Ostpolitik)*, the Soviet Union renewed its calls for such a conference. Formal negotiations began in 1973, and in the summer of 1975 representatives of thirty-five countries, including all of those in Eastern Europe except Albania, signed the Final Act in Helsinki.

Since the Helsinki accords did recognize East Germany and did guarantee all current European borders, it appeared that Soviet policy had been crowned with success. Many conservatives in Europe and in the United States condemned the Helsinki accords as simply another caving in to Communist domination of Eastern Europe on the pattern of Yalta, and oppositionists in Eastern Europe feared the same thing. But one section of the accords turned the tables on the doubters and on the Soviets as well. The so-called "Basket Three" of the agreements committed all signatories to respect "civil, economic, social, cultural, and other rights and freedoms, all of which derive from the inherent dignity of the human person."[54] Not only did this portion of the agreement, which went into great detail concerning the exact rights and freedoms envisioned by the agreement, give Western powers an excuse to upbraid the Soviet Union and its allies periodically about their failure to live up to its terms, but it gave dissidents within Eastern Europe and the Soviet Union a legal basis to insist that their governments uphold human rights. Helsinki Watch committees appeared in the Soviet Union, Poland, and elsewhere. The most significant initiative was Charter 77, which appeared in Czechoslovakia.

The immediate impetus that led to Charter 77 was the arrest and trial of members of a rock music group called The Plastic People of the Universe.[55] Long-haired, antiestablishment, and generally indistinguishable from dozens of similar groups in the West, in Czechoslovakia the Plastics' aggressive nonconformity, vulgarity, and rejection of normalcy profoundly shocked a regime intent on maintaining a Victorian standard of morality. Václav Havel loved rock music for its vibrancy and freedom—he was a Lennonist rather than a Leninist. For him and his friends the Plastics "were simply young people who wanted to live in their own way, to make music they liked, to sing what they wanted to sing, to live in harmony with themselves, and to express themselves in a truthful way."[56] Outraged by the government's crude attack on the musicians, Havel and his friends mobilized support for the imprisoned musicians abroad among a wide circle of European artists, writers, and intellectuals.

Despite the international outcry, the Plastics were convicted. Frustrated, but encouraged by the support they had found abroad, twenty to thirty Czech intellectuals began meeting secretly late in 1976 to see if a next step was possible. The group was enormously varied. It included a former high party official, Zdeněk Mlynář; an antidogmatic Communist writer, Pavel Kohout; a revolutionary socialist, Petr Uhl; a Catholic writer, Václav Benda; and Havel himself, who had never been a Communist. Despite their diversity, they were able to agree on a long-range antipolitical strategy, which they made public in a relatively brief document on January 1, 1977. "Charter 77 is not an organization," they stated. "It has no rules, permanent bodies, or formal membership. It embraces everyone who agrees with its ideas, participates in its work, and supports it. It does not form the basis for any oppositional political activity."[57] The thrust of this nonorganizational document was to insist that the Czechoslovak government follow all the international agreements, including the United Nations Declaration on Human Rights and the Helsinki agreements, that it had signed in regard to human rights. Three spokespersons were designated to bring instances of human rights failures to the government's and the public's attention. In contrast to the clandestine modus operandi characteristic of the hyperrationalist political tradition, all 243 of the original signatories of the charter indicated their intention to live "as if" they were free by signing their real names and adding their addresses. Overt, aboveboard, and nonideological, Charter 77 was the epitome of the antipolitical style of opposition.

Civil Society in Poland

In Poland an antipolitical form of resistance began to emerge in the early 1970s almost without Poles being aware of it. Inspired in part by Kołakowski's article "Hope and Hopelessness," Jacek Kuroń identified the development in 1974 in an article entitled "Political Opposition in Poland." Kuroń reiterated the point that in a system that seeks to control the everyday life of its citizens, simply living that life honestly is itself a political act. The preservation of culture, the reading of literature, and the discussion of philosophy constitute political opposition precisely because they ignore politics in a state that insists on saturating everything with politics. In fact, if enough individuals were to draw together into social activities of their own choosing outside of state compulsion, it might be possible to create a civil society that achieved much or all of the goals of democratization without transforming the state through traditional means at all.[58] As Adam Michnik put it shortly after Kuroń's article appeared, the opposition should no longer address itself to the totalitarian state, trying to change the immutable, but to the independent public, or at least to a public living "as if" independent. Polish antipoliticians proposed abandoning traditional political programs in favor of creating a "real day-to-day community of free people."[59]

What did these abstractions mean in practice? The most important answer came in 1976. Gierek's overheated investment policy during the first five years of his regime, coupled with his insistence on increasing real wages, left him with few options with which to address economic problems, which remained pressing. He did cut the rate of investment after 1975, and he found surreptitious ways to cut the growth in real wages, but until 1976 he resisted taking the most reasonable step, from the macroeconomic point of view at least, of raising food prices and decreasing subsidies. In that year, however, the increasingly clear evidence of trouble finally convinced him to take even that potentially fatal step. On Saturday, June 24, 1976, a compliant Sejm (the Polish legislature) accepted the government's recommendation to raise food prices as of Monday, June 26. To no one's surprise, the strikes began as soon as workers reported for work on Monday.

Unlike 1970, however, when the government improvised its repression, in 1976 the regime was well prepared. The largest strike broke out in Radom, a sizable industrial city and a provincial capital. Workers in Radom had not undergone the learning process that the coastal workers had in 1971, and instead of occupying their plants and forming interfactory strike committees, they marched into town. During the afternoon of the very first day of this demonstration, June 25, the government flew in special police units, and by 7:00 P.M. about two thousand persons already had been arrested. Although almost no one died in the confrontations in Radom and elsewhere, the police used calculated brutality to cow the strikers. A common tactic, used also in 1970, was to run detainees through a "path of health" each time they were taken somewhere. This meant walking along a long line of police officers, each of whom was required to hit the prisoner once.[60] In the days and weeks that followed, courts sentenced hundreds of strike participants and sympathizers to fines and jail terms up to ten years, and hundreds more suffered retributions in the form of dismissal, call-up into the army, and assignment to "Centers of Social Rehabilitation." Despite this show of force, the government revealed its fear and weakness by rescinding the price increases only one day after they had been imposed.

Also unlike 1970, the intelligentsia—inspired by the Helsinki accords, in the early phase of working out new notions of civil society, and a little bit guilty about their relative passivity in 1970 and 1971—responded vigorously to the Radom suppressions. In mid-July a group of people met at Adam Michnik's vacation studio and formed a committee to defend the workers at their trials. Even before this Committee for the Defense of Workers (Komitet Obrony Robotników—KOR) formally came into being in September, a growing number of intellectuals spontaneously began offering legal assistance to the accused and financial assistance to their families. KOR organized and sustained these efforts.

Despite KOR's obvious political significance, its origin lay in a "simple impulse of compassion," as Stanisław Baranczak puts it, and its founders conceived it as an antipolitical organization.[61] According to one of its most important organizers, Jan Józef Lipski, KOR's mission was threefold: to "appeal above all to ethical values and to general moral standards rather than political attitudes"; to act openly, including revealing the names of all participants; and to conduct its activities within Polish law, relying on the Helsinki accords and the Polish constitution. From the beginning, therefore, KOR's goal was not simply to assist workers, although during its first year it considered direct, one-on-one help its most important practical work, but to "stimulate new centers of autonomous activity in a variety of areas and among a variety of social groups." In other words, whereas KOR was founded originally in response to a specific need to defend unjustly arrested workers and to help their families, as the first year of activity wore on many members realized that the widespread response their relief efforts had evoked offered an unexpected opportunity to turn the abstract notion of civil society into a concrete reality.[62] Accordingly, in September 1977 KOR changed its name to the Social Self-Defense Committee "KOR," retaining the original initials to indicate continuity with its original functions.[63] The term "self-defense" indicates how completely the organizers had abandoned any identification with the party and state. The state and the party had become the usurpers against whom society must defend itself.

Beyond their work with the strikers in Radom, the most important sphere of KOR's activity became underground publishing. The original models for underground publishing under socialism were the Russian samizdat publications of the 1960s. *Samizdat* means self-publication *(samstvennoye izdatelstvo)* as opposed to publication by the state *(gosudarstvennoye izdatelstvo)*, which was abbreviated *Gosizdat* and was the name of the Soviet state publishing company.[64] It achieved currency in the 1960s when a handful of brave Soviet oppositionists began publishing the *Chronicle of Current Events*. In Eastern Europe such efforts were rare until the 1970s, and even then they achieved real significance only in the northern tier of states. In Czechoslovakia Ludvík Vaculík took the lead in 1972 when he established his publishing enterprise *Petlice* (Padlock), which put together typewritten novels, philosophical works, and other forms of belles lettres.[65] By 1987 *Petlice* had produced four hundred volumes of this sort. Vaculík's effort laid the groundwork for an explosion of illegal publications in Czechoslovakia after the founding of Charter 77.

In both the Soviet Union and in Czechoslovakia the state reacted vigorously to underground publishing, making it difficult for oppositionists to operate in volume. In Poland, however, under Gierek's less compulsive leadership, the authorities limited themselves to harassment rather than to obliteration. The initial model of the underground press in Poland was KOR's *Biuletyn Informacyny* (Information Bulletin). In 1977 Jan Lityński and other KOR activists began *Robotnik* (Worker) as a four-page news sheet printed on a mimeograph machine in some four hundred copies. A little more than a year later it was publishing twelve pages every two weeks in approximately twenty thousand copies and the paper was being distributed in factories throughout Poland. Inspired by this example, KOR members on the Baltic began publishing their own version, *Robotnik Wybrzeża* (The Coastal Worker). Copycat local publishing efforts elsewhere suggested that *Robotnik* was beginning to have an impact on the more active factory workers in the major urban centers.[66]

Equally significant was Mirek Chojecki's creation of the Independent Publishing House (Niezależna Oficyna Wydawnicza—NOWA) in August 1977.[67] Chojecki's purpose was strictly cultural, and over the next few years he put together an all-star list of Polish and foreign authors. From its founding until the spring of 1980, NOWA published fifty-five separate volumes averaging two hundred pages in length in editions averaging two thousand copies. This huge achievement was only one of a number of significant publishing efforts. By 1979 twenty-five illegal journals were appearing, each with a circulation of over forty thousand copies a year.[68] At the same time, *Robotnik* achieved a nationwide circulation of approximately fifty thousand a week.[69]

How was such an extensive illegal effort possible? First of all, KOR supported a number of printing enterprises financially, at least at the start. KOR received its funds primarily from individual donations, a significant number of which came from people of Polish descent living abroad. Both Leszek Kołakowski and Włodzimierz Brus actively solicited funds in exile for the committee, for example. But the biggest problem was technical, not financial. Printing and distributing such a large volume of illegal material was a major organizational problem. Foreign contacts provided some machinery, particularly small duplicators and the like, and some of the biggest jobs were done on state printing presses on off hours or by sneaking them through other press runs. But most of the printing was done by a relatively small number of trained persons who hid out in basements, apartments, peasant houses, and barns, and transported their paper, machines, and stock from place to place to avoid the police. Each publication built up its own network of clandestine distributors, mostly students and workers.

An important ingredient in the relative success of KOR and its publication efforts was that Gierek decided not to push the underground to the wall, or, as some would have it, Gierek was so indecisive that he was unable to make a decision to do so. Despite many thoroughly unpleasant cases of arrests, beatings, and dismissals, Gierek's regime was, in comparison to the regimes in neighboring countries, relatively tolerant. The police made a large number of arrests and harassed people they knew were leaders, sometimes even beating them. In the four years from 1976 to 1980, for example, Mirosław Chojecki suffered a subcutaneous hemorrhage over half his face in a beating by "unknown perpetrators," dramatically escaped from thugs who were about to throw him down a staircase, spent five months in jail, had his apartment searched fifteen times (during which many of his belongings, including money, were confiscated), and was personally searched at least eighty times under a variety of pretexts, including burglary. But NOWA continued to publish, its readers were not arrested, and no one was sent to a death camp.

In contrast to the pinched, suspicious, and puritanical Gomułka,

Gierek was an optimist who believed in his ability to inspire confidence, which he attempted to do by innumerable visits to villages and factories. Without humor, and not in any way spontaneous, he perceived himself as the patron of the Polish working class. "Comrades," Gierek said in a speech to workers in Katowice in November 1979, "you know me well enough to know that nothing linked with the life of the working people slips by me. Your difficulties . . . keep me awake at night."[70] Familiar with the ways of the West, Gierek understood that intellectuals need to criticize, but he felt confident he could confine their complaints to a normal level of academic whining. Although he was the sort of man who avoided making decisions, Gierek believed in his ability somehow to bring Poland through whatever problems it might encounter. Dazzled by what he took to be brilliant success in bringing in foreign loans and raising the standard of living during his first four years in office, he became unwilling to damage his reputation as the builder of a new Poland by provoking confrontations. For him, harassing opposition movements in the late 1970s was simply one of the costs of doing business that could be left to those responsible for it, not a campaign directed from the top to unmask and crush enemies.[71]

KOR was instrumental in two other efforts that promoted the emergence of civil society in Poland during the late 1970s. The first was the Flying University, created in the fall of 1977. In November of that year the Information Bulletin of KOR announced that a number of prominent intellectuals, including Adam Michnik and Jerzy Jedlicki, would offer free lectures on such subjects as "The History of People's Poland" and "Contemporary Political Ideologies" at locations and dates obtainable from KOR. Despite their clandestine quality, the response to these lectures was enormous, and the police took them seriously. In 1979 lectures by KOR leaders such as Kuroń and Michnik had eventually to be canceled because of the violent interventions of police goons. Another organization, the Society for Scientific Courses (*Towarzystwo Kursów Naukowych*—TKN), formed by a group of scholars, continued their activities, even publishing academic studies in order to fill in the "white spaces" in Polish scholarship. The underground journal *Res publica* (Public Affairs), later the first legal independent publication in Eastern Europe and today a leading Polish journal, began publishing in 1979 as a direct outgrowth of the lecture series begun by Jerzy Jedlicki, Marcin Król, and others.[72]

The second significant initiative of KOR activists was the creation in 1978 of the Founding Committee for the Free Trade Unions of the Coast (Komitet Założycielski Wolnych Związków Zawodowych Wybrzeża). In 1977 activists in Gdańsk attempted to memorialize the workers killed in the riots of 1970 by placing a wreath at Shipyard Gate No. 2 at 2:00 P.M. December 16, exactly seven years after the tragedy. Only about one thousand persons showed up, but the event marked the beginning of the emergence of the Gdańsk shipyard as the premier symbol of worker resistance in Poland. In April 1978 three of the same activists who had organized the memorial boldly proclaimed the creation of a committee to found an independent trade union to defend the "economic, legal and humanitarian interests of the working population."[73] The core group of this new organization provided some of the most important leaders of Solidarity in the 1980s, including Andrzej Gwiazda and his wife Joanna Duda, Bogdan Borusewicz, Bogdan Lis, Anna Walentynowicz, and, shortly after its formation, Lech Wałęsa. Two other such committees existed by 1980, one in Katowice, the other in Szczecin.

By conviction, most of the KOR activists considered the working class to be the basis of a stable civil society. Despite their disillusionment with socialism, a high proportion of KOR activists had been Marxists in their youth, and many retained their orientation toward class analysis. The very term civil society, as they used it, derived from Hegel and Marx and had overtones of class struggle—the working class in cooperation with the intelligentsia on one side against the "new class" of state and party apparatchiks on the other. Adam Michnik explicitly based his program of "new evolutionism," the gradual expansion of civil and human rights in Poland, "on faith in the power of the working class,"[74] and the name *Robotnik* evoked a tradition of socialist newspapers dating back to 1884.

This orientation of what Michnik called the "lay left" was not, however, the only orientation of oppositionists in the late 1970s. For example, in March 1977 a group of Catholic activists established the Movement in Defense of Human and Civil Rights (Ruch Obrony Praw Człowieku i Obywatelstwa—ROPCiO). A separate underground organization, the Polish League for Independence (Polskie Porozumienie Niepodleglosciowie—PPN), called for a peaceful Europe and a reunited Germany, while the Confederation of Independent Poland (Konfederacja Polski Niepodległej—KPN), advocated a policy of national independence free of Soviet domination and party dictatorship. Both PPN and KPN accepted the major human rights goals of KOR, but their emphasis on Polish political autonomy put them in direct conflict with the Soviet Union—an extreme position for 1976, in contrast to KOR's seemingly more realistic policy based on the evolution of civil society.[75] A number of other groupings, often associated with a publication, came into being as well, creating the initial elements of the rich variety of political views that characterized Polish politics after 1989. The political pluralism of today's Poland had its origins in these pre-Solidarity activities.

All of these oppositional efforts had their impact, particularly in the symbolic sphere, since they represented the efforts of independent people to assert themselves in a difficult situation, but they did not yet profoundly tap the dissatisfactions of Polish society. Many university students, always the first to be mobilized, were involved in opposition, and some of their professors helped them. Only a small portion of the intelligentsia were overt oppositionists, but most of them were at least aware of what was going on and of the issues.[76] Among workers, however, only those in the major industrial centers were directly affected. A small number of activists around papers like *Robotnik* informed a fairly broad stratum of workers in the major factories; but among the peasantry, the artisans, the pensioners, and the medium and small enterprises, KOR and the other oppositional organizations were foreign enterprises conducted elsewhere by other people.

Pope John Paul II and the Polish Catholic Church

Before 1980 Polish civil society was not mobilized primarily by the intelligentsia or by the working class, although progress was being made, but by a thunderbolt from abroad that galvanized the entire Polish population, young and old, rural and urban. On October 16, 1978, a puff of white smoke emerging from the chimney of the Sistine Chapel at St. Peter's in Rome announced that Cardinal Karol Wojtyła, formerly archbishop of Kraków, had been selected Pope John Paul II, the first non-Italian pope in 455 years.

The Polish Catholic church was the only church in Eastern Europe to maintain and even enhance its position in the generation after World War II. The Orthodox churches of Romania, Bulgaria, and Serbia, steeped in an ancient tradition of "harmonious concert" with state authorities, found ways to live with the Communist regimes and became kept institutions, docile before the state, narrow ethically and intellectually, and retrograde in their national parochialisms. The Romanian church particularly profited from its slavish policy when, in 1948, the Romanian government forcibly disbanded the Eastern Catholic church, arrested thousands of its priests and believers, and turned its assets over to the Orthodox church. Forty years of overwhelming pressure so decimated the Eastern Catholics, who numbered 1.7 million in 1948, that in 1990 some seriously questioned whether that faith could be re-established in Romania.[77]

In general, Catholics took the opposite tack and vigorously opposed the Communists. In Croatia and Slovakia, however, the church was seriously compromised by its relations with the Germans. When Croatian Archbishop (later Cardinal) Alojzje Stepinac refused to deal with Tito's new government, he was jailed, thus beginning a hostile pattern of confrontation between the church and state in Croatia that lasted forty years. In Hungary Cardinal József Mindszenty had been a forthright anti-Nazi, but he was also a forthright anti-Communist, and stubborn besides, so he spent not only the war years in prison but many postwar years there as well. After 1956 he took refuge in the American Embassy in Budapest, where he lived for the next fifteen years.

Poland was the only East European country where the church found a way to work with the Communists. Catholicism has been a fundamental aspect of Polish sensibilities from the time of the original conversion a thousand years ago, but Poland has always contained a number of other faiths, both in the early modern period and in the interwar period. After World War II, however, with most of the Jews dead and the Ukrainians and White Russians behind the Soviet border, Poland became almost entirely Catholic. For a few years after the war both the government and the church avoided direct confrontation, but when the Vatican decreed in 1949 that followers of communism should be excommunicated, the Polish government went on the attack, nationalizing church lands and instituting heavy censorship.

Rather than marking the end of church independence in Poland, however, nationalization proved to be the beginning of a fluctuating relationship of repression and accommodation, during which the church carved out an independent position. In 1957, as part of his renegotiation of Poland's social contract, Gomułka reached an agreement with Cardinal Stefan Wyszyński that permitted the church to publish and pursue pastoral activities. Two main directions of lay Catholic activity emerged, the first being a "liberal-intellectual" group centered around the Kraków newspaper *Tygodnik Powszechny* (Universal Weekly), the philosophically oriented journal *Więź* (Bond, as in "bond of friendship"), and the more sociologically oriented journal *Znak* (Sign). The second was the "popular-traditionalist" group around the officially permitted organization Pax.[78]

Cardinal Wyszyński also broadened the influence of the church during the 1960s through a vigorous pastoral policy. During a ten-year celebration called the Great Novena, designed to celebrate the millennium of the Polish adoption of Christianity in 966, the famous Black Madonna of Częstochowa was taken on a visit to every diocese in Poland, thus putting a significant portion of the population in touch with the Catholic version of antipolitical opposition. Wyszyński believed that only moral renewal would free Poland, and he proved very successful in propagating his messianic vision of romantic Polish nationalism. In 1978 the church had almost twenty thousand priests on the job and more than five thousand students in Catholic seminaries, a number that far exceeded the total in these categories in all the rest of Eastern Europe combined.[79]

After 1968 the church began to throw its substantial moral and organizational support toward the opposition. In 1968 cardinals Wyszyński and Wojtyła both protested the way the students had been treated, and in 1970 and 1971 the church spoke out against the atmosphere of governmental intimidation. *Więź*, under the editorship of Tadeusz Mazowiecki, opened its pages to opposition writers, who usually wrote under pseudonyms and who were unable to publish in official outlets.[80] Mazowiecki followed an editorial policy that stressed moral factors rather than a narrowly conceived Polish national Catholicism. On the occasion of the repressions of 1976, Cardinal Wyszyński condemned the brutal methods of the police and characterized contributions to KOR's relief efforts as "the duty of all people of good will, and especially of a Christian community."[81] In the following year Cardinal Wojtyła permitted the Flying University to hold lectures in church buildings in Kraków, which effectively shielded those sessions from state interference. These linkages prompted Adam Michnik to suggest in 1977 that a close look at the sermons of Cardinal Wyszyński and other documents published by the Polish episcopate showed that the social policies found there, especially those showing concern for the civil rights of workers and postulating a true social and political equality, "are almost totally in accord with, or at least do not contradict, the program of reform conceived by the democratic left."[82]

Onto this already well-prepared ground the naming of Wojtyła as Pope John Paul II burst like a joyful bombshell. Poles felt a thrill of pride and stature at the unexpected news. Almost immediately negotiations got under way for a visit of the new pope to his homeland on the nine hundredth anniversary of the martyrdom of St. Stanisław, the patron saint of Poland, which was to take place in May 1979. The regime absolutely refused to permit a visit at that particular moment, since in the popular mythology Stanisław was martyred for opposition to tyranny, but it could not prevent a visit entirely. The government was well aware of the threat John Paul II represented to its diminishing moral authority, as these revealing excerpts from instructions given to teachers who were party members in Warsaw attest: "The Pope is our enemy. . . . Due to his uncommon skills and great sense of humor [John Paul II] is dangerous, because he charms everybody, especially journalists. Besides, he goes for cheap gestures in his relations with the crowd, i.e. puts on a highlander's hat, shakes all hands, kisses children, etc. . . . We must strive at all costs to weaken the Church activities and undermine its authority in the society. In this respect all means are allowed and we cannot afford any sentiments."[83]

The government's efforts to manipulate media coverage and otherwise to downplay the pope's triumphal visit, which took place in June 1979, only further damaged its credibility in the face of the public's overwhelming response. One million people turned out for the first pontifical mass, held symbolically in Victory Square in Warsaw, to this point "one of the most revered spaces of the official Communist ritual."[84] In the week that followed hundreds of thousands of ordinary Poles embarked on pilgrimages to holy places at which the pope appeared, and literally millions of people saw and heard the pope give dozens of homilies and sermons in the most historic centers of Polish religious and national life. John Paul II stressed the right of the individual to dignity both as a human being and as a worker, and in advocating the christocentric religious themes for which he has become known made explicit linkages to a Polish national tradition that in the nineteenth century conceived of Poland as the Christ of nations.[85] To some his concept of "man in society" sounded very similar to KOR's notion of an independent society.[86]

The "psychological earthquake," as Viennese Cardinal König put it, of the pope's visit proved to the party, to the opposition, and to society at large that the old language of redemption struck the hearts of Poles with incomparably greater force than the new one.[87] One of the most characteristic features of Communist rule was the debasement of ordinary political language. *Sovereignty* had come to mean loyalty to the Soviet Union; *freedom*, absence of choice; *reform*, cosmetic administrative reorganizations; and *economic success*, standing in lines for hours to buy substandard goods. "We are being drowned in a sea of double talk," said the program of the Confederation for an Independent Poland. In that atmosphere of falsity the pope's vibrant Christian rhetoric, delivered in a stylish literary Polish that contrasted sharply with the stereotyped and hackneyed Communist idiom, flew like an arrow to the emotional and spiritual heart of millions of Poles. The very appearance on the streets of these millions surprised many people who had harbored doubts about the regime but felt that they were alone and outnumbered by the state. "Different people found that they were not alone," as one participant put it.[88]

The experience of the pope's visit proved the accuracy of Havel's prediction that anything that touched the hidden sphere of authentic human need would speak to people in a fundamental way. "If a better political model is to be created, then perhaps more than ever before it must derive from profound existential and moral changes in society," Havel said.[89] The antipoliticians had begun the process of creating a civil society in which such a moral change could occur, but John Paul II's visit to Poland suddenly jolted millions of Poles to their first awareness that this was indeed a proper sphere in which to begin the hopeless enterprise.

Solidarity

Solidarity turned out to be the organizational embodiment of that enterprise. The initial disturbances that led to its creation began, as one might guess, over meat. One of the devices the government introduced in 1976 to bring food prices more in line with costs without raising prices across the board was the opening of commercial shops, where premium cuts of meat were sold at prices considerably higher than those in the state stores. At first only 2 percent of the meat was sold that way, but by 1979 the proportion had crept up to 19 percent. Starting in 1979 the government reluctantly and cautiously began to seek other ways to slow the growth of real wages. To defuse the protests that an austerity program would provoke, Gierek authorized local authorities to grant striking workers raises and similar benefits on their own authority. This would pacify strikers without involving the central government in a generalized pay raise.[90] Gierek had not given up his idea that the workers could be bribed; he just turned a society-wide inoculation into a series of spot cures. As one aspect of its belt-tightening, the government decided to increase the proportion of meat going to the commercial shops by 2.5 percent, an increase that was actually less than the annual increase since 1976, and to adjust prices for inflation. The result was a significant de facto increase in the cost of meat. Obviously nervous about the decision, officials introduced the change without announcement, simply permitting a low-ranking bureaucrat to make a statement after the event.

Almost immediately, workers in the Ursus plant near Warsaw came out in protest, followed quickly by others. During the next six weeks Jacek

Kuroń, in touch with factories around the country by telephone and reporting to Western newsmen, counted more than 150 work stoppages throughout the country.[91] Most of them were relatively short, since managers were able to settle them with raises of 10 and even 20 percent, but railway traffic was disrupted and production, already shaky, declined. Kuroń and the KOR activists did what they could to publicize the increasing breakdown of the regime's control over society, since the official press confined itself to brief mentions of "temporary work interruptions." Surprisingly, the government took no preventative measures against KOR, and in the middle of a mounting crisis Gierek even went off to the Soviet Union for his annual three-week vacation.

At the Lenin Shipyard in Gdańsk organizers were unable to bring workers out in June over the meat issue, but in mid-August the shipyard management conveniently provided KOR with a cause by firing Anna Walentynowicz only a few months before her retirement. Since Walentynowicz was a popular crane operator and a well-known activist, her sacking was the perfect pretext for action. For the previous two years activists like Bogdan Borusewicz had learned how to get in touch with significant numbers of workers through such tactics as passing out leaflets on commuter trains and distributing *Robotnik Wybrzeża*. Now *Robotnik Wybrzeża* printed a demand for the reinstatement of both Walentynowicz and Wałęsa, who had been fired in 1976, adding demands for increases in wages, family allowances at the same level as those received by the police, and a memorial to the victims of the 1970 strikes. Early on the morning of August 14 Borusewicz and his small team distributed six thousand leaflets publicizing these demands, and this time the shipyard workers responded. A large crowd gathered in the yard's main courtyard, where the director of the factory stood up on a bulldozer and promised negotiations if the workers returned to their jobs. This tactic had worked throughout Poland in the previous six weeks, and it almost worked now. But just at this moment a second man crawled up onto the bulldozer, tapped the manager on the shoulder, and said. "Remember me? I worked here for ten years, and I still feel I'm a shipyard worker. I have the confidence of the workers here."[92] Indeed he did. Lech Wałęsa had arrived, and "with the matchless impudence of a natural leader," he proceeded to take charge of the strike.[93]

Wałęsa (pronounced Va-WEN-sa) was a real proletarian. An electrician with six children at the time, he literally spoke the workers' language, an uneducated and rough Polish that sounds distinctly lower class to intellectuals. Born and brought up on a poor, minuscule farm where he had to walk four miles to school "barefoot as often as not," he left home at age sixteen to become an electrician.[94] After training and military service, he took a job in his home region only to leave for Gdańsk at the age of twenty-five after a disappointing love affair. Good with his hands and talented at making friends, he signed on as an electrician at the Lenin Shipyard. Laying cables in the bowels of ships and living at first in a mildewed workers' barracks full of drunken and violent young men, he managed to find a sympathetic companion, married, and began to raise a family.

Two years after coming to Gdańsk, Wałęsa's audaciousness and intuitive ability to grasp a situation, as well as his strong sense of what workers wanted and needed, propelled him to a leadership position in the strikes of 1970 and 1971. The shooting of four workers outside the gates of the Lenin Shipyard moved him deeply and the memory of shouting "we will help" to Gierek along with the other workers in 1971 came to embarrass him. Over the next few years he became a tireless organizer. Wałęsa was not an ideologue or a theorist. He simply wanted to get people involved in standing up to the state. Some of his actions were dramatic, such as plastering his jalopy with copies of the Polish Constitution of May 3, 1791, the most democratic of its day; others were simpler, such as marching to church every Sunday with his growing family. But mostly he simply talked with as many people as possible, even strangers on buses, whom he approached for carfare when released from his periodic forty-eight-hour detentions. Finally in 1976 he was fired from the shipyard, but he continued tirelessly to organize. When others established the Founding Committee for Free Trade Unions on the Coast in 1978, he joined their work. By 1980 he was perhaps the best-known personality in the workers' section of Gdańsk in which he and his family lived.

When Wałęsa first spoke to the crowd of workers on August 14, 1980, therefore, they recognized him and cheered, but two days later, after hours of negotiation and indecision, the strike committee he headed decided, as had many other strike committees elsewhere over the past two months, to accept a pay raise. Wałęsa announced the end of the strike over the shipyard's loudspeaker system, and the director told the workers to go home, which most of them started to do. But during that two days representatives of strike committees from other factories in the region had flocked to the Lenin shipyards. They appealed to Wałęsa to keep the Lenin Shipyard out in solidarity with them. "If you abandon us we will be lost," pleaded the leader of the Gdańsk public transport garage.[95] As the workers began filing out, Wałęsa sensed their unease with the settlement, and in one of those instinctive decisions that have made him Poland's most successful posttotalitarian politician, he suddenly realized that the strike should continue.[96] Rambling around the shipyard on a trolley with two colleagues, he convinced about one thousand workers to stay on, and so the strike continued.[97] Within twenty-four hours Wałęsa and his colleagues formed the Interfactory Strike Committee (Miedzyzakładowy Komitet Strajkowy—MKS) with two members from each of the increasing number of enterprises on strike in the Gdańsk area. By August 18 some two hundred factories from the region had joined the Interfactory Strike Committee. When a young design student gave the movement a name by producing a striking logo based on the word *solidarność* (solidarity), the Rubicon was crossed.[98]

The Interfactory Strike Committee quickly formulated a list of twenty-one demands, including the right to strike, selection of foremen on the basis of talent rather than party service, better health care, and more meat. But the first and most fundamental demand was the same one that workers had raised in 1970 in Szczecin: a free and independent union.[99] Gdańsk members of KOR such as Joanna Duda Gwiazda, Bogdan Lis, and Bogdan Borusewicz, who had been in close touch with the coastal workers and who had called forth the crucial strike, supported this demand and helped formulate it, but KOR activists who were not at the scene found the demand for a free union dangerously radical, even "senseless." Adam Michnik was preparing to go to Gdańsk and tell the workers to abandon such impossible expectations when his arrest prevented him from doing so. "*We* knew that independent, self-governing trade unions were impossible in a Communist system," Michnik reminisced later about himself and Jacek Kuroń, "but the workers didn't know. That's how Solidarity arose, without us and against us, although we always considered it to be our [KOR's] child. An illegitimate one, you might say."[100] Not all the Warsaw intellectuals felt that way. Tadeusz Mazowiecki, the noted Catholic editor, put together an appeal signed by sixty-four intellectuals, later joined by hundreds more, placing "the entire progressive intelligentsia" on the side of the strikers. Arriving in Gdańsk late on August 22 to assist the strikers in their negotiations, Mazowiecki and historian Bronisław Geremek quickly understood the force of the workers' demand for a free union. Within two days five other Warsaw intellectuals joined Mazowiecki and Geremek, and the Interfactory Strike Committee accepted them as an advisory group.[101]

At first the government hoped to deal with the Gdańsk strikes as it had with the others, sending a middle-ranking negotiator to divide the strikers with relatively minor concessions. But the rapid formation of the Interfactory Strike Committee, publication of the twenty-one demands, and the firmness of the workers' resolve made that impossible, and soon the deputy prime minister arrived. After several days of tense but not always hostile discussions, the final agreements were drafted.[102]

After a brief but bitter internal struggle in which Gierek's insistence on a negotiated settlement won out over those who wanted to use force, the government proved willing to concede most of the strikers' goals. On the strikers' side, the negotiating team also proved willing to make concessions that permitted the party to acquiesce.[103] In the agreement promulgated on August 31, the section in which the Interfactory Strike Committee received the right to set up "new independent and self-governing unions" also included a provision that the unions would "recognize the leading role of the Polish United Workers' Party in the state."[104] The phrase "in the state" was artfully designed to be acceptable to the party as supporting its primary position and interpretable by Solidarity as restricting the party's sphere to political activities, leaving civil society open to Solidarity. Hotheads from KOR and KPN, the nationalist group, temporarily upset the applecart when they claimed that conceding the leading role of the party in any sphere made the entire notion of an independent union—and by extension an independent society—meaningless. Wałęsa successfully countered with the argument that it was better to get permission to establish an independent union and to work out its actual role in practice than it was not to get agreement at all. "This is just a matter of words," he said. "It's practice, only practice, which will tell how this agreement will work."[105]

The Gdańsk agreement, along with two others signed at Szczecin and Jastrzębie, became known as the Social Accords. Together they represented a giant failure of Gierek's policy of stuffing a sausage in the mouth of the workers.[106] Here was a genuine strike document growing out of a significant experience of self-activization among the coastal workers that put the issue of dignity first. Solidarity's fundamental demands were independent, self-governing unions, the right to strike, and freedom of expression, while higher wages and improved working conditions came only down the list. "History has taught us that there is no bread without freedom," the Solidarity program of a year later said. "What we had in mind were not only bread, butter and sausage but also justice, democracy, truth, legality, human dignity, freedom of convictions, and the repair of the republic."[107] Within days of the accords, Gierek paid the political price for his mistake. On September 5, 1981, Stanisław Kania, an wily apparatchik with little popular standing, replaced him as prime minister.

Solidarity's 469 Days

The coastal strikers had been so involved in the issues of their strike and so cut off by the government from the rest of the country that at first there was no plan to make Solidarity a national movement. But the opening provided by the Social Accords brought dozens of delegations representing strike committees from all over Poland to Gdańsk to visit Solidarity's new headquarters in the Morski Hotel. The question they had to confront was this: Should the Solidarity unions that were popping up everywhere remain locally based or should Solidarity be united into a single union with a national headquarters? Karol Modzelewski argued forcefully that only a national body would have the organizational strength to stand up to the party, whereas partisans of the Gdańsk experience held that only if local unions organized themselves autonomously would real democracy be possible. Typically, Wałęsa spoke on both sides of the issue, but also typically, he found a solution that satisfied both sides. This was to keep the local organizations strong but to form the National Coordinating Commission to coordinate policy on a national level. Late in September the new commission submitted Solidarity's statutes to the Warsaw Provincial Court for registration as a legal body.

When the judge to whose court Solidarity appealed for registration as a legal entity refused to approve the union's application, Solidarity called a short demonstration strike in which three million workers throughout the country participated, thus using the registration crisis to draw workers from the small and medium-sized enterprises into the movement for the first time. After six weeks of tension Solidarity finally agreed to add the first few sentences of the Gdańsk accord in which it accepted the leading role of the party in the state to the statutes as an annex. On this basis the statutes were formally accepted, and Solidarity became a fully legal entity.

In a few short months Solidarity had achieved something not only unprecedented in postwar Eastern Europe but seemingly impossible. As Kuroń put it later, "I thought it was impossible, it was impossible, and I still think it was impossible."[108] A vanguard party, basing its legitimacy on its claim to be the single true representative of the working class, had permitted the creation of a bona fide workers' movement outside of its control that commanded the loyalty of millions of Polish laborers. It was, as many observers noted, the first genuine workers' revolution in history. But even though Solidarity struck at the very basis of the Leninist party, it was still a partial revolution, in fact hardly a revolution at all, since the revolutionaries self-consciously limited themselves to what they claimed were nonpolitical activities. They not only feared the possibility of Soviet intervention if they threatened the government too directly, but they respected the antipolitical roots of the movement. Solidarity was a "moral revolution," as Andrzej Gwiazda put it, not a political one, and the social accords explicitly stated that Solidarity was "not to play the role of a political party."[109] But politics, after all, is the space in which social power is apportioned. That is what politics is about: power. With actual control over the workers in its hands, it was only a matter of time before Solidarity found itself unable to maintain the fiction that it was merely a labor union.

From the beginning Solidarity sought a partnership with the government, or even a kind of tripartite corporate arrangement, with the church as the third entity. But the government continued to issue important decisions without consulting Solidarity or informing the public, and it continued to make it as hard as possible for the union to achieve its goals, which at first remained relatively limited. The only tool the union possessed was the general strike. During the registration crisis a short strike had proven useful, but its very success momentarily hid from the Solidarity leadership something that European labor leaders had long since learned: the general strike is a cumbersome weapon. If it is used, it runs the risk of failure or of provoking widespread conflict, including perhaps class or civil war, and even, in the case of Poland, foreign intervention. But if it is not used, the intensity of purpose that unites the workers behind the concept begins to decay.

For the first six months of Solidarity's existence the threat of a general strike remained credible. Actual strikes and the menace of more secured the release of a printer arrested for possession of an embarrassing state document. Wildcat strikes and the threat of a demonstration general strike got the government to roll back its unilateral decision that workers would have to be on the job two Saturdays every month, a decision that was inconsistent with the Gdańsk agreement. A general strike warning finally, after a long struggle, induced the regime to permit the registration of Rural Solidarity. In each case tortuous negotiations backed by the threat of strikes resulted in victories for Solidarity, but in each case the victories required important concessions as well. After the release of the arrested printer, Solidarity's leadership had to prevail on angry local unions not to strike; the rollback of the two-Saturday rule meant that Solidarity had to accept a one-Saturday rule; and Rural Solidarity was not registered as a union but only as an association.

Wałęsa's role in all this was central and contradictory. Solidarity was extremely democratic. Its discussions were open to the point of chaos; it ran scrupulously fair elections; and its newspaper, when it was finally allowed to appear in April 1981, carried differing views. On the other hand, Lech Wałęsa was not much of a democrat. Negotiating with members of the government or with Cardinal Wyszyński, often alone, he decided on what concessions could or could not be made without informing even those around him, let alone the rank and file. This may be a highly efficient way to negotiate, and even necessary in some circumstances, but by the spring of 1981 a growing number of Solidarity activists had tired of Wałęsa's insistence on maintaining unity rather than acting democratically. As the one who negotiated the compromises, Wałęsa had to convince his executive committee and the workers in general to go along, something they often did only reluctantly. And, since he realized that Poland's declining economy could not stand the constant work stoppages that volatile local grievances were causing, this militant union leader spent a sizable portion of his time during the Solidarity period hopscotching around the country trying to convince workers not to strike. This could only go on for so long before Wałęsa ran into dissatisfaction and opposition from within the ranks.

That moment came in March 1981 in Bydgoszcz. When Solidarity activists and representatives of Rural Solidarity, which was trying to achieve legal status, refused to leave a meeting of the local government council that had reneged on its promise to hear them, security forces cleared the protesters out in a manner reminiscent of the "paths of health" of 1976. Three participants were badly injured. Many Solidarity activists already were furious at the patent unwillingness of the government to treat the union as a partner, and the Bydgoszcz incident, relatively trivial in itself, pushed them over the edge. Demands for an immediate general strike rained down on the leadership. Trying to avoid an unambiguous confrontation with the government, which he thought would result in bloodshed, Wałęsa successfully proposed instead a four-hour warning strike and a full general strike four days later if the demands for punishing the offenders were not accepted.

On March 27, 1981, as negotiations began, the four-hour strike proved a formidable success, with work stopping almost completely throughout the country. It was a remarkable demonstration of the breakdown of the government's hold over its citizens. Meanwhile, Wałęsa closeted himself with Mieczysław Rakowski, the editor of the Warsaw paper *Polityka* and a Communist who managed to be simultaneously a critic of the regime and one of its most dangerous supporters. After very difficult negotiations, interspersed with an acrimonious central committee meeting, Rakowski and Wałęsa, who grew heartily to dislike each other, reached an agreement. Only hours before the general strike was to begin Andrzej Gwiazda appeared on television with Wałęsa at his side and read the none-too-satisfactory compromise agreement they had agreed upon. The strike, which had been carefully prepared and for which the union was psychologically ready, was off. In return the government promised to investigate the Bydgoszcz event, to permit Rural Solidarity to operate even if it was not officially registered, and to look at the possibility of releasing some political prisoners.

To most Solidarity activists, it looked like the government had prevented the strike by the same old methods of insubstantial promises and insincere assurances, and Wałęsa faced a pent-up storm of bitter criticism. Karol Modzelewski, one of the movement's most penetrating analysts, resigned as Solidarity spokesman. Andrzej Gwiazda, whose personal relations with Wałęsa had been deteriorating, quickly regretted his participation in the compromise and wrote an open letter attacking Wałęsa for ignoring democracy in the union. Anna Walentowicz, over whose case the movement had begun, became a critic and was dropped as the Gdańsk representative to the National Coordinating Commission.

The original antipolitical purposes of Solidarity created frustration because they conflicted with the actuality of Solidarity's position in Polish society. The Bydgoszcz agreement was in the antipolitical tradition. It merely sought redress from the government and did not make any structural proposals for change. By this time, however, many Solidarity activists had become convinced by the government's continued unwillingness to treat the union as a true partner that only political reform would make it possible to achieve the economic gains they all wanted. This was one of Gwiazda's basic arguments. On his side, Wałęsa feared that giving up the self-limiting character of the revolution would only result in bloodshed and possibly even Soviet intervention. Pressured by an increasingly intransigent government that itself was under intense pressure from the Soviet Union, Wałęsa had decided against a general strike in favor of following the antipolitical path originally set out by KOR. "We don't know yet if I was right, or those who took another view," he said. "In my opinion the risk was too great."[110]

After Bydgoszcz, the many factional elements that an organization of ten million persons is bound to contain came to the surface in Solidarity. Wałęsa never fully lost the confidence of the workers, but from the early spring of 1981 Solidarity moved inexorably in the direction of political confrontation. But confrontation takes two sides, and during this same period the government firmed up its position as well. During the late fall of 1980 and in the first few months of 1981 there was a real danger that the Soviet Union might intervene, as it had in Czechoslovakia in 1968. Ryszard Kukliński, a high-ranking Polish defector, has confirmed that the Soviets were ready to invade Poland on December 8, 1980 (or perhaps December 12). Warnings from President Jimmy Carter and other Western leaders were so firm, however, and the cost in lost credits likely to be so high, that, apparently at the last minute, Brezhnev decided to give the Poles another chance to handle the problem on their own.[111] The appointment in February 1981 of Defense Minister General Wojciech Jaruzelski as prime minister temporarily reassured the Soviets, and Jaruzelski promised in private to prepare a plan for imposing martial law.

Pressured externally by Brezhnev, the Polish party found itself pressured internally by reform elements.[112] A movement of "horizontalists," so called because local organizations coordinated their reform ideas without conferring with higher party organs, spread rapidly. In April 1981 it began to attract the attention of the Western press, which praised it, and the Soviet press, which reacted strongly against it, both for the same reason: the horizontalists threatened the higher party apparatus. The pattern of unanimous voting at party plenums began breaking down, and local party units expressed their dissatisfaction by replacing about 50 percent of their first secretaries in the first half of 1981. Party leader Stanisław Kania tried to straddle the fence between impatient reformers and irritated hardliners but, in the end, without success.

In September and October, Solidarity took a major step toward becoming a true political movement, although it continued to deny such an intent. In a lengthy two-part convention, it adopted a program that, if implemented, would destroy the Polish United Workers' party. The "October Program" retained some aspects of self-limitation. It remained opposed to private ownership of large industry, specifically rejected the creation of political parties, and steered clear of calling for an independent Poland. But its other proposals showed its true intent: social ownership rather than state ownership of the means of production; private ownership in agriculture and small business; a second chamber in the legislature to accommodate nonparty needs; and free local elections. "Pluralism of views and social, political, and cultural pluralism should be the foundation of democracy" in Poland's "Self-Governing Republic," the program asserted. Wałęsa was re-elected to lead the union to the realization of these goals, but his relatively slim 55 percent margin suggested that the elements pushing for confrontation were becoming stronger.

Just after the end of the Solidarity national congress early in October, the Polish United Workers' party held its congress. Consistent with the new spirit of democracy provoked by the horizontalists, in July the party had changed its electoral rules to add secret balloting and to require more than one candidate for party positions. Under these new rules, the relatively uncontrolled elections to the party congress in October returned "remarkably few officials and apparatchiks," making the congress, in the opinion of one observer, "largely uncontrollable."[113] Angered by the Solidarity congress and frustrated by the declining economic situation, delegates indulged in a wholly uncharacteristic surge of criticism of Kania. When, on the third day, the central committee adopted a sharply critical resolution, Kania interpreted it as a vote of lack of confidence and resigned. Into his place stepped General Jaruzelski, minister of national defense since 1968 and prime minister since February 1981. In Jaruzelski the party found what it wanted: a strong leader but not a Stalinist one.

One of the first steps Jaruzelski took was to meet with Lech Wałęsa and the newly appointed primate of Poland, Cardinal Glemp. It is almost certain that none of the parties in this meeting expected much from it, but there were many who hoped that party, church, and people could achieve a tripartite partnership of some kind. But the time for partnership with Solidarity remained almost a decade in the future. In fact, it was almost at the very moment of meeting with Glemp and Wałęsa that Jaruzelski decided to put the lid back on Polish society by declaring a "state of war," the Polish equivalent of martial law.[114]

The State of War

The confrontation, when it came, was not unexpected, but it was a surprise nonetheless. By the end of November an increasingly intransigent government faced an increasingly agitated Solidarity. At the factory level local unions had begun demanding the removal of party units from the factory premises, and at the national level leaders such as Jacek Kuroń, who had been counseling caution from the beginning, began to advocate the creation of an alternative political party. To make the tension worse, the economy was rapidly sliding downhill. Debt had increased to over $25 billion, and servicing now took up almost all the hard currency produced by exports, which were down in any event. Industrial production dropped 19 percent from the previous year and total national production dropped 12 percent, declining for the third consecutive year. The standard of living was now worsening, having declined to its 1974 level.[115]

By early December, Solidarity leaders felt a confrontation was coming, but they had difficulty imagining its potency and extent. Despite repeated but vague warnings from Wałęsa that they underestimated their opponent, most Solidarity activists did not differentiate between Solidarity's power as a representative of society and the government's power as the wielder of the forces of social control. They were right that Solidarity was much stronger than the government in the minds of most Poles. They were wrong that this made the government incapable of acting.

On the cold evening of December 12, 1981, the National Coordinating Commission of the Solidarity union was meeting in Gdańsk for the second day of discussions on how to respond to Jaruzelski's apparent determination to provoke a confrontation. Only a week before, the government had secretly recorded a disputatious Solidarity meeting at Radom, the most inflammatory portions of which it repeatedly broadcast to make the case that Solidarity was plotting the overthrow of the state. Most of the participants in the Gdańsk meeting anticipated that the Sejm, scheduled to meet three days later, on December 15, was about to agree to emergency measures, and they were discussing how to respond—with a general strike, perhaps. Despite the tenseness of the situation, few of the assembled activists believed themselves in any imminent danger. When the meeting broke up at midnight, most of them simply went home or took their chartered bus back to the hotel. A few of them, including Zbigniew Bujak, Wiktor Kulerski, Władysław Frasyniuk, and Bogdan Lis, for various reasons did not go home immediately. They turned out to be among the few who escaped the roundup.

The lightning strike by Jaruzelski's forces on the night of December 12–13 was well planned, professionally executed, and almost completely successful.[116] Just after midnight security forces surrounded the Gdańsk hotel in which Solidarity leaders were staying and took them all into custody. Throughout the country the security forces arrested activists in their apartments (including Wałęsa), searched trains (where they missed Frasyniuk, whom a friendly engineer had let off the train in time), cut off telephone and other communications, and patrolled city streets with an intimidating show of force. "How long can the [government's] hand extended in accord be met with a clenched fist?" Jaruzelski asked in an unconscious reversal of the actual state of affairs.[117] Declaring that "our country stands at the edge of an abyss," Jaruzelski advised the nation that civilian power had passed to the Military Council for National Salvation (Wojskowa Rada Ocalenia Narodowego—WRON), which consisted of twenty-one high-ranking officers. He reimposed full censorship, re-established the six-day work week, placed coal mines under military control, and created military courts empowered to impose lengthy jail sentences for such offenses as spreading false information.

Despite their equivocal experience earlier in the year, Solidarity leaders still considered the general strike their ultimate and most devastating weapon. With a majority of Poland's work force as members, including many in the military and the police, they had incorrectly assumed that the government would not mount a direct attack on them because the security forces would not obey. If they did obey, the union would proceed to shut the country down. Thus they were caught almost completely unprepared for the government's action. They had not taken steps to secure their printing presses, for example, or their monetary resources. No shadow network of underground links and safe houses had been arranged, and few preparations of any kind had been made at the local and shop level. Consequently, the large number of vigorous strikes that burst out around the country had an episodic character and were put down relatively easily by a government that proved willing and able to use whatever force was necessary, including shooting a number of miners at the Wujek mine.[118] Worst of all, Solidarity was "not mentally prepared. Nobody imagined that this seemingly weak government would prove strong enough to turn the police ... or the army ... on us."[119] Wrapped up in its own internal politics, which had become increasingly contentious, and confined by a style of thinking that bound it to acts of the working class, Solidarity proved momentarily unable to meet the challenge of overt force.

2

The Gang of Four and Their Nemesis

Solidarity's collapse under the weight of martial law ended the third major attempt of East Europeans to escape from the Stalinist embrace in the direction of pluralism, and the least violent. The Hungarian Revolution of 1956 was a bloody event. More an emotional outburst of rage against the Soviet Union than a calculated effort to achieve an attainable goal, the Hungarian Revolution erupted suddenly after only a few months of relatively superficial oppositional activity, although its passion clearly bespoke deep hostility both to Russians and to the Soviet system. When, in the first days of the revolution, Soviet troops temporarily withdrew, Hungarians could not restrain their hunger to reject Soviet tutelage and to turn westward. A few days later the Red Army returned and began shooting, and the Hungarians shot back. This was revolution such as Delacroix might have painted it—a bare-chested Imre Nagy leading his people over the barricades to liberty. In good romantic fashion, the result was not victory but death—a heroic death, but death nonetheless.

Twelve years later, the Czechs and Slovaks, having learned, in a sense, from the Hungarian experience, explicitly denied they were trying to replace the Soviet system. They claimed to be merely reinterpreting the style with which socialism presented itself, emphasizing the humane rather than the mechanistic side of Marx. More than a year of economic reforms and months of vigorous oppositional activity preceded the surprise denouement. When the invasion came it was not only Soviet troops but also Warsaw Pact soldiers who invaded, and they did not enter shooting; neither did the Czechs and Slovaks shoot back, although they did offer bitter passive resistance. Despite the emotions it raised and the hopes it engendered, the Prague Spring was a peculiarly Czech revolution—sensible, solid, and, when finished, justified with ironic satisfaction as an honorable defeat.

The Solidarity movement was even longer in preparation and much longer in execution. The Poles, having learned the impossibility of replacing their Socialist regime from the Hungarian experience and of reforming it from the Czechoslovak experience, decided instead to bypass it. Independent society would be a democratic sphere unconnected with the all-encompassing state. More cautious than their predecessors and more willing to compromise, Solidarity's self-limiting revolution was the most measured of the three. Perhaps because of this it managed to bring most of the working population of Poland into its fold and to go a long way toward creating the self-governing independent society it set as its goal.

Solidarity was a much shrewder, a much more subversive, and a much more powerful movement than either the Hungarian Revolution or the Prague Spring, and it provoked a milder form of intervention. Solidarity was put down not by foreign invasion but by Polish police—self-repression of the self-limiting revolution. During the martial law period Poles had more leeway for opposition than their Hungarian brothers did in the first few years after 1956 or the Czechs and Slovaks had for many years after 1968. Solidarity was a soft revolution, but that softness was its greatest strength because it educated a generation of activists and it gave almost the entire nation a taste of running its own affairs. Eventually, this is what made the breakthrough in Poland in 1989 possible.

The three great revolutionary moments of the post-Stalinist period all occurred in countries that were traditionally Catholic (or Protestant—but not Orthodox), historically part of one of the Germanic empires, and economically linked to the rest of Europe by traditional trade patterns.[1] Southeastern Europe, which was traditionally Orthodox, historically related to the Ottoman Empire, and relatively new to economic development, experienced no such outbursts.[2] Neither Bulgaria nor Romania produced significant dissidence, let alone the emergence of an independent society, although scattered moments of violent rage occasionally pierced the placid surface of Romanian life. The reason for this is not to be found in some sort of historical determinism through which semi-oriental countries are fated to follow a path of underdevelopment but in specific postwar arrangements and in the policies pursued by the leaders of the two countries.

Neither Romania nor Bulgaria had a lengthy tradition of democracy or of capitalist relations, but both achieved independence in the nineteenth century, created parliamentary systems, and by the interwar period began at least a modest turn toward industrialization.[3] In these ways they did not differ substantially from Greece, which, despite pockets of extreme wealth and a few major cities, was no better governed than Romania and Bulgaria up to World War II and not more prosperous either. But Greece, which had been a client state of Great Britain since the nineteenth century, returned to England's protection in 1944, whereas Bulgaria and Romania, both closely linked with Russia from the nineteenth century, remained in the Soviet sphere after World War II.

After Stalin's death, neither Bulgaria nor Romania experienced breaks in their leadership as Poland and Hungary did, and neither experienced significant internal reforms. In Bulgaria, the Stalinist Vŭlko Chervenko lost his position as party leader in 1956, but he remained an important political force until Todor Zhivkov consolidated both party and state leadership in his own hands in 1962. In Romania, Gheorghe Gheorghiu-Dej, a convinced Stalinist who vigorously opposed Khrushchev's relative moderation, stayed in power until his death in 1965, when his protégé Nicolae Ceauşescu succeeded him. Zhivkov and Ceauşescu stayed in power right up until the fateful months of November and December 1989. All of these leaders, from the early ones through Zhivkov and Ceauşescu, firmly believed in the fundamental Stalinist tenets of collectivization, industrialization, and democratic centralism (that is, strict party control). Within a decade of Stalin's death both Romania and Bulgaria had pushed their agricultural collectivization drives to completion and had embarked on successive five-year plans that stressed heavy industry. The huge metallurgical combines at Galaţi (Romania) and Kremikovtsi (Bulgaria) could compete with Socialist enterprises anywhere for their waste of resources, propaganda excesses, and wretched inefficiency. Neither the Bulgarian nor the Romanian party had any patience with euphemisms such as "United Workers' party" or "Socialist Workers' party." They called themselves simply the Bulgarian Communist party and (after 1965) the Romanian Communist party.

The men who governed these two countries for twenty-five years and more had similar backgrounds and careers. Both Todor Zhivkov and Nicolae Ceauşescu were of peasant origin and received their education primarily in the Communist opposition rather than in formal schools. Zhivkov may have completed secondary school, whereupon he became a printer; but Ceauşescu left school at age eleven to become a shoemaker's apprentice and, eventually, supposedly, an electrician, although he was not very handy.[4] Both suffered arrest and spent the war years in their own countries, either in prison, in the case of Ceauşescu, or in Bulgaria's small partisan movement, in the case of Zhivkov, emerging from the war years with impeccable revolutionary resumes. Ceauşescu had been a prisonmate of Gheorghiu-Dej and became his protégé, whereas Zhivkov became party boss of Sofia. At the time they achieved full control of their countries, neither man had ever left his native land and both understood the world primarily in terms of the simplistic catechisms they had learned as young Stalinists. Their rise to the top of their parties is prima facie evidence that they both had considerable political talent, but neither man was particularly charismatic. The curiosity is that they remained in power for so long and led their countries in such different directions.

Zhivkov's Quiet Bulgaria

There is not a great deal to be said about the development of Bulgarian politics under Todor Zhivkov. By a constant process of reorganization and reshuffling, by pitting occasional challengers against each other, and by demoting upstarts, Zhivkov maintained his personal power and sustained the authority of his party for more than thirty years, an entire generation. His only two tricky moments—and neither of them threatened the party's hegemony—were a rumored army coup in 1965 and a purge associated with the dismissal of Boris Velchev in 1977. In foreign policy Zhivkov hewed closely to the Soviet line.

Economically, Zhivkov was an inveterate reformer. Bulgaria conducted major reform campaigns in 1963, 1965, 1968, 1970–1971, 1978–1979, 1982, and 1985–1987. But since for Zhivkov "reform" meant rationalizing and perfecting centralized planning, none of them led to anything. In general the Bulgarian economy remained closely tied to that of the Soviet Union, which was Bulgaria's largest supplier of fuel and ore, its most consistent buyer of machinery (such as fork-lift trucks and electronics equipment), and a major market for its agricultural products. Bulgaria's moderate success in producing relatively advanced industrial products was made possible by the importation of technology and raw materials from the West, particularly from West Germany, which in turn led to the accumulation of a significant foreign debt. By the end of the 1970s debt service was taking approximately 40 percent of Bulgaria's hard currency earnings. Other East European countries found it difficult or impossible to solve their debt problems, but at the end of the 1970s Bulgaria began paying off its obligations and by 1982 had succeeded in halving the debt. Aggressive selling of agricultural goods throughout the world helped in this endeavor, but the primary method of redressing the Bulgarian balance of trade was to resell at the world price oil imported cheaply from the Soviet Union. Hard currency oil profits and energy supplies for domestic use were the most tangible way that Bulgaria profited from being the Soviet Union's most loyal follower.

Collectivization was successful enough in Bulgaria that in the 1960s agricultural production increased at a rapid rate, although growth fell off during the 1970s, thanks in part to the creation of agroindustrial complexes. These huge, overadministered agricultural enterprises employed tens of thousands of farm workers and covered five to ten thousand hectares of land.[5] The idea was to put food processing facilities, and eventually even research and technical facilities, under the roof of the cooperative that actually grew the crops, thereby increasing specialization, upgrading technical proficiency, and improving production. The agroindustrial complexes suffered the normal bureaucratic inefficiencies, but in general they were successful enough to make Bulgaria one of the best fed countries in Eastern Europe and to permit Bulgaria to earn foreign exchange by exporting agricultural products. Despite the chronic shortage of housing typical of centrally planned systems, the Bulgarian standard of living moved upward noticeably in the period of Zhivkov's rule.

Very little oppositional activity of any kind developed in Bulgaria, either in the pre-1968 period characterized elsewhere by revisionist Marxism or in the post-1968 period characterized elsewhere by antipolitical opposition. No major strikes disturbed Zhivkov's Bulgaria, and no samizdat literature or oppositional tracts rippled the subsurface of public life. Even rock and roll music was late and pallid in Bulgaria. Zhivkov did not achieve this quiescence solely with repression, as Ceauşescu did, although the Bulgarian secret police kept a close eye on society and occasionally a recalcitrant opponent went to prison. But normally a slip did not mean Soviet-style punishments. When philosopher Zhelyu Zhelev's book *Fascism*, which was an obvious aesopian piece, appeared in the 1970s, this future president of Bulgaria had to live in his family village for a while, but when he returned to Sofia under the protection of Liudmila Zhivkova, Todor Zhivkov's eccentric daughter, he took up a position in the Institute for Culture, where he pursued a restrained career as a philosopher. In another case, when in 1968 authorities banned Radoi Ralin's *Hot Peppers*, a collection of short poems, pointed aphorisms, and clever drawings, because it contained, among other things, a cartoon of a pig whose tail looked suspiciously like Zhivkov's signature, both Ralin and the book's cartoonist, Boris Dimovski, suffered "invisible conspiracies" that made their lives difficult, but within a few years they were able to write and publish again.[6]

But these were exceptional cases. In general little or no opposition existed in Bulgaria. One of the most common explanations for this seeming anomaly is the orientalist argument that Eastern Orthodoxy is morally passive, emphasizes form rather than substance, and therefore does not provide suitable cultural soil for initiative and risk taking. In this view Bulgarian culture is uncongenial to the kind of ethical stands taken by Charter 77 or the drive toward independent society characteristic of Catholic Poland.[7] This view is analogous to the explanation given by many people in the Balkans that their various failings are attributable to the legacy of four hundred years of Ottoman occupation. There may well be some truth in these assertions, but they are so widely accepted that they have come to stand in the way of more ordinary analysis that would be offered for other countries.

One reason for the weakness of the Bulgarian opposition was that the Bulgarian Communist party had a long, indigenous history and therefore was not perceived as a foreign imposition. The Bulgarian party came into existence in 1891 and had its own Bolshevik-like wing (the Narrows) as early as 1903. Another reason was the relatively positive feelings Bulgarians have toward Russians. Since the Russian army achieved independence for Bulgaria in the nineteenth century, Bulgarians did not look on Russians with the same kind of hostility as did other East Europeans, and since Soviet troops entered Bulgaria only briefly at the end of World War II,

Bulgarians did not have the same opportunities for developing a hatred of the invader as occurred elsewhere.

A change in social stratification also helped the Communists in Bulgaria. A very high proportion of the postwar Bulgarian intelligentsia were men and women who emerged from poor backgrounds and had the postwar changes to thank for their rise to position. This was not an accident, because class criteria were used to ration education in Communist Bulgaria, thereby almost wiping out a generation of middle-class students in favor of ones from peasant or proletarian backgrounds. Those who benefited from this policy had every reason to support the system that had given them their chance to prove themselves. Without a strong set of traditional linkages with the West but with a stake in the system, the new Bulgarian intelligentsia often saw itself as peripheralized from European concerns, both geographically and culturally. The isolation in which Zhivkov kept the intellectuals during his years only added to this sense of detachment. In consequence, they often did not look upon the activities of oppositionists elsewhere as something that concerned them.[8]

Certainly an important reason for the lack of overt opposition in Bulgaria was the political skill of the leader himself. Western authors have tended to patronize Todor Zhivkov, characterizing him as "modest and well-meaning," or "colorless and plodding," or "sluggish and inept."[9] This is in contrast to evaluations of János Kádár, who was admired for his clever policies that kept Hungary calm and satisfied after the devastation of 1956. Kádár was of peasant origin too, and with a proletarian youth, but by 1970 he had transmuted himself, in legend at least, into a practical and gifted leader.

Zhivkov, on the other hand, fell into a category that is difficult for educated Westerners to understand and to esteem—the sly Balkan peasant. When he read pronouncements or speeches written for him by others, his speech was faltering and wooden; but when he spoke off the cuff he had a common touch that suggested his real talent, which was manipulating people. Zhivkov did not permit intellectuals particularly large material gains, although some stars lived well. Instead he cultivated and flattered them. He met periodically with writers, actors, academics, and students; liked to tell self-deprecating stories about his own lack of education; and found ways to flatter and to reward individuals at the right moment. Zhivkov used this special talent to minimize opposition without introducing particularly brutal methods, while at the same time the Bulgarian economy inched modestly forward. As Maria Todorova puts it, "Zhivkov managed to implement a successful policy of dividing or corrupting the intelligentsia while not creating martyrs and saints."[10] No workers' strikes, no samizdat publications, and no overt dissidence disrupted Bulgarian public life, and the credit, if it be that, goes to Todor Zhivkov. Of course, at the same time he deserves credit for the rest: a cult of personality, coupled with luxurious living for himself and an egalitarian wage system for the rest of the country; a dullness in public life; serious and ignored pollution; nationalist outbursts against Yugoslavia and Turkey; a xenophobic internal policy against national minorities; closed borders; and all the other dreary markers of "real existing socialism."

Megalomania in Romania

Bulgaria fared better than did its neighbor Romania, where Nicolae Ceau-şescu came to power in 1965. Insofar as Ceauşescu was known at all in 1965, he was perceived as the most loyal and energetic servant of his predecessor, Gheorghe Gheorghiu-Dej. That postwar leader had embarked Romania on a quite different course than the one followed by Bulgaria, which was always a loyal supporter of the Soviet Union. After Soviet troops finally left Romania in 1958, Gheorgiu-Dej took advantage of the conflict between China and the Soviet Union, as well as the Cuban missile crisis, to turn Romania away from direct dependence on the Soviet Union. He began to reorient Romanian trade a bit toward the West, and he encouraged historians to rekindle traditional interpretations of the Romanian past. Most important, in 1963, after several years of controversy, he rejected Nikita Khrushchev's plan to integrate the economies of the CMEA (Council for Mutual Economic Assistance—the economic association of the Soviet bloc).

Khrushchev's plan would have made Romania responsible for supplying the Soviet bloc with agricultural goods and raw materials in return for which it would receive machinery and industrial products from the other members of CMEA. Such a policy would have prevented the construction of the great steel mill that all Stalinists considered the sine qua non of modernity and independence. Gheorgiu-Dej, Stalinist to his core, saw Khrushchev's integration plans as yet another Soviet effort to thwart Romania, whose future he believed he had assured by signing an agreement with an Anglo-French consortium to develop a huge steel mill in Galaţi. A series of anti-Soviet pinpricks, such as publishing a reinterpretation of the Soviet invasion of 1944 that gave most of the credit for "liberating" Romania to Romanian rather than to Soviet forces, prepared the way for the publication in 1964 of a "Statement of the Romanian Workers' Party." "No party has or can have a privileged place," the statement said, "or can impose its line and opinions on other parties. . . . It is the sovereign right of each socialist state to elaborate, choose, or change the forms and methods of socialist construction."[11] This independent line marked Romania as the maverick of the Soviet bloc in Western eyes. No matter how despotic Ceauşescu later became, the United States and others clung to the vision of a nonconformist Romania until the late 1980s.

When Nicolae Ceauşescu came to power, then, he inherited a party whose independent stands toward the Soviet Union had created a modest but genuine popularity for itself. Not only were many people proud of the renewed Romanophile direction of national politics, but the economic picture seemed hopeful. The devastation of the postwar years had been repaired, a reasonably successful collectivization process was complete, and the device of placing new industries relatively evenly around the country rather than simply in the urban centers shielded the peasantry from the worst side effects of industrialization.[12] Ceauşescu began his rule by claiming to be in favor of increased democracy, Socialist legality, and cultural openness. He encouraged letter writing to newspapers, staged huge conferences of workers, suggested increased material incentives for the peasants, called for a "confrontation of viewpoints" to improve science, and promised more intellectual diversity.[13] From 1968 to 1972 he even permitted private businessmen to lease state restaurants and similar services for their own profit. Western observers who had begun to look at Romania in a more favorable light were particularly impressed when in 1967 Romania was the only bloc country not to break with Israel during the Six Day War and even more so in 1968 when Ceauşescu refused to permit Romanian troops to participate in the invasion of Czechoslovakia.

The abrupt ending of the Prague Spring had the opposite effect in Romania from the one it had in east central Europe. Instead of convincing the intelligentsia that there was no hope of reforming socialism, Ceauşescu's stirring indictment of the invasion of Czechoslovakia convinced many Romanian intellectuals that Ceauşescu was opening up new possibilities for Romania. Many of them joined the party for the first time. In that same year some young writers tested the new sense of hope by putting their own candidates forward for leadership of the writers' union, demanding an end to censorship and calling for more democracy in publishing.

But the hopes of the late 1960s came to nothing. Not only were the young writers unsuccessful in 1968, but three years later, after a visit to North Korea and China, Ceauşescu closed the door on his early promises. The "July theses" of 1971, which called for a tightening of discipline in cultural affairs, began the process whereby the Ceauşescu regime took on that peculiar version of unreality that characterized it over the next twenty years.

Nicolae Ceauşescu was never personally popular, even at the beginning of his rule. A rigid and authoritarian man, he had none of the folksy charm of Todor Zhivkov and little of the flexibility of János Kádár. He read his speeches with a slight stutter and in a monotone, punctuating his talk with weak little arm movements and often emphasizing the wrong word. Without any spark of spontaneous warmth, Ceauşescu began early to manufacture demonstrations of public support through a variety of artificial means. One strategy was to visit the countryside often, theoretically to hear popular concerns and to mingle with the people. In actuality he paid not the slightest attention to the real concerns of the population, from which his increasingly regal manner isolated him, and the vivacious demonstrations of support that always greeted his appearances were rigidly choreographed. By 1980 party organizers were putting together massive spectacles of adulation that involved literally millions of active participants in what one observer called "a permanent ceremonial enacted by the entire country in front of a single spectator."[14]

The central device in what Katherine Verdery calls Ceauşescu's symbolic-ideological strategy of social control was the creation of a cult of personality to end all cults of personality.[15] At the beginning of his rule the media mentioned other public figures prominently, but by 1973 the main news item in every television broadcast or newspaper became the daily rounds of President of the Republic Nicolae Ceauşescu, as he was always referred to, and his wife, Comrade Academician Doctor Engineer Elena Ceauşescu. The rise of Elena to equal billing in the daily barrage of effusive praise was particularly irritating to Romanians.[16] If Nicolae's self-promotion was difficult to stomach, at least he had seized power on his own merits. Elena, on the other hand, was despised for using her husband's position to advance her own pretentions. Supposedly an engineer, although it was difficult to find anyone who had known her as a student (the only proof that has been found documenting her educational achievements was one showing her completion of the fourth grade),[17] she ruthlessly promoted her own quite fraudulent reputation as a great scientist and came to be a formidable power in her own right. By the mid-1970s she was being characterized as an "outstanding activist of party and state, eminent personage of Romanian and international science."[18] A less charitable opinion was that of Mark Almond, who described her as a combination of Lady Macbeth and Trofim Lysenko, the Soviet scientific charlatan.[19]

Even the praise of Elena pales before the fatuous adulation heaped on her husband.[20] As Walter Bacon has pointed out, this adulation typically contained five elements: "party praise of the leader, evidence of his theoretical genius, proof of his paternalistic relationship with the masses, reminders of his heroic revolutionary past, and demonstrations [usually in the form of ever-upwardly arching graphs] of his leadership's accomplishments."[21] By the 1980s Ceauşescu had become the "torchbearer among torchbearers," "unique as a mountain peak," and even "our famous lullaby trill." His brilliance was legendary, his figure unique and impressive, his personality passionate and fascinating, and his moral endurance fabulous—all qualities tempered, of course, by his "saintly modesty."[22]

While one may speculate about the needs that drive a man to revel in such absurdities or about the functional rationality of deifying the leader in an undeveloped society, it is clear that two basic and incompatible ideas underlay Ceauşescu's worldview—the primitive and one-dimensional Marxism that he had learned as a semieducated revolutionary in the 1930s and an equally primitive and self-serving nationalism. If Stalinism was the reductio ad absurdum of the idea that human reason could transform the world, as suggested in the Introduction, then Ceauşescuism is the reductio ad absurdum of Stalinism. Heavy industry, collectivized agriculture, and strict social controls enforced by an aggressive and sizable security police constituted the pillars of his socialism. Above all, Ceauşescu believed in the virtues of a proletarian and revolutionary party, which must take the lead in building a "multilaterally developed socialist society." The party's duty was to extend its control over as many aspects of public and private affairs as it could. In Poland the successes of KOR and Solidarity in mobilizing civil society made independent society a realistic candidate for political partnership. In Romania, by contrast, the party's constant invasion of public space after 1971 left no room for an independent society to emerge. Even within the party Ceaușescu left no free space, because he insisted that party affairs be run only by sycophants whose loyalty to him was outspoken and abject. By placing their deadening hands on every public and private act, this "sycophantocracy," as Bacon calls it, squeezed all spontaneity and vivacity out of Romanian public life.

From his first speeches in 1966 and 1967, however, Ceaușescu did not rely primarily on Marxism to mobilize Romanians and to legitimate his rule. He took the nationalist card originally dealt him by Gheorghiu-Dej and raised it, as he did so many other things, to new heights of vulgarity, linking the ideas of nation, party, and leader into one indissoluble conception of Romania. Since every nationalism privileges certain cultural practices over others, control of the historical narrative is always a point of contention. Ceaușescu took close personal control over the Romanian narrative, often presenting the "correct" view of the nation's past in major speeches. He maintained that continuity and unity were the bedrocks "of *any* theoretical, ideological and political educative activity" of the party.[23] Continuity referred to the questionable thesis that a direct line of historical transmission linked the Dacians, who inhabited Transylvania in pre-Roman times, and the Socialist Republic of Romania. Between the Dacians and the present, every major Romanian historical figure had added his special quality to the Romanian character, which became most fully represented in the preeminent historical figure of Nicolae Ceaușescu. Staged meetings between himself and important kings from the Romanian past were only the most comic among the devices Ceaușescu used to demonstrate his unimpeachable genealogy as the most fully developed realization of the Romanian spirit. Reports of these encounters never mentioned that Ceaușescu was actually meeting an actor, and not, say, Michael the Brave. Paintings showed Ceaușescu radiant in a semicircle of the ancient rulers.

Unity referred to the constant longing for unification into one state that allegedly had motivated Romanians from Dacian times. This characteristic may have needed particular stress because, in fact, the three main Romanian lands had never been firmly united until the twentieth century. In any event, after World War II the Romanian Communist party became "the continuer of the centuries-old struggle of the Romanian people for the country's independence, for the formation of the Romanian nation and of the unitary national State, for the acceleration of social progress."[24] Romania's entire history had to be promoted as a two-thousand-year-long aspiration to be united under the direction of the party and its leader.

Katherine Verdery argues that Ceaușescu and his party did not impose their exaggerated nationalist discourse on Romania simply as a way of justifying their rule. Rather, the party was successful in finding a discourse "inscribed in and emanating from many quarters of Romanian society" and that therefore constituted an already existing field of contention it could seek to control.[25] The measure of the party's success in using this strategy was that even its opponents, when offered a minimal opportunity to raise their heads, tended to conduct their arguments using nationalist symbolism. This had the effect of confirming the terms that the state had already appropriated, so that by their very use of nationalist categories the potential oppositionists lent subtle support to the centralizing character of the regime.

In fact, however, there was little opposition in Romania. Norman Manea, one of the few oppositionist writers, has said that after Ceauşescu came to power some writers tried to write nonpolitically, but they became so involved in the details of how to do this that they lost track of their literary aims, becoming preoccupied instead with politics rather than esthetics and thereby entering into the cage provided for them by the regime.[26] The only oppositionist who became even moderately known in the West was the novelist Paul Goma.[27] After several years of difficulties with the regime, in 1970 Goma attempted to publish a novel in which he seemed to model an unsympathetic character on Elena Ceauşescu. This marked the end of his public career. In 1977 he circulated a letter of solidarity with Charter 77, but he could gain the signature of only two ethnically Romanian intellectuals (a number of others signed, but they were Romanians of German, Hungarian, or Jewish descent who had been denied emigration visas). Goma was arrested, interrogated, and forced to emigrate.

One of the reasons so little opposition emerged in Romania may have been that Romania, like Bulgaria, boasted few powerful Marxist thinkers. This may have been a function of the extremely small number of leftist intellectuals existing in Romania before the war, so that when the Communists came to power they boasted no prominent thinkers of European stature. In places like Poland and Hungary it was often just these figures who provided the intellectual basis for a revisionist Marxist opposition before 1968. Even opposition after 1968 in those countries can be understood as benefiting from the failure of the revisionists, against whom the antipoliticians could react.[28] Michael Shafir argues, therefore, that the presence of the pre-1968 revisionists who were "capable of formulating demands in an 'elite penetrative' jargon" was a necessary, though not sufficient, condition for inducing change in Eastern Europe.[29] Since these did not exist in Romania there was little movement toward reform before 1968, and no failed revisionism to react against with an antipolitical strategy after 1968. Shafir suggests three other possible explanations for the lack of an opposition in Romania: an Ottoman tradition of dissimulation; the intellectuals' willingess to enter into nationalist discourse, and the lack of restiveness within the working class.

There is another factor: the extraordinarily thorough penetration of Romanian society by the infamous *Securitate*, Ceaușescu's huge and ubiquitous secret police. The true extent and organization of this shadowy but powerful organization has yet to come to light, but all foreign travelers to Romania were painfully aware of its presence—friends interrogated after social visits, film taken from cameras locked in suitcases inside locked hotel rooms, menacing interviews with insinuating officials. It has been said that a good political machine thrives on the visibility of its rewards and the certainty of its punishments. Ceaușescu's punishments were not ultimate— he killed only a few of his opponents—but they were certain: harassment, demotion, transfer, house arrest, and prison. The Securitate penetrated deeply into the fabric of Romanian society, creating a pervasive atmosphere of fear by continually testing the loyalty of every citizen in the country and intimidating all but the most foolhardy. "The reason why most attempts at opposing the Romanian regime were dissipated in improvised, transient, isolated explosions," Manea writes, "was the virtual impossibility of establishing the very foundations of genuine social dialogue."[30]

Romania's economy suffered from the same deficits as the other centrally planned economies, but with two significant and unusual twists. In the 1960s Romanian officials became alarmed about the country's declining birth rate, which by 1965 had dropped below the point needed to sustain a growing labor force. Other East European countries facing a similar problem in the 1960s expanded their social benefits programs to encourage women to bear children. Hungary and East Germany in particular coupled economic reform with positive incentives to encourage births.[31] But Romania took a perversely original and unorthodox approach: in 1966 it decided to increase the labor force by banning abortions.

Abortions had become much easier throughout Eastern Europe after the Soviet Union reliberalized its laws late in 1955.[32] Since contraceptive devices, while not illegal, were impossible to obtain in Romania, with the legalization of abortion there in 1957 it became the only readily available method of birth control. Thus the number of abortions surged from about 130,000 in 1958 to 1,115,000 in 1965, or more than four abortions for every live birth, the highest rate reported up to that time for any country in the world.[33] Ceaușescu found this unsatisfactory. Both he and his wife had a strong puritanical streak that they periodically pitted against drinking, smoking, and frivolity in general. The Ceaușescus insisted on a carefully measured and controlled organic diet and watched their weight carefully. This puritanical streak probably influenced their decision to ban abortions.

The instantaneous impact of the ruling in 1966 was the near doubling of the country's birth rate in one year. But the new rule did not halt illegal abortions, or even legal ones, which were still permitted in cases of incest and threats to the mother's health. By the mid-1970s the rate had crept back to about one legal or illegal abortion for every live birth, a higher rate than in any other East European country.[34] Within a decade the birth rate declined into the range it had been in 1960, and by the mid-1980s it was back where it had been when the restrictions were put in place. The costs in human terms of Ceauşescu's natalist policy were enormous, especially in the 1980s, when many mothers, unwilling or unable to care for their unwanted children, simply abandoned them. The discovery after 1989 of orphanages filled with thousands of wretched children living in medieval filth was the single most horrible revelation to come out of any formerly Communist country in Eastern Europe. And it goes without saying that Ceauşescu's brutal policy had no effect whatsoever on Romania's economic growth.

The second peculiar aspect of Romanian economic development under Ceauşescu revolved around Romania's main natural resource, oil. The Romanian oil fields were the largest in Eastern Europe outside the Soviet Union and had provided the basis for a strong Romanian oil industry throughout the twentieth century. In the 1970s, however, output began to decline due to well exhaustion at a time when Romania, pursuing its emphasis on heavy industry, had greatly increased its refining capacity. Where to get the oil? The logical place would have been the Soviet Union, but because of Romania's independent policies from the 1960s, the Soviets refused to sell Romania oil at the preferential prices that other members of CMEA enjoyed. The solution was to cultivate oil-rich countries such as Iraq, Iran, Libya, and Algeria. During the 1970s trade with these countries increased significantly, until by 1980 it consisted of more than one-quarter of all Romanian foreign trade (trade with CMEA countries and with the developed world each consisted of about one-third of Romanian foreign trade). At the same time, however, the world price of oil skyrocketed in the oil crises of 1973 and 1978. Trying to maintain its import schedule, Romania ran up a foreign debt of $10.2 billion by 1981, forcing Romania to become the second East European country (Poland was first) to reschedule its debt.

At that point, however, Ceauşescu made another idiosyncratic move—he decided to pay off all Romania's foreign debt by 1990. This economically unsound decision was quite consistent with the narrow moralism with which he propagated his natalist policies, with the pride with which he emphasized Romania's uniqueness, and with the provinciality of his self-image. Romania was not going to have to depend on anyone. This draconian decision could only be implemented by dramatically cutting imports and greatly increasing exports, even if it meant impoverishing his own people, and it made Romania the most miserable and despised country in Europe in the 1980s.

Nicolae Ceauşescu and his wife Elena were surely the least attractive among a none-too-attractive rogues' gallery of East European Communist leaders, and they fell into an entirely different category from the intellectually and morally vigorous leaders of the East European opposition. But in a strange way Ceauşescu had his affiliation with the revolutions of 1956,

1968, and 1980 too, for he was also seeking a way to lead his country out of the Soviet grasp. Unfortunately for the Romanians, however, he traded an evolving Soviet domination that eventually produced Gorbachev for a megalomaniacal version of inward-looking totalitarianism that crushed the human spirit and left Romanians with few social resources to cast off the evil thing when an opportunity finally presented itself. In 1968, when Ceauşescu achieved great popularity in Romania by refusing to participate in the invasion of Czechoslovakia, one Romanian prophetically observed, "We have been so preoccupied with the danger of Soviet occupation that for all practical purposes we have pre-occupied ourselves."[35] In escaping the domination of a foreign power, Romanians fell headlong into the grasp of a more vicious homegrown version of that very domination.

The First Workers' and Peasants' State on German Soil

When the West wrote off Bulgaria and Romania after World War II, the Communist regimes of those countries were able to establish such strong control over their societies that the Soviet Union never had to come to their rescue. The Soviet interventions in 1953, 1956, and 1968 came not in southeastern Europe but in east central Europe. Despite these interventions, in two of the Soviet clients, Poland and Hungary, an independent society emerged that eventually challenged the party's exclusive right to rule. But in the other two cases, Czechoslovakia and the German Democratic Republic, the interventions succeeded in imposing or reinforcing restrictive regimes that maintained a social control quite comparable to that maintained by Ceauşescu and Zhivkov. Unlike their Balkan counterparts, the leaders of the two conservative regimes of east central Europe were educated men. Gustav Husák was a rather brilliant Communist lawyer of middle-class origins from Slovakia, and Erich Honecker received a substantial education, albeit more in party schools than in ordinary educational institutions. But the regimes they presided over were sufficiently similar to those of Zhivkov and Ceauşescu that Charles Gati has lumped all of them together as the "gang of four," the backward-looking neo-Stalinists who continued to apply the failed lessons of the 1950s well into the 1980s.[36]

The most obvious problem that faced the German Democratic Republic was summed up in the first word of its name: German. Created in 1949 by the Soviets as a counterpoise to the Federal Republic of Germany and deprived of formerly German lands to the east, the GDR always suffered from an inferiority complex as the semilegitimate poorer relation of its western counterpart. Whereas the Federal Republic presented itself simply as "Germany," the best the German Democratic Republic could do was to present itself as "the first workers' and peasants' state on German soil." For twenty years the West German governments of Konrad Adenauer and his Christian Democratic successors encouraged this sense of inferiority by preventing diplomatic recognition of East Germany by the international community. Shortly after West Germany became a fully recognized sovereign state in 1954, its foreign minister declared that the Federal Republic would break relations with any state that granted diplomatic recognition to East Germany. Since it was already clear that West Germany was on the verge of a rapid economic resurgence, this so-called Hallstein Doctrine diplomatically isolated East Germany until the 1970s.

Isolation assumed a physical dimension in August 1961, when, alarmed at the large numbers of its citizens working in West Berlin and leaving for West Germany, the East German government constructed a huge wall through the center of Berlin. More than twenty-five miles long and twenty feet high in many spots, the Berlin Wall succeeded in slowing the flow of emigrants, but it failed to prevent the stagnation of East German population growth and was a grotesque public relations disaster in the bargain. Between 1949 and the construction of the wall roughly 2.7 million East Germans, or approximately one-seventh of the country's population, registered as refugees in West Germany, whereas in the following decade only half a million succeeded in making the journey. Nonetheless, East German population did not grow. In 1989 it remained about 17 million, approximately where it had been in 1961 and less than it had been in 1949. Worse, the wall became "a permanent, massive, anti-Communist propaganda exhibition" to which tourists—from presidents to ordinary citizens—flocked from all over the world.[37]

East Germany's diplomatic isolation ended in December 1972, when initiatives from West Germany led to the signing of the Basic Treaty committing the two Germanies to "normal, good-neighborly relations on the basis of equality."[38] Worldwide diplomatic recognition followed rapidly, as did admission to the United Nations and participation in the Helsinki Accords of 1975.

The man who signed the Basic Treaty for East Germany was Erich Honecker, from 1971 the leader of both the Socialist Unity party and the state. The son of a militantly left-wing coal miner from the Saarland, Honecker joined the Communist party at age seventeen at the beginning of the Great Depression and as a young man attended the Comintern School in Moscow. He survived the war because he spent the ten years from 1935 to 1945 in a Nazi prison, much of that time in solitary confinement. Despite the reserved manner that this experience reinforced in Honecker, his unswerving loyalty to postwar leader Walter Ulbricht and to the Soviet Union permitted him to rise rapidly through the party ranks to become, by 1958, the politburo member in charge of army affairs and internal security.

Honecker took over from Walter Ulbricht in 1971 because he was more willing to follow the Soviet policy of détente than his predecessor, but in many ways Honecker was more rigid than the none-too-flexible Ulbricht. He quickly declared that the German Democratic Republic was a "class society of a special type," reported that Ulbricht's economic reforms had created "serious industrial 'distortions' that might take 'years to overcome,'" and began to replace Ulbricht's technically competent bureaucrats with administrators with purely party backgrounds. Honecker's view, which he maintained until Gorbachev's time, was that absolute loyalty to the Soviet Union was the "decisive criterion of fidelity to Marxism-Leninism."[39] An unpretentious man in private, much more able to relax with friends and even servants than had been Ulbricht, Honecker's public persona of a dedicated and rigid neo-Stalinist well suited the Brezhnev years.[40]

One of the most important benefits of the Basic Treaty Honecker signed in 1972 was that it provided for direct monetary payments to East Germany. By the late 1970s these payments, when added to the liberal credits that West Germany had provided since the 1950s to facilitate inter-German trade, reached the substantial sum of 600 million marks a year. One analyst has calculated that by the end of the 1980s East Germany and its citizens were receiving as much as six billion marks in various West German subsidies and advantages a year, or more than 15 percent of its "produced national income."[41] Part of this benefit came from the willingness of the European Community to consider East German goods imported into the Federal Republic as having been produced there, thus freeing those East German products from the tariffs to which they would otherwise have been subject.

But opening relations with West Germany in 1972 gave new urgency to an old problem: how to encourage East Germans to distinguish positively between themselves and the West Germans? The East Germans had vigorously advocated unification in the first years after the war, but unification in a socialist state, arguing that the West Germans were exclusively to blame for the division of Germany. As time passed, however, and the hope of Stalinizing West Germany became increasingly absurd, West Germany turned the tables by defining unification not as a mutually agreed upon federation, as Stalin had suggested in 1952, but as the incorporation of the smaller, poorer, and weaker East Germany into West Germany, a solution obviously unacceptable to the German Democratic Republic. Erich Honecker recognized this problem and found a logical if unrealistic solution: he denied that a single German nation existed. Under modern conditions, he argued, there were two Germanies, a bourgeois one and a socialist one. "There is no German question at all," one of his ideological spokesmen said in 1973. "Rather there are two sovereign, socially opposed, and independent German states and nations."[42]

The methods that the dogmatic Honecker favored for "fencing off" (*abgrenzung*) East Germany were to improve the "political-ideological education of party members and all workers in the spirit of socialism" and to integrate East Germany as fully as possible into the CMEA in partnership with "the other countries of the socialist community."[43] *Abgrenzung* also meant forbidding key groups of functionaries to have contact with "foreigners" (that is, West Germans) and maintaining "guest books" of foreign visitors. "Germany" was eliminated in favor of the "German Democratic Republic" and schoolchildren had to be taught to hum the national anthem because it contained the verse "Arisen out of the ruin and headed for the future, let us serve Germany, our united fatherland."[44]

Honecker was enough of a realist to understand that it was not sufficient simply to assert that capitalism was bad and socialism good. East German life actually had to get better. The paradoxical result of the policy of *abgrenzung*, therefore, was that East Germany entered into competition with the West to improve life under socialism, while at the same time trying to create the illusion that East Germany constituted a nation of its own. There was nothing intrinsically impossible about this effort. After all, Austrians speak German and consider themselves part of a Germanic cultural world, but they remain Austrians, not Germans. East German historians began to assimilate such great figures of the German past as Johann Sebastian Bach, Martin Luther, and Frederick the Great into their own history; East German television received orders to produce shows more competitive with the West German television offerings that most East Germans were able to view; consumer goods and housing received renewed emphasis; the most vigorous writers were permitted to travel, publish, and even live for extended periods in the West; and extraordinary accomplishments in international sports competitions gave East Germans some highly visible successes to be proud of.

For a while Honecker's stiff-necked new programs seemed to succeed. East Germany entered the world stage, its sovereignty apparently secured by the Helsinki Accords, and its economy improved to the extent that in the 1970s it was deemed to be the tenth largest in the world. Some observers even began to notice a sense of a distinct East German identity.[45] But as in the rest of Eastern Europe, by the end of the 1970s the veneer of success began to wear thin. Due to massive financial aid from West Germany, East Germany did not face the same debt problems that Poland, Romania, and Bulgaria did, but the stricter centralized controls that had been reimposed under Honecker were wreaking their usual havoc—overinvestment, inefficient pricing, soft budget constraints, and the rest.

Disaffection in East Germany bore a family resemblance to the dull sullenness of the Romanians in the 1980s or the isolated apathy of the Bulgarians, but it differed in several ways from that found in southeastern Europe. For one thing, because of East Germany's proximity to the West, rock music made much greater inroads there than in southeastern Europe. All East European regimes recognized the subversive nature of this music, which tended "to be hard driving and given to half-resolved or even unresolved dissonances," as one historian puts it. The regimes wanted triumphant or nonevocatory music, not music with lyrics displaying "consistent and unmitigated subjectivity" or private feelings and perceptions.[46] In October 1977, a year after the conviction of the members of People of the Plastic Universe in Czechoslovakia, a riot at a rock concert in East Germany turned anti-Soviet, and the regime reacted with repression, but at the same time it also had to permit an increasing amount of sanitized rock music of its own, thus chipping away at its claim to cultural hegemony.

Also unlike southeastern Europe, revisionist Marxist thinkers criticized the regime. One of the first to do so was Wolfgang Harich and his associates, who proposed, on the basis of the Polish and Hungarian examples of 1956, to abandon the collectivization of agriculture and to replace the bureaucracy with a democratic socialist party. Harich received ten years in jail for his trouble. In 1963 a more interesting revisionist appeared, the physicist Robert Havemann. A lifelong Communist activist who had known Honecker in prison during the war and who already had a reputation as a courageous critic of the regime, Havemann delivered a series of lectures in Leipzig and Berlin during 1963 and 1964 in which he lacerated the German Democratic Republic for being dogmatic rather than dialectical and for inhibiting the freedom of scientific inquiry.[47] At the same time Havemann was very critical of bourgeois materialism, especially privately owned automobiles. "Socialism should offer human beings different perspectives," he said in a later interview, "not those of greater consumption but of greater liberty and development."[48] Havemann lost his university position for these lectures and was placed under severe house arrest—security personnel occupied the house next door and one across the street; everyone entering the street was interrogated; and sometimes as many as five cars followed him on his regulated and restricted trips to visit relatives.

The failure of the Prague Spring did not turn Havemann in the direction of antipolitics. He interpreted the preinvasion period as proof that socialism and democracy could exist side by side if hostile forces did not interfere. The most famous Marxist critic of the German Democratic Republic, Rudolf Bahro, a career party man who in 1977 smuggled his secretly written book *Alternatives* to the West, did not agree.[49] He thought the Prague Spring proved the bankruptcy of socialism as it was practiced in Eastern Europe, but this did not propel him in the direction of antipolitics either.[50] Much like Kuroń and Modzelewski more than a decade before, Bahro proposed legalizing opposition within the workers' party, creating workers' councils, and increasing direct democracy in the party. In addition, he suggested that all white-collar workers spend four to six weeks doing manual labor, that wages be equalized, and that the Communist party be replaced by a league of Communists. Like Havemann— and Harich too—Bahro criticized the regime for attempting to compete with capitalism in consumer goods. "It is better to know than to have," is one way he put it.[51] Exciting though Bahro's ideas were to the European Left, by the time they appeared they were already obsolete, not to mention utopian and naively coercive. The human rights movement was already underway in Poland and Czechoslovakia, and Marxism as a living political ideology had long since embarked on its steep and slippery path to oblivion.[52]

If the lack of revisionist critics was one of the reasons for the absence of an antipolitical opposition in Romania and Bulgaria, the same cannot be said for East Germany. Nevertheless, antipolitical opposition was thin there as well. The most vigorous form of organized opposition was the unofficial peace movement that emerged in reaction to the increasing militarization of East German society in the late 1970s and early 1980s. The Soviets and their allies had always held that since, by definition, their regimes favored peace, any expressions of pacifist sentiments outside the official peace organizations were "objectively" antipacifist.[53] Thus the regime disapproved when the evangelical churches spoke out increasingly after 1968 on that subject. In the early 1980s a small pacifist movement protected by both the Protestant and Catholic churches reacted publicly against the introduction of such measures as widespread civil defense exercises, teaching army songs in nursery school, hand-grenade throwing in sports classes in the fourth grade, and ninth- and tenth-grade paramilitary training. Although it presumably was within the capacity of the *Stasi*— *Staatssicherheitsdienst* (State Security Service)—to crush the pacifists (some one hundred pacifists were arrested in 1983), the government permitted the churches to provide some shelter for the movement.[54] The Protestant churches did provide a home for pacifists in East Germany, but at the same time they also "served to domesticate and channel such dissent."[55]

Why did these weakly organized protest movements—environmental and feminist groups existed as well—not develop the same kind of antipolitical thinking as their colleagues in Czechoslovakia and Poland? A significant reason was that the regime dealt with its small number of critics both harshly and cleverly. In addition to arresting and imprisoning dissidents, authorities often simply threw them into the West German briar patch. "One has to say that the demonstrators are mainly people who want to leave the GDR," one activist lamented late in the 1980s. "They have now learned that if one takes part in a demonstration, one quickly gets out of the country."[56] Continually demoralized by this tactic, the oppositionists could not count on significant support from East German writers either. Many writers opposed Honecker's regime but they tended to oppose it in terms of revisionist Marxism and in the 1980s often from the vantage point of comfortable and lengthy stays abroad. Critical of the cultural norms of Western capitalism, although willing to endure them periodically, these authors did not evolve in the direction of antipolitical pluralism and therefore did not generate the kind of moral strength or political challenge that proved valuable to Czech oppositionists.

But probably the most important reason no movement for an independent society took hold in East Germany was the country's proximity to the West, which had two complementary effects. First, when East German writers, almost all of whom began from leftist assumptions in the first place, peeked over the wall by means of their television sets, they did not like the consumer society they saw on the other side. For reformers in other parts of Eastern Europe, democracy, constitutionalism, and civil liberties were more or less empty concepts, icons standing for all that was good about the West but without experiential meaning. In East Germany the West was a concrete and sometimes not-altogether-appealing country literally within sight. East German oppositionists hated their regime and wanted to replace it, but not with a crass materialism. They were therefore inclined to stick to specific reform objectives that could have application in both East and West, such as the peace movement, rather than to speculations based on Western ethical precepts.

The closeness to West Germany had just the opposite effect on ordinary citizens. East Germans had access to Western television, were visited by millions of relatives and friends from the other side every year, and suffered the humiliation of heavily armed borders constantly patrolled to keep the young and vigorous from emigrating. The ordinary East German, despite a certain defensiveness and pride in some of the country's successes, envied the brightly lit, colorful, and vivacious Kurfürstendamm in West Berlin, which contrasted so starkly with the dimly lit gray façades lining the almost empty Unter den Linden in East Berlin. Alienated from a false regime that gave them no hope of a normal future, hundreds of thousands of East Germans could conceive of no better solution for their personal lives than escape to the West.[57]

"Normalization" in Czechoslovakia

The fourth of the neo-Stalinist regimes in Eastern Europe, Czechoslovakia, went through a trauma that no other East European state experienced—invasion by their Warsaw Pact neighbors. At first, party leader Alexander Dubček, who was none too agile a politician, had hoped he would be able to save some of the reforms outlined in the April program. In fact, during the first months after the Warsaw Pact invasion, borders remained relatively open while discussion of the new laws on decentralizing industry and on workers' self-management proceeded. A new law making Czechoslovakia a federal state actually went into effect on January 1, 1969. But from the beginning it was obvious that the Soviets were not going to permit Dubček room for maneuver. Only two weeks after the invasion, special Soviet envoy V. V. Kuznetsov told the Czechoslovaks that "the process of normalization means, first of all, the complete exposure and stamping out of the subversive activities of the right-wing, anti-socialist forces."[58] By October Dubček had to sign a treaty authorizing the "temporary" stay of Soviet troops in his country, and by the end of the year no further references to the April program could be heard. In March 1969 Gustav Husák replaced Dubček, who disappeared into obscure retirement.

Eight months earlier, Husák would have been a completely unexpected appointment. A loyal Communist who spent time in a Nazi prison during World War II, Husák had been sent to prison again during the Stalinist purges of the early 1950s as a bourgeois nationalist. He reentered politics only in April 1968, when he emerged from obscurity in Slovakia to become deputy prime minister. During the Prague Spring Husák established a reputation as a moderate reformer, but in fact he was a pragmatic and austere politician with an authoritarian streak and a hunger for power, more like Władisław Gomułka than Edward Gierek. He also had one quality that the Soviets admired greatly—the ability quickly to grasp the new power situation. On the occasion of a later trip to Moscow, when Brezhnev personally dressed down the Czechoslovak delegation, Husák allegedly remarked: "We came; we saw; we lost."[59] From the beginning Husák understood that resistance to the Soviets was impossible and began to court their support.

Husák was far from being the worst possible successor to Dubček. On the extreme fringes Moscow nurtured a group of "ultras" who explained the reform period as an imperialist plot and spoke of vengeance. Slightly less extreme but still unstinting in his loyalty to the narrowest kind of Brezhnevism was Vasil B'ilak, who stated his view succinctly in May 1971: "Never again must we give [the reformers] the slightest opportunity to assert themselves."[60] Finally, there was the head of the Czech party, L'ubomir Štrougal, who over time inclined moderately toward reform. Among these possibilities Husák was the most pragmatic, the one who recognized the necessity of following a Moscow-oriented line but at the same time realized that he had a disaffected and unsettled country to run. Husák was never able to dispense with his adversaries, but on the other hand they were never able to overthrow him. Eventually all sides came to accept a unique situation of duarchy, B'ilak the hardliner and Husák the moderator, because it preserved the stability of the top party organs, although Soviet support of B'ilak's constant pressure to increase the harshness of the "normalization" process consistently carried the day. "Others," writes Vlad Kusin, "imprinted their stamp on the history of the [1970s] through [Husák's] good offices and over his signature."[61]

Milan Šimečka called "normalization" a process of "civilized violence."[62] The massive purge that began in 1970 under B'ilak's direct command led to interviews with a million and a half party members and forced resignations from almost five hundred thousand of them. Most important from the point of view of public life, the Husák-B'ilak regime mounted an all-out attack on cultural institutions. The Prague broadcasting station lost fifteen hundred employees; forty-five of the eighty editors of the party paper were dismissed; every literary and cultural journal—some twenty-five of them—was closed; twelve hundred scholars connected with the Academy of Sciences lost their positions; and five university departments, including sociology, were abolished altogether. Other actions were equally destructive of social trust: all members of the state and federal legislatures were reselected; crude historical revisions, such as ripping out offending pages in textbooks, were undertaken in primary education; and a militant campaign of aggressive atheism began.[63]

But, as Šimečka points out, no one was killed. There was no third degree, no physical torture. Interrogations took place during normal working hours. One could continue to occupy one's flat after dismissal. "When bugging devices were installed in people's flats, it would be done without damage to the furniture."[64] Victims left their jobs with a handshake and simply found menial work as street sweepers, window washers, and boiler stokers. In part because of this paradoxically civilized method of persecution, the dismissals and humiliating social descent of so many affected not only the losers but everyone around them. Caution, adaptation, removal became the order of the day. At first a few former Communists tried to salvage the idea of reform socialism, but late in 1971 and early in 1972 the police arrested some 200 of them and courts sentenced 47 of these to a total of 118 years in prison. Thus ended "socialism with a human face" as a viable idea among the Czech intelligentsia. It was in this severely demoralized atmosphere, which the regime created as the condition of its own existence, that the ethical message of the tiny antipolitical movement described in the last chapter began to take shape.

"Normalization" was not simply repression, however. The second prong of the Husák-B'ilak policy resembled that of Poland's Gierek or East Germany's Honecker during the same period: buy off the population with material benefits without modifying the command structure of the economy or the party's dominant position. Because of the residual effects of the beneficial reforms made in the 1960s, growth continued into the first half of the 1970s and the Czechoslovak government did not overextend itself with Western credits. Debt built up, but by 1980 it remained the lowest per capita in Eastern Europe. In addition, the "normalizers" occasionally did the right thing. In 1969, for example, prices were adjusted successfully, thus bringing them more in line with actual costs than in some other East European countries.

But the "normalizers," still in thrall to the obsolete ideas of the 1950s, found it impossible to let the economy alone. In agriculture they did their best to kill the goose by merging agricultural units into larger and larger industrial-style enterprises, each under stricter political control, much like the East Germans and the Bulgarians. A campaign against the less than 10 percent of the farm population that was still private, most of it in remote western Slovakia, reduced the number of private farmers by more than half. Even the semisacred private plot came under pressure. Unsurprisingly, the respectable agricultural growth of the period from 1965 to 1975 began to taper off. In industry the Husák-B'ilak regime managed to avoid the worst mistakes of Gierek in Poland, but by 1980 the growth rate was declining and the familiar problems of quality control, energy inefficiency, and trade deficits presented the regime with intractable, indeed insoluble, problems.

Whatever the difficulties, Husák-B'ilak managed to keep real wages rising, and ordinary Czechs and Slovaks were sufficiently satisfied with daily life that for almost twenty years the opposition generated by Charter 77 activists did not strike deep roots in Czechoslovakia. This was not because the population accepted or liked the regime but because ordinary people were convinced that any overt display of "living in truth" would have unpleasant financial and emotional results. Ordinary Czechs considered the oppositionists simply foolish. Workers repairing the flat of Zdena Tominova, for example, rather than showing sympathy for her resistance to the regime, laughed at her stupidity. "Piss on their slogans when their backs are turned," was their advice.[65] The overwhelming majority of Czechoslovak citizens simply went about their private lives and let it go at that. And so did the authorities. No longer did the state ask that one believe. Its own operatives themselves no longer did. "Fanaticism," as Milan Šimečka put it, "grew weary and died."[66] All one had to do was conform in public, and then a reasonably comfortable private life was possible. Until the very last moments of its existence in 1989, this was the social contract the Communist leaders of Czechoslovakia offered their citizens.

Mikhail Gorbachev: The Improbable Reformer

In 1985 an aging cohort of rigid neo-Stalinists still ruled the four most conservative East European countries. Ceaușescu, Honecker, Husák, and Zhivkov had succeeded in keeping themselves in power but not in addressing any of the serious problems their countries faced. The information revolution posed insurmountable new problems for their already none-too-viable economies, their citizenry had long since concluded their regimes were false, and even the ruling elites themselves had lost their confidence.[67] The socialism that in the 1950s could be presented as a plausible developmental and social ideology now appeared to the overwhelming majority of the people of Eastern Europe to be a hollow and outworn shell in which the ruling bureaucracy encased itself simply to maintain its own privileges. Leonid Brezhnev had passed on in 1982, but his generational and ideological brethren, the administrators of civilized violence, had not.

In March 1985, however, a new leader appeared in the Soviet Union who did change direction, a substantial and unexpected change that had fateful consequences. After the incompetent and doddering Konstantin Chernenko, Mikhail Gorbachev was a surprising, almost unbelievable new leader. His "intellectual capacity and flexibility, his ability to learn on the job, his powers of argumentation, charismatic appeal, serenity in the midst of social turmoil, faith that turbulence will 'smooth out' in the long run, his sustained, single-minded motivation and irrepressible optimism, his energy, determination, and tactical political skill" marked Gorbachev as one of the world's most remarkable leaders in the second half of the twentieth century.[68] Even before coming to power Gorbachev had spoken of the need for "deep transformations" in the Soviet economy and of the need for "wide, prompt, and frank information" in a Socialist democracy. Almost as soon as he came to power he began speaking about the need for substantial economic reform and about the necessity for honesty in public affairs, not only in the sense of combating alcoholism or the corruption of the Brezhnev years but in the sense of bringing society into the public debate.[69] He initiated a daring foreign policy based on what he called "new thinking," proposing an entirely new European alignment in which the Soviet Union would be a partner, not an antagonist. At the close of a meeting with French president François Mitterand only seven months after taking power, Gorbachev put his goal succinctly: "The Soviet Union seriously intends to change the situation in the world."[70]

After eighteen years of the gray rule of Leonid Brezhnev and more than two years of rule by dying men, the Western world was perplexed, if not astonished. Where had this man come from? Could they believe him? Was it possible for a hyperrationalist system to restructure itself, especially one in which many ancient traditions of Russian autocracy seemed reproduced in modern guise? The initial reaction was skepticism and doubt. The United States ambassador to the Soviet Union thought that Gorbachev's words seemed new but that the substance would amount to nothing. Right-wing observers scoffed at the lack of specifics in his talk of economic reform, and more balanced analysts wondered if a system so completely demarketized could change in a way that would be acceptable to the huge bureaucracy of the ruling party. Even Gorbachev himself, when asked in February 1986 if the Soviet Union was beginning a "new revolution," replied, "Of course not. I think it would be wrong to formulate the question in those terms."[71]

The question itself suggests the wonderment of observers at this unexpected blazing star. But Gorbachev's emergence from the grayness of the Soviet bureaucracy was not, as Soviet analysts used to say, an accident. He represented a vigorous element in the Communist party that for some years had been anxious to rectify the serious economic and strategic problems they knew faced the Soviet Union at the end of the 1970s. These realists did not reject socialism, and none of them intended to destroy the Soviet Union. They began from the premise that the Soviet Union had made important progress since Stalin. When the great dictator died the Soviet economy was in a shambles, the standard of living below that even of tsarist times. The thaw introduced by Khrushchev and the efforts to improve economic performance in the late 1950s and the 1960s raised both morale and living standards in a way that Soviet citizens could readily observe. Under Brezhnev it was the peasants' turn to enter the mainstream of Soviet life, as their incomes increased and they obtained coverage under the national health plan. Increased military spending gave the Soviets an impressive space program and vastly increased their strategic power, especially under Brezhnev, who concentrated on building up the Soviet missile force and in creating a blue water navy.

The realists could be proud of other Soviet successes as well, such as the integration into city life of a phenomenal influx of new residents from the countryside and the education of its population. Before World War II some 56 million Soviet citizens lived in cities, and the overwhelming majority of workers and peasants had only four years of schooling or less.

By the mid-1980s the number of Soviets living in cities had risen to 180 million, and more than 80 percent of manual laborers had finished more than four years of education.[72]

This vast social revolution had fundamental implications for the possibilities of economic and political change in the Soviet Union. Workers born around 1910 had entered the work force as manual laborers, often in agriculture, and remained primarily engaged in physical labor most of their lives.[73] Workers born around 1930 entered a somewhat more complex economy and often were employed in industry, where more than manual skills were needed. But two thirds of the workers born around 1950 entered what Soviet sociologists called the "intellectual labor force" and never encountered physical work. In other words, as the Soviet economy modernized, the kinds of problems ordinary citizens faced changed dramatically, and the skills they possessed to cope with change became more developed.

A similar kind of generational differentiation existed among the leadership. In the late 1970s Jerry Hough enumerated four post-Khrushchevian leadership generations in the Soviet Union.[74] The first was Brezhnev's generation, born before 1910, the members of which moved up during the Stalinist purges. The second comprised those born between 1910 and 1918, including Yuri Andropov and Konstantin Chernenko, who were thrust upward during the war. The third generation, born between 1919 and 1926, was missing due to the horrible slaughter of World War II, thus leaving a significant educational and experiential gap between men like Chernenko and the members of the fourth generation, who were born after 1926, a group that included Mikhail Gorbachev. As early as 1959 Edward Crankshaw recognized that the men of this generation were different.[75] Party functionaries in the first two generations "survived either because they were too stupid to be considered dangerous, or because they brought sycophancy to a fine art, or because they were as cunning as the fox." The post-1926 generation, however, was "relaxed and easy in manner, often with a pleasantly ironical approach to life, and very much in touch with realities of every kind."[76]

The advance scouts of this generation, and Gorbachev was among the first of them, began to enter the top leadership in the late 1970s. By coincidence, just at this time Soviet economic growth rates began to decline for the first time since Stalin's death. The very success of absorbing the huge influx of men and women into the cities made further gains by the addition of labor problematic. Faltering in its developmental plans and needing to improve its efficiency, the Soviet Union was confronted with dynamic technological challenges that its lumbering economic system was ill-prepared to meet.

The Soviet economy suffered all the usual disabilities of a command economy. Gorbachev himself outlined some of these in his book *Perestroika,* published in 1987. In the 1970s, he said, "the country began to lose momentum" because of declining efficiency, excessive use of energy and raw materials, waste of capital, poor consumer products, a wage-leveling mentality, lack of long-range planning, inability to attack important social needs such as housing, unproductive agriculture, and a decline of ideological and moral values that grew from reliance on the propaganda of success rather than on honest accomplishments and gains. Sounding more like a Western sovietologist than the general secretary of the Communist party, Gorbachev concluded that the "country was verging on crisis."[77]

These problems had not been unknown to the men around Leonid Brezhnev, nor were they unobserved elsewhere in the Soviet bloc.[78] But unlike the younger generation of realists, Brezhnev was unwilling, and perhaps unable, to think his way to a possible solution. The five-year plan for 1981–1985 recognized that growth was declining, but its authors could come up with nothing better than to promote heavy industry and to insist for the umpteenth time on better planning. Writing in 1981, the American economist Abram Bergson realized that this strategy was not only likely to fail, as it had in the past, but also to make the need for more dramatic reforms apparent. "Failure to fulfill even [this] comparatively modest plan," Bergson wrote, "could make more impelling the case for finally taking an action that the leadership has evidently resisted so far: to initiate a radical reform of the planning mechanism."[79]

The plan in fact did fail, as Soviet productivity continued to drop and the West mounted increasing technological pressure. In 1979 NATO, at the insistence of President Jimmy Carter, decided to base new nuclear cruise missiles in Western Europe to match the SS-20 missiles that Brezhnev had stationed two years earlier in Eastern Europe, and in 1981 Ronald Reagan began a substantial American military buildup, including later the Strategic Defense Initiative, a proposal to construct a high-tech missile defense system. Apparently about to be outspent and outengineered in the one area the Soviet Union could claim to be pre-eminent—military power—the Soviets had to face up at the same time to their wretched performance in providing consumers with usable shoes and dresses, as well as their dismal record in providing housing. In all areas, from energy production through military balance to consumer goods, it was clear to many Soviets that their economy was in trouble.

Gorbachev's selection in 1985 as general secretary instead of the Brezhnevian candidate, Viktor Grishin—it was not a foregone conclusion that Gorbachev would win—constituted an explicit decision for economic reform.[80] After a fairly slow start, Gorbachev installed changes of such magnitude that they produced the collapse of the Soviet Union he was trying to save. But Gorbachev's remark to the French journalist that he was not involved in revolution was correct, at least in terms of his aspirations. Perestroika, the Russian term for "restructuring," was not a marketizing reform, despite occasional rhetorical flourishes to the contrary. Of the four basic principles of perestroika that took shape in 1987, the first was that the Soviet economy would remain centrally planned.[81] The remaining proposals evoke eerie echoes of the 1960s: the success or failure of enterprises was to be based on economic criteria; incomes were to reflect productivity; enterprises were to be autonomous in their economic decisions; and workers were to participate in management decisions. Despite their amazement at the energy with which this fascinating new Soviet leader began putting these shopworn ideas into effect, most Western observers predicted from the beginning that perestroika would fail in substantially transforming the Soviet economy. They were both right and wrong. Perestroika did fail in reforming the centrally planned economy, but by completely disrupting the Soviet system perestroika cleared the ground for the creation of a new economy based on market principles. This unexpected result may become one of the classic examples of an unintended consequence.

Despite the sound and the fury, for the first three or four years Gorbachev's economic reforms bore a strong familial resemblance to those of his predecessors, all of whom had come to grief over the same difficulty—genuine economic reform always threatened the position of the party and therefore always lost out. Gorbachev's originality was not that he understood this linkage—by now everyone understood it—but that he accepted the challenge that everyone else had avoided: reforming both society and the party in order make the economic reforms work. The first tactic in the overall reform strategy was the policy of openness, or glasnost.[82] Gorbachev believed as a matter of principle that the people should have more say in how society should run, both because they were capable of adding to Soviet society and because it was the right thing to do. Glasnost "enhances the resourcefulness of the working people," he said in 1984, and "is evidence of confidence in the people and respect for their intelligence and feelings, and for their ability to understand events for themselves." Looking back on his reforms later, he said, "This is why we started everything in the first place—so a human being can feel normal, can feel good, in a socialist state. So that he will feel above all like a human being."[83] A more instrumental view might be that he hoped to draw the intelligentsia to his side by permitting them the kinds of freedoms they could only have dreamed of under previous regimes.

Since glasnost was contrary to decades of Soviet experience, it got off to a slow start. But the nuclear accident in Chernobyl in April 1986 shocked and mobilized the Soviet leadership, which realized that their efforts to conceal the enormity of the accident greatly increased the suffering and correspondingly decreased their credibility. The main signal that openness actually would be tolerated was the release late in 1986 of the great moral critic Andrei Sakharov from exile. By late 1986 and early 1987 previously unheard-of things started happening: new editors at a resuscitated *Novy Mir* (New World) and at *Moscow News* began expanding the limits of censorship; daring economists suggested that real markets were needed; films critical of dictators and specifically of Stalin were taken off the shelf and shown to enthusiastic audiences; television news programs turned to factual reporting; even tourist maps were redrawn correctly instead of with purposeful errors. To a Soviet population used to massive disinformation these simple steps were stunning. For seventy years the Soviet regime had encouraged apathy and conformity as two of its best supports; now Gorbachev sought to shake off the dullness, to create the excitement and enthusiasm that would draw in the creative powers of the intelligentsia and marshal the working enthusiasms of the people.

But still the economic reforms were stuck, blocked by the inertia of the enormous economic and political bureaucracy. By 1988 Gorbachev concluded that only a reform of the political system could bypass this bureaucracy and create popular enthusiasm. In a remarkable series of maneuvers he cajoled and browbeat the party and then the government into creating a new Congress of People's Deputies elected on the basis of secret ballot in openly contested elections.[84] By including "the broad masses of the working people in the management of all state and public affairs," Gorbachev believed he would "complete the creation of a socialist state based on the rule of law," reform the party, and legitimize perestroika all at the same time.[85] After wooing the intellectuals with glasnost, the elections would woo the people with *demokratsiya*. The gratitude and enthusiasms unleashed by these changes would create the public space in which the needed economic reforms could be accomplished.

During 1988 and 1989 Gorbachev translated this scheme into something resembling actuality. On May 25, 1989, a competitively elected Congress of People's Deputies convened and in full view of an engrossed nationwide television audience proceeded to engage in bona fide political contestation. Within two years the political chaos this contestation unleashed had so devastated the Soviet Union that it completely disintegrated.

What did these dramatic, not to say astonishing, events mean for Eastern Europe? One thing they almost certainly did not mean was that the Soviet Union was prepared to give up its hegemony over the region. What Gorbachev the reformer of socialism saw, when he looked at Eastern Europe, was a set of countries run by men of Chernenko's generation using Brezhnev's ideas. How could Gorbachev rejuvenate socialism when his small but vital socialist partners on the periphery were suffering from the same economic problems and lack of legitimacy that Brezhnev had brought to the Soviet Union? Perestroika had to come to Eastern Europe as well, but not in a way that would allow the East European countries to slip their ties to socialism or to the Soviet Union. "To threaten the socialist system," Gorbachev said in a speech to the Polish party in 1986, "means to encroach not only on the will of the people, but on the entire postwar arrangement and, in the last analysis, on peace."[86]

Ever since Khrushchev had apologized to Yugoslavia in 1955, Soviet and East European leaders alike, albeit in different contexts and with different meanings, had claimed that each socialist state was free to pursue socialism in is own way. In 1969, less than a year after the invasion of

Czechoslovakia, an international meeting of Communist and workers' parties in Moscow declared that "all parties have equal rights. . . . There is no leading center of the international Communist movement."[87] Gorbachev did not seem to be taking a dramatic initiative in 1987 when he wrote that "the entire framework of political relations between socialist countries must be strictly based on absolute independence," especially when he pointed out, much as the 1969 program had, that despite this independence, the East European countries and the Soviet Union needed to achieve a "harmonization of initiatives" that would lead to "mutual advantage and mutual assistance" under the umbrella of CMEA, which should "coordinate economic policies" and develop "normative standards for the integration mechanism."[88] After all, Gorbachev wrote, the "socialist community has everything it needs" for doubling and even tripling productivity by the year 2000.[89]

Even Gorbachev's most famous phrase, "the creation of a common European home," which he first used in a visit to England in 1984 before becoming general secretary, could be interpreted as simply an extended gloss on Leonid Brezhnev's similar statement in Bonn in November 1981. Speaking against the NATO decision to place cruise missiles in Western Europe, which in Brezhnev's view turned Europe into a field of military operations, the Soviet leader had said, "Whatever may divide us, Europe is our common home. Common fate has linked us through centuries, it links us today too."[90]

Observers both East and West saw nothing very new in Gorbachev's initiatives.[91] Commenting late in 1987, two Western analysts argued that Gorbachev's policy had "the clear goal of exploiting the Eastern Europeans to serve his [Gorbachev's] domestic economic goals. His success in this venture would also entail more effectively integrating the bloc, [thus] enhancing long-term Soviet domination of its allies."[92] In Poland, Dawid Warszawski (the pseudonym of Konstanty Gebert) wrote the following: "Gorbachev's failure would result only in the continuation of the status quo. If he succeeds, however, we can expect that domestic liberalization in the USSR will be accompanied by a turning of the screw in the peripheral areas as a sop to the CPSU conservatives." Jan Zaleski agreed. If Gorbachev succeeds, Zaleski wrote early in 1987, Poland would be totally absorbed into the Soviet orbit.[93]

But Gorbachev's initiatives took on enhanced meaning in the framework of the fundamental change that he made in the traditional Soviet policy of hostility toward the West. Only four months after coming to power, he indicated that his foreign policy would not follow the old paths when he replaced Andrei Gromyko, the most senior foreign minister in the world, with Eduard Shevardnadze, a brilliant and free-thinking Georgian politician with little experience in foreign policy but with no skeletons in foreign service closets. The two newcomers to power, in collaboration with Alexandr Yakovlev, Gorbachev's most important reformist advisor, immediately "began looking for ways in which we might live," as Gorbachev put it later.

Ever since 1917 the Bolsheviks had presented a hostile face to a world they believed threatened them. Stalin's successors pursued his two-camp policy in modified form even after his death. The result of these seventy years of hostility had been to surround the Soviet Union with enemies and to distort its economy with military expenditures. Such hostility in the thermonuclear age seemed to the new leaders potentially disastrous in case of war and debilitating in case of peace. Soon after coming to power, Gorbachev invited the United States to join the Soviet Union's moratorium on nuclear testing, and by December 1987 the United States and the Soviet Union had signed a treaty eliminating intermediate-range nuclear missiles from their inventories.

Military doctrine, however, was only part of Gorbachev's new thinking. Slowly, over the first three years of his rule, he came to believe that Soviet self-interest could best be served by abandoning the two-camp idea. Dialogue and competition were what was needed, not imposition from one side or the other. "The interdependency of survival is of cardinal importance" is how the Soviet ambassador to the United States phrased it.[94] "The conflict between two opposing systems is no longer the decisive tendency in the present age," Shevardnadze said in 1988.[95] Europe was not to be the exclusive domain of the Western nations, but the common home of Soviet and East European peoples as well. By 1988 Gorbachev had gone beyond Brezhnev's ritual statements and made the theme of a common European home the basis of his foreign policy. Openness to the West was not only right, he thought—and he stressed the ethical dimension in his statements and speeches—but it also had the possibility of important strategic advantages. Lessening arms expenditures would release resources for productive investment. Friendship with Europe would open up possibilities for mutually beneficial trade and especially for needed economic credits. And, best of all, lowering the temperature of international politics would lessen, perhaps even eliminate, the justification for keeping so many American troops in Europe. Perhaps the "New Thinking" could achieve with honey what Soviet policy had clearly failed to do with vinegar—eliminate the American presence on the continent.

Few people in Eastern Europe realized the full implications for themselves of Gorbachev's new grand strategy, which did not become clear to the most perspicacious of them until late 1988 or even 1989.[96] But Gorbachev did not clearly recognize the implications of his new ideas for Eastern Europe either. He did not intend to bury socialism, but to revivify it. "If we can bring people back into the socialist system instead of alienating them," he said as late as July 1989, "we can give socialism a second wind."[97] In all likelihood he hoped that men like himself would come to power in Eastern Europe, mini-Gorbachevs who would shake up their tired regimes and restore popular support for socialism, just as he was convinced he was doing in the Soviet Union.

Since Gorbachev believed in socialism, he did not understand the depth of its moral failures, and he never suspected the magnitude of East European popular hostility to it. One reason may have been that he was not receiving completely accurate assessments of the public mood from his representatives there. Ambassadorships and similar high-ranking diplomatic jobs in Eastern Europe were the preserve of the party rather than of the professionals of the foreign office.[98] Soviet representatives in Eastern Europe who were "former party officials appealed to higher party levels in all questions, bypassing the Ministry of Foreign Affairs."[99] These representatives depended heavily on local party sources for their information rather than conducting their own research. As late as spring 1989, for example, no one in the Soviet embassy in Prague was in contact with even the moderate opposition in Czechoslovakia, and Soviet observers came out onto the streets to observe events for themselves only several days after the decisive events of November 17.[100]

The enormous popularity that Gorbachev's candor and charm before the cameras created, especially outside the borders of his own country, also may have helped convince him that reform communism was still possible in Eastern Europe. Gorbachev in the late 1980s was the most charismatic Soviet leader since Lenin. Enthusiastic crowds from London and New York in the West to Budapest and Prague in the East turned out to shout "Gorby! Gorby!" Gorbachev almost certainly misinterpreted these reactions to his star quality as support for perestroika, when in fact it represented hostility toward a bureaucracy that refused to budge. Instead of indicating a possibility of revivifying socialism, the demonstrations actually indicated disgust with "real existing socialism."

But none of this was clear in 1987. No matter what sort of intriguing possibilities lurked in Gorbachev's rhetoric or in his popularity, and no matter how seriously policy makers such as West Germany's foreign minister Hans-Dietrich Genscher took glasnost and perestroika, almost all analysts in the West were certain of one thing: under no circumstances would the Soviet Union give up its hegemony over Eastern Europe.

> Control of East Central Europe is a source of immense pride and security to the Soviets, the most tangible evidence of their great victory in the war; and that victory remains the most powerful legitimating experience of the soviet Communist system. . . . Hegemony over East Central Europe compensates the Russian people for their enormous sacrifices in the war and their enduring grievances since its end. It validates the Soviet system to itself. Any Soviet yielding of the area not only would undermine the ideological claims of Communism . . . and degrade the Soviet Union's credentials as a confident global power, but also would gravely jeopardize a basic internal Soviet consensus and erode the domestic security of the system itself.[101]

Joseph Rothschild, the author of these lines written in 1987, lacks neither foresight nor analytical ability. Indeed, the loss of Eastern Europe *did* undermine the ideological claims of communism, degrade the Soviet Union's power, and gravely jeopardize Soviet consensus. But in 1987 the unthinkability of these outcomes led sensible and clear-headed observers of Soviet behavior to the conclusion that the Soviets would never abandon

Eastern Europe. This line of thinking made Gorbachev's initiatives difficult to interpret at the time and confirms the enormous originality of what he eventually permitted to happen. Norman Stone, writing in the *Sunday Times* in November 1987, pointed out that the logical consequence of perestroika, the relaxation of the Brezhnev Doctrine, and the abandonment of Moscow's "monopoly on truth" was "to dismantle the Berlin Wall and remove troops from Eastern Europe."[102] Stone did not seem to think that was going to happen. Gorbachev probably did not either.

3

The Momentum of Change in Hungary

Mikhail Gorbachev's prodding sent chills down the spines of the gang of four. He received the cheers of the crowd in April 1987 when he visited Prague, but only nervous smiles from Gustav Husák. When he visited Bucharest shortly thereafter, his discussions with an antagonistic Ceau-şescu reached such a pitch that security guards entered the conference room to check on the safety of their chief. In Bulgaria, Todor Zhivkov tried to ignore perestroika and glasnost by claiming that Bulgaria had undertaken those kinds of reforms long ago, and in East Germany, Erich Honecker was sufficiently edgy to ban at least one Soviet publication because it was too critical of the system he stood for.

In Poland and Hungary, however, Gorbachev's initiatives found a creative response. Different leaders and broad social movements differentiated these two countries from their conservative neighbors. In Poland the evolution of an independent society pioneered by KOR and Solidarity proceeded apace after 1981, despite martial law. By 1989 General Jaruzelski realized that the only way to deal with the severe social and economic problems facing Poland was to enter into an authentic partnership with Solidarity. In Hungary János Kádár's politics of reconciliation permitted the growth of a significant autonomous sector in the Hungarian economy, the re-emergence of reformers in the party itself, and the elaboration of a set of popular issues that mobilized urban segments of society in favor of change. The avalanche that swept away the Communist regimes of Eastern Europe began in these two countries.

Hungary Turns Its Economy Westward

Of all the Communist parties in Eastern Europe, the Hungarian was the most reform minded. Perhaps this was because, unlike the Polish party, it had not been destroyed by Stalin in the 1930s. Its ranks contained fewer first-generation peasant apparatchiks, and it lost fewer of its intellectuals to opposition than did the Polish party.[1] Even in the depths of Kádár's repressions after 1956 the government abandoned compulsory deliveries of agricultural produce, and when recollectivization was undertaken in the early 1960s it was done by trying to offer the peasants incentives rather than strictly by brute force. The New Economic Mechanism (NEM) was the most lasting and important economic reform undertaken in Communist Eastern Europe. Despite a step backward in 1972, by the late 1970s Hungary appeared to be prospering. For the first time since World War II, a socialist state began to get decent press in the West about its consumer products, which not only compared favorably with those seen elsewhere in the Soviet bloc but were readily available in decent shops in central Budapest. East European organizations contrived to hold their meetings in Budapest if possible so that they could combine some retail grazing with their business meetings, while at the same time a Hilton hotel with all the amenities helped convince foreign visitors that Kádár's Hungary was the least dreary of the East European capitals. Statistically the situation had its positive aspects as well. Between 1970 and 1978 national income, measured in volume of goods produced, increased about 6 percent per year and real consumption rose about 4 percent per year.[2]

But not far beneath the surface of this apparently successful picture lay some very disquieting difficulties. Not least among them were the disruptions caused by the oil embargo that Arab states imposed in 1973. In 1974 Hungarian planners had to reassess the decline they had permitted in their coal mining industry, and by 1975 they were forced to begin importing expensive oil from the world market. The Soviets were willing to continue to supply their CMEA partners with energy at reasonable cost (prices were set at the average of the last five years of world prices, which amounted to a substantial subsidy to East European users during a period of rising prices) if they would invest in projects designed to increase Soviet energy production. In Hungary's case this meant sinking substantial investments into the massive (and inefficient) Orenburg natural gas complex and the 2,700 mile pipeline that connected it with Eastern Europe. With its own economy facing significant labor shortages, Hungary had to send thousands of its most highly trained specialists to economically disadvantageous employment in the Soviet Union.[3]

At the same time, Hungarian foreign trade took a turn for the worse. The Hungarians tended to blame Soviet pressure for their problems, but under conditions in which the government always responded to pressure for subsidies or other favorable concessions, enterprises had little incentive to scramble in the international arena for export markets and no incentive to limit the importation of goods that would help them meet their quantitative targets. The most egregious example of such a condition was a system of preferential taxation in the iron and steel industry that permitted individual firms to show a "profit" even though the hard currency costs of imported raw materials were greater than the hard currency receipts from the sale of the finished products.[4] Under such conditions it was only natural that imports tended to rise uncontrollably. During the 1970s Hungary had a negative balance of trade with convertible currency countries every year but one, and its terms of trade declined by approximately 20 percent.[5] Terms of trade constitute a rough approximation of how well an economy is maintaining its competitiveness in the world market. A decline of 20 percent means that to sustain the quantitative level of imports Hungary achieved in the early 1970s it had to export 20 percent more of its own goods by the end of the 1970s. In effect, this meant that Hungary was paying excise tax to the world economy of about 20 percent.

By 1977 Hungarian economists were able to convince the politicians that something had to be done to correct the foreign debt situation. Between 1970 and 1979 Hungarian debt rose from about $1 billion to $9.1 billion.[6] Poland and Romania attacked their debt problems by suspending payments and rescheduling in 1980 and 1981 and by taking other steps that had a long-term negative effect. Poland turned to Soviet trade and Ceauşescu decided to pay off his debt completely. Hungary, however, found a much more creative solution. In 1982 it became a member of both the International Monetary Fund (IMF) and the World Bank, which opened the door to a series of bridging and other loans that tided Hungary over its worst debt crisis. In other words, Hungary decided to attempt an opening to the world market a good ten years before the revolutions of 1989.

Joining the IMF was easier for Hungary than it would have been for other East European countries because Hungary had already introduced the kind of austerity measures the IMF favors for overextended countries. A report discussed by the central committee in October 1977 explicitly recognized that Hungary was going to have to improve its position in the world market.[7] On the basis of the ensuing discussions, in 1979 the politburo reversed the centralizing course adopted in 1972 and re-entered the path initially set out by the New Economic Mechanism. It cut back on consumption, squeezed the money supply, lowered the rate of investment and tried to encourage producers to raise their export levels. In a statement almost diametrically opposed to the one made by Gierek in Poland a few years earlier, Deputy Premier Ferenc Havasi outlined the new policy: "Economic growth, production and development, as well as living standard improvements, must be subordinated in the interest of improving our international financial balance."[8]

Autonomous Economic Activity

Hungarian leaders were willing to begin another round of reforms in 1979 in part because successes in areas of the economy in which they had permitted the most flexibility over the past twenty years encouraged them. A good example, surprisingly enough, was socialized agriculture. The final campaign to collectivize agriculture took place in Hungary between 1958 and 1961. Although officials used coercion, at the same time they realized that the best way to get peasants working was to make the new cooperatives profitable. Abandoning compulsory crop deliveries, the collectivizers permitted the cooperatives to mechanize on their own rather than through the Stalinist machine tractor stations and replaced the grossly ineffective system of workdays credit with monthly cash wages. It was with considerable surprise that a representative of the agricultural ministry reported in 1960 that "one of our best methods is regular cash advances."[9] Most significant, in the 1960s cooperatives received the right to enter into auxiliary businesses, which they did with a vengeance, at first trying food processing, then related light industry such as furniture making, quarries, and lumber yards, and eventually completely unrelated and detached businesses, such as producing computer power supplies. Over the years, despite setbacks in the 1970s, these auxiliary enterprises, which were not run by the same rules as state industries but rather as part of the collectives, developed considerable autonomy and often became quite profitable.

A second niche in which productivity and output increased through the 1960s and even during the centralizing period of the 1970s, was the *second economy*. The meaning of this term is elusive. There is debate over whether it should encompass only legal activities or also informal activities, which are often technically illegal. Here the term means any economic activity, legal or informal, through which individuals or households obtain income outside the official socialized sector.[10] Every economy, no matter how regulated, experiences inefficiencies that present opportunities for enterprising persons to profit. Even in the most restrictive economy, if there are shortages there will be efforts to cope: black markets, bribes, pilfering, slacking off on the job, and working hard after hours for cash payments. In open societies, the range of activities allowed to fill these gaps is wide, and entry into profit-making activities is relatively easy, although far from unregulated. In centrally planned economies, however, the range of permissible enterprise can be extremely narrow and entry very difficult. Despite this, the chronic shortage of goods that is characteristic of these economies inevitably leads to parallel markets—methods of acquisition that fall outside regular channels.

The difference between Hungary and its more conservative neighbors, such as the German Democratic Republic, was that the Hungarians broadened the range of permissible activity in parallel markets. As early as 1957 government regulations allowed individuals to lease some service-oriented, state-owned shops and permitted self-employed craftsmen to contract for work in the public sector.[11] In some ways, these rules had not significantly affected economic activity, since by 1981 only about 1,900 leased shops, 1,500 of them restaurants, existed.[12] On the other hand, by that time building cooperatives not directly run by state enterprises were constructing 60 percent of all new apartments.[13] Naturally, as in the other socialist economies, a large number of artisans were making extra money by private work on their own account. By 1982 one observer could write that Hungary was not only "a world of salaried workers, but rather one of small independent workers operating on the rationally and strategically ordered free market. It is increasingly the spirit of enterprise that characterizes the economic strategy of these small independent workers."[14]

A third example of autonomous economic activity, and one that had a great deal of influence in convincing reformers that private enterprise could be integrated into their socialist system, was the family-oriented farm. In an arrangement known as the "family work organization," cooperatives assigned certain holdings to those who actually worked them rather than treating the peasants simply as an agricultural proletariat. This arrangement was particularly effective for animal husbandry. Collectives worked out what amounted to thousands of tiny feed lot arrangements and mini-breeding stations that benefited both sides, with the families growing the stock and the cooperatives processing and marketing the meat. Other enterprising peasants used their small household plots very effectively in other ways, such as by growing tomatoes or other hothouse vegetables for town markets, or mass producing eggs.

These activities produced an unexpected pattern of social differentiation. One of the developmental goals of communism was to get marginally employed peasants off the land and into more productive factories where they would form the new proletariat.[15] The idea was to turn "the entire population into salaried workers and [to abolish] independent labor."[16] The effort was generally successful, but in the 1950s and 1960s Eastern Europe's rural population declined more slowly than it should have at a time of rapid industrial expansion. Hungary and other countries as well remained "underurbanized" because many peasants used factory employment as simply one aspect of an overall family strategy to maximize their benefits from the centrally planned system. In a typical case the husband might commute a long distance to factory work using public transportation that the regime had created in part to minimize its capital expense of constructing housing. As an employee of the factory he received retirement and other social benefits. Meanwhile, his wife remained a member of the cooperative, thereby retaining the family's right to a plot and to forage for their cow. Instead of becoming proletarians, these workers adopted an intermediate position—peasants and workers at the same time.[17]

In the 1970s Hungary's rural population actually started to increase, as marginally urbanized individuals and families who had found "hiding places," or "parking orbits," as Iván Szelényi calls them, began to sense greater opportunity in small-scale but marginally free agriculture rather than in factory employment. The regime's investment policy in the 1970s, which placed new manufacturing plants around the country rather than concentrating them near Budapest, helped in this process. The old type of family subsistence farm almost completely disappeared, but a vigorous stratum of small-scale farmers turned more and more of its attention to the intensive cultivation of tiny plots, marketing the produce instead of consuming it. Rather than sliding into proletarian status, as the planners had originally anticipated, or staying in some intermediate position as worker-peasants, these vigorous businessmen reversed their social vector in the direction of becoming genuine entrepreneurs. Rather than consuming their product or working for a wage, they were accumulating and investing capital, sometimes quite a bit of it by Hungarian standards. Szelényi estimates that a typical rural entrepreneur might have accumulated between $20,000 and $40,000 by the early 1980s, not much by Western standards but equivalent to twenty to forty times the annual salary of an average Hungarian worker.

A fourth arena in which working people had achieved a certain amount of autonomous experience by 1980 was the shop floor of factories. From the beginning of centralized planning, one of the basic jobs of management was to conduct "plan bargaining." The best way to fulfill one's plan and receive bonuses was to bargain with the bureaucracy for an easy plan. Sociologists investigating Hungarian work conditions in the late 1970s were surprised to find key workers on the shop floor itself conducting similar negotiations. The "countervailing power," as Burawoy and Lukács put it, that skilled workers possessed permitted them to negotiate with the apparently much more powerful factory administration for better schedules, choice holiday accommodations, and similar perquisites. A number of studies have shown that factory workers could be divided into two groups—these elite workers who found ways to maximize their rewards and the much larger force of regular workers without much power, able only to withhold their labor (that is, not work very hard).[18] This division mirrored the division in the countryside between the relatively small number of entrepreneurial farmers and the very much larger population of state farm and cooperative members.

By the end of the 1970s, therefore, when the leadership decided that Hungary's economic future depended on restoring some of the reforms of NEM and on turning toward the world market, a significant substratum of enterprise and autonomy already existed in Hungary. This did not constitute exactly a civil society as the Poles thought of it, although sociologist Elemer Hankiss spoke of a "second public sphere" that included the second economy.[19] No strikes or dramatic confrontations emotionalized this still inchoate phenomenon, but an active segment of the Hungarian population, perhaps not any smaller than in Poland and certainly larger than in any other East European country, lay in wait, ready to take advantage of whatever opportunities might come its way.

Reform, Austerity, and Anxiety

The Twelfth Congress of the Hungarian Socialist Workers party, held in March 1980, set the new directions for the 1980s—greater democracy and legitimation of the second economy. "We can best strengthen the country's economic power," said Sándor Gáspár, the head of the trade unions' national council, "if we rely on democracy, on the clash of opinions and interests, and on the increased participation of the working population."[20] Despite the understandable skepticism that greeted calls for greater democracy from a centralizer like Gáspár, the gradual return to favor of reformers in the party did lead toward a modest increase in democracy. Agricultural cooperatives received more leeway in electing their leadership, the national electoral law was changed to require multiple candidates and secret elections, and elected bodies were permitted a larger role at the local level. Politburo member Mihály Korom characterized this last reform as an effort to fulfill the "commitment by the party to implement the policies of socialist democracy."[21] Elemer Hankiss later said, "We have sufficient reason to suppose that there were people in the political elite who really meant it, who sincerely thought that it was time to make the electoral system more democratic."[22]

The second significant decision of the Twelfth Congress was to recognize explicitly what everyone had known for a long time: the second economy was a significant asset. "During their spare time," said the relevant resolution, "a certain percentage of the workers participate in work that is useful to the national economy and to the individual. This is a supplementary source of our development that . . . enhances the growth of the nation's wealth."[23] Legitimation of the second economy led in 1981 and 1982 to a series of laws authorizing a number of "intermediate property forms."[24] These included simplified procedures for establishing subsidiaries and small spin-off businesses, legalization of associations of enterprises and cooperatives, and an auction of franchises for state-owned restaurants and similar service enterprises to build on the principle established in 1957. Most interesting of the alternate forms of ownership were three new types of small businesses: nonagricultural cooperatives of fewer than one hundred members; business work partnerships, in which no more than thirty persons created a business as a second job; and enterprise business work partnerships, or partnerships among employees of an enterprise that contracted its services back to the enterprise during off-hours.

To assist these new enterprises, the government established a number of financial intermediaries, including some oriented toward venture capital, such as The Innovation Fund, The Enterprise Fund, Young Investors Association, and the Small Business Innovations Association.[25] In 1983 enterprises received permission to sell bonds to each other, while at the same time Hungary enacted Eastern Europe's most liberal joint venture regulations.

These innovations were very successful. The number of shops leased from the state grew from fewer than 2,000 in 1980 to 11,500 in 1986. The 10 percent of Hungarian restaurants in private hands by 1986 turned an operating profit in that year equal to the entire operating profit of the other 90 percent of Hungarian restaurants that remained in public hands.[26] The successes of the work cooperatives and partnerships were equally startling. By 1986 the first of these had grown in number from 200 to 10,000, mostly in engineering, light industry, and construction, while the second had grown from nothing to 11,000. Together these two types of new businesses employed 110,000 persons.[27] By 1985 one hundred bond issues existed, and a small bond market had opened in Budapest.

The most interesting of the innovations was the enterprise business work partnership. These partnerships constituted the "household plots of industry," as one central committee member put it.[28] Skilled employees could join together to contract their services to the enterprise in which they worked. They retained their ordinary jobs and kept their ordinary hours, but after quitting time the partnership worked on its own, often performing the same job at the same location. Instead of contracting with an outside firm for a rush order of architectural drawings, for example, firms would contract with one of their own enterprise business work partnerships. Since such contracts tended to be for specialized products and highly skilled services, the same trained workers who had been best able to apply "countervailing power" in the 1970s were best prepared to create the new partnerships. This had the tendency to intensify the social and economic divisions between them and ordinary workers, who had neither the technical nor the social skills to put together the complex partnerships. Among the skilled workers, however, the partnerships were very popular. Some large factories had as many as 150 of them, and by the end of 1986 21,490 partnerships with 267,000 members were adding one-third to one-half of their regular wages to their annual income through work in their partnerships. Managers liked the system too. Not only did they get quality work from the partnerships—productivity was substantially higher than during regular working hours—but they paid them from funds not accounted as wages, thereby increasing their flexibility.[29]

By the mid-1980s the various alternate forms of ownership had become a vital part of the Hungarian economy, producing about one-third of the national income.[30] More important, participants in these forms were forming a new sense of themselves and their possibilities. David Stark has traced these changes in one enterprise work partnership.[31] When the eighteen skilled machinists formed this particular partnership their goal was to show that they could produce sophisticated machines without the suffocating and inefficient interference of managers and engineers. Earlier, in selective bargaining on the shop floor, "the tool-makers had sought to get the best price for their *time;* in establishing the partnership they sought the best price for their *skills.*" But once they proved they were more efficient and more precise than the plant at large, able to produce to close tolerances for the export market, management started giving them only the most difficult and demanding jobs on which the profit margins were the smallest. Eventually this led to a crisis in which the partnership fired its original representative, who had been one of the most respected machinists, and hired a new one, a young and ambitious engineer who was not a worker at all. At the same time they used their key positions as highly skilled craftsmen to convince management that they should be able to contract outside the factory, and for the first time they began to investigate the market value of the products they made. In other words, from seeking a proof of their worth as workers, the toolmakers had progressed to thinking like businessmen and had begun their exit to the private economy.

Hungary, therefore, was structurally very different from Poland. Whereas in Poland an opposition presenting itself through a working-class union sought to create a civil society by cultural means, in Hungary economic reforms introduced by a Communist party were creating a new stratum of quasientrepreneurs among factory workers that paralleled a process of bourgeoisification in the countryside. The reform process was also educating many other workers to the pressures of the market and to the norms of pluralist interactions. Hungary proved more successful in attracting foreign investment and in marketizing its economy than Poland after 1989 because in Hungary the process was already well under way before 1989, whereas in Poland work structures and consciousness remained only slightly changed in the 1980s.

Nevertheless, the alternate forms of ownership in Hungary remained parasitic on the centrally planned system. Few of the new businesses were stand-alone enterprises. They depended on the cooperatives or other enterprises to provide the facilities and the supply and distribution networks within which they worked. The mixed forms of ownership were beginning to influence Hungarian society through a process that Iván Berend calls "hidden pluralization," but in themselves they were not able to solve the structural problems of the centralized system, since to a certain degree they owed their success to the inefficiencies caused by the regime's inability to solve those problems.[32]

Looking back, it seems clear that the Hungarian reforms set the stage for relatively good economic development after 1989. But at the time, what most Hungarians noticed was a declining standard of living brought on by the policy of austerity. Kádár was cleverer in dealing with prices than either Gomułka or Gierek, who provoked riots by keeping prices stable for years and then adjusting them suddenly, without warning. In Hungary price changes took place periodically and usually with lengthy preliminary preparations. This more sensible policy had prevented sudden outbursts of rage but not a steady deterioration in morale, since between 1978 and 1984 real wages fell about 7 percent.[33] A significant portion of the population was prospering in the private sector, but a majority was feeling pinched by the falling real value of wages. Rising prices also reduced the value of social benefits, and those on pensions particularly suffered.

Almost as important as real losses in creating uneasiness were anxieties about the future. Bankruptcies began in the late 1970s, when the Csepel Steel Trust began laying off workers. In August 1984 the large Office Equipment and Fine Mechanics Enterprise near Budapest closed, reassigning its twelve hundred workers elsewhere, and Tungsram, the large light bulb company purchased after 1989 by General Electric, announced that it had laid off three thousand of its twenty-six thousand workers over the past eighteen months and planned to lay off twelve hundred more shortly.[34] Failures of this magnitude were a new experience for Hungary and undercut one of the most popular promises of the socialist regimes, job security.

Strangely enough, at the same time real wages were falling and uncertainty increasing, consumption was rising.[35] How was such an anomaly possible? The answer was that approximately 75 percent of Hungarians received income from the second economy. To preserve their standard of living Hungarians were frantically working extra hours, very often at what amounted to two full-time jobs. Specialists speculate that the decline in life expectancy of Hungarian men, which began in the late 1970s, can be attributed primarily to the deleterious impact of continuous overwork.[36] Working double time as real wages at the primary workplace fell, or seeing purchasing power evaporate and for the first time fearing actual unemployment, ordinary Hungarians in the mid-1980s no longer felt as buoyant as they had a decade earlier.

The Thirteenth Party Congress, held in March 1985, did not offer them much solace. Kádár had to admit that the standard of living had declined, and speaker after speaker criticized the government for its inability to prevent inflation or to provide adequate housing. But the congress took no major new steps, instead announcing the continuation of the austerity policy. When Kádár said in his closing remarks that in any event it was necessary to adhere to the principles of "socialist centralism," many realized that the hero of the 1970s, now seventy-three years old and starting to decline, was in touch with neither the new vibrancy of the semiprivate sector nor the new energy emanating from the Soviet Union. Speculation began to appear both in the party, where a vigorous discussion was developing over strategies of reform, and in the opposition, which was becoming increasingly defined, whether Kádár would be able to retain his control.

The Democratic Opposition

The beginnings of a Hungarian opposition can be traced in the late 1960s to a few individuals like Miklós Haraszti and to the "Budapest School" of humanistic Marxist philosophers. Haraszti was an original, the son of Communist parents who found inspiration as a young man in the New Left of the 1960s, flirted with the North Vietnamese version of communism, and for a time professed Maoism, all in his efforts to find a purer brand of communism for Hungary. The Budapest School is the name given to the group of students surrounding György Lukács, one of Europe's most creative Marxist theorists. Lukács was a magnetic personality who managed to survive 1956, even though he was minister of culture in Imre Nagy's short-lived cabinet. He returned to Budapest University and gathered around himself a particularly brilliant circle of young philosophers. Powerful thinkers as well as clever writers and skillful polemicists, the members of the Budapest School were foremost among those who found the basis for their critical stance in the young Marx.

In 1972, when party hardliners reasserted themselves, one of the sacrifices they demanded was a disciplining of the Budapest School, whose reputation, if not actual behavior, seemed to present a threat to the party's omniscience. When they refused to submit to criticism at a closed party session, eight of Lukács's most prominent students lost their university positions and four of them emigrated.[37] Not long after that authorities detained the novelist György Konrád and the sociologist Iván Szelényi for writing a book entitled *Intellectuals on the Road to Class Power*.[38] The two authors argued that a new class was emerging, just as Milovan Djilas said it would, but that class was the intellectuals, both those in power and those who would like to get into power. "We thought," Szelényi said later, "that the system would be good if intellectuals had power, that there is nothing wrong with intellectuals having power—the only problem with socialism is that it is not the intellectuals who have power."[39] Konrád was restrained from publication and Szelényi went into exile. At about the same time economic reformers such as Rezső Nyers were being demoted from the politburo.

These purges were notable because of their relative rarity. Whereas in Czechoslovakia during the 1970s thousands of scholars were working as doorkeepers and window washers and in Romania the enforced calm was almost complete, in Hungary the last significant political trial came in 1973, when Miklós Haraszti was sentenced to eight months in prison for having given a few friends copies of his powerful personal account of the debilitating piece-work system he found in a factory where he had worked for six months.[40] Occasional unreconciled opponents might end up working for a fire extinguisher company, police might rough up ordinary workers caught writing graffiti, and a few thinkers deemed theoretically threatening, such as Lukács's students, might be ostracized, but if one did not overtly challenge the regime it was possible to think moderately independent thoughts and to survive quite well.

An identifiable opposition movement, as opposed to dissident individuals, began to cohere in Hungary about the same time as in Poland. In 1976 Hungary's first typewritten samizdat publication appeared, an essay by Iván Szelényi on housing with an introduction by János Kis and György Bence. Discussion circles had been meeting for several years, and in 1977 about thirty intellectuals signed a petition in support of Charter 77. In September 1978 these disparate activities took concrete form when the Hungarian version of the "Flying University" held its first lecture, a discussion of the seminal populist thinker István Bibo given by the historian Miklós Szabó. In a short time these Monday night talks, which went on for many years, were being held in mid-town Budapest apartments that could hold as many as four hundred listeners in their separately wired rooms.[41] About 1978 László Rajk, son of the man of the same name juridically murdered in the purge years, began opening his apartment one evening a week to sell oppositional literature.[42] Rajk would lay out copies of recent publications in this "samizdat boutique," as he called it, and customers, whose names were never taken, would indicate which ones they wanted and how many copies. During the next seven days Rajk's team of copiers would reproduce the texts and next week the buyers would return and pick up their purchases. In 1979 Ottilia Solt and some colleagues launched the Fund for the Assistance to the Poor, Hungary's first independent charitable organization. Of course the fund was also profoundly political, since even the very use of the term "the poor" was at that time unacceptable to the regime. "What we really did with the foundation for the poor," says Haraszti, "was to change the language."[43]

With the coming of Solidarity in Poland, the handful of persons involved in these initiatives began thinking of how they could expand their activities. At the turn of the year 1980–1981, twenty-five of them met in a Budapest apartment to discuss a suggestion that they begin a journal. Despite the many negative opinions expressed, the most poignant of which was that they had no vital issue capable of mobilizing popular support, the meeting led to a year-long series of discussions among a group of about seven persons that in December 1981 produced Hungary's first and most important opposition journal, *Beszélő* (Speaker).[44] Just as KOR did in Poland, the editors printed their names and addresses. "We have nothing to hide," was their motto.

The key figure in *Beszélő* was the Budapest School philosopher János Kis, who later became chairman of the Alliance of Free Democrats and whom friends consider one of the finest minds in Central Europe. Kis set out the journal's main goal as the encouragement of civil society, which he believed was the only sound basis of genuine democratization. The modest first issue of five hundred, printed in a film critic's summer home outside of Budapest, received considerably more publicity than its tiny print run warranted when the editors thoughtfully sent a copy to Radio Free Europe in Munich. Shortly thereafter the volatile Gábor Demszky, who later became *Beszélő*'s publisher as well as competitor and who in 1990 became mayor of Budapest, established AB press, the Hungarian equivalent to Vaculík's Petlice Press. In 1983 Demszky began publishing another opposition journal, *Hírmondó* (Messenger), which was somewhat less forbidding than the sophisticated *Beszélő*.

These activists and others like them, including a small peace movement, expressed a wide variety of opinion, ranging from humanist Marxism to Hungarian populism. Taken together they constituted a new phenomenon in Hungary, belated perhaps in relation to Poland and Czechoslovakia, but considerably ahead of Bulgaria and Romania: a democratic opposition.[45] The goals of this incipient opposition were at first quite modest. Simply "to maintain an unbroken tradition of opposition" or to follow the motto "what can be done should be done" was enough at first.[46] Very few of the oppositionists who raised their heads in the early 1980s favored marketizing reforms, and most felt that any sort of true democracy was a pipe dream, but they did hope to maintain pressure on the state by presenting independent opinions.

By 1985 this minuscule opposition, whose most active membership was probably fewer than a hundred, whose sympathizers numbered in the low thousands at best, and whose message was a sophisticated one aimed primarily at intellectuals, began to have a modest impact. Falling real wages were changing the Hungarian mood from one of self-satisfaction at living in the "happiest barracks in the socialist camp" to one of discontent. Over the next three years these discontents crystallized in two general areas: the party itself, where reformers, already in the majority after the Thirteenth Congress in 1985, successfully pressured for change from within, and in the democratic opposition, which was able to formulate popular causes and to mobilize the public in a way the party eventually had to take seriously.

Party Reformers

Reformers such as the economist Rezső Nyers resurfaced within the party in the late 1970s, and in 1982 Imre Pozsgay, hitherto a not particularly distinguished minister of culture, became chairman of the Patriotic People's Front (PPF), the party's mass organization, which he began to use as a platform for advocating reform. Increasingly, the term "pluralism" crept into party discussion. In 1985 an interviewer for *Mozgó Világ* (Moving World) could say that the term had become a "fashionable expression." But in 1985 pluralism did not mean multiparty pluralism, a concept that still seemed unrealistic and utopian, but socialist pluralism, which meant "monism moderated by pluralistic elements," as one advocate put it.[47]

The elections of June 1985, the first held under the 1983 law that required multiple candidates, provided both an example of what "socialist pluralism" meant in real life and an indication of what kind of pressures for self-activation bubbled beneath the surface of Hungarian public life. For this election, authorities adopted the principle proposed in 1968 for Czechoslovakia, assigning the National Front, or in Hungary's case the PPF, the task of running the nomination process, which was open except for the stifling stipulation that all candidates had to adhere to the PPF's platform. Direct interference kept the most radical candidates from achieving nomination, but the process was still vigorous enough so that about half the constituencies nominated independent candidates, often directors of agricultural cooperatives who were perceived as fighting the bureaucracy despite their party membership. Forty-three independent candidates entered parliament and a number of prominent figures, including a former prime minister, went down to defeat.[48] It was not exactly democracy, but the elections produced more political mobilization than Hungary had seen since 1956 and more real differences of viewpoint in the Hungarian parliament than existed at the time in, for example, Mexico. In 1989 this parliament adopted the revolutionary changes that finished communism in Hungary.[49]

Hungary's administered democratization fit well with the new thinking coming from the Soviet Union. The Hungarian press was very positive about perestroika, which the Soviets had formally adopted early in 1986, and it became downright enthusiastic in June 1986 when Gorbachev visited Budapest. Gorbachev showed his interest in Hungarian reform shortly thereafter by sending a delegation of Soviet economists, headed by one of his most brilliant reform minds, Abel Aganbegyan, to Budapest to discuss the Hungarian experience with Rezső Nyers and his team. By 1987, the question was not so much reform versus recentralization, but rather what sort of reform to implement and how fast it should proceed.

The main stumbling block now became the old reformer himself, János Kádár. In the new conditions of the 1980s, Kádár looked more like the child of the Stalinist era that he actually was than the moderate who had found a way to make Hungary prosperous. Crowding him were two sorts of reformers, those like Károly Grósz, who believed that somehow the economy could be saved without damaging the right or ability of the party to rule, and more radical advocates of pluralization, like Pozsgay and Nyers. Grósz saw economic reform as the solution to the political problem; Pozsgay and Nyers saw political reform as the precondition to the solution of the economic problems.

Late in 1986 Pozsgay began the debate that led to 1989 with a frontal attack entitled "Turning Point and Reform," a report he commissioned from the PPF, which he headed. This remarkable document, which was known to the elite but was not published, listed the serious economic difficulties Hungary was experiencing; the squandering of labor, energy, raw materials, and capital; the inability to adjust to world trends; and wasteful investment allocation. It went on to make a startling proposal to fix them: introduce the profit motive through marketizing reforms. Admitting the total failure of centralized planning, the sixty-page paper advocated equal legal treatment for all forms of property, opening Hungary entirely to the world economy, cutting back demands from CMEA, and permitting prices and wages to fluctuate according to supply and demand. For this to happen, the report concluded, political change was needed. No party should be above the law, individual rights should be protected, and an independent judiciary should be introduced.[50]

Realizing that the terms of public debate were changing and that a space was opening into which it might inject its ideas, *Beszélő* published its own proposal for change in June 1987. In this lengthy article, entitled

"A New Social Contract," János Kis and his two coauthors argued that the time had come for Hungary to move from the tactic consensus that had marked the Kádár years to open negotiations that would work out the compromises needed to create a new social contract. Political pluralism, self-management in the workplace, national self-determination, and neutrality in foreign policy were the principles on which this contract should be based.[51]

If "Turning Point and Reform" advocated what amounted to a turn toward capitalism in the economic sphere, "A New Social Contract" advocated the separation of powers in the political sphere. In 1987 it was still necessary to assume that the party would continue to be a powerful force, if only to placate the Soviet Union, so the authors of "The New Social Contract" suggested that the party become the executive power, responsible for putting laws into effect and for conducting foreign policy, but that the legislature become the true representative of the people, freely elected, authorized to establish public policy through legislation, and competent to call the government to account. They also proposed an independent court system. Clearly several steps beyond socialist pluralism, "The New Social Contract" sought a new legal and constitutional basis for pluralism based on the American example, or as the Hungarians might put it, on Montesquieu. It is doubtful such a scheme could have worked in practice, at least insofar as the party retained its Leninist coloration, but "The New Social Contract" was an important step in the evolution of oppositionist thinking from reform Marxism to real pluralism.

The aging Kádár found it difficult to respond to the reformers in his party and to the challenges of the democratic opposition, but he gave no indication that he had any intention to step down. In what some have interpreted as an effort to embarrass his most serious rival, in June 1987 he elevated Károly Grósz to chairman of the council of ministers, where presumably economic difficulties would bring him to grief.[52] Rather than drifting with events, however, the workaholic Grósz proved to be a capable administrator and leader. He criticized both the bureaucracy and the workers, the first for mishandling the economy, the second for low productivity. Creating a stabilization plan of his own, he began working within the committee structure of parliament and stressing the functions of the state as opposed to the party, giving the impression that perhaps the government, which he headed, should be separated from the party, which he did not, so that it could put his program into effect.

In a strange way, Grósz's approach to the legislature complemented the proposal of "The New Social Contract" to enhance the parliament's role in a separation of powers. To this point the Hungarian legislature had been such a rubber stamp that the first time someone had wanted to register a "nay" vote, it turned out that there was no procedure established to count votes. Renewed interest in the legislature's role came to the surface in September 1987, when Grósz prepared a proposal to install a turnover tax, similar to that levied by West European states, and an income tax. The proposal had economic merit, but on the other hand the income tax in particular brought home to the population at large the enormous cost of the failures of centralized planning. One hundred prominent intellectuals, many of them never previously identified with opposition, sent an open letter to each member of parliament, which was just convening to consider the measures. "It must become possible to decide issues like sharing out of unavoidable sacrifices by means of open debate," the letter said. Only real marketization economically and full democratization politically would create the appropriate conditions for improvement, it continued. "Decisive initiatives are demanded."[53]

At first Grósz summarily rejected the right of the signatories even to send such a letter, and the legislature passed his tax bills routinely without opposition. But in the newly mobile atmosphere of Hungarian politics, Grósz could not sustain his rejection of the right to make proposals to the legislature. Almost immediately he had to state publicly that he really wanted to continue a dialogue with the opposition. "We do not have a monopoly of wisdom to solve Hungary's problems," he said not very convincingly. One month later he described lack of political competition as "one of the shortcomings of [Hungary's] political life."[54]

He did not have long to wait for that lack to be remedied. In 1986 a number of critics of the regime, including not only the democratic opposition but populist poets and other conservative and even nationalist writers, met in the town of Monor. About a year later, in September 1987, Imre Pozsgay invited the more conservative of these critics to meet again. Inspired by such nationalist poets as Sándor Csoori, about 170 center and right-wing oppositionists gathered in the unlikely small town of Lakitelek to discuss "Turning Point and Reform" and to hear a talk by Pozsgay advocating constitutional guarantees for free speech. This was an important moment in the maturation of Hungarian pluralism, because it clarified the differences between the democratic opposition and the populist opposition.[55] At the time feelings ran high, since the democratic opposition, which was not invited, saw Lakitelek as an effort to undermine the solidarity of the anti-regime forces. They were right, but precisely for that reason Lakitelek also presaged the pluralization of Hungarian politics.[56] The Communist reformer Pozsgay was building support among the more conservative non-Communists in preparation for the moment when he might ask them to join in a centrist coalition against the hardliner Communists on the right and the democratic opposition on the left.

The Democratic Opposition Finds Its Voice

If 1987 was the year in which Hungarians started inching down the slope of political reform, 1988 was the year they slipped over the edge of the cliff. In 1987 even János Kis believed that "a multi-party system is still a distant dream."[57] But by the end of 1988 Kádár had been deposed, dozens of new clubs and organizations had appeared, the regime was on the verge of permitting political parties, and the Hungarian Socialist Workers party had moved away from its claim to be the sole legitimate political force. Struggles over power and debates about declining real income and low productivity occupied party members, but during 1988 the democratic opposition finally found the issues it had lacked up until that point. Three major campaigns created the psychological substrate of their success: environmental opposition to the Gabčikovo-Nagymaros Dam; concern over Hungarians living elsewhere, particularly in Romania; and struggle for control of the symbolic representations of the national past.

In 1977 Czechoslovakia and Hungary signed an agreement to construct a huge system of dams, resevoirs, and canals over a 138-mile stretch of the Danube River that ran through their two countries. The massive project, first proposed in the Stalinist era and quite in the tradition of gargantuan heavy industrial investments, was designed according to the apex principle. Instead of operating continuously, water would be discharged twice daily through the dam at Gabčikovo in Czechoslovakia, creating a fifteen-foot-high swell that would continue down the river to a second dam at Nagymaros, where it would be stopped and used a second time for generating power.

Not until January 1984 did a handful of Hungarian environmentalists begin to discuss this formidable rearrangement of the Danube. Forming the Danube Circle to fight the dam, they argued that the project would completely disrupt the ecology of the region, ruin the acquifers, and flood the historic Hungarian capital of Visegrád.[58] During that year and the next other small protest movements took up the issue. Their agitation, as well as cost-benefit studies suggesting that Hungary would increase its energy production only modestly through the project, helped the government decide to stretch out the dam's construction, but it did not give up the idea.

Late in 1985 an announcement that Hungary had signed an agreement with Austria to construct the Nagymaros dam stunned the Danube Circle. The Austrians had wanted to build their own Danube power project, but when environmental opposition made that impossible they offered to finance most of the Nagymaros dam in return for receiving 70 percent of the construction contracts and 1.2 million kilowatts of electricity a year for twenty years after completion, which was substantially all of Nagymaros's production.[59] This announcement greatly dispirited the environmentalists, who now believed their cause lost, but in February 1986 they nonetheless held their first small demonstration march along the river, which the police managed to disperse quietly, and took out a full-page advertisement in the Viennese paper *Die Presse* to put some pressure on Austrian consciences.

The democratic opposition joined the dam issue not only because it was one they could believe in but because they found that a significant number of people otherwise unwilling to enter into political debates, to say nothing of becoming oppositionists, were willing to come forward on this issue. In September 1988 they were able to bring thirty thousand people onto the streets of Budapest, while at the same time several members of the legislature began demanding that the issue be put to a national referendum. When a governmental agreement to discuss the dam at the October 1988 legislative session came to nothing, a rash of demonstrations produced a petition of protest containing seventy thousand signatures. The contrast with Czechoslovakia, which tolerated little or no opposition to the dam, suggests how far Hungary had come by the end of 1988.

The opposition also found the alleged mistreatment of Hungarians living outside Hungary, particularly in Transylvania, a useful issue. Nicolae Ceaușescu's policies in Transylvania during the 1980s provoked emotional reactions, especially since the Hungarian government continued to maintain correct relations with Romania. When Ceaușescu announced his village reconstruction plan, which proposed to bulldoze thousands of villages and to replace them with "modern" apartment complexes, many Hungarians interpreted the plan as an effort to destroy Hungarian culture in Transylvania, although in the end no Hungarian villages were actually razed. Still, the difficult position of the Hungarian Protestants and Catholics in Orthodox Romania and the restrictions placed on Hungarian cultural figures there all were grist for the opposition press. Inflaming the situation even more was the influx of refugees, who by 1987 were slipping across the border in substantial numbers. In that year a small group of activists created a refugee aid group, in February 1988 five hundred people gathered at the Romanian embassy in Budapest to protest Ceaușescu's policies, and in June 1988 some thirty thousand people demonstrated in Budapest against the village reconstruction plan and the Hungarian government's lack of action, the largest demonstration in Hungary since 1956.

Anti-Romanian demonstrations the government did not find unsettling. In fact, the government tried to coopt the anti-Romanian feeling for its own purposes. But demonstrations on unauthorized holidays, the "struggle over public memory" as Tamás Hofer calls it, almost unhinged the regime.[60] After coming to power the Communist government, quite naturally, had installed its own holidays—Liberation Day on April 4; May Day on May 1; Constitution Day on August 20; and October Revolution Day on November 7. But in the 1980s the opposition began to attempt celebrations on other days: March 15, which was the traditional national holiday commemorating the Hungarian Revolution of 1848; June 16, the day on which Imre Nagy, leader of the 1956 uprising, had been executed; and October 30, the traditional date for the beginning of the 1956 revolution. All three dates had the added emotional power of being anti-Russian, because in all three cases Hungarians fighting for national independence had been crushed by Russian (or Soviet) troops. In 1985 the government permitted a small group of students to demonstrate on March 15, even directing apartment managers to put out flags for the occasion. But the next year police attacked students who attempted to march and arrested a number of them. After a relatively subdued dem-

onstration in 1987, in 1988, despite detention of eight leading members
of the opposition, some ten thousand people turned out for the March 15
demonstration.

The day of Imre Nagy's execution proved an even more volatile date.
The government was very sensitive to any efforts to reinterpret what it
characterized as the "counterrevolutionary" and "reactionary" revolt of
1956. Not only did the regime's legitimacy depend on the legitimacy of
the Soviet intervention, but since János Kádár was directly implicated in
Nagy's execution, any re-evaluation of 1956 presented a personal problem
for him. On the occasion of the thirtieth anniversary of the 1956 revolution
(October 30, 1986) the police took extraordinary precautions to insure
that the opposition would not use the occasion for a hostile demonstration.
But in trying to defuse the situation by a media campaign that passed the
blame for 1956 and its aftermath primarily onto the shoulders of a
"clique" surrounding Mátyas Rákósi, the old Stalinist leader, the regime
only served to call further attention to the event. Its defensiveness could
not compare in emotional impact with the opposition's much more powerful presentation of the revolution simply as an uprising of the Hungarian
people in defense of the nation.

By careful monitoring, the government was able, both in 1987 and in
1988, to prevent large demonstrations on June 16, but it could not make
the issue go away. The opposition insured it would not when at the 1988
demonstration, Miklós Vásárhelyi, an old associate of Nagy's and now a
vigorous member of the democratic opposition, announced the creation
of the Committee for Historical Justice, consisting primarily of relatives of
the executed leaders from 1956. Later that year Judit Ember's publication
of eleven hours of filmed interviews with surviving family members of the
Nagy group capped a flood of personal reminiscences about the period.
By the end of 1988 the only position acceptable to the democratic opposition was the full rehabilitation of all participants and victims of repression
in 1956, a possibility the government continued to reject as out of the
question.

Party Reformers Take Control and Opposition Parties Form

In May 1988 the Hungarian Socialist Workers party finally, after a long
spring of obvious maneuvering and speculation, relieved the increasingly
senile János Kádár of his position as general secretary, bumping him up to
the purely decorative and newly created title of president of the party.
Károly Grósz, backed up by a restructured politburo including Pozsgay
and Nyers, replaced him. In retrospect Grósz proved to be a transitional
figure, but at the time his accession was a major event, welcomed in both
the East and the West. In economic matters Grósz was a pragmatist. "I
want a Hungary that is open, integrated into the world and that is in the
mainstream of . . . intellectual and economic trends," he said. In politics
he was in the traditional mold. Democratization would take place in Hun-

gary only "in the context of a one-party system," he asserted.[61] The special brutality with which the police broke up the small June 16 demonstration in 1988 lent substance to those words, as did Grósz's description of that demonstration as an "incitement toward fascist propaganda, chauvinism, and irredentism."[62]

With the accession of the reformers, however, a Hungarian perestroika began in earnest. Imre Pozsgay was put in charge of summing up the party's experience of the past twenty years and preparing a program for the next twenty, which guaranteed that the pressure for reform would increase. Pozsgay also held responsibility in the politburo for the media. Editors accordingly found they needed less and less self-restraint to stay out of trouble. In July 1988 the party drastically cut back on the nomen-klatura, the list of jobs for which party approval was needed, and Grósz announced that Hungary would soon adopt a law on associations that in principle would permit opposition parties to form. By fall the official press was publishing stories about strikes and similar, formerly forbidden sub-jects, and in November the party reliquished control over the national youth organization. Finally, in December, bowing to pressure, the gov-ernment announced that March 15 would henceforth be a national holiday.

The new openness under Grósz led to a proliferation of clubs and associations during 1988.[63] At the time, the Democratic Trade Union of Academic and Scientific Workers (Tudományos Dolgozók Demokratikus Szakszervezete—TDDSz), billed as the first independent trade union in Eastern Europe since Solidarity, received a great deal of attention because of the Polish experience, but several other organizations turned out to be more important. In September 1988 the same group of populist figures who had met with Pozsgay in Lakitelek the previous year and who had met regularly ever since returned to Lakitelek to create the Hungarian Democratic Forum (Magyar Demokrata Forum—MDF). They even received permission to publish a newspaper sympathetic to their cause, *Hitel* (Credit—so called to resonate with a book written in the nineteenth century by the aristocratic liberal István Széczenyi). Earlier in the year a number of embryonic groupings of the democratic opposition came together to create the Network of Free Initiatives, which quickly spawned the Alliance of Free Democrats (Szabad Demokraták Szövetsége—SzDSz). The Free Democrats were a Western-oriented liberal counterpart to the more nationalist and populist Democratic Forum. Under their pres-ident János Kis they advocated European-style democracy and Hungary's withdrawal from the Warsaw Pact. Another important group that formed in 1988 was the Alliance of Young Democrats, usually called by its Hun-garian acronym FIDESz (Fiatal Demokraták Szövetsége—pronounced FEE-dess). Designed as an alternative to the official Communist youth organization, FIDESz restricted its membership to those between the ages of sixteen and thirty-five. "FIDESz wants to represent three basic values," one of its organizers said: "Nation, Socialism, and Democracy," of which the last was the most important.[64] Somewhat to the left of the Free Democrats, FIDESz also stood squarely behind the creation of a pluralist society in Hungary.

The Democratic Forum (MDF), the Free Democrats (SzDSz), and the Young Democrats (FIDESz) became the nuclei of the three main political parties of post-1989 Hungary, but they were far from the only new organizations founded in 1988. Groups ranged from the Stalinist Ferenc Münnich Society, consisting of old-line centralizers, through the short-lived New March Front, founded with the help of Rezső Nyers to rally liberal reformers close to the government, to the Independent Smallholders' party and the Social Democratic party, recreated from remnants of the past, and smaller movements such as the Republican Circle, the Openness Club, and literally dozens of others. Most of these organizations were very small. The largest among them, the Democratic Forum, claimed only about twelve thousand members by mid-1989, while the Free Democrats claimed only four thousand and the Free Democrats only two thousand, almost all of these students and intellectuals in Budapest. But together they represented an unprecedented flourishing of political pluralism in Hungary.

Gorbachev Gives the Green Light

The quickening of economic and political ferment in Hungary in 1988 was indigenous, depending on developments peculiar to Hungary, but during that year the Soviet leadership passed an increasing number of signals that it was prepared to accept major changes.[65] While on a tour of the United States in mid-1988 Abel Aganbegyan stressed the Soviet Union's need for a free "commodity market" regulated by supply and demand, advocated introducing market mechanisms, and proposed putting Soviet enterprises on a profit-and-loss basis.[66] About the same time Oleg Bogomolov, another of Gorbachev's chief advisors, said at a meeting in the United States that "the administrative-state model of socialism, established in the majority of East European countries during the 1950s under the influence of the Soviet Union, has not withstood the test of time" and admitted that the "hegemonic aspirations of the Soviet leadership" had deformed socialism in Eastern Europe.[67]

From June 28 to July 1, 1988, the Soviet party held its Nineteenth All-Union Party Conference, surely one of the most important it ever held. Gorbachev pursued two tactics at the conference. On one hand, he solidified his position as the most powerful figure in the Soviet Union by creating the office of president, to which he was duly elected later, and on the other hand he proposed the creation of a new legislature, the Congress of People's Deputies, that would select the Supreme Soviet after having been elected itself by open and contested elections.

Answering Gorbachev's summons for "lively and demanding" legislative sessions rather than ones filled with "long-winded speeches," delegates to the Nineteenth Party Conference offered proposals that were nothing short of astonishing.[68] One delegate rose to demand the resignation of Politburo member Andrej Gromyko and three other old-line leaders; another called the leaders of Uzbekistan criminals; and dozens of speakers complained about living conditions, national slights, censorship, and everything else they could think of. More amazing, a good deal of this was televised to the entire nation. For the first time ever Soviets in 1988 saw their leaders debating real differences. And when Gorbachev's proposals were adopted at the end, the vote was not unanimous.

East European leaders watched the Nineteenth Conference closely. Erich Honecker and Nicolae Ceauşescu rejected its message completely. But talk about democratization, "the all-around enrichment of human rights," establishment of "the rule of law," and separation of party functions from those of the state could only persuade Hungarians that the Soviets supported the increasing pace of reform in their country. Gorbachev's military policy reinforced this growing suspicion that the Soviet Union would not intervene with force. Late in 1987 the Soviets made it clear they were looking for a way out of their debilitating and demoralizing war in Afghanistan, and in February 1988 Gorbachev announced Soviet troops would be leaving. The first troops actually left on May 15. When Grósz visited Moscow just after the Nineteenth Party Conference Gorbachev apparently told him that the Soviet Union intended to withdraw some of its troops from Hungary, where some sixty thousand soldiers had been "temporarily stationed" since 1946. By the end of the year the two countries had reached an agreement to do so, and the first Soviet troops boarded their trains on April 25, 1989. If these and other hints that the Soviet Union had no intention of intervening militarily in Eastern Europe were not clear enough, Gorbachev made them so at his United Nations speech of December 7, 1988, which can be taken as his official repudiation of the Brezhnev Doctrine. "It is obvious," he said, "that force and the threat of force cannot be and should not be an instrument of foreign policy. . . . Freedom of choice is [mandatory,] a universal principle, and it should know no exceptions. . . . The growing variety of options for the social development of different countries is becoming an increasingly tangible hallmark of these processes. This applies to both the capitalist and the socialist systems."[69] Given all these green lights, the surprising thing is not that Hungary continued on its path toward pluralization but that with the exception of Poland it was the only East European country to do so, at least for the moment.

The Reformers Win the Battle for Historical Memory

By early 1989 the more radical reformers in the party were gaining the upper hand. The legislature finally passed a law on associations that would permit the creation of political parties, and in January Pozsgay leaked a central committee historical commission report calling the 1956 uprising a "popular uprising against an oligarchic system of power which had humiliated the nation." Going even further, Pozsgay asserted that the socialist path "was wrong in its entirety," surely a remarkable statement for a member of the politburo. Grósz instantly rebuked Pozsgay for his statement, but the Soviets did not back him and he could not make his criticism stick. This is the moment when Pozsgay realized that the Soviet Union was not going to intervene, no matter what happened.[70] A few weeks later, when his report appeared in print, it said, "Under the Stalin regime the ideal of international communism was turned into a merciless imperial program. In the shadow of this endeavor, Marxist humanism completely vanished." The system Stalin installed was built on "bloody dictatorship, bureaucratic centralism, fear and retribution."[71]

The central committee never actually adopted this report, but it was perfectly clear that a significant portion of the party had moved from a position of "socialist pluralism" to a position of rejecting the basis of its own existence. The central committee confirmed that this indeed was the case when in February 1989 it agreed to eliminate the phrase "the Marxist-Leninist party of the working class is the leading power of society" from the draft constitution it was preparing. Since the Leninist claim that the party, as the vanguard of the proletariat, was the sole repository of truth constituted the legitimating basis of the hyperrationalist system, the Hungarian reformers now seemed to have staked their future on their ability to control the emerging pluralism and to devise an electoral scheme that would permit them to retain power. The hyperrational pathway from the Enlightenment was coming to an end.

The outcome of the battle of the holidays suggested that retaining power would be a difficult task, since in February 1989 the government totally caved in, not merely permitting a celebration on March 15 but adopting it as a national holiday in place of November 7 (Day of the October Revolution) and deciding to disinter Imre Nagy and permit his ceremonial reburial on June 16, 1989. The opposition, emboldened and vigorously organizing themselves to be prepared for the elections they now anticipated would be coming in 1990, turned the first of these holidays into a magnificently symbolic celebration. Actually there were, in effect, three celebrations on March 15, 1989. The first was the official government ceremony, for which the quite respectable figure of thirty thousand turned out. Second was the completely unpolitical and anticelebrational movement of some two hundred thousand Hungarians who used the holiday weekend and the relaxed border regulations to travel the 150 miles to Vienna, where they paralyzed the center of the city in a massive shopping splurge.

The third celebration was a march of some one hundred thousand persons organized by the opposition movements in Budapest.[72] Organizers meticulously planned this march so that over a five-hour period it stopped at six locations in central Budapest that had significant links to both Hungarian revolutions, the one of 1848 and the one of 1956. For instance, the first stop was the statue of Sándor Petöfi, the poet of the 1848 revolution whose statue marked the spot where the demonstration of October 23, 1956, started. The last stop was Batthyány Square, the traditional end point of antigovernment demonstrations in 1956 and once again a memorial to a hero of the 1848 revolution. The government had placed its water cannons along the parade route in anticipation of intervention, but in the end it chose to interpret this clever and ambiguous symbolic display as a national historical celebration that was not inconsistent with its rule. The opposition saw it as a massive morality play. By touching on as many interlinked markers of Hungarian history as possible, it hoped to rekindle memories of a liberal and democratic past interrupted by war and communism. Whether their interpretations of 1848 and 1956 could stand the test of historical analysis is less important than their success in finding the appropriate symbols and rituals in the Hungarian cultural tool kit to reshape public memory to the disadvantage of the regime.[73]

The last in this series of public demonstrations that capped the Hungarian declaration of independence from post-Stalinist norms took place on June 16, 1989. A massive state funeral attended by the prime minister, the president of the national assembly, and two hundred thousand others reburied not only the remains of Imre Nagy and several of his colleagues, but the entire Kádárian pretense that Communist Hungary had been an independent Communist state. The somber and sometimes even tearful mood of the huge crowd testified to the depth of the emotional burden of powerlessness and humiliation that Hungarians had felt since 1956. With Gorbachev beaming unseen in the background, the Soviet press correctly reported that Nagy's humane reburial served "the purpose of national reconciliation and rallying which is so necessary now for the Hungarian people."[74]

4

Solidarity: The Return
of the Repressed in Poland

By 1989 the changes underway in Hungary gave promise of transformations such as had never before been seen in a Communist country. The party had promised to give up its monopoly role, a multiparty system was in the offing, marketizing economists were in the ascendancy, and, best of all, the Soviet Union had made it clear that it would not intervene. But in the spring of 1989 the world was not looking primarily at Hungary. Instead its gaze was focused on the remarkable political events in the Soviet Union. Even the withdrawal of the last troops from Afghanistan in February after almost ten years of futile bloodshed, an otherwise notable event, was eclipsed by the open election to the Congress of People's Deputies in March and the raucous meeting of that body and of the Supreme Soviet two months later. The spectacle of relatively open elections and truly contentious debate in the motherland of Leninism overshadowed the less dramatic internal evolution in Hungary, which even acute observers did not grant a high likelihood of success in any event.[1]

The stirring re-emergence of Solidarity in 1988 and 1989 also overshadowed the relatively undramatic Hungarian events. In June 1989 the Polish United Workers party lost every seat it contested in an election for the national legislature and even many that were not contested. Three months later Tadeusz Mazowiecki became the first non-Communist prime minister in Eastern Europe since Petru Groza left office in Romania in 1952. Unlike Groza, however, Mazowiecki was no puppet. He represented the broadest genuine coalition of social forces ever brought together in Poland. To those who had not been following events, the change seemed almost instantaneous, but the coming to power of Solidarity in 1989 was the climax of a Polish trialogue that had been going on for more than a decade. The three participants in this trialogue were the party and the state, which had the strongest hand on paper, conducted a well-conceived and cleverly executed policy, and won a good many of the individual contests; the church, which followed a conciliatory and practical approach at the top that brought it many benefits and an oppositional approach in many local parishes that assisted in the creation of an independent society; and Solidarity, which was overpowered on occasion, confused on others, and split internally, but, to the amazement of even itself, emerged in 1989 as the winner.

Jaruzelski's Dual Strategy of Normalization

Despite the brutality of the first days and weeks of the imposition of martial law in December 1981, when most of the Solidarity leadership was arrested, enterprises militarized, miners shot, telephone communications interrupted, and strikes broken by specially trained forces, Jaruzelski's overall strategy of normalization differed fundamentally from that of Gustav Husák in Czechoslovakia after 1968. Jaruzelski did not attempt to restore a neo-Stalinist regime in Poland, not even to restore Gierek's regime. In a curious way he realized the importance of Solidarity's contributions to Polish public life, confirmed the necessity of the social accords of 1980, and in due time even accepted the idea of pluralism.

Jaruzelski initially maintained that because of its "juvenile emotional dynamism" Solidarity had become an unreliable and impossible candidate for partnership with the party and had pushed the economy to the wall with unreasonable wage demands. It had to be suppressed because it had "trodden on the law, ruined the economy, waged a struggle against the party and the Government, and also insulted the Sejm."[2] But from the beginning, when the police took Lech Wałęsa to Warsaw and were unable to get him to appeal to the people for calm, Jaruzelski understood that it was Solidarity, not the party, that enjoyed the support of the nation. During the first few weeks of martial law the general presented himself as minister of defense, prime minister, and chairman of the new Military Council for National Salvation but never as head of the party. "When the Party began to reappear publicly in 1982," David Ost argues, "there was never any question that it could run things by itself. That notion had been discredited forever."[3] To compensate for this lack Jaruzelski and his advisors complemented their repression of Solidarity, which they pursued vigorously for years, with a sophisticated strategy of attracting support through superficially reasonable offers of cooperation and of creating new organizations that simulated independent institutions.

One of the first steps in this dual policy was to regain control of the intelligentsia. Immediately after the introduction of martial law all media and educational institutions had to undergo "verification," a process in which each employee was interviewed concerning his or her attitude toward the regime and toward Solidarity. Over two thousand persons in the media lost their jobs for failing this test, and those who stayed had to sign a loyalty oath by which they also resigned from Solidarity.[4] Not everyone was fired or intimidated. Some prominent television actors, for example, stopped appearing in popular soap operas, which led to their shows' cancellation. But eventually, by disbanding the artists' union, the writers' union, the film board, and the association of journalists, the government restored its control over the means of public discussion.[5]

Having broken the media, Jaruzelski then proceeded gradually, over a period of years, to open it to varied comment. Local or small-circulation journals received the most freedom at first, and national television the least, but over the next few years independent intellectuals could, if they did not associate themselves too openly with Solidarity positions, publish increasingly outspoken pieces. In this way, a number of intellectuals were able to play a role in making Poland a variegated society without actually entering into illegal activities.

Jaruzelski also sought an accommodation with the Catholic church, which in 1981 received a new, more amenable primate, Archbishop Józef Glemp.[6] Over time, the regime had considerable success in dealing with Glemp, but during the first months of martial law the church, while always expressing its concern for peace and nonviolence, came down on the side of a more pluralist society. On April 4, 1982, the primate's social council adopted a report pointing out that any social contract was impossible without popular support and that therefore the state must recognize society as an active subject, which meant holding truly free elections. In September the episcopate circulated a sermon to be read throughout the country that called for an end to martial law, amnesty for the imprisoned, and renewal of dialogue. Individual priests often supported opposition activities directly, and the church's pastoral activities, which included creating special ministries for workers and for farmers as well as patronizing artists and supporting youth movements, gave life to the idea of an independent society during the worst years of martial law.[7]

But Archbishop Glemp was more equivocal. Pursuing his own agenda of strengthening the church's position in what was, after all, still a Communist society, Glemp decided early on that he would side with the regime. Glemp's most obviously self-interested and divisive decision came in November 1982. Pope John Paul II had been scheduled to make his second visit to Poland in 1982, but with the imposition of martial law it had been postponed. Glemp considered this visit of the utmost importance, so in return for the government's approval of the trip he agreed to make the announcement only two days before underground Solidarity had called for a demonstration strike. Glemp confirmed the feeling of many activists that his call for calm at that moment had betrayed Solidarity when, a month later, he suggested that actors should stop their boycott of state productions.[8]

Underground Solidarity

Initially, the regime did not contemplate completely abolishing Solidarity, which was only "suspended." Jaruzelski hoped that the determined use of force would demonstrate the futility of rejecting the party's leading role and encourage an accommodation on the party's terms. By isolating Solidarity's leadership, Deputy Prime Minister Mieczysław Rakowski said, "people who think realistically and, most important, [who] are committed to socialism would come to prevail."[9] This was not an unreasonable hope, since historically Communist regimes had been quite successful in taming social organizations like unions and had never had difficulty finding ambitious people willing to serve them. But, like every other Communist regime in Eastern Europe, the Polish leadership had no idea of the depth of its own illegitimacy in the eyes of the public, even though this should have been obvious after the Solidarity experience. It took seven years for them to realize that it was not inexplicable fanaticism that caused hundreds of activists to reject repeated offers of emigration visas and thousands of others to write, print, and distribute oppositional newspapers and journals. A deep sense of humiliation and injustice permeated society and sustained the oppositionists' principled behavior.

The tone of Solidarity's resistance was set almost immediately in the first months of martial law. Despite the regime's best efforts to decapitate the union, a handful of activists eluded capture and took the union's struggle underground. The new Solidarity leaders became so not by election or by choice but by virtue of accidentally escaping the December roundup. It was fortunate, therefore, that the senior figure remaining at large in the Mazowsze region, the one that contains Warsaw and is therefore the most important in Poland, was twenty-eight-year old Zbigniew Bujak. The thirteenth son of a peasant family, Bujak had become technician at the Ursus tractor works, where his instinctive understanding of politics had brought him to high position despite his youth. Bujak considered Václav Havel's essay, "The Power of the Powerless," the theoretical underpinning for his activity. Later he said that he saw in the victories of Solidarity and Charter 77 "an astonishing fulfillment of the prophecies and knowledge contained in Havel's essay."[10] In Bujak's view, underground Solidarity's hope lay in continuing the tradition of KOR and of the self-limiting revolution by constructing an independent society outside the parameters of ordinary politics. Many disagreed. Jacek Kuroń, for example, wrote from prison that the imposition of martial law called for more confrontational resistance:[11]

> A well-organized, mass resistance movement is the Poles' only chance. . . . For this reason—in contrast to our strategy before August 1980—we must now organize around a central nucleus and accept its discipline. . . . Throughout the many years of my opposition activity I have always argued against the use of force. Therefore I now feel duty-bound to state publicly that in the present circumstances preparation to overthrow the occupation by a concerted, collective action would be the least of all possible evils.

Bujak and one of his colleagues, teacher Wiktor Kulerski, rejected Kuroń's view that a centralized organization was needed to combat state terror.[12] "Local groups and social circles in the community should organize . . . to build a system of social structures independent of the state," wrote Bujak. These actions should include the creation of mutual aid committees, independent publications, and educational and cultural networks. We do not need to choose between revolution or compromise, Kulerski added.

> Instead of organizing ourselves as an underground state, we should be organizing ourselves as an underground society. Not into a movement directed by a central headquarters requiring absolute discipline, but into a loosely structured, decentralized movement composed of mutually independent groups, committees, etc., each of which would be largely autonomous and self-directed. . . . Such a movement should strive for a situation in which the government will control empty shops but not the market, employment but not the means to livelihood, the state press but not the flow of information, printing houses but not the publishing movement, telephones and the postal service but not communication, schools but not education.

"This road is not one of rapid and stunning success," Bujak said. But "structures rich in form last the longest. . . . A democratic society, with abundant forms of social life and activity, can defend itself against various defeats, while a totalitarian society is very frail, and every setback threatens its viability."[13]

Bujak's and Kulerski's views represented the dominant position of what Aleksander Smolar has called the "legitimist" opposition, that is, the opposition "perceived by its adherents as the continuation of legal Solidarity."[14] When leaders of this persuasion still at large in four regions of Poland met clandestinely in April 1982, they did not create a centralized party organization but rather a Temporary Coordinating Commission (Tymczasowa Komisja Koordynacyjna—TKK) to coordinate the activities of those independent local unions that were still trying to maintain their identity underground. TKK entitled its first programmatic statement, which it published at the end of July 1982, "The Underground Society," an ironic play on the term *independent society*. The program called for a boycott of official organizations and for alternative observances of significant anniversaries, while at the same time emphasizing the importance of independent culture.

Underground Solidarity succeeded most dramatically in the sphere of culture, the same arena in which KOR had excelled before 1980. NOWA remained in existence and continued to print the best Polish authors, including those in emigration. By 1984 it boasted two hundred full-time employees. The first issue of *Tygodnik Mazowsze* (Warsaw Region Weekly), the main Solidarity newspaper underground, appeared only two months after martial law began. *Tygodnik Mazowsze* carried the debate between Kuroń and Bujak, and until it came into the open in 1989 it remained the most authoritative vehicle of the legitimists. Using at least six separate presses, the four-page, letter-size newspaper published between fifteen and forty thousand copies a week depending on paper supplies, a schedule that it maintained over the entire period of its underground existence, rarely missing an issue. Another significant Solidarity outlet was *Niezależny Serwis Informacyjny* (the Independent Information Service), Solidarity's equivalent to the Associated Press. By 1984 Bujak estimated that more than one million Poles were reading oppositionist papers.[15]

Some of these papers were not Solidarity publications. In Wrocław, for example, Kornel Morawiecki, who believed the relatively accommodating position of the legitimists did not represent the true interests of the working class, founded Fighting Solidarity (Solidarność Walczanca). Morawiecki was against any dialogue with the regime and went so far as to suggest that activists sabotage Soviet bases and communications, conduct propaganda among the army, and obstruct the armaments industry on the model of the Polish Home Army during World War II. This would prove to the Soviet Union, he thought, that its "direct rule" over Poland was not functioning and should be replaced by "weaker Finlandization."[16] On the other side of the fence, the Circles of Social Resistance (Komitety Oporu Społecznego—KOS) rejected even the idea of writing a political program, which its adherents maintained would only put them in the same ethical category as the ruling party. "We are not fighting for a better tomorrow," KOS leaders said, "but for a better today. . . . A free Poland is not a point in time or space from which we are separated by a wall of external force. It is a possibility asleep here and now inside each one of us."[17] KOS, which published a successful antipolitical newspaper throughout the 1980s, later became the founder of Poland's antiwar and pacifist movements.

Other groups less committed to socialist values argued that to be a self-governing republic did not have to mean creating an egalitarian workers' self-management or a trilateral corporate settlement among Solidarity, the church, and the party. Independence from foreign pressure and the recognition of real Polish sovereignty in a Catholic context were the goals of these activists. Aleksander Hall, an organizer of the nationalist Young Poland movement who joined Solidarity only after the imposition of martial law and then left it again early in 1984, presented this "unrealistic" argument with great skill in *Polityka Polska* (Polish Politics), while others pushed an even more nationalist line in *Niepodległość* (Independence). The nationalists all emphasized the Catholic nature of the Polish experience, but the group around the journal *Głos* (Voice) was explicitly Catholic in orientation. *Wiadomosci* (News) argued that the church should have its own agenda and called criticism of Glemp "irresponsible" and "baseless" since the church was following a consistent policy of peace. More radical proposals came from *Wyzwolenie* (Liberation), which considered Poland to be under occupation, and *Słowo Podziemne* (Underground Word), which advocated "developed liberalism," including a multiparty system, depoliticization of the church, and the partition of the Soviet Union into a number of independent states.[18]

Widespread grassroots support for Solidarity contrasted markedly with the relative lack of response generated by Charter 77 in Czechoslovakia. Within a year of the imposition of martial law in Poland hundreds of small groups, a few of them slipshod and ineffective, a few stalking horses organized by the police, and still others ingenious in starting a newspaper or handing out broadsides, emerged all over the country. Graffiti appeared; speakers organized discussions during intermissions at plays; clandestine lecture courses began again; students flashed the forbidden "V" sign in public places; volunteers collected Solidarity dues in factories; unofficial art exhibits took place. In Swidnik almost everyone in town took to leaving their houses for a walk at the time the evening news was broadcast, which so irritated the authorities that they declared a curfew when the news was on, whereupon the town began taking its stroll during an earlier newscast. In Warsaw first old women and then students began placing flowers in the form of a large cross in Victory Square to memorialize the late Cardinal Wyszyński. Each night the police would clear the square and wash away the flowers. And the next morning first one old woman and then another would appear with her carnations and the process would be repeated. By mid-1982 the authorities had to close off the square to end the "battle of the crosses." "Everywhere else," one university lecturer commented, "people think history is something that happens to strangers, while here it is what happens to . . . us and our friends."[19]

At first, those Solidarity leaders still at liberty believed that a compromise between the state and civil society based on the Social Accords of 1980 could be worked out. But it did not take them long to realize the impossibility of an early agreement. Solidarity's dilemma became how to pressure the government into accepting the union without becoming a political movement itself. The legitimists never solved this problem—it was insoluble—but in the beginning their favored strategy remained, as in the days of legal activity, the general strike. This was a problematic strategy under conditions of legality, but underground, with all the difficulties of communication and contact that condition implied, it proved impossible.

The Temporary Coordinating Commission (TKK) began to lose track of the public mood almost immediately. On May 1, 1982, for example, it called for citizens to boycott official celebrations and to go to church. Instead, in Warsaw some fifty thousand protesters marched in spontaneous counterdemonstrations against the official ceremonies. Two days later, on the anniversary of the Polish constitution of 1791, ten thousand more people assembled. Similar demonstrations throughout Poland led to the arrest of approximately three thousand persons. The demonstrations took TKK by surprise, but it decided to try to take advantage of the continued willingness of citizens to put themselves on the line by offering the government a deal: lift martial law and drop the suspension of the union and TKK would appeal for an end to strike activity. When the government rejected this rather naive offer and added that it would never negotiate with Solidarity, *Tygodnik Mazowsze* called for demonstrations on the second anniversary of the union's formation, August 31. But the protests failed. Authorities dispersed the smaller-than-expected crowds and arrested some four thousand persons.

The government's success in repressing these demonstrations, as well as its ability to handle dozens of smaller strikes, work stoppages, and other spontaneous actions, gave credence to Jaruzelski's claim that he had won "the battle of the winter." In July 1982 Jaruzelski showed his growing confidence by beginning to release detainees and to loosen some of the martial law restrictions. Over time, a balanced combination of vigorous repression on the one hand, including militarizing factories and mines and firing strike leaders, and the staged release and pardon of detainees on the other hand, succeeded in suggesting to the population that stability was returning and Solidarity was losing.

And yet by the middle of the summer of 1982 Jaruzelski and his team realized that their original idea of isolating the leadership of the union in order to attract the "realistic" element had failed. The union, far from accepting defeat, had only become more determined than ever to maintain its independence underground. Therefore, on October 8, 1982, the government disestablished Solidarity and introduced new rules by which independent unions could be formed. Having failed to get Solidarity to accept the party's leading role, the regime decided to establish "self-governing" unions that would. These unions retained the right to strike, although not for political reasons, and they were forbidden to create national organizations for two years. In their first year they managed to enroll about 2.5 million workers.

The spontaneous reaction of the Gdańsk shipyard to the new union law was to go out on strike, but the underground leadership proved unable to respond effectively. By October 12 the strike was broken and the shipyard militarized. Now, closing the barn door after the horse had been stolen, TKK called a one-day national protest strike for November 10 with a general strike threatened for 1983. The one-day protest strike fizzled, undermined in part by Glemp's announcement of the Pope's visit two days earlier. On November 12 Jaruzelski trumped the reeling union by releasing his most famous detainee, Lech Wałęsa.[20]

Permissible Pluralism

One year after the declaration of martial law Solidarity was profoundly disoriented. The old Solidarity, the democratic union of ten million members, was clearly finished. It began to dawn on the opposition that a daunting amount of slow and difficult work would be required to create an independent, pluralist society that could present itself for full partnership with the state. Sensing he had the opposition on the run, Jaruzelski pushed ahead with his balanced strategy of repression and artfully timed concessions. A typically two-sided act was the announcement in July 1983 that because conditions had stabilized he was lifting martial law and releasing a number of detainees. At the same time he changed the constitution to permit the head of state to declare a state of emergency without consulting the Sejm or any other body, adjusted a number of laws to permit a continuation of strict police control, and kept a few of the main leaders of Solidarity in detention.[21]

Government representatives continued to denigrate Solidarity as nonexistent, lacking reasonable advisors, corrupt, illegal, and antisocialist. They pressed forward with trials of the most prominent activists and tried to subvert the leadership with offers of emigration and petty harassment. Lech Wałęsa, although no longer in prison, bore the brunt of these negative tactics. He was prevented from returning to work, investigated for alleged tax irregularities, detained for short periods, and barred from speaking at rallies. His flat was searched, his assistants had their driving licenses revoked, and he was constantly attacked in the press for his hostile and uncooperative attitude, dismissed as "totally discredited" and without any further role in Polish politics, and ridiculed for his contacts abroad as "the self-appointed American ambassador to Poland."

And yet, in the midst of all of this hostility, Jaruzelski tacitly adopted perhaps the most fundamental principle underlying Solidarity's program. The party continued to insist, as it would until 1989 and as it had to as a Leninist organization, that it remain the leading political actor in society. But it no longer insisted that it be the *only* actor in society, a crucial difference that set it on the slippery road to extinction. While suppressing Solidarity with his right hand, so to speak, Jaruzelski struggled with his left hand to devise a kind of pluralism the party could control. The first of these "organs of permissible pluralism," as George Kolankiewicz calls them, were the new "self-governing" unions. Late in 1982, Jaruzelski created a second such organ, the Patriotic Movement for National Rebirth (Patriotyczny Ruch Ocalenia Narodowego—PRON). A revised version of the old Front of National Unity, which PRON replaced, PRON was supposed to reflect a "pluralism of views and the differentiation of interests" while seeking a coalition with various forces in society, not including Solidarity, of course.[22] With the constitutional amendments of July 1983 it became the official organization "for uniting the patriotic forces of the nation . . . and for the cooperation of political parties, organizations, social associations and citizens."[23]

Neither Wałęsa nor the rest of the opposition submitted to Jaruzelski's stick or succumbed to his carrot, and, more remarkable given the provocations, the legitimists did not abandon the moderate position first laid out by Bujak and Kulerski in 1982. "The aim of our struggle remains the same," TKK's statement of January 1983 said: "A SELF-GOVERNING REPUBLIC."[24] The methods that would lead toward that end, the statement continued, remained the refusal to participate in lies, the cultivation of independent thought, and preparation for a general strike. "Pluralism and openness are the mark of the Solidarity movement," the program reiterated.

Despite this bravado, the democratic opposition felt in 1983 that things were going badly. In reading over some of the analyses of that year and the next, one is struck by how often a mood of despair flows over the activists. They are tired; the people are going back to their regular concerns and are becoming apathetic; the government has just won another battle; the interior polemics are becoming debilitating; the future is far away. But the difference between 1972, when Leszek Kołakowski had asked how one hopes in a hopeless situation, and 1983, when it was possible to read and write and scheme, was palpable. And in 1983 Solidarity had one asset that it did not have in 1972: Lech Wałęsa.

In the letter he wrote to General Jaruzelski when he left prison, Wałęsa signed himself as "Corporal Lech Wałęsa," but everywhere else he presented himself as the elected head of independent Polish society. The government's characterization of him as a man who had lost all influence was wildly incorrect. Wałęsa constituted a separate opposition movement all by himself. Always ready to talk with the government and believing that negotiations in which compromises would have to be made were in the end inevitable, he had an uncanny knack for presenting himself as society's most uncompromising oppositionist. In April 1983 he caused a sensation when, despite almost constant surveillance, he contrived to arrange a secret three-day meeting with TKK. In November, he did it again. The embarrassed government put out the patently absurd explanation that since Solidarity no longer existed and Lech Wałęsa was a private citizen, the meeting could only be considered a social occasion, a position Wałęsa confirmed with a wink.[25] In October 1983 he received the Nobel Peace Prize, which the government found a bit more difficult to explain away as a social occasion. At a time of declining optimism in the opposition, the Nobel Prize was an enormous psychological lift. "Our wings have caught the wind," is the way Wałęsa put it.[26]

In the long run, of course, Wałęsa was right, but in the mid-1980s it might have been more accurate to say that the wind was going out of Solidarity's sails. During 1983 and 1984, actors drifted back to work, PRON's public role expanded, and the government achieved increasing legitimacy by broadening the limits to public discussion. In November 1984 unions created under the October 1982 law formed the National Trade Union Accord (Ogólnopolskie Porozumiene Związków Zawodowych—OPZZ) and elected Alfred Miodowicz its chairman. OPZZ, Miodowicz said, "will not have anything to do with restoring the old organizational structures of the trade union movement, nor returning to old mistakes."[27] Consumer goods such as soap and sugar reappeared in shops, and ordinary social life returned to normal.[28] Average citizens no longer felt the same obligation to be unhappy that they did in 1982. Jaruzelski, Rakowski, and others began to appropriate the symbolism of Solidarity, giving speeches at places sanctified by the Solidarity movement and prohibiting Solidarity activists from doing so. Under the slogan "Social Accords: Part of Our History," they argued that martial law had been the only way to save the agreements of 1980, which the regime claimed it had now incorporated into the Polish experience by means of the new unions.[29]

Victories in the local elections of 1984 and the national elections of 1985 also gave the regime confidence. These elections were conducted under new rules similar to those the Hungarians used in 1985, with PRON acting as the organizer and lightning rod, but the choices offered were more restricted than in the Hungarian case and the results more foreordained. Still, the elections were not entirely without drama. There was a contest, but it was over how many turned out to vote rather than who got elected. The government laid down the gauntlet in 1984 by saying that if 70 percent of the electorate voted it would consider the election a success. Taking up the challenge, Solidarity called for a boycott.[30] After the elections both sides claimed they won, but Solidarity's claims were the less convincing. In the local elections of 1984 the government reported that about 75 percent of the population voted, and in the national election of 1985, in which it set a goal of raising that percentage, it announced that 79 percent had voted. Solidarity, which with difficulty conducted its own surveys in selected voting areas, claimed that the actual numbers were only about 60 percent in both cases. Even if Solidarity's figures were correct, they did not show the kind of massive rejection of the regime that free elections were to show later. Government spokesman Jerzy Urban could argue with some justice that the 1984 election was "evidence of the social support for stabilization, social calm, and our country's development along the socialist road" and that the 1985 vote represented "a vast acceptance by the majority of the permanence of the system and the government's political line."[31]

We can suspect that the government's analysis of the 1985 election was faulty, but at the time Urban's view—that it ended a period of crisis—found wide acceptance. At the very least it gave Jaruzelski enough confidence to take another step along his road of normalization. During the Sejm that met in November 1985 he resigned as prime minister, a position he had held since 1981, but retained the office of chairman of the Council of State (president) and turned the cabinet over to Zbigniew Messner, an economist who formed a government that consisted primarily of technicians rather than party stalwarts.

The Murder of Father Jerzy Popiełuszko

As Jaruzelski continued to move Poland toward a superficial stability, the leadership of the Catholic church continued to move toward supporting him, with one important exception: Pope John Paul II. The pontiff's June 1983 visit, the announcement of which had been so controversial, drew large and enthusiastic crowds. Without mentioning the banned labor union by name, John Paul II made many pointed references to his personal "solidarity" with the church and with his homeland while suggesting that "the events that followed August 1980" had a moral character and that trade unions were "an indispensable component of social life."[32] "Social justice consists of respect for and implementation of human rights for all members of society," he said.[33] Surprisingly, all three sides expressed satisfaction with the visit: the government considered it proof that the outside world was beginning to accept normalization as a respectable process; the church was pleased with a visit of its spiritual leader; and Solidarity found the pontiff's positive references to its goals gratifying. In April 1985, John Paul also appointed a strong Solidarity supporter as bishop of Wrocław, which was one of the main centers of opposition activism.

Cardinal Glemp, on the other hand, sided with the regime. Glemp saw himself as a pragmatist seeking to improve the position of the church in Poland through pastoral work rather than through the sort of romantic and insurrectionary resistance that had led Poland to disaster in past centuries. His personal politics were those of *Endecja,* the conservative National Democrat party of the interwar period, and accordingly he was suspicious of the leftist origins of Solidarity.[34] In a 1984 interview in São Paolo, Brazil, for example, Glemp said that Wałęsa had lost control of Solidarity because the union "was a sack into which everything had been thrown, all the opposition Marxists, all the Trotskyites, and then all the careerists and Party members."[35] Even allowing for Glemp's notorious penchant for impolitic statements, obviously his sympathies did not lie with the Solidarity of Adam Michnik and Jacek Kuroń. His style was to maneuver behind the scenes to gain advantage for the church by lobbying for a new law regulating church–state relations, by creating an agricultural fund that the church would administer, or by re-establishing diplomatic relations between Poland and the Vatican. Although he failed to achieve all his objectives in these campaigns, on balance he was not unsuccessful. Jaruzelski granted the church wide access to television at Easter and provided substantial funds for building new churches. By 1984 nine hundred churches were under construction with regime financing.[36] But these concessions had their price. Glemp disciplined priests the government had complained about, and he even ordered the wording of some hymns changed.[37]

In some local parishes the picture was completely different. Mieczysław Nowak, for example, became so well known for his forthright sermons to workers in Ursus that Glemp transferred him. Henryk Jankowski, Wałęsa's confessor, was famous for his flamboyance.[38] The most charismatic parish priest was Father Jerzy Popiełuszko, who since January 1982 had been celebrating a monthly "Mass for the Fatherland" in Warsaw's St. Stanisław Kostka church. As many as ten thousand of the faithful would gather on these occasions to hear Popiełuszko talk about the "tears, injuries, and blood of workers" and to suggest that "the hopes of 1980 are alive and are bearing fruit."[39] Needless to say, Popiełuszko was not popular with the regime. He had been detained by the police, upbraided by Cardinal Glemp, and formally charged with abuse of religious freedom and with harboring concealed arms.

On October 20, 1984, Popiełuszko disappeared.[40] Two days later four policemen were secretly arrested; after a week Interior Minister General Czesław Kiszczak announced that an investigation was under way; and after ten days the body was found. The whole nation was shaken—including, apparently, generals Kiszczak and Jaruzelski. The title of Bujak's and Kulerski's editorial in *Tygodnik Mazowsze*, "We Are All Guilty," may have been rhetorical, but the deeper strands of the murder, if there were any, remain unclear. The most common belief, besides the obvious one that the state decided to kill Popiełuszko, was that his murder was part of an antiregime plot by hardliners. The party contained a conservative faction, called the "Cements," who would have been capable of it, but no real evidence has surfaced to sustain the argument. It is almost certain, however, that neither Jaruzelski nor Kiszczak ordered the killing or knew of it ahead of time.[41]

The most remarkable thing about the tragedy was that the government decided to put the four policemen who abducted and killed Popiełuszko on public trial. For over a month early in 1985 a fascinated and absorbed national television audience tuned in every night for excerpts from the trial, in which they learned juicy details of the private and highly privileged lives of the security police. In the end the four officers were convicted and sentenced to terms in prison ranging from fifteen to twenty-five years (the sentences were subsequently substantially reduced).

The conviction of Popiełuszko's killers was an important moment in the development of the Polish trialogue. On the surface in 1985 it seemed that the party/state and Solidarity were completely at odds. The government constantly maintained that it would never negotiate with Solidarity, and even after granting a conditional amnesty in the middle of 1984 it found ways to rearrest many of the most important activists and put them on trial. On their side, the oppositionists refused to accept the regime's legitimacy, and most leaders who remained underground did not respond to the 1984 offer of amnesty. But in a curious way the two sides were communicating, and, all appearances to the contrary, it was the government that was starting to move, not Solidarity. Jaruzelski's decision to convict his own security police of Popiełuszko's murder went beyond the earlier efforts to create organs of permissible pluralism. His admission that he could not simply ignore public opinion, as government spokesman Jerzy Urban had tried to do at first by ridiculing those who had expressed concern for Popiełuszko's safety, pushed him a bit further down the track toward real pluralism.[42]

As in many things Jaruzelski did, however, the trial served a dual purpose. It was not only a method of gaining credibility with the public but also part of a strategy of gaining full control over the party by weakening its most conservative elements. In 1985 and into 1986 he removed many high-ranking officials who opposed his relatively moderate policies toward the intelligentsia and the opposition. In November he succeeded in replacing hardline foreign minister Stefan Olszowski, and in January 1986 he recalled Stanisław Kociolek, a Stalinist, from his position as ambassador to the Soviet Union.[43] During the same period General Kiszczak quietly reassigned perhaps two hundred of the most recalcitrant security officers. With the hardline faction tamed, the Tenth Party Congress, held in June 1986, looked for all the world like any one of the well-orchestrated and completely predictable congresses conducted at the height of the party's powers. In fact, it was the beginning of a new, accelerated phase of change.

The Expansion of Permissible Pluralism

For Jaruzelski consolidation did not mean exercising greater social control, as it had for Husák in Czechoslovakia, but enhancing his ability to open the party further to society. In August and September 1986 he finally granted a full and complete amnesty to all persons detained under martial law, even those who had stayed underground for long periods of time, such as Bujak, who had finally been arrested in May 1986, and Michnik, who had been under threat of trial for five years. This step put the ball in the opposition's court, because full amnesty met the first condition Solidarity had set for negotiations. A significant number of activists, both inside and outside Solidarity, had long since decided that any cooperation with a Communist government was impossible, even immoral, and they quickly announced that they had no intention of coming out from underground. The legitimists, on the other hand, granting that it would be premature to abandon underground activities altogether, argued that it was important to meet the government's initiative at least half way. "We must not waste this opportunity," Jacek Kuroń argued.[44]

Wałęsa was a master at finding ways to accommodate apparently contradictory viewpoints. This time he decided on a dual strategy, partly public, partly underground. On September 11, 1986, ten days after the definitive announcement of the amnesty, he created the Solidarity Provisional Council (Tymczasowa Rada Solidarności—TRS), which he chaired. Of the seven other members, at least five were fresh from prison.[45] This did not make Solidarity a legal entity, but it did bring a portion of its activities out into the open. At the same time TKK continued its underground operations under anonymous leadership. Regional councils were given the option of staying underground with the TKK or of going public with the Provisional Council. This new situation of both open and clandestine possibilities, in which organizations of all kinds sprang up, upset many oppositionists. Steeped in a culture that assumed society's interests were one and should be represented by a single organization—not only did the Leninist party claim this but the name Solidarity itself implied it—many activists shrank from the uncontrolled pluralism of local initiatives. But the legitimist leadership stuck to its guns. If the government was going to moderate its hostility in practice, Wałęsa would revise Solidarity's approach also, bringing some of its organs into public view, not overpowering local initiatives from the center, and moving always in a direction that kept in view the main chance—a power-sharing arrangement.

Jaruzelski's next step was to attempt a power-sharing arrangement of his own. In the fall of 1986, after consultations with the church, he proposed creating a Social Consultative Council attached to the Council of State. Consisting of fifty-six selected "representatives of Polish society," the council was to be a forum for "open and unrestrained" discussion of political, economic, and social issues that would advise and inform the president of society's views. Very few independent intellectuals chose to participate in the council, evaluating it as what David Ost calls a "piddling concession."[46] But a handful of prominent persons did join, including the chairman of the Catholic Intellectual Clubs (who resigned from the clubs to do so) and Władysław Siła-Nowicki, a noted civil rights lawyer who had spent time in jail under both the Nazis and the Communists and had been a legal advisor to Solidarity. As the price of his participation, Siła-Nowicki extracted a promise that the proceedings of the council would be published. This proved to be an astute move that expanded the public space considerably. Once the council started meeting in 1987, Siła-Nowicki and some other members turned it into such a lively forum of debate that "no less an authority than Wrocław Solidarity leader Władysław Frasyniuk said that many Solidarity activists were avidly reading the Council's reports, often more eagerly than they read the underground press!"[47]

Indeed, everyone was reading the press with increasing interest because, consistent with his turn toward a more open society, from about 1986 Jaruzelski significantly liberalized censorship. Concurrently with the takeoff of glasnost in the Soviet Union and the increasing openness of the Hungarian press, the Polish press began to undertake discussions of the theory of totalitarianism, to criticize the government's economic performance, to float radical marketizing and pluralizing reforms, to discuss sensitive historical subjects, and to publish previously forbidden authors such as Milan Kundera and George Orwell. In March 1987 the government even legalized the underground journal *Res Publica,* which had originated as a samizdat publication in the 1970s. By late 1987 the executive director of Helsinki Watch observed that Poland was "the freest country in the Eastern Bloc."[48]

The change in Jaruzelski's approach, or at least the intensification of that side of his policy that had sought since 1982 to preempt Solidarity's support with the public, brought significant international gains, which was surely one of the important reasons Jaruzelski undertook the policy. When martial law descended, President Ronald Reagan had imposed economic sanctions on Poland, including lifting its most favored nation trade status. These made it difficult for Poland to negotiate with the international agencies that held its debt. Gradually, with each partial amnesty, the United States relaxed its pressure, although as late as 1985 Polish-American relations were still not good. But in 1986 Reagan acquiesced to Poland's admission to the International Monetary Fund, and early in 1987, after consulting with Solidarity activists, he restored Poland's most favored nation trade status. By September 1987 relations had improved to the extent that Vice-President George Bush visited Warsaw, where he talked not only with General Jaruzelski but also with Lech Wałęsa.

During 1987 Poland's relations with the Soviet Union improved as well, as the Polish party under Jaruzelski became, along with the Hungarian reformers, the most open supporter of Gorbachev's reform plans among the East European leaders. At a meeting in Moscow in April, Jaruzelski and Gorbachev signed an agreement on cooperation that included a commitment to investigate the "blank spots" in Soviet-Polish history, such as the decimation of the Polish Communist party by the Comintern in the late 1930s, the deportation of over one million Poles from Soviet-occupied eastern Poland in 1940–1941, one of whom had been Jaruzelski himself, and the massacre of thousands of Polish officers at Katyn Forest near Smolensk in 1940. In effect, Gorbachev's policy of glasnost was providing Jaruzelski with an opportunity to increase his popularity at home by assuming some anti-Russian postures, which during the course of 1987 he did.

In 1987 the pope visited Poland for the third time in ten years. While the visit was not the violently emotional event that the visit of 1979 had been, John Paul continued to draw hundreds of thousands, millions even, to his sermons. By continually speaking of human rights, pluralism, and free association and by granting Lech Wałęsa a private audience, John Paul made it clear that he strongly favored an intensified course of reform. Even if Cardinal Glemp had written off Solidarity and even if the episcopate attempted to ban Solidarity banners from the crowds attending the pope, the visit added to the heightened sense of potentialities that characterized Poland in 1987.[49]

In this new atmosphere it was the government that seemed to retain the reform initiative, not the opposition. In Hungary the democratic opposition found three issues around which they successfully rallied support, but these were not available in Poland. Without significant Polish enclaves in bordering countries, Solidarity could not draw on the issue of persecuted Poles abroad, although there was some grumbling about German attitudes toward Poles. Environmental issues were an important part of the underground press, but activists lacked a powerful single issue like the Gabčikovo-Nagymaros dam on which to focus attention. And whereas the opposition did mount demonstrations on holidays like May 3 (the date of the Polish constitution of 1791), these demonstrations never developed the momentum of the March 15 movement in Hungary or the significance of the anniversary of Imre Nagy's execution.

Economic Failures and a Break in the Logjam

For all the apparent progress of permissive pluralism and the seeming softness of Solidarity's support, Jaruzelski's stabilization of Poland was an illusion. Nowhere was this more obvious than in the economic sphere. By 1986 lines for the purchase of ordinary goods were becoming common once again, and Adam Michnik characterized 1988 as a time when "everybody's fondest dream was to be able to locate a roll of toilet paper."[50] Jaruzelski had inherited a seriously sick economy. At the beginning of martial law official figures for 1981 showed overall production down by 12 percent from the previous year, which itself had not been that good, and foreign trade was $2 billion in deficit. A career military officer, Jaruzelski had little idea how to deal with this "picture of colossal chaos," as the party newspaper *Tribunu Ludu* called it in January 1982.[51] His first efforts were drastic and martial. Noting that the export of coal, Poland's primary source of foreign currency, had fallen precipitously in 1981, he inducted all coal miners into the army and literally forced production back to a reasonable level. Efficiency did not improve, but by compelling the miners to work longer hours production did rise. By 1983 national income had begun to grow again, but the hope now was simply to maintain the levels of the early 1970s, not to create any socialist utopias.

Consistently with his line that he was only implementing the reforms of the Solidarity period without the disruptive activity of the union, Jaruzelski adopted economic reforms worked out before the imposition of martial law. Those reforms, which had been created by five hundred economists with vastly differing views, were haphazard, inconsistent, and futile, despite their nod to the Hungarian experience.[52] They called for wider use of market mechanisms but retained central planning; they emphasized self-management but left power in the factories in the hands of enterprise directors; and they praised the freeing of prices but continued to control most of them. Without a strong notion of economics himself, Jaruzelski probably did not understand these failings, and he certainly could not provide the insight to overcome them. When problems emerged he appointed special commissioners, often military men, to fix them according to the old methods of direct command, so that despite much talk of reform, direct intervention in the economy actually increased during the 1980s.[53] Since, as Martin Myant concluded, "the essence of the system of management was barely altered," the results were predictable: debt continued to rise, investment and wages rose much faster than productivity, trade with the West dropped dramatically, and the standard of living barely stabilized.[54]

The most damaging aspect of Jaruzelski's economic policy was a turn back to the Soviet Union. Hungary's solution for its debt problem was to open itself somewhat to world markets, a decision that laid the groundwork for relatively rapid economic progress in the 1990s. Jaruzelski, by contrast, believed that he could sidestep the constraints imposed by Western sanctions and by Poland's poor international credit through expanding trade with the Soviet Union. By 1985 some three hundred of the largest production facilities in Poland had become essentially appendices to their Soviet counterparts, and 37 percent of Polish industrial production was going to the Soviet Union.[55] Unable to import new technology from the West and tied into the slipshod Soviet market, Polish industry became less and less able to compete even in the sheltered CMEA marketplace. Poland's eastward reorientation during the 1980s was one of the most onerous economic legacies of the Jaruzelski period. When the Soviet market completely collapsed in 1990, Poland was left with an enormous trade deficit and many large, obsolete industrial plants oriented in the wrong direction.

When by 1986 it had become clear that ad hoc interventions to fix the economy were not working, Jaruzelski used the occasion of the Tenth Party Congress to propose a "speeding up of the process" into a "second stage" of reform. Prime Minister Messner's first proposal to the Sejm in October 1986, however, was so strongly centralizing that a storm of protest from economists and editorial writers forced its withdrawal. By this time it was clear to almost everyone that more contact with world markets and less interference from the center were required. After further input from the various party organizations concerned with the economy, in April 1987 the Commission of Economic Reform published a package of 174 measures for debate, and in October of that year Prime Minister Messner placed the final program before the Sejm.

In many respects these "second stage" reforms were quite similar to those of 1981, but in at least two regards they constituted a significant step forward. First, they proposed a reorientation of Polish trade away from the ruble market by re-emphasizing exports and by switching from direct to indirect controls on foreign trade, something Włodzimierz Brus had called for more than twenty years previously. Second, they proposed expanding the possibilities of joint ventures and permitting the creation of private firms with an unlimited number of employees. The first reform was important, but the second was fundamental. For the first time in socialist Poland the principle of private capital would be established in law.

Public reaction to the revised proposals varied. Since the plan called for austerity measures, including significantly higher prices, OPZZ, the National Trade Union under Miodowicz, which was emerging as a populist advocate of short-term worker interests, complained that incomes policy did not adequately compensate the worker for the price rises. OPZZ also opposed the introduction of private property as a matter of principle. Many Solidarity economists, on the other hand, had evolved to the point of advocating a mixed economy of both public and private property. But Solidarity continued to insist that without a democratization that would break the power of the nomenklatura, no economic reform was possible. The first necessity in Polish politics, it argued, was political reform, which meant primarily bringing Solidarity into a real partnership with the party in conducting public affairs.

The party agreed that democratization was needed, but it was not ready to bring Solidarity on board quite yet. "This government is willing to share power," the editor of *Nowi Drogi* (New Roads) noted; but, he added, "not on a 50–50 basis. The party will hold the deciding power."[56] "Pluralism in a socialist framework" now became the government's watchword. Despite the derisive comments of the opposition, this idea constituted a great advance over martial law, not to mention over Stalinism. Its first test came only shortly after the economic reform measures reached the Sejm. In October 1987 Messner surprised both the opposition and some party members by announcing that the government would conduct a referendum on November 29, 1987. The referendum asked two specific questions: Do you favor the package of economic reforms just placed before the Sejm even if it means two or three years of sacrifice? and Do you favor the Polish model of "profound democratization?"

Politically, the referendum was an astute move. If it succeeded, Jaruzelski could go ahead with price rises and other painful changes. If it lost, he could present himself to the Western powers from whom he was seeking debt relief as having done the best he could but having been defeated by a shortsighted public. The referendum once again put Solidarity on the spot. "If we say yes, we're giving allegiance to something we don't trust," one Solidarity activist said. "But we also cannot say 'Don't vote,' or we would be portrayed as against reform."[57] The results shocked everyone. Sixty-eight percent of the electorate voted, and almost two-thirds of them voted yes. But since the positive votes on the two questions came to only 44 percent and 46 percent respectively of the total electorate, the government declared that the propositions had lost. General astonishment! Had the government intended to lose? Why else would it fail to falsify the vote as it had presumably done in the past? Was it a devious plot to court the West? A provocation of some kind? Or did the apparat draw back at the last minute at the prospect of the social unrest that real reform might provoke?

Whatever lay behind the government's unexpectedly ethical handling of the vote, the referendum of November 1987 broke a logjam. Shortly after its completion the Warsaw Regional Executive Committee of Solidarity declared that "all of us in Solidarity realize at last that we have entered a new phase . . . we know for certain: the war is over. . . . The Polish referendum proves that the restructuring of the economy, of social ties, and of public life cannot be achieved against the wishes of society. . . . We are ready to enter [into an 'anti-crisis'] pact for the common good, but on one condition: that our right to express and represent social interests is respected."[58] In January 1988 *Polityka* published an open letter by Jerzy Holzer, a prominent Solidarity historian, urging that Jaruzelski and Wałęsa agree to an "historic pact" to rescue the nation, and shortly thereafter historian Bronisław Geremek, one of Wałęsa's closest advisors, suggested an "anti-crisis pact" between the government and Solidarity.

The government too was more conciliatory early in 1988. For example, in January it announced legislation to permit public service for conscientious objectors to the draft, thus responding to protests that a new movement of young people called "Freedom and Peace" had generated in 1988.[59] In March the party formally acknowledged that the organized anti-Semitic campaign of 1968, which it now admitted for the first time, was a "political error" contrary to the tradition "of Polish tolerance" and "contradictory to Marxist ideology."[60] Solidarity, however, remained outlawed, its leaders harassed, and many official statements indicated that whatever plans for "pluralism in a socialist context" the government might have, they did not include the union.

Strikes and the Roundtable

Then, once again, in the familiar Polish way, strikes intervened. The referendum's defeat did not mean the need for reform had disappeared. On February 1, 1988, Messner's government went ahead with price increases that pushed the cost of food up 40 percent. Protests erupted, and with the coming of the spring strike season at the end of April substantial work stoppages took place in Silesia and Gdańsk, among other places. Massive wage increases settled some of the strikes, but security forces finally had to storm Nowa Huta, the steel mill in Kraków, to end the strike there, and a few days later an uneasy compromise worked out with the participation of Lech Wałęsa ended a nine-day strike in Gdańsk. Solidarity had not foreseen or organized these strikes, nor did it support them wholeheartedly. In Gdańsk Wałęsa merely said, "I am not on strike, although I am not against it." The stoppages shook the Solidarity leadership because some of the most vigorous of the younger strikers were not only not part of the Solidarity movement, they were even hostile to the old Solidarity leadership, "the senators" who in their view no longer represented the real needs of the young workers.[61] Some Solidarity analysts tried to pass the strikes off as a provocation undertaken by the government to permit the workers to let off a little steam in an easily controllable way, and Wiktor Kulerski believed that the strikes, being outside the control of the union, had completed the destruction of the myth of Solidarity as a mass movement.[62]

But Kulerski was wrong in two ways. He was right that the old Solidarity, unified more in the memory of an intelligentsia that cherished an ideal of social cohesion than it had been in reality, no longer existed. But this was not necessarily bad, because what had taken its place was a vibrant and vigorous independent society in which dynamic citizen initiatives of all kinds were emerging, including those of the angry young workers. Constant pressure applied by the opposition since the days of KOR, coupled with Jaruzelski's willingness to respond to that pressure, had produced a real opening of the public space. In its own way Poland was becoming a pluralist society, still at this point in a socialist framework but moving with increasing speed in the direction of a fully open society. Kulerski was also wrong in suggesting that the myth of Solidarity was dead. In fact, that myth, actualized in the person of Lech Wałęsa, remained the union's greatest strength, as the second wave of strikes in August showed. Still illegal, divided into competing regional councils, unable to attract the youngest and most radical workers, and outmaneuvered by a regime that was more intelligent and incomparably better at manipulation than its predecessors, Solidarity (especially its logo) remained the symbol of the emerging independent society and Wałęsa remained its personification.

The power of these Polonified representations of freedom and hope contrasted sharply with the complete lack of emotional attachments the regime could bring to bear, so much so that it had almost completely abandoned its dependence on ideology. Since 1986 at the latest, party leaders had "recognized the opposition as a lasting element on the country's political map," and in cautious ways they had been putting out feelers to that opposition ever since.[63] That is why, when in August 1988 a second wave of strikes erupted, this time much more severe and much more widespread than in May, the government, realizing that these strikes introduced a qualitatively new element into the social equation, finally decided, after almost seven years of stonewalling, that it was time to negotiate openly with Solidarity, the enemy whom, at least, it knew.

At first Minister of Defense General Kiszczak announced drastic measures just short of martial law, but, after a crucial politburo meeting on the morning of August 26, during which Jaruzelski proposed a roundtable discussion with the opposition without conditions, on August 27 Kiszczak publicly offered Solidarity direct political negotiations rather than simply economic discussions.[64] The next day Jaruzelski attacked Messner's government and called for "a courageous turnabout" in policy. On August 31 Kiszczak called Wałęsa to Warsaw and offered to discuss even the legalization of Solidarity if Wałęsa would get the workers to return to their jobs.

Wałęsa knew he could not refuse such an offer, even though breaking a strike yet one more time might undermine his authority. Indeed, Kiszczak is alleged to have said after meeting with Wałęsa that he did not think the Solidarity leader could produce, and Bronisław Geremek reports that Wałęsa's closest advisors thought he had made a terrible mistake.[65] But Wałęsa's greatest strength as a politician has been his sense of timing. Like his radical opponents in the opposition, such as Gwiazda and Leszek Moczulski, Wałęsa could be intransigent, but where he rose above them was in his understanding of when the moment for a deal had arrived. This time he correctly saw the possibility of a major breakthrough. Besides, he never lacked confidence that he could talk to the people. In three days of shouting, arm waving, and nonstop negotiations, the workers were back on the job and the government was committed.

Under the new circumstances, Messner, the economic technician who had failed to fix the economy, had clearly outlived his usefulness. On October 17 Mieczysław Rakowski replaced him as prime minister. Rakowski is one of the most curious figures in Polish politics. Well known in the West as a liberal Communist because of his editorship of *Polityka*, which occasionally published critical views, he produced interesting analyses on occasion, as in 1987 when he warned of a "revolutionary upheaval" in Eastern

Europe unless its ruling parties abandoned "useless ideas and outdated concepts." But among oppositionists Rakowski was considered a slippery opportunist who had behaved badly in the negotiations at the time of the Bydgoszcz crisis in 1981. His dislike of Wałęsa, whom he once called an "organ grinder," boded ill for creating a true partnership with the union.[66]

Rakowski was a more aggressive prime minister than Messner had been, both in economic terms and in his dealings with the opposition. He withdrew some of the crucial economic reforms still before the Sejm, resubmitted them in more radical form, and got them through. By making certain kinds of privatization easier these new rules facilitated the bailout of nervous members of the nomenklatura into semiprivate enterprise. Accommodating to the desires of his colleagues to enrich themselves, Rakowski presented an unyielding face to the opposition, although in the long run he favored a deal. It was just that by nature Rakowski was a hard-nosed negotiator. Solidarity leaders were little surprised, therefore, when the new prime minister announced, as he had in 1982, that the government would negotiate only with the "constructive opposition" and not with "aggressive anti-Communists" like Władysław Frasyniuk, Jacek Kuroń, Adam Michnik, and the like, all of whom were included in Solidarity's proposed negotiating team. When Wałęsa quite naturally rejected that condition the preliminary meetings about organizing a roundtable were postponed indefinitely.

The consensus of opinion seemed to be that the government would, as it had in the past, continue to find excuses why it could not meet with Solidarity, always probing for a slip on Wałęsa's part that would permit Rakowski to blame him for scuttling the talks. But Wałęsa did not slip, even when Rakowski blandly announced that in order to further the process of improving economic efficiency, the Lenin Shipyards in Gdańsk— cradle of Solidarity and Wałęsa's workplace—would be closed. The shipyard was not closed, although its workforce began a steady and permanent decline, but this not particularly subtle maneuver depressed even the relatively moderate opposition activists. "The very idea of coming to an agreement . . . is politically and socially finished," said Zbigniew Bujak.[67] For the more radical oppositionists, Rakowski's move simply confirmed their position that it was pointless, even traitorous, to negotiate with a regime that, in their view, had no intention of real reconciliation and would only break its agreements.

At the very time of this apparently discouraging series of events the shape of a compromise was taking form. Late in 1988 Rakowski, according to his own account, conceived of the idea of a Gorbachev-style election in which the party would retain control but would be able to claim an electoral mandate.[68] He proposed the idea to Jaruzelski. After private discussions with Rakowski and other government representatives, Catholic emissaries brought the proposal to the Solidarity leadership.

The delay these machinations caused in the start of the roundtable discussions provided Wałęsa's team valuable time to organize itself into a more cohesive bargaining unit. Wałęsa gathered his associates around him in a "Citizens' Committee," with subcommittee chairmen forming what amounted to a shadow cabinet. He was able to shrug off the frustrations of dealing with Rakowski and to maintain that a negotiated partnership was not only possible but was the only route to a revived Poland. In 1985 Wałęsa had said, "In the more or less near future the government will be induced to negotiate, it will not be able to do otherwise. . . . Whether the meeting takes place now or later is unimportant. The meeting is inevitable."[69] When such a meeting became possible in August 1988 and critics attacked him for negotiating with the enemy, he responded: "I would negotiate with the devil himself if it would help Poland."[70]

One of the dramatic moments of the interim period between the initial offer and the actual beginning of the roundtable came in November when Alfred Miodowicz, head of OPZZ, challenged Wałęsa to a television debate. Wałęsa immediately accepted, despite the worries of his associates, and overwhelmed his opponent from the official unions by calling on Poles to cast off the "tail end of Stalinism" and return to pluralism. "Let's not make people happy," he said. "Let's give them freedom."[71] In January 1989, with the basic outlines of a deal moving into place and backed by strong public approval, Wałęsa had every reason to be confident that the government would accept Solidarity one way or another.[72]

Jaruzelski had somewhat more trouble making his preparations. Having gotten his government into the proper position in October 1988, in December 1988 he had Rakowski tell a central committee plenum that the party needed to find a new approach to trade union pluralism, by which he meant that after insisting for years it was impossible, he nonetheless intended to legalize Solidarity. Messner had gone quietly, but the reaction in the party to this proposal was furious and outspoken. The December plenum broke up without making a decision and reconvened in mid-January 1989. Most of the speakers at this second session rejected trade union pluralism with such vigor that it appeared Jaruzelski's resolution might fail. At this point the general rolled out his heavy artillery, threatening to resign and to take General Kiszczak and General Florian Siwicki, minister of national defense, with him. Alarmed lest their strongest political figures abandon them and also not quite ready to forego long-held habits of following the leader, the central committee voted 142 to 32, with 14 abstentions, to lift, "in conditions of national agreement, restrictions on creating new trade unions."[73] The conditions set for negotiations were potentially onerous, but they were not impossible. Solidarity had to define itself "as part of socialism," break relations with extremist groups, and forego foreign financial aid, but no mention was made of excluding people like Michnik and Geremek. A few days after the plenum Wałęsa accepted the restrictions not as conditions but rather as the regime's statement of its negotiating position, and on February 6, 1989, the discussions began.

The symbolism of a roundtable (it actually existed—a huge, round table twenty-eight feet in diameter and seating fifty-seven persons, although it was only used for the opening and closing ceremonies) was that it minimized the confrontational aspects of the negotiations and suggested the community of interests of all Poles. This is why the government insisted that several agencies, not just Solidarity, the government, and the party, participate in the negotiations. Of course the church was represented; a demoralized and now obviously obsolete PRON was there; and the two tame political parties, the United Peasants' party and the Democratic party, had their representatives. Several independent intellectuals completed the roster of fifty-seven main negotiators. Even the underground media, such as *Tygodnik Mazowsze* and Radio Solidarity, which were technically illegal, could be found furiously interviewing participants in hallways and cloakrooms. All in all, over the next two months more than five hundred persons took part in the various sessions and subsessions organized around the three main working groups discussing union law, economic issues, and political reorganization.

Despite the size and extent of the negotiations, no one doubted that the roundtable discussions were primarily about politics. The basic deal had already been cut at the highest level. Solidarity would be legalized, and an election would be arranged in such a way as to insure the party's continued predominance. This is why Wałęsa, when asking Geremek to represent him at the political working group rather than the union working group, apologized, saying the great victory would come at the union group where Solidarity would be recognized, whereas it was in the political group that the demoralizing compromises on elections would have to be made.[74] In fact, it was in the political subgroup that the most important decisions were thrashed out, particularly the agreement to create a senate, which Wałęsa later told Geremek was "our greatest success." While discussions went on in hundreds of specialized meetings in dozens of subcommittees, direct meetings continued between Wałęsa and Kiszczak, both of whom proved to be conciliatory and receptive negotiators. Their discussions were no longer about whether Solidarity would re-enter public life but under what conditions. Solidarity knew that the government was offering it a new social contract: legalization and minority representation in parliament, which would mean accepting coresponsibility for an economic program and any hardship it might cause, in return for validating elections and the creation of a strong presidency, which would mean, presumably, that the party would retain ultimate control over the political process. Two months after the official negotiations began, Wałęsa formally accepted the offer.

Solidarity Takes Power

The accords announced on April 6, 1989, met Solidarity's first and foremost demand since December 13, 1981: relegalization of the union, a step that registration on April 18 completed. An economic plan was announced as well, as were promises of greater access to the media, a more independent judiciary, and freedom of association. Accordingly, one week after the talks concluded, *Tygodnik Mazowsze* published its last underground issue, revealing the hitherto unknown names of its staff and reappearing in a few weeks as *Gazeta Wyborcza* (Election Gazette) under the editorship of Adam Michnik. Interestingly, given the complete predominance of men in the Solidarity structures, "it turned out that the overwhelming majority of these journalists who had been driving the regime crazy with their defiant irrepressibility were women."[75]

There is no question, however, that the constitutional innovations were the most important part of the accords. The agreement created a bicameral legislature consisting of the newly created Senate, to be elected in an open and free ballot, and a lower house, the Sejm, to be selected by a "nonconfrontational" election. This meant that 65 percent of the seats in the Sejm would be contested only by the Polish United Workers' party (PUWP) and its satellite parties on a single list, and 35 percent of the seats would be elected from among opposition or independent candidates. In four years (1993) all elections would be completely free. The Senate would have a veto power, which the Sejm could override by a two-thirds majority (that is, slightly more than 65 percent). The two houses of the legislature would elect a president, whose powers were significantly enhanced.

This remarkable agreement clearly resonated with the first relatively open elections Gorbachev held in the Soviet Union at roughly the same time. But the Polish arrangements went much further than the Soviet ones, conceding substantial representation to the opposition. On the other hand, by agreeing to an election in only two months, Wałęsa seemed to give the government apparatus every chance to dominate the disorganized and squabbling opposition. "Solidarity . . . cannot count on mass enthusiasm to make up for its organizational disadvantages," said one analyst.[76] Even Wałęsa himself complained. "None of us want these elections," he said. "They're the terrible, terrible price we have to pay in order to get our union back."[77] And those were the optimists. The radical faction "Fighting Solidarity," which opposed the very concept of reconciliation with the Communists as "tantamount to reconciliation with captivity," called for a boycott of the elections. As one skeptic put it, "I don't trust the Communists. That's the basis of my political analysis."[78]

Many believed that the party, with its organization and funds, held a significant advantage, but its campaign proved to be lifeless. While at Solidarity headquarters eager volunteers bustled in and out and mimeograph machines thumped all day long, at party election headquarters bored typists sat idle at their machines. Communist party campaign posters appeared in every color but red, and official candidates tried never to mention that they were party members. Despite these obvious indications of malaise, many party people seemed to think they would do at least all right in the elections, while many Solidarity activists worried that a public they had been calling apathetic would not respond. Wałęsa, the optimist, hoped Solidarity could win about two-thirds of the contested seats. In any event, as John Tagliabue reported in the *New York Times,* Poland's "bold experiment in democracy poses no immediate threat to the Communist Party's monopoly on power."[79]

The election results, therefore, were a sensation. After a runoff, Solidarity candidates won all of the 161 seats they contested in the Sejm and all but one of the 100 seats available in the Senate. Even more amazing, since the election procedures permitted voters to cross off names they did not want, 33 of the 35 major Communist figures, including Prime Minister Rakowski, General Kiszczak, and OPZZ leader Miodowicz, failed to get the required 50 percent of the vote in the first election on June 4. Since the voting rules stipulated that in such a case a candidate could not stand again in the runoff, it meant that most of the main party leadership would not be represented in the Sejm. Realizing that "too big a percentage of our people getting through would be disturbing and might force a fight on us," Wałęsa immediately entered into negotiations that permitted the defeated men to run again, but in the end they withdrew anyway.[80]

The magnitude of the voters' rejection of the Communists was overwhelming. This was no quibbling over whether 60 percent or 78 percent of the populace showed up to vote. Could the Communists possibly continue in power in the face of such utter annihilation at the polls? For Solidarity the problem was different: how to deal with sudden and unexpected prosperity. "I face the disaster of having had a good crop," Wałęsa quipped. "Too much grain has ripened for me and I can't store it all in my granary."[81]

Almost immediately after the election Jaruzelski proposed that Solidarity enter into a coalition government, but Wałęsa refused. At this point very few Solidarity leaders believed the union should enter the government, let alone seize the opportunity to form their own government. Their plan was to provide a responsible opposition, learn parliamentary tactics, and win the election of 1993. Tadeusz Mazowiecki, writing in *Tygodnik Solidarność* (Solidarity Weekly), argued that it would be a mistake to enter into a government in which "the army and the police are still in the hands of the ruling party." In his view Solidarity was strong enough to "enforce reforms" in parliament without taking on the responsibility of government.[82] Adam Michnik was one of the few who believed that Solidarity should grab for the brass ring. He surprised and even angered many when early in July he suggested in his paper *Gazeta Wyborcza* that to satisfy the Russians the Communists should retain the strengthened office of president but Solidarity should form the government. His slogan, "Your President; Our Premier," reminds one of "The New Social Contract," the proposal of the Hungarian opposition in 1987 that suggested giving the Communists the executive branch and the opposition the legislative branch in a system of separated powers. Even Michnik's idea, the most radical of the postelection period, remained self-limiting, not yet quite able to countenance the idea of completely eliminating the Communist party, still apparently the strongest element in society.

During the period between the elections and the final selection of

Mazowiecki as prime minister, Poland experienced its first taste of real politics since the 1930s, and maybe before. With each side uncertain of its support and unclear about the consequences of its actions, the outcome was far from certain. The first order of business was for the Sejm to elect a president. Jaruzelski, fearing public resentment of his role in imposing martial law, declared he would not run, even though the strong presidency had been expressly created for him. Even within his own party he faced so much opposition that his advisors thought he might fall as many as fifty votes short in the Sejm. He proposed General Kiszczak for president. But this choice proved even more unpopular, and, after lengthy negotiations and assessments of strength, Jaruzelski finally returned as the sole candidate. On July 19, after a delay of almost two weeks, the Sejm elected him president. Wałęsa told members of the Citizens Parliamentary Club (Obywatelski Klub Parlamentarny—OKP), the organization of Solidarity members in the Sejm, to vote as their consciences dictated, which for most of them meant voting against their great enemy of the last ten years. Obviously, however, the Solidarity leadership had decided that after having rejected Kiszczak, stability required Jaruzelski. When, during the actual voting in the Sejm, careful counting revealed the general was about to lose, just the requisite number of senior Solidarity representatives invalidated their negative ballots to permit Jaruzelski to receive exactly 50 percent plus one of the valid votes cast.

The vote for president revealed three things: first, Solidarity intended to keep its power-sharing agreement with the Communists; second, it had the power to disrupt that agreement; and third, the United Peasants' party and the Democratic party, some of whose members had voted against Jaruzelski, were not firmly in the Communist camp any more. All three of these factors influenced the hardball politics that followed Jaruzelski's election.

Now Jaruzelski tried to install Kiszczak as prime minister. On August 2 the Sejm approved the nomination, but only after extreme pressure from Jaruzelski held wavering representatives from the United Peasants' party and the Democratic party in line behind his proposal. Without any possibility of including Solidarity members in his cabinet and facing incipient rebellion from the traditional coalition of satellite parties, Kiszczak found it impossible to form a government. He suggested that United Peasant party chairman Roman Malinowski take his place, but this old war-horse had become completely unacceptable to everyone, even to many members of his own party. This was the moment when it finally sank in for many party leaders that the end was in sight—even Malinowski could not make it! Wildcat strikes and a one-hour protest strike led by Solidarity exacerbated the situation. Adding to the tension, the Rakowski government decided this was a good time to marketize the food distribution system. When it lifted price controls on food, froze farm subsidies, and ended meat rationing on August 1, prices shot up and the public reacted.[83]

In this tense and unresolved situation, Wałęsa brought forward a new proposal designed to take advantage of the increasing restiveness of the satellite parties while at the same time reassuring the Communists. On August 7 he announced Solidarity would be ready to form a coalition with the satellite parties that would produce a parliamentary majority for an opposition cabinet. The defection of the satellite parties was an eventuality no one had foreseen. Conditioned to think of the United Peasants' party and the Democratic party as completely subservient to the PUWP, no one had considered the consequences of allocating 27 percent of the seats in the Sejm to them and only 38 percent to the PUWP. Now, by bringing those two parties into its own coalition, Solidarity proposed turning the roundtable on the Communists, so to speak. Naturally the Communists complained bitterly, and even *Izvestia* reproached Solidarity for breaching the agreement.[84] On August 15 Wałęsa responded by suggesting the opposition would be willing to form a government with the Communists controlling those ministries concerned with "the physical continuity of the state," that is, the ministries of defense and interior, traditionally the keys to social control in Communist states. At the same time he attempted to reassure the Soviets that Poland must remain committed to the Warsaw Pact. Solidarity was now proposing a coalition government, but with the balance of power in their own favor—a reversal of Jaruzelski's offer of June.

Jaruzelski, apparently assured of a strong position as president and noting that the Soviets were taking a wait-and-see attitude, accepted. Wałęsa proposed three candidates for prime minister of the new government: Bronisław Geremek, the historian; Jacek Kuroń, the grand old radical accommodator; and Tadeusz Mazowiecki, the Catholic intellectual and advisor to Solidarity from the days of its formation in 1980. Of these, only Mazowiecki, the devout Catholic intellectual, was satisfactory to the church, which added its final note to the trialogue of the 1980s at this point. On August 18 Jaruzelski announced that he had accepted Kiszczak's resignation, and the next day he asked Tadeusz Mazowiecki to form a government.

According to the *New York Times,* Rakowski, who became head of the party in July when Jaruzelski became president, opposed the idea of a Solidarity government.[85] Jerzy Urban predicted privately (and correctly) that if the Communists went into opposition they would lose power altogether. On August 20 a caucus of the central committee demanded representation in a future government that would correspond to the party's "political and state potential."[86] At this point Mikhail Gorbachev provided a last nudge in a telephone conversation with Rakowski. This conversation has evoked considerable interest, since it seems to be a specific intervention by Gorbachev at a key moment that drove the final nail in the coffin of the Polish United Workers' party. The initiative for the call, however, came from Rakowski, not from Gorbachev. About two weeks after Rakowski became head of the party he requested a meeting with Gorbachev through the Soviet embassy, a completely normal request for a new head of an East European Communist party. About a week after that, on August 21, the embassy alerted Rakowski that Gorbachev would call the next day. When he did, the two leaders spoke for about forty minutes.

According to Rakowski, Gorbachev said that a meeting at that particular moment would not be opportune, due to the events going on in Poland, but he did want to hear about the development of the political situation. Gorbachev was particularly critical of the Polish party leadership, saying that a new one would have to be built because the old one was "crap" and "not accomplishing anything."[87] The two men did not speak specifically of the recent decision to form a government dominated by Solidarity, Rakowski claims, and Gorbachev said the Soviet Union intended to maintain its firm support of Jaruzelski. Only if Solidarity specifically turned against the Soviet Union would policy toward Poland change. At the end of the conversation Gorbachev shrugged off Nicolae Ceauşescu's question (suggestion, really) whether the Soviet Union would invade Poland by saying (with justification, as it turned out), "Ceauşescu fears for his skin."

In 1982 Rakowski had said "sooner or later we'll have to live with them, I'm afraid."[88] That time had come. On August 24, 1989, the Sejm overwhelmingly approved Tadeusz Mazowiecki's cabinet and installed him as the first non-Communist prime minister of an East European state in almost forty years. The sad-faced Mazowiecki was so overwhelmed that he fainted during the ceremonies. No wonder. The dramatic turn of events had left the entire world somewhat lightheaded.

5

The Glorious Revolutions of 1989

August is vacation month in Europe. Parisians abandon their city to the foreigners and head for the countryside; Germans flock to the warm waters of Spain and Greece; the English working class repairs to Brighton. Much the same used to happen in Communist Eastern Europe. Yugoslavs overwhelmed their beautiful Adriatic Coast, while Czechs loaded their families in their cars and began their search for inexpensive camping grounds. Traditionally, East Germans were partial to the Bulgarian coast, flooding into the attractive Black Sea Coast resort of Varna. East Germans liked to vacation in Hungary, too; well over one hundred thousand used to vacation there annually. In August of 1989, however, a significant number of East German visitors were attracted to Hungary not by the bucolic beauty of Lake Balaton but by the possibility of finding a way into Austria. Hungary began letting its own citizens visit Austria freely early in 1989, and on May 2 Hungarian border guards began to dismantle the cement, barbed wire, barricades, and obstacles that lined the border between Hungary and Austria. What these East German vacationers realized was that in Hungary, unlike Berlin, where the wall remained in place, the Iron Curtain—the ugly commonplace of a divided Europe—was starting to come down.

Since the construction of the fortified Hungarian border restraints in the mid-1960s, only about three hundred people had successfully crossed into Austria, whereas Hungarian authorities had caught more than thirteen thousand potential escapees.[1] Now that the barrier was being dismantled and Hungary was plunging ahead with reform, East Germans found that they could slip into Austria with relative ease and within a day finish their journey to their real destination, West Germany. By the time the great onslaught of vacationers hit in August, Austria had already registered 237 such persons, although the actual number probably was much higher. During August the numbers grew exponentially, totaling perhaps as many as six thousand by the end of the month. On one memorable day, August 19, more than two hundred picnickers celebrating "European unity" charged an unattended border gate and burst into Austria en masse. By the last ten days of the month thousands of East Germans were gathered along the border looking for ways to sneak across.

At the same time these East Germans were leaking into Austria, other East Germans were showing up at West German diplomatic offices in Hungary, Czechoslovakia, Poland, and even in East Berlin itself, to get their German passports. The Federal Republic considered all Germans automatically citizens of West Germany and issued passports to East Germans virtually on demand. Until 1989, however, the passport was useless, because East Germany had agreements with its Warsaw Pact allies not to honor a West German passport that did not have a valid entry stamp on it. If you did not get into Czechoslovakia on a West German passport you could not get out on one. In the summer of 1989, however, grasping much better than their government the magnitude of the changes under way in the Soviet Union and elsewhere, East Germans began to camp out in West German embassies, which, according to long-established and rigidly observed convention, were considered sovereign German soil. Early in August the Federal Republic had to close its mission in East Berlin because more than 130 East Germans had entered and asked for asylum. A few days later it closed its embassy in Budapest because 180 people had shown up for the same reason. By the end of the month the Prague embassy closed down as well.

Hungary's Negotiated Revolution

Hungary had become a focal point for these hopes not only because it was dismantling its border fences but because reform was accelerating there. While the democratic opposition succeeded in bringing tens of thousands of demonstrators onto the streets and in creating new political groupings, Karoly Grósz's government searched for a way to control the emerging dialogue. Claiming that the Hungarian Socialist Workers' party (the Communists) represented the entire community whereas each opposition group could claim to represent only a small portion of society's interests, Grósz proposed creating a multiparty democracy that would include all those parties willing to accept the legitimacy of socialism.[2] When none of the important new parties—the MDF (Hungarian Democratic Forum), the SzDSz (Alliance of Free Democrats), and FIDESz (Alliance of Young Democrats)—would accept that condition, he tried picking them off individually, offering this one a small bribe or a promise while harassing that one, differentiating between what he called a genuine opposition and a divisive one. Early in April he convened a roundtable of "harmonization and reconciliation" stacked with sympathetic groups.

No bona fide opposition party attended Grósz's roundtable. Instead, eight rival opposition groups that had cooperated successfully in organizing the huge demonstration of March 15 came together on March 23 to found an Opposition Roundtable, the purpose of which was to face the party/state with a united front, thus thwarting Grósz's divide-and-rule tactics. The success of the negotiated revolution in Hungary can be laid to the unity these disparate groups maintained for the next few months, which was just long enough to prevent the regime from ramming through a phony multiparty constitution and to create a workable political agreement for the future.[3]

Fittingly, after the tactics Grósz had been attempting, the opposition's success in creating a united front accelerated the division of the Hungarian Socialist Workers' party both at the top and at the bottom. Just as the "horizontal" movement had appeared at the local party level during the Solidarity period in Poland, so in 1989 local party "reform circles" in Hungary began sending messages to the top that the Communists needed to offer a better program if they were to have any hope of restoring their credibility. In Poland, Party Secretary Kania was able to stifle the horizontalists in 1981, but in Hungary in 1989 such a solution was no longer possible. In April and May so many party members began to announce that they had seen the light and were converting to the reform position that the writer Péter Esterházy complained of a traffic jam on the road to Damascus.[4] A politburo reshuffle in April foreshadowed the final victory of the radical reformers, which came in June, when a new four-member presidium dominated by Rezső Nyers, Imre Pozsgay, and Miklós Nemeth took over direction of the Hungarian party.

With the accession of the real reform Communists, the way was now open for serious roundtable discussions to begin, which they did on June 13, 1989. Technically the discussions were three-sided, including the party, the opposition, and the party's satellite organizations, such as the labor unions, but no one had any illusions about who was confronting whom. A reforming Communist party was negotiating with the representatives of society, or at least groups who claimed to be those representatives, for the purpose of initiating a "peaceful and lawful evolution towards a constitutional multiparty system."[5] In a public television debate a few days after the start of the discussions, Imre Pozsgay said that the party now accepted the principle of a democratic electoral system with free elections and rival parties. If it did not dominate the elections scheduled for 1990, he said, it would seek to form a coalition. Recognizing the hollowness of the party's traditional claims of omniscience and abandoning the principles of hyperrationalism, Pozsgay and his colleagues now began to try to pull the mantle of European social democracy over their shoulders. By accepting the ideas of parliamentarianism, democratic socialism as practiced "according to Western European ideas," and—mirabile dictu—market economics, they began distancing themselves from the ghost of Stalinism as rapidly as they could.[6]

Roundtable discussions began at a moment of unusual unity among the opposition. Solidarity went into the Polish roundtable discussions as the recognized representative of a large portion of Polish society, but in Hungary none of the opposition groups had widespread backing in society. All of them, therefore, united behind a demand for free elections through which they could establish political legitimacy. The reform Communists, already conceding the necessity for some kind of election, concluded from the Polish experience that it would be dangerous to fix the proportions of representation in advance. With their large and ubiquitous organization, well-known leaders, and truly reformed program, they believed they could win, or at least run very strongly, in an open election. It was a risk, but the stakes were high—becoming the first Communist party to achieve legitimacy through the ballot box.[7]

By mid-1989 free elections were no longer an issue in Hungary, but almost everything else was. During the roundtable discussions the party concentrated on economic problems, hoping to get the opposition to share responsibility for a deteriorating economic situation and for the unpopular reforms that would be needed to correct it. The opposition insisted on presenting political demands, such as eliminating the Workers Guards, which were an armed force in every factory, and getting party cells out of the workplace.[8] After three months of difficult negotiations, in September 1989 the conferees agreed to overhaul the legal system, depoliticize the army, and cut the size and competence of the Workers Guards.

On one issue, however, no agreement could be reached. The final roundtable agreement, which the Hungarian Parliament enacted into law on October 20, 1989, called for a new president to be elected directly by a nationwide vote on November 26, with parliamentary elections to follow ninety days thereafter. This provision for a strong president, that is, one with a national mandate, was a victory for the Communists, who calculated that Imre Pozsgay would be able to win a popular election, thus putting the party in a good position to dominate the parliamentary elections. Public opinion surveys indicated that this strategy could succeed. One poll taken early in November showed that 53 percent of the voting public backed Pozsgay.[9]

When the parties of the center and right, led by the Democratic Forum (MDF), did not object to this arrangement and signed the roundtable agreement, the parties of the left—the Alliance of Free Democrats (SzDSz) and the Alliance of Young Democrats (FIDESz)—suspected them of cutting a deal with the Communists. Since candidates from the Democratic Forum had won all four of the by-elections held in 1989, the Forum had reason to hope it would win substantial representation in the new parliament and become the dominant opposition party, potentially even the partner of the reform Communists in a powerful ruling coalition. In return for backing an electoral method that would put a Communist in the presidency, the Democratic Forum could hope to get the prime minister's portfolio. These calculations reflected the belief common in the summer of 1989 that the Communists would remain a vital factor in Hungarian politics.

The Free Democrats and the Young Democrats refused to sign a roundtable agreement that agreed to a quick presidential election.[10] As soon as the other parties signed the agreement on September 18 the Free Democrats undertook a petition campaign to force a national referendum on the question of how the president would be elected, whether by popular election or by parliament. The Free Democrats argued that Hungary needed a weak president, that is, one elected by parliament, because strong presidents would constitute a threat to democracy. It may be assumed that they also hoped that if they could prevent Poszgay's election they might be successful enough in the later parliamentary elections to outflank the Communists and the Democratic Forum and to elect their own president. In little less than a month they obtained far more than the one hundred thousand signatures required to force a referendum.

In the meanwhile the Communists began to streamline themselves for the open politics to which they had agreed. Károly Grósz did his best to resist the pressure of the newly created Reform Circles Alliance, which consisted of Communist reformers from all over the country, but Grósz's day had passed. A special party conference held early in October 1989 elected Rezső Nyers to replace him as head of the party. When the conference then proceeded to vote overwhelmingly to drop the word "Workers" from the party's name, making it the Hungarian Socialist party (HSP), unrepentant hardliners stalked out to continue the old party under its old name. The reformers were unconcerned. They anticipated voters would reward them for shucking off their hardline colleagues and for turning resolutely in the direction of social democracy.

Shortly after the special party congress had tried to turn the Communists into a European party of social democrats, the parliament, consisting almost entirely of Communists elected in 1985, changed the name of the country from the People's Republic of Hungary to simply the Republic of Hungary, approved the changes to the constitution agreed to at the roundtable discussions, and declared that Hungary was "an independent, democratic legal state in which the values of bourgeois democracy and democratic socialism prevail in equal measures. All power belongs to the people, which they exercise directly and through the elected representatives of popular sovereignty."[11] Even before the fall of the Berlin Wall, Hungarians had put in place the basic elements of their negotiated revolution.

One important item remained: the referendum, which asked, among other things, do you favor election of the president by the national assembly?[12] The referendum put the Democratic Forum on the spot. It did not feel it could advocate a yes vote because that would be against the interests of its Communist ally, but it hesitated to advocate a no vote because that would be too public an endorsement of the Communists. Doing their best to ignore the referendum, Forum leaders called for a boycott. The Free Democrats turned this tactic against them with the effective slogan: "Who stays home, votes for the past." In a surprise, the newly recreated Small-holders party, which later entered the government as the Forum's coalition partner, decided to side with the Free Democrats and called for a yes vote.

Perhaps the Smallholders provided the edge, because the election turned out to be very, very close. Nothing so clearly shows how suddenly democratic values had penetrated the public space in Eastern Europe, or at least how impossible it had become to ignore them, as the scrupulousness with which the votes were counted in this election, which was a disaster for the government. Out of more than four million votes cast the yes votes prevailed by a margin of only 6,100 votes—a squeaker, but one that dashed the hopes of Imre Pozsgay and the reform Communists.[13] Instead of being swept into office on a wave of appreciation for bringing about the negotiated revolution, he, and everyone else, had to wait. The longer the wait, the more it sunk in that the old days were gone. By the time the parliamentary elections came in March and April 1990, the voters gave the former Communists and their collapsed Socialist party a mere 8.5 percent of the seats in the new legislature. The unrepentant hardliners did not get any.

The Collapse of the Berlin Wall

By the summer of 1989 Hungarian political elites were well into negotiations on how to make Hungary a pluralist society. They had powerful incentives to continue the process and a quite specific reason to be sympathetic to the East German refugees. In the previous two years Hungary had taken in seventeen thousand persons fleeing Ceauşescu's regime in Transylvania, and it was anxious to put the rights and needs of these mostly Hungarian refugees in the best light. In March 1989 Hungary announced it was acceding unconditionally to the 1951 United Nations' Convention on Refugees and the follow-up protocol of 1967.[14] Having accepted these international norms the Hungarians could not very well claim that those fleeing Romania were true refugees and those fleeing East Germany were not. Despite many negative comments in the Federal Republic about its ship already being full, in mid-August West German officials began negotiating with the Hungarians about means of accepting more refugees. On September 1 Hungarian Foreign Minister Gyula Horn personally flew to East Berlin to repudiate the long-standing travel agreement with the German Democratic Republic. On September 11 the announcement came: all East Germans waiting in Hungary and any who wished to do so in the future could cross into Austria and make for West Germany. Eleven thousand people immediately crammed themselves into buses, trains, and chugging two-stroke Trabant cars and set out for arrival centers already prepared for them in West Germany. The East German regime shrilly denounced what it called an outrage against international agreements, but the Hungarians were not ruffled. One week later American President George Bush announced he was making Hungary's most favored nation trading status permanent.

The frenzy to flee reached its climax in September when thousands of East Germans crowded into the reopened West German embassy in Prague. Climbing over walls, sitting shoulder to shoulder in the garden, almost falling out of the windows, some thirty-five hundred of them had gathered by the end of the month. Desperate to get this problem behind him so that it would not ruin the fortieth anniversary of the formation of the German Democratic Republic, which was coming up on October 7, Honecker announced on September 30 that the East Germans holed up in the Prague embassy could leave on the condition that the sealed trains in which they traveled to West Germany passed through the German Democratic Republic. As they did so, the refugees would be "expelled" for "humanitarian reasons." When the trains passed through Dresden fulfilling this farcical technicality, police had to beat back hundreds of desperate citizens trying to jump onto the trains and escape. The only result, especially after all of East Germany saw the rapturous arrival of the emigrants on West German television, was that a few days later the Prague embassy began to fill up again.

This constant desire of East Germany's most active citizens to leave the country conflicted with what some outsiders thought was the success of the country's economy. Western analysts ranked East Germany as the tenth largest industrial power in the world. But East Germans were not convinced.[15] They could talk with the large number of West German travelers who visited the German Democratic Republic in the 1990s; they could watch West German television, which blanketed the country (except for one valley near Dresden, which therefore became known as "the valley of the clueless"); and they could see the difference between their own money and deutschmarks, which were in widespread circulation in East Germany. When they compared their own scruffy currency—cheap in appearance, insubstantial in feel, and, in the case of coins, clunky in sound—with the valuable, well-printed, and solid-feeling West German money, they received an unavoidable daily reminder of East German economic inferiority.[16] Irwin Collier likens the East German economy to the commercial sailing industry of the nineteenth and early twentieth centuries. Commercial sailing ships underwent significant technological change under competition from steam-powered vessels, increasing their efficiency dramatically, but they could never match steam-powered vessels because there came a point beyond which sail technology could not go. Collier suggests that the German Democratic Republic was a dynamic system as well, one that made significant improvements, but that the inherent limitations of centralized planning and single-party domination made it just as impossible for it to compete with the market system as it proved impossible for sailing vessels to compete with steam-powered ships. He suggests there was more pathos than intended in the plea of an East German Communist party leader late in 1989 who exhorted his colleagues "to get the wind back into our . . . sails."[17]

During the great exodus of 1989, the Western press emphasized the economic reasons for escape, as did the West Germans themselves, sometimes referring to East Germans as "banana-fresser"—a condescending and derogatory way of denigrating the animal-like eagerness with which East Germans fell upon common consumer articles when they first arrived in West Germany. But it is not a crime to want a decent apartment or varied and nourishing food. The reason so many wanted to flee East Germany was not fundamentally economic, however. They were fleeing a stifling sense of powerlessness, the regime's deadening insistence on capitulation, and the enervating denial of all possibility of idealism and hope.

Two particularly debilitating events deepened this despair in 1989. The first was the election of May 7, 1989. At a moment when the Soviet Union had already conducted its first open election and Poland was preparing to do so, after opposition groups had specifically advised the public on how to vote negatively, and following scattered exit polls that showed significant negative voting, Honecker's protégé, the toothy Egon Krenz, blandly announced that 98.95 percent of the vote in that election supported the government list.[18] The regime compounded the despair this absurd result produced one month later when it strongly approved of the massacre of Chinese students in Tiananmen Square. Over and over again East German television played "a Chinese documentary that praised the heroic response of the Chinese army and police to the perfidious inhumanity of the student demonstrators."[19] The regime made its point all too well. Upon arriving in West Germany in September many young refugees, 40 percent of whom were between the ages of twenty-two and twenty-nine, explained their flight by saying, "In East Germany there is no future" and "Nothing will happen in that country soon. We do not feel like waiting twenty years."[20] "Do you intend to keep putting us off until doomsday?" one impassioned nineteen-year-old had asked in 1982. "What about the shining city on the hill?"[21] In September and October 1989 tens of thousands of East Germans took their road to the shining city through Hungary.

But many stayed, and it was they, not the ones who left, who toppled the Berlin Wall. The opposition groups that became active in East Germany in the 1980s were small and ineffective. In June 1989 the State Security Service, or Stasi, estimated that some one hundred and sixty groups, including pacifists, feminists, and environmentalists, existed in the GDR. In all of these only about twenty-five hundred persons were involved, of which six hundred held leadership positions. The Stasi identified only sixty persons as hard core activists.[22] The environmentalists did not find a mobilizing issue with the mass appeal of the Nagymaros dam, and Honecker's state itself pre-empted the historical discourse by a campaign in the mid-1980s that co-opted Luther, Frederick the Great, and Bach into its own pantheon of historical predecessors.

But an opposition did exist, influenced by the traditional left and generally suspicious of the capitalist West. The thirty activists who gathered in East Berlin on September 10, 1989, to create the New Forum as a platform for democratic forces throughout the country did it specifically to prevent the "wild fire" of emigration from gutting the country any further.[23] Like the other activists of Eastern Europe ten years before them, they chose an antipolitical name and a moderate program. The New Forum claimed it had no intention of becoming a political opposition, although some of its members dreamt of perhaps putting a slate together for the 1991 elections. It simply sought "a democratic dialogue about the tasks of the constitutional state, the economy, and of culture."[24] Although the East German courts summarily rejected their petition of registration, thousands of people signed their manifesto and the New Forum temporarily moved to center stage in the increasingly chaotic East German public life.

Much more important than this first emergence of an embryonic democratic opposition were the massive public demonstrations that took place throughout East Germany in October. These were not, as Honecker would have hoped, demonstrations celebrating the fortieth anniversary of the formation of the German Democratic Republic, which took place on October 7. Of all the public celebrations that modern authoritarian states have forced on its people, none were as surrealistic as this fortieth anniversary. With his countrymen fleeing by the tens of thousands, the question of German unification peeking out from behind the rostrum, and political opposition swelling, the ailing Honecker paraded around East Berlin with a Soviet leader who told him "life punishes those who come too late."[25]

The real demonstrations, the ones that brought Honecker and his state down, grew out of a traditional peace service that had been held before small gatherings in the St. Nikolai Church in Leipzig on Monday afternoons since 1982. There had been arrests in Leipzig in 1988 and early in 1989, but just at the time the Hungarians opened their borders and the New Forum was coming into being the character of these Monday afternoon prayers for peace changed. On September 4 some fifteen hundred persons gathered after the prayers, some of them demanding the right to leave East Germany but many for the first time chanting "We are staying."[26] When a similar gathering took place the next Monday the police arrested fifty persons, but with little effect. On Monday, September 25, eight thousand persons gathered to walk through the center of Leipzig, and on October 2, ten thousand persons marched, shouting "We're staying here," singing "We Shall Overcome," as well as the "Internationale," and chanting slogans such as "Legalize New Forum" and "Gorbi, Gorbi."[27]

During Gorbachev's visit, which took place on October 7 and 8, security police responded to protesters who demonstrated against the fortieth anniversary celebrations in many towns and cities throughout the country in the traditional manner—breaking heads and making arrests. "Give those pigs a sound beating," the head of the security policy is alleged to have said.[28] What would the authorities do on October 9 at the next Monday demonstration in Leipzig? It was rumored that Honecker had signed Secret Order Number 8/89 directing all security agencies, including the army, to prevent hostile actions and provocations by any means.[29] Sensing the imminent danger of a Chinese solution, Kurt Masur, director of the Gewandhaus Orchestra and one of Leipzig's most respected citizens, called several other prominent persons together that Monday afternoon and worked out an appeal for peaceful dialogue. It is still not known exactly who received this appeal and approved it—Egon Krenz later took credit for it but it is more likely that local officials made the decision—but the security forces withdrew. That evening, after the regular 5:00 P.M. prayers, more than fifty thousand people peacefully marched through Leipzig chanting, among other things, "We are the people."

The Leipzig demonstration of October 9 was the crucial moment when the Socialist Unity party lost control of East Germany. Convinced now that they were free to vent their frustrations in public, crowds began gathering regularly in towns throughout East Germany. Tens of thousands gathered in provincial cities and the by-now traditional Monday night marches in Leipzig grew to seventy thousand, then to over one hundred thousand, and then to three hundred thousand. The most spectacular of the marches came in East Berlin on November 4. At least half a million Berliners thronged the streets carrying banners with all manner of slogans, ranging from the historical ("1789–1989") through the light-hearted ("I want to visit my girlfriend in Holland") to the bitter ("Stop privileges"). Most significantly, the crowd changed its chant from "We are the people" to "We are one people," indicating that as far as they were concerned not just the party but the entire country should be thrown on the ash heap of history.

The situation had passed beyond crisis. This was revolution, and not by an opposition party—the brand-new and still weak New Forum was pulled along by events—but by an entire people. When the Leipzig crowds chanted "We are the people," they did not have to add "And you are not." Even the most blinkered party member got the message. But having adamantly resisted any change for years, the best the party could come up with was to replace Erich Honecker, who stepped down on October 18. Egon Krenz, hitherto known as a hardline, unimaginative bureaucrat, took his place. Smiling broadly at all times, Krenz did his best. In a frantic forty-four days in office he fired Stalinists, visited Gorbachev (who gave him scant support, telling him that pluralism of opinion was a good thing), reshuffled both the Council of Ministers and his politburo, opened the Czech border, and generally beat a rapid retreat in a disorderly effort to stave off complete collapse.

The climactic moment came on the evening of November 9, when the politburo approved, apparently without much discussion, a vaguely worded addendum to a new set of rules for permanent emigration that said "private trips abroad can be requested without fulfilling requirements."[30] This casual act proved to be, as Egon Krenz said later, a "slight mistake."[31] When, a few minutes before 7:00 P.M., the politburo's press spokesman was winding up his press conference, a reporter asked him about the new travel law. The spokesman replied by reading a note from Krenz saying "private trips abroad can be applied for. Permits will be granted promptly." The reporters' interest perked up considerably. Did this apply to travel to West Berlin? The spokesman did not know. Despite restrained television reporting of this exchange, the rumor began to spread on the streets that a momentous decision had been made, and crowds began to gather at the Wall. The border guards, uninformed about any change in the rules, themselves began to be influenced by the rumors, and when the pressure of the crowds increased, their officers simply decided to yield and to let people through to the other side. By midnight hundreds of thousands of ecstatic people were pouring through the Wall and a delirious celebration, joined in by both *Ossies* and *Wessies*, as the East and West Germans refer to each other, engulfed the entire city.

The exhilaration generated by the fall of the Berlin Wall—for in a matter of hours people were chipping away at it and in a matter of days and weeks it was being dismantled—is beyond description. In that one night the entire picture of Europe constructed in the mind of almost all of its citizens for forty years underwent an irreversible phase shift. Every situation seems semipermanent to those who are living through it, and the postwar settlement, which was always implicit rather than explicit—no treaty formally ended World War II with Germany—was no exception. Despite the rhetoric over the years about the desirability of German unification or the injustice suffered by the peoples of Eastern Europe under Communist rule, the cost of actually changing the relationships established in the first few years after the war was always far too high. No one who had experienced World War II could feel really comfortable with the idea of a united Germany, especially since West Germany had become the most powerful country in Europe. Each time a serious confrontation occurred in Eastern Europe the West wisely decided that it was not worth risking World War III to intervene. But with the sharp crack of champagne bottles spraying corks on all sides of the Wall, on the night of November 9–10 the unification of Germany suddenly seemed not only possible but likely, and the future of the Communist regimes of Eastern Europe suddenly seemed very bleak indeed.

Zhivkov's Fall in Bulgaria

Almost unnoticed in the euphoric hangover on November 10 was the announcement that Todor Zhivkov, leader of Bulgaria since 1954, had resigned under pressure to be replaced by long-time Foreign Minister

Petŭr Mladenov. Zhivkov's departure had no direct relationship to the fall of the Berlin Wall, but it was part and parcel of the reform momentum that the Polish and Hungarian developments had evoked even in the farthest reaches of Eastern Europe.

In the early and mid-1980s Bulgaria became notorious in the West for being Eastern Europe's most notorious venue for real-life spy stories. In the late 1970s Georgi Markov, a Bulgarian oppositionist, died in London when someone injected him in the leg with a poison pellet shot through an umbrella point. Bulgarian authorities denied responsibility and the matter remains under investigation, but few considered the deed to be the work of the International Red Cross.[32] Then the trial of the would-be assassin of Pope John Paul II in Rome hinted that the Bulgarian secret police had fronted for the KGB in that plot and revealed that sleepy Sofia had become the home base of a number of arms smugglers and dope runners, all probably in collusion with the authorities.

Corruption was not alien to Todor Zhivkov's regime but probably did not go as far as plotting to kill the pope. Just about the time of the attempt on the pope's life in 1981, Zhivkov reached the peak of his success.[33] Despite the oil price disasters of the 1970s, Bulgaria had succeeded in lowering its external debt to a sustainable $1.8 billion (mid-1983 figure). By adopting the Motorola family of microchips instead of the Intel family adopted by the rest of CMEA (Council of Mutual Economic Assistance) and by entering into a number of cooperative agreements with Hitachi and Toshiba, the Bulgarians created a successful computer industry, carving out a niche for themselves at the high end of the East European user spectrum. Since the Soviet space program used Bulgarian computers, the value of computer exports to the Soviet Union rose substantially in the 1980s.[34]

Zhivkov had great faith in science and technology, but he also understood the difference between talking about a technological revolution, which kept him in a position of control, and actually producing one, which might threaten his position by creating economic pressure for political change.[35] Purposefully ineffective reform was the hallmark of Zhivkov's Bulgaria in the 1980s. When in 1982 he introduced a plan he called the New Economic Mechanism, perhaps hoping some of the Hungarian successes would rub off on Bulgaria, he spoke at length about the scientific-technological revolution as the key to Bulgarian progress, sounding very much like Walter Ulbricht in the 1960s. At the Thirteenth Party Congress in 1986 he emphasized again that the "further development of socialist society would depend on the scientific-technological revolution."[36] Presenting himself as a reformer pushing for modern methods who was at the same time sensitive to changing winds in the Communist world, he had no difficulty in responding to Gorbachev's perestroika and glasnost with Bulgarian equivalents: *pereustroistvo*—"the work of the party, the work of the people," as he put it early in 1988—and glasnost, limited however by the principle that openness could never be used as a "subjective mirror of those . . . not on the right track."[37] Never breaking stride, he announced again, as countless party documents had in the past, that he would increase the degree of economic self-management, eliminate distortions and deformations, and guarantee the professionalism of party cadres at all levels.[38]

These familiar pronouncements did not work because they were not supposed to work. Out of ideas, Zhivkov clung tenaciously to personal power and to the rhetoric with which he had justified it for thirty years. As the price of Soviet oil rose in the 1980s and Bulgaria could no longer achieve a positive balance of trade by reselling cheap Soviet oil at world prices, Zhivkov turned to the inevitable remedy: borrowing. By 1989 Bulgarian debt had ballooned to over $10 billion and the country's economy was in a downward spiral.

For reasons that remain obscure, in 1984 and 1985 Zhivkov, probably on his personal authority and without much discussion even in party circles, began a brutal assimilation campaign against the ethnic Turks living in Bulgaria. Comprising close to a million persons and constituting about 10 percent of the Bulgarian population, these Turks were not an unassimilated and indigestible mass of foreign peoples. They lived mainly in two rural areas, where their ancestors had resided for centuries, and were Islamic in custom, if not always practicing their faith punctiliously. Most of them spoke Bulgarian as well as Turkish, and the educated among them were often quite assimilated to Bulgarian culture. They had been living at peace with their neighbors for several generations and were among Bulgaria's most industrious and efficient agricultural producers.

Bulgarian policy toward minorities had been intolerant since 1956, when Zhivkov began to put his stamp on Bulgarian politics.[39] Zhivkov did not insist on the same level of absurd personal identification with the national past as Ceauşescu did in Romania, but the elaborate celebration of the thirteen hundredth anniversary of the founding of the medieval Bulgarian state and an exclusive focus on the Bulgarian past in the history department of Sofia University confirm that Zhivkov relied heavily on nationalist forms of legitimation. The presumption of this worldview was that everyone who lived in Bulgaria was really Bulgarian.

The first decision reflecting this view was to stop counting Macedonians separately in the census. The 1956 census had counted almost one hundred ninety thousand Macedonians living in Bulgaria, but in the 1960 edition of the same census the table listing population by nationalities was omitted, never to return.[40] Next, over a period of years, the regime forced Bulgarian-speaking Muslims, called Pomaks, to change their names to more Slavic-sounding ones. This campaign reflected the parochial orientalism characteristic of Bulgarian nationalism. Asserting that Islam is an obscurantist faith that stands in the way of modernization, officials cited the economic progress of the Pomaks in western Bulgaria since 1960 as proof that the assimilation policy had been correct. The final push was Zhivkov's turn against the largest "backward" minority, the Turks, per-

haps because after thirty years he felt it was time to have the census scheduled for 1985 show only Bulgarians living in Bulgaria.

The campaign for the reconstruction of names, as Bulgarian officials
called it, was conducted secretly and in the absence of foreign observers.
After it was over the government announced that a spontaneous ground
swell of pride in Bulgaria had swept the countryside. All Bulgarians with
Turkic and Arabic-sounding names had voluntarily and willingly registered
new, authentically Bulgarian names with the authorities.[41] In fact, many
Turks vigorously resisted the name changes and the Bulgarian army intervened. Stories of people crushed by tanks began filtering out of the Turkish
regions, and international human rights organizations reported that the
reconstruction of names had cost approximately one hundred lives. Prime
Minister Georgi Atanasov is said to have remarked privately that it was
necessary to finish with the Turkish question by "flame and sword" once
and for all.[42]

For four years the Bulgarian government stonewalled negative international reaction to its minorities policy, particularly ridiculing the "hypo-
critical tears" and "nationalist propaganda" coming from Turkey. In May
1989, however, a group of Bulgarian Turks calling themselves the Democratic League for the Defense of Human Rights began a series of hunger
strikes, work stoppages, and demonstrations against the persistent pressure
by the government to eliminate and transform their cultural and religious
customs, including the right to use Turkish in elementary schools. Suddenly Zhivkov, perhaps overly defensive at his weakening political position,
turned angry. Turkish families were told to pack their belongings and
leave, often on only a few hours' notice. From May into July authorities
forced some three hundred thousand persons to leave Bulgaria literally
overnight, taking with them only what they could carry or cram into their
small cars. Even though more than half of these unwilling refugees
returned to Bulgaria within a year, the damage both to ethnic relations
and to the Bulgarian economy was incalculable. One of the reasons that
1990 was a bad year economically for Bulgaria was that a significant portion of its most productive citizens were sitting in Turkish refugee camps.

Many among the Bulgarian intelligentsia found the reconstruction of
names a distasteful tragedy and today blame Zhivkov for poisoning ethnic
relations, but until mid-1989 very few spoke in public against it. Early in
1987 six longtime activists sent a letter to a meeting of the Conference on
Security and Cooperation in Europe (CSCE) protesting human rights
abuses in Bulgaria but to little effect, except to cause their own exile. One
year later, associates of those who had written the CSCE formed the Independent Association for the Defense of Human Rights, but, since it was
perceived as being pro-Turkish, it did not have a widespread impact.

The mainstream of Bulgarian opposition emerged over a different
issue, the environment. In April 1987 the journal *Literaturen Front* (Literary Front) publicly mentioned the problem of air pollution in Sofia for
the first time. That fall the same journal reported that a few people had

gathered in Ruse to demand that the Romanian chemical plant across the Danube River in Giurgiu stop its constant and excessive emanations of chlorine gas.[43] "Give us fresh air," the demonstrators cried. In December 1987 and January 1988 activists in Ruse staged an exhibition, combining forty drawings and paintings of ecological decline with dreadful data on the environmental situation in the city, in which all the vital statistics were in decline. The emboldened Ruse activists then produced a short film called *Dishe* (Breathe), which they showed in Sofia to groups totaling perhaps two thousand intellectuals.

Concurrently with these initiatives a four-part series in *Trud* (Labor) chronicled the corrupt practices of a certain Mihaylov family in the small town of Etropole. The sensitive issue in the articles, although they did not mention this directly, was the knowledge that the Mihaylov family was linked with Zhivkov's son Vladimir. The prospect that future articles might reveal deeply corrupt practices at the very top of the Bulgarian leadership was obviously what Zhivkov meant by "subjective mirrors of people on the wrong track," and he reacted strongly. The editor of *Literaturen Front* was fired, and for good measure, three or four party members, including the wife of the speaker of the national assembly, were expelled for signing the environmental appeal of the Ruse group. Zhivkov announced an offensive against the intelligentsia, calling a central committee plenum for May 1988 for the purpose of "restructuring intellectual life."

Zhivkov was not able to make good his demand for a plenum in May because an internal party fight suddenly surfaced. Zhivkov had always claimed that he was the first to try perestroika in the 1960s but that 1968 had shown its failings. In the 1980s he continued to maintain that Bulgaria had been the first country to reform and that reforms were going further there than anywhere else. By 1987 and 1988 this claim was wearing thin. In 1988 Stoyan Mikhailov began to argue in party circles that Zhivkov's reforms were not original at all and that those in the Soviet Union had gone much further and deeper. The fight was bitter—supposedly Zhivkov even wrote letters of resignation—but without a history of preparation over the years party critics were not yet able to oust the wily Zhivkov. When the plenum finally took place in July, Zhivkov was able to force Mikhailov out, along with Chudomir Aleksandrov, heir apparent and a frequent critic of the slowness of pereustroistvo.

During his long career Zhivkov had faced and defeated many challengers. The ouster of Mikhailov and Aleksandrov was another one of these moments. But at this same plenum, during which he once again emerged victorious, the first conversations took place among members of a faction that finally, after so many others had failed, forced Zhivkov to resign. A contentious issue in the politburo during the last years of the regime was agricultural policy. Some members of the politburo had come to the conclusion during the 1980s that a system in which an efficient cooperative was penalized by being made to turn over its surplus to the state while an inefficient one was rewarded with subsidies was never going to work properly. These individuals were not reformers in the Hungarian sense but simply a few persons who wanted to give the peasant more control over the land and its produce while otherwise maintaining the system. After discussions of this issue became so heated in the politburo that they turned into shouting matches, the realization that Zhivkov would never accede to real changes led to the first conversations among those who finally found a way to replace him.[44]

In trouble with an as-yet entirely informal and behind-the-scenes reform faction, by 1989 Zhivkov no longer had the support of a significant portion of the intelligentsia either. For more than thirty years he had successfully cultivated the Bulgarian intellectuals. In 1988 he lost them. No group in Eastern Europe was more aware of the progress of reform in the Soviet Union than was the Sofia intelligentsia. Many educated Bulgarians speak Russian, and all can read it; there is a Russian language high school in Sofia; and since the late 1970s the city even had a separate television channel broadcasting in Russian. By 1987, for the first time in postwar Eastern Europe, Soviet newspapers began to sell out in Bulgaria on hot news days. Aware of what was going on in the Soviet Union, frustrated by the obvious falsity of its own government's mouthing of glasnost, and agitated by minor repressions against editors, professors, and students, the Sofia intelligentsia began to create a belated democratic opposition.

The first rumblings emanated from Sofia University late in 1987 when four persons, three of them old-line Communists, were expelled from the party for criticizing Zhivkov at a meeting of faculty party members.[45] The case created a stir among the faculty, many of whom began discussing how to defend the rights of the expelled. In March some of these faculty made contact with the Ruse environmentalists. These initiatives led in the fall of 1988 to the creation of the Club for the Support of Perestroika and Glasnost, an "unofficial association of individuals" formed by about one hundred faculty members in an antipolitical spirit. Prominent members included the philosopher Zhelyu Zhelev, the respected and formerly sanctioned poet Blaga Dimitrova, and the *Hot Peppers* collaborators, Radoi Rolin and Boris Dimovski.

The government reacted to the formation of this club with near panic, calling its members "disinformants," "traitors," "extremists," and "anti-Bulgarian," but opposition among the intelligentsia continued to grow. By March 1989 it was said that nine opposition movements existed, including a new independent labor union, *Podkrepa,* and the heir of the Ruse group, Ecoglasnost. When in 1989 Zhivkov began expelling Turks, the intelligentsia did not keep their concerns to themselves as they had in 1984–1985. On July 4, 1989, 121 persons, including the most prominent members of the Club for the Support of Perestroika and Glasnost, sent an appeal to the national assembly calling the government's expulsion of the Turks "contrary to our national character, humiliating for our national dignity, and disruptive of our tradition of tolerance." On August 1 they sent an even tougher statement.[46]

For the first time in his regime, Zhivkov could no longer count on the intelligentsia to remain silent. In October 1989, Ecoglasnost, which had expanded its program to include opposition to a hydroelectric project near the famous Rila monastery and other similar issues, embarrassed the regime by holding a public demonstration during an international conference on the environment that was being held in Sofia. The police responded with some arrests and detentions, provoking international protests. On November 4, the same day as the massive demonstration in East Berlin, Ecoglasnost was able to respond by assembling four thousand people outside the national assembly to demand democratic reforms.

In the end it was not these oppositional activities—although they were by far the most extensive Bulgaria had experienced since World War II—that brought Zhivkov down.[47] Former Prime Minister Georgi Atanasov states that the effort to replace Zhivkov began in the summer of 1989, when Atanasov, Petŭr Mladenov, Andrei Lukhanov, and General Dobri Dzhurov began to discuss the possibility at the annual fête for the diplomatic community held in Smolyan. Mladenov had been minister of foreign affairs since 1971 and was frustrated because he felt Zhivkov was not sympathetic to the opening toward the West that Mladenov believed necessary. Lukhanov was an intellectual Communist who still believed that it would be possible to create a social democratic party that could introduce reforms without giving up the party's primary role. Dzhurov, the minister of defense, was an old partisan colleague of Zhivkov's who was not afraid to talk back to the party leader. All of them were frustrated not only at Zhivkov's unwillingness to move with the times but with the promotion of his son Vladimir to the central committee position in charge of culture. For some time Dzhurov in particular had opposed the influence of Zhivkov family members, and Zhivkov's efforts to win him over with appointments benefiting Dzhurov's own family had failed.

Late in October Lukhanov took what he called "a calculated risk" by speaking more or less openly to a few colleagues in the politburo. Late in October, Mladenov also took a chance. He had been working hard to advance Bulgaria's application to the General Agreement on Tariffs and Trade (GATT) and to widen other similarly needed openings to the West. Greatly irritated by an order from Zhivkov to rebuff the American ambassador, who had been encouraging the democratic opposition, Mladenov sent Zhivkov a letter of resignation. In surprisingly vigorous language Mladenov accused the Bulgarian leader of dragging the country down into "the same pigs' trough as the rotten dictatorial family regime of Ceauşescu."[48] Zhivkov brought the letter to the politburo, where it received agitated discussion, but he decided to forgive Mladenov and not to accept his resignation.

On November 4 Mladenov traveled to China for a scheduled diplomatic visit. Some have speculated that he must have stopped in Moscow en route to discuss the situation with Gorbachev, but Atanasov says that the only contact the faction had with the Soviets was Atanasov's visit to the Soviet Embassy on November 4. When the Soviets gave the green light by not reacting to the information that Zhivkov would be replaced at the central committee plenum of November 10, the Soviet-trained Dzhurov moved four loyal army units into Sofia to insure that the change would go smoothly.[49]

During the week before the November 10 meeting of the central committee, Lukhanov and others began speaking to Zhivkov in general terms about resigning. After taking some soundings of his own, Zhivkov agreed, but without setting a date. Finally, at the politburo meeting of November 9, Zhivkov found himself facing a majority against him, a majority that controlled the army. When he got up at the central committee meeting on November 10 to announce his resignation, it seemed to those present that he did so willingly. Mladenov, the most presentable of the main plotters, stepped into his place as head of the party.

The streets greeted Mladenov's accession with joy. Over the next year the center of Sofia became a huge debating society, full of street corner discussions, serious meetings, and exuberant rallies. Mladenov responded in a manner that can only be described as amazing for a man who had been at the center of single-party Communist power for almost twenty years. He announced that Bulgaria had to become a modern, democratic, and pluralist state and countered the skepticism these promises evoked by reinstating all dismissed party members and expelling Zhivkov from the party, renouncing the party's leading role in society, permitting widespread freedom of speech, calling for free elections for the spring of 1990, and, by the end of December 1989, agreeing to the by-now traditional East European transition device—roundtable discussions with the opposition. On its side, the opposition, which now consisted of nine major organizations and dozens of miraculous flowers that had sprung from the hitherto barren Bulgarian soil, had already come together under the leadership of Ecoglasnost and Podkrepa to form the Union of Democratic Forces. Bulgarians jumped with alacrity on the bandwagon that was heading, they hoped, back to Europe.

Czechoslovakia

One country that had not jumped on the bandwagon, at least by the time the Berlin Wall fell and Zhivkov left power, was Czechoslovakia. This once prosperous democracy had been in what Charter 77 activists called "a death-like torpor" since 1968.[50] The Husák/B'ilak team changed its tune very little from the time it fully consolidated its power in the early 1970s until December 1987, when Husak stepped down as party chairman (he stayed as president) in favor of Miloš Jakeš and Jan Fojtik pushed aside B'ilak as chief ideological watchdog. Czechoslovakia was not in the same kind of acute economic difficulty as were the other states of Eastern Europe. Husák had isolated his country from the world economy, increasing trade with the other socialist countries to almost 80 percent of total foreign trade. Whatever long-term harm this parochialism did to the Czechoslovak economy, it had the advantage of making it less necessary for Czechoslovakia to borrow in the West.[51] During the 1980s Czechoslovak foreign debt was the lowest in Eastern Europe, remaining at the manageable figure of between $3 and $4 billion through the end of 1988. Czechoslovak planners, despite their lack of interest in private farming or alternative forms of cooperative property, managed to keep relatively plentiful supplies of food in the stores, even meat. In 1989 one of the arguments the regime used to defuse public dissatisfaction was to compare the Czechoslovak standard of living to that of Poland, where long lines for simple groceries were commonplace. And yet the economy was not vigorous. Growth had dropped off dramatically in the early 1980s and did not recover well. Even Husák had to admit that some changes were necessary, but when they were introduced in 1987, the year Gorbachev visited Prague to shouts of "Gorby, Gorby," they were modest even by the standards of the 1960s. When Jakeš came to power he loyally proclaimed Czechoslovakia's interest in *přestavba*, the Czech word for perestroika, but in fact very little changed.

As in East Germany, however, it was not economic disappointments that pushed the Communists aside but massive gatherings of hundreds of thousands of citizens on an almost daily basis. When this happened in East Germany no clearly identified new leaders existed. In Czechoslovakia obvious and natural leaders were available for the transition to democracy: the veteran members of Charter 77 who had been keeping the antipolitical flame of democratic hope flickering for more than a decade.

Charter 77 was never a large movement. Constant harassment had kept its membership down to that small number of people who were willing to "live in truth" no matter what the consequences. A few thousand people at the fringes, a few hundred near the center, a few dozen real leaders, and one at the very center—Václav Havel. There have been few figures in European politics quite like this man. A writer by birth, a philosopher by inclination, a playwright by profession, and a moralist by conviction, under ordinary circumstances Havel would never have been a politician, let alone president of his country. He would be a philosopher, writing, as he did during his longest prison stay, about "the mysterious multiformity and infinite 'elusiveness' of the order of Being, which . . . simply cannot be grasped and described by a consistent system of knowledge,"[52] or he would be enriching the theater of the absurd with a family of plays about "the basic modalities of humanity in a state of collapse."[53] Even under the special circumstances of growing up in a revolutionizing state, he had no inclination to be a politician. He was a writer whose mission was "to speak the truth about the world I live in, to bear witness to its terrors and its miseries—in other words, to warn rather than hand out prescriptions for change."[54]

The pudgy and unathletic son of a successful Prague businessman, Havel felt an outsider even as a child because of the privileges his family position gave him.[55] When the Communists came to power his class origins made his outsider status official. The regime seized his father's property in 1948 (it was returned in 1991) and Havel had to take a job as a laboratory assistant rather than entering high school, although he did eventually receive a high school diploma after several grueling years of night school. After some desultory studies of public transport and a difficult two-year stint in the army, he began to work as a stagehand in Prague's ABC Theater, from which point he found his voice as a playwright. During the 1960s he produced some of his best-known plays at the Theater on the Balustrade.

There was never any question in Havel's mind that he was a writer. From the time he first learned the alphabet he wrote and associated with people who wrote. At fifteen he formed his first intellectual group, which put out its own typewritten magazine, and by twenty he had already raised his voice at the Second Congress of the Writers' Union of Czechoslovakia to call party reformers hypocrites when they said they wanted to open windows to truth and yet refused to listen to those who sought to tell the truth. From that point on, driven to investigate the human condition and to live his life in accordance with what he found, Havel simply went from one logical decision to another, writing down his thoughts in a powerful and effective prose as he went, often stopping to drink a beer or to watch a play with his friends. They never sat down and decided to be oppositionists, he said in 1978, but had "simply done certain things which we had to do or which seemed to us to be proper."[56] "When a person behaves in keeping with his conscience, when he tries to speak the truth, and when he tries to behave as a citizen even under conditions where citizenship is degraded," he said on December 7, 1989, the day he agreed to stand for president of Czechoslovakia, "it may not lead to anything, yet it might. But what surely will not lead to anything is when a person calculates whether it will lead to something or not."[57] As his sometime antagonist, novelist Milan Kundera, has said, Havel's life was "one gradual, continuous process, and it gives the impression of a perfect compositional unity." Havel's life is that rare case, Kundera said, "where comparing a life to a work of art is justified."[58]

The clarity and moral attractiveness of Havel's views, which he expressed in such powerful essays as "Letter to Dr. Gustav Husák" and "The Power of the Powerless," identified Havel as the most eloquent of the East European antipoliticians, not only to observant Westerners and aspiring oppositionists but to the Husák/B'ilak regime as well. The authorities countered Charter 77 with harassment, house arrests, preventative detainment, forced exile—all the varied methods of the police state. Some of the harassed reacted with insouciance, as did Ludvík Vaculík, who describes his interrogations with a light but devastating touch in *A Cup of Coffee with My Interrogator*.[59] But special attention was reserved for Havel and the other Charter 77 spokespersons. In 1979, despite indignant protests from abroad, a Czechoslovak court sentenced Havel and five prominent activists, all of whom, ironically, were also members of a group called the Committee for the Defense of the Unjustly Persecuted (Vybor na obranu nespravedlive stihanych—VONS), to lengthy jail sentences. Havel was released in March 1983 only when he contracted pneumonia after having spent almost four years at exhausting hard labor.[60]

Charter 77 was not an organization, although it had its organizers abroad, and it was not even a movement, although some used that term. It was a group of people with a wide range of viewpoints united by a moral attitude. "We were crazy, impractical madmen and adventurers who voluntarily gave our names and addresses to State Security," said Miroslav Kusy, one of the few Slovak activists.[61] Havel's ability to express the moral dimension of living in truth was what made him the natural leader of an inherently leaderless initiative. The ability to overlook programmatic differences and to unite in their effort to live the truth made Charter 77 what Petr Uhl, a Trotskyite sentenced to five years in the 1979 trial, called "a school for diversity."[62] Another of those convicted in 1979, given three years, was Václav Benda, a practicing Catholic who believed that one had to go beyond the abstract ideal of ethical choice and make a true community possible by creating a "parallel polis."[63] In their personal lives, Benda said, people should attempt to establish independent structures in areas such as education, culture, and information.

The differences among these three men, one a Trotskyite, another a conservative Catholic, and the third a nonpolitical philosopher/artist, suggest that Charter 77's strength lay not in a specific ideology but rather in its moral conviction. Charter 77 brought together people of diverse views who could agree on one overriding point: the regime was false. This belief, as well as a conviction that overt political opposition would be pointless in the face of repression backed by Brezhnev's Soviet Union, permitted them to subsume their differences under the general umbrella of Charter 77's focus on human rights and to accept the admonition to live in truth.

Appealing as this adage was to foreigners contemplating it from the comfort of their libraries, it was too rarified in theory and too difficult in practice to overcome the fear the Husák regime generated among the vast majority of Czechoslovaks, including even most intellectuals. Living in truth was Charter 77's greatest strength because the regime was powerless against it, but it was also its greatest weakness because such a life was far too difficult for most people. Why do the people not protest the obvious and daily injustices they suffer, Havel asked in his letter to Husák? Because, he answered in "The Power of the Powerless," if they do not conform the regime will "spew them from its mouth." Havel, Uhl, Benda, and others were willing to be spewed, but most people understandably were not.

In Slovakia Charter 77 had only a limited response. There the important issue remained a lurking Slovak nationalism that in the twentieth century had become closely linked with Catholicism. During the 1930s and 1940s the success of the Slovak People's party, whose leader had been a Catholic priest, fused Slovak national feeling with the church. Religious practice remained stronger in Slovakia, where 70 percent of the people baptized their children in 1984, than it did in the Czech lands, where only 30 percent did so.[64] The connection between religion and nationality in the Czech mind, even though 40 percent of Czechs consider themselves Catholic, is primarily with the Protestant movement of Jan Hus and the cosmopolitan morality of the Bohemian Brethren of the fifteenth century. The decline of religiosity among the Czechs was amply demonstrated in 1989 at one of the great street meetings. When a dissident priest tried to lead the crowd in singing the old Czech Wenceslas hymn, "most of crowd either [did] not know the words or [were] reluctant to sing them."[65] Under great pressure from the Communists, neither the Catholic church nor the minority Protestant faiths, which constituted about 10 percent of the population, was able to provide the sort of succor to an opposition that the Polish Catholic church provided to Solidarity or even as much as the Evangelical (Lutheran) church did to the East German peace movements.

In the 1980s, however, when the regime increased its pressure on the church in response to the dual threats it felt emanating from Poland and from a revivified papacy under John Paul II, a backlash developed among Catholics. Cardinal František Tomášek, who is Czech and who remained vigorous despite being in his eighties, took his lead from Rome and began, as he had not under previous popes, to speak out. In 1985 he invited John Paul II to the celebrations of the eleven hundredth anniversary of the death of Saint Methodius who, with Saint Cyril, brought Christianity to the Slavs. When the authorities refused permission for the visit, more than one hundred thousand Czechs and Slovaks turned up at the ceremony at Velehrad anyway.[66] Later that year Tomášek responded to crude attacks on him in the party press with an open letter in which he said, "The church here is not the center of political opposition. All it wishes to do is carry on its pastoral and missionary work. . . . Talking of peace and disarmament would only become relevant and effective when justice and respect for human rights prevail."[67] Then in the spring of 1987 the church announced a "Decade of Spiritual Renewal." That year more than one hundred thousand participated in the Velehrad pilgrimage. Late in 1987 a group of Moravian Catholics began circulating a thirty-one-point petition calling for the separation of church and state and for freedom of religion in general. When Cardinal Tomášek appealed to Catholics to sign this petition, saying that "cowardice and fear are unworthy of a true Christian," the phenomenal number of six hundred thousand persons throughout Czechoslovakia signed within six months.[68] Organizing such a massive endeavor, and planning for the needs for food and sanitation of a large number of pilgrims, gave organizers precious experience in self-activization outside of state structures. This unintended consequence of Catholic activism was one of the few instances of a broad civil society developing among the Czechs and Slovaks.

Opposition in Czechoslovakia, then, headed in two not necessarily compatible directions during the 1980s. The first was the elegant and highly ethical community of mostly secular intellectuals, primarily Czech, who attracted considerable sympathetic attention in the West. Many Czechs had heard of Havel and of Charter 77, primarily through foreign radio services and attacks in the controlled media, but the movement's antipolitical message provoked no mass response.[69] Slovakia, on the other hand, had only a few Charter 77 activists and little of the creative and artistic ferment that was characteristic of Czech culture. But in Slovakia hundreds of thousands of people took part in pilgrimages and risked signing a petition the government wanted to suppress, a petition that sought freedom, but under the aegis of the Catholic church.

In 1988, the hitherto antipolitical opposition in Prague began to turn to active political confrontation. A regular underground newspaper, *Lidové noviny* (People's News), began appearing in January 1988, and about the same time Petr Uhl, Jan Urban, and others established the East European Information Agency. Sections of the agency in Hungary, the Soviet Union, Poland, and Czechoslovakia exchanged news and disseminated it to Western agencies such as Radio Free Europe, the Voice of America, and the BBC. In October a group calling itself the Movement for Civil Liberties announced its manifesto, the first sentence of which read, "The time has come to get involved in politics."[70] Praising the antipolitical work of Charter 77, the signatories argued that the time had come for concrete work to create "Democracy for Everyone," which was the title of their manifesto. In 1988 Czech activists were putting their cards on the table, as Havel phrased it, moving from the advocacy of human rights into political activism, even though they knew this would mean confrontation with the government. "We need to fill up the jails," Jan Urban said.[71]

But as Havel also said, the regime was putting its cards on the table too. Prague party boss Miroslav Štěpán summed up the government's view in December 1988 as he personally supervised the spraying of demonstrators with water hoses on Human Rights day: "There will be no dialogue."[72] Party leader Miloš Jakeš claimed that Czechoslovakia supported Gorbachev's policies of perestroika and glasnost, and this may well have been one of the reasons many observers noted an increased willingness of Czech citizens to speak out in 1988. On the other hand, Jakeš got rid of Prime Minister L'ubomir Štrougal, who had been considered a moderating influence in the Husák/B'ilak years. Jakeš's new cadre was younger and less experienced than its predecessors, and its policies were more conflicted. The government permitted Alexander Dubček, the hero of 1968, to receive an honorary degree in Bologna, for example, and allowed somewhat more leeway in the kinds of plays produced. But it also rounded up oppositionists in preventative detention at every potentially tense moment. Whether these hesitant and poorly executed policies were an effort to introduce a Jaruzelskian dual strategy of carrot and stick or whether they were simply a result of incompetence is unimportant. They were too little and too inept, only convincing Timothy Garton Ash that the regime was exhibiting the fatal vacillations of an *ancien regime* in its last years. In November 1988 he predicted the Jakeš regime would not last another ten years—and probably many fewer.[73]

The revolutionary year of 1989 started in Czechoslovakia on a familiar note: the arrest and imprisonment of Václav Havel. One of the martyrs of the Prague Spring had been a young student named Jan Palach who had shocked the world by burning himself to death in Wenceslas Square on January 16, 1969. Palach was not the only one to attempt this sacrificial act, but his name became one of the symbolic rallying points of democratic initiatives throughout Eastern Europe. The Independent Association for the Defense of Human Rights in Bulgaria chose January 16, 1988, to announce its creation, for example, and when Jan Kavan established a publishing house in London to circulate Charter 77 writings abroad, he called it Palach Press.[74]

On January 15, 1989, some four thousand persons defied a government ban and attempted to gather at the place of Palach's sacrifice. They gathered a day early to highlight the differences between the pretentions of the government, which on this day was signing a new accord on human rights at the Vienna meeting of the Conference on Security and Cooperation in Europe (CSCE), and the realities of its repression. Undeterred by the potential for negative foreign reaction, Prague police charged the crowd, arresting almost one hundred persons and beating many more. For the next five days police did battle with street crowds ranging in size from five hundred to five thousand, fulfilling Jan Urban's hope by filling the jails with hundreds of demonstrators. Among them was Václav Havel. In February a Prague court sentenced him to nine months in prison for antisocial activities.

The newly restive activists did not consider Havel's sentencing a defeat, calculating that the trial of only Havel—none of the other arrested persons was put on trial—was a sign of weakness. The duration of the demonstrations was also encouraging. At his trial Havel spoke of how surprised and impressed he was when on January 16 many uninvolved passersby joined in to protest the brutality of the police.[75] Earlier he had warned the authorities that "the situation is more serious than they think." Now, he said, "I suddenly realized that the situation was more serious than I myself had thought."[76] Outside observers were not so sure. German journalists writing early in 1989 saw little hope that Czechoslovakia would democratize in the foreseeable future and could identify no potential political leaders among the opposition.[77] The authorities supported that view. As late as September 1989, at a time when East Germans were crowding into the West German embassy in Prague, Jan Fojtik told a visiting American official that Havel was "morally insignificant and had no popular appeal. Communism would prevail."[78]

In Czechoslovakia the battle of the holidays did not go as well for the opposition as it had in Hungary. The effort to commemorate and mourn the invasion by the Warsaw Pact on August 21, 1989, was actually less successful than the spontaneous demonstration of 1988. In Bratislava an effort of a handful of Slovak Charter 77 activists, among them Jan Čarnogursky and Miroslav Kusy, to lay flowers on the spot where Russians had killed a fifteen-year-old girl in 1968 ended quickly with their arrest. The incident received little publicity, and the demonstrators stayed in jail until the November events.[79] Neither the Soviet nor the Czechoslovak regime seemed willing to give an inch on their interpretation of the 1968 invasion as a rescue of socialism from counterrevolution, although by 1989 some Soviet historians and other public figures were admitting a Soviet mistake.

But the regime could not contain tension and anticipation. Everyone knew about the Polish election. Late in June four authors, including Havel, released a statement entitled "A Few Remarks" that called for freedom of assembly, a free media, and open discussion, among other things. Within two months twenty thousand persons had signed it, the first time such a document had obtained widespread support outside the narrow circle of dissidents.[80] Late in the summer, as East Germans crowded into their embassy in Prague, a harvest of little Trabant automobiles, abandoned on the streets each night, seemed to spring up each morning like mushrooms, providing visible proof to thousands of Prague citizens that events were on the move.[81] With huge demonstrations occurring in East Germany in October, many Czechs in the Moravian capital of Brno felt that surely something big would happen on October 28, the traditional celebration of the formation of the Czechoslovak republic in 1918, and they crowded into the center of town. The tension was almost unbearable, as for several hours police and citizens milled around together, but nothing happened. Perhaps in the spring, some hoped.[82]

On Friday evening, November 17, the official Socialist Youth Union, in cooperation with a newly formed independent student organization that had been recognized only in September, organized a student ceremony in Prague to commemorate the fiftieth anniversary of the murder of a Czech student by the Nazis.[83] It could have been expected that this gathering might produce a confrontation, especially since there had been minor demonstrations on November 15, but the authorities could not very well cancel this traditional anti-Nazi ceremony. The meeting provoked real interest among students because, for the first time, representatives of both the official student organization and its newly formed independent rival were going to be permitted to speak. When the rally first formed at a student living area, the speakers began to call for reforms, removal of the Jakeš regime, and democracy. Several thousand of the thirty thousand participants decided not to stop with lighting candles at the Vyšehrad cemetery, as originally planned, and spontaneously set out for the traditional demonstration point, Wenceslas Square. As they were coming up Narodny Street, near the Magic Lantern theater, the police blocked their way and brutally beat a number of students. The news quickly spread around Prague that many students had been badly injured and one even killed.

Later investigations showed that no one had been killed, but this rumor, reported soon by Radio Free Europe on information provided by Petr Uhl, provided the spark that set the nation aflame.[84]

The two main political movements that were shortly to take power formed themselves within little more than forty-eight hours of the November 17 events. On Sunday, November 19, a group of Slovak writers, artists, and intellectuals met in a Bratislava art gallery and formed Public Against Violence (Verejnost' proti nasiliu—VPN), while the previous evening in Prague, Havel convened a meeting of the main opposition groups, including even the revisionist Communist movement *Obroda* (Rebirth). The assembled company created Civic Forum (Občanské Fórum—OF) "as a spokesman on behalf of that part of the Czechoslovak public which is increasingly critical of the existing Czechoslovak leadership."[85]

If an independent society had been slow in forming in Czechoslovakia in comparison to Poland and Hungary, it almost caught up in the ten days following the November 17 events. On the very night of the confrontation actors in Prague called their colleagues from around their country. The next day a meeting of four hundred theater people voted to go on strike. The sign "On Strike" in front of theaters throughout the Czech lands had a powerful psychological impact. Theaters also provided convenient meeting places, as well as mimeograph machines and other equipment, to local Civic Forum and Public Against Violence groups, which formed within days in many places.

Naturally the Prague students, especially those in law and the arts, responded immediately to what they quickly began calling "the massacre." Students fanned out across the country with copies of a videotape showing the police beating the demonstrators. By Sunday videos of "the massacre" had arrived in Brno, Bratislava, and elsewhere. On Monday students throughout the country went on strike, formulated demands, and even created a computer network to keep in touch.[86] Within days small groups of students were knocking on the doors of factories and visiting villages to bring their message of freedom. Sometimes the people's militia did not let them into the factories, and sometimes peasants called them criminals and troublemakers; but the cumulative effect of these small teams speaking hitherto forbidden words was tremendous.[87] The presence of well-known theater personalities in the teams that went to the factories and villages provided convincing evidence to ordinary citizens that something very unusual was happening. Pushed by the students' enthusiasm and the growing response their strike and demonstrations had evoked, Czechs and Slovaks suddenly knew that after East Germany and Bulgaria it was their turn. On Monday night, November 20, hundreds of thousands of people jammed into Wenceslas Square chanting "This is it" and "Now is the time." Within just seventy-two hours, the seemingly vertical Czechoslovak domino had entered its accelerating arc of fall.

As huge crowds gathered every night in Wenceslas Square and similar crowds took to the streets in provincial cities like Brno and Bratislava, the party attempted to salvage the situation by jettisoning Jakeš and Fojtik and forming a new government.[88] Meanwhile, in a frantic series of nonstop meetings held in the Magic Lantern Theater, the newly formed Civic Forum proceeded in a remarkably open and sensible, albeit chaotic, way to create a new public program for Czechoslovakia, one not only consistent with Charter 77's notions of ethical pluralism but also with the practical notions of electoral democracy and, through the vigorous and persuasive prodding of Václav Klaus, the free market.[89]

Different people have different memories of when they became convinced the regime was finished.[90] Some thought so from the beginning, others remember when Alexander Dubček, looking, as Garton Ash puts it, as if he stepped out of an old black-and-white photograph, appeared together with Havel on the balcony of the Socialist party publishing house in the middle of Wenceslas Square. The crowds cheered him ecstatically, honoring him as a symbol of honorable resistance to the Soviets, even if they found his idea of socialism with a human face passé. Others cite the moment when Prague party leader Štěpán tried to rally the workers of a huge local factory against the students by telling them, "We do not intend to be dictated to by children." "We are not children," the workers roared back. Then there was the moment when the people's militia, which played a very important role in the Communist seizure of power in 1948, came from the provinces into Prague and Brno but proved completely unusable, ashamed, as interviewed participants said on television, to be there. And finally there was the two-hour general strike, called for lunch hour on November 27 so as not to interfere with work. (It was a very Czech revolution—the Prague demonstrations did not start until after working hours for the same reason.)

The great success of the general strike convinced even the last doubters that this was indeed it.[91] Two days later the federal assembly overwhelmingly voted to revoke the constitutional articles guaranteeing the party's leading role, which had been one of the prime demands of the student strikers from the beginning. When a week later the new prime minister, Ladislav Adamec, put forward a so-called coalition government containing almost no oppositionists, the Civic Forum was able to force its rejection. On December 9 Gustav Husák finally resigned from his by now purely symbolic office of president, and the next day, only three weeks after the initial student march, a coalition government dominated by non-Communists took power. After brief negotiations and some constitutional fudging, Alexander Dubček was co-opted as the chairman of the national assembly, which thereupon unanimously elected Václav Havel the new president of Czechoslovakia. On January 1, 1990, Havel opened his address to the nation with these words: "I do not think you appointed me to this office for me, of all people, to lie to you." Thus did the end of what Garton Ash calls "the most delightful" of 1989's revolutions, the velvet revolution, pose a newly difficult challenge for its inspiration and leader: living in truth at the top.[92]

The End of the Ceauşescus

Nicolae Ceauşescu lived at the top for twenty-five years, but never in truth. In the 1980s his regime became one of the world's most notorious dictatorships, and he himself became as far removed from reality as any ruler in modern times. During this period Ceauşescu bent the entire country to the task of paying off Romania's foreign debt. The variety and pettiness of the devices he implemented to do this were endless. To increase the export of foodstuffs, which would provide hard currency, he introduced rationing in 1981. Ceauşescu and his wife Elena were themselves fanatical about their diets. In 1982, after accusing Romanians of being too fat, he created a Rational Nourishment Commission to reduce the population's caloric intake through a "program of scientific nourishment." For the rest of the 1980s the food situation for ordinary Romanians deteriorated so dramatically that by the end of the decade simply getting any kind of food at all required substantial effort for every family.

Energy was another enervating problem. The Romanian economy expended about twice the energy per capita of its neighbors, but, due to the high concentration of grossly inefficient heavy industry, little of this energy found its way into households. In order to make sure industry had enough, Ceauşescu forbade citizens from having more than one 40-watt light bulb per room. Cities and towns were barely lit in the evenings. In the winter the common central heating plants kept the temperatures in apartments in the mid-fifties—that is, when heat was available, which was sometimes only a few hours a day. Apartment dwellers in the cement urban conglomerations favored by Communist planners everywhere could routinely go without hot water for a month. In a few cases people froze to death in their own apartments.[93]

In a renewed effort to add labor to the already fully employed economy, Ceauşescu trotted out his natalist policy of the 1960s.[94] Despite laws against abortion, by the early 1980s Romania was experiencing more than one abortion per live birth (oral contraceptives were illegal, and other contraceptives were not available). Cracking down once again, Ceauşescu ordered random gynecological examinations of Romanian women at their workplaces to insure that they were having their menstrual cycle and, if not, that they carried their pregnancies to term. Divorce became almost impossible, and married couples without children had to pay a special tax. The death rate of women went up, mainly through botched abortions, and the number of abandoned and orphaned children increased dramatically.

Ceauşescu's efforts to conserve foreign currency went to humiliating extremes. International employees had to remit half their earnings to the government. Approved and loyal scholars attending foreign meetings received no foreign currency while abroad. Yet if they wished to stay overnight in the facilities of a Romanian embassy while en route home (by Romanian airlines, of course), they had to pay hotel rates in foreign currency. On one occasion, a personal aide of General Ilie Ceauşescu, Nicolae's brother, spent the night in a railroad station when he could not come up with the required foreign currency on his way home from a conference.

All of these measures, and more, reflected Ceaușescu's adamant belief that the way to economic progress was through the vision and rational planning of the party. "We cannot let each enterprise produce according to its wishes or contract what it wants," he said at the 1984 party congress. Progress will come only with "an increase in the role played by the state," and, he promised, the security police would "take measures against anyone who violates order, the laws and norms of social coexistence." But Ceaușescu's "norms of social coexistence" were in fact simply those schemes he devised to force Romanians to follow his orders. Is productivity down? Introduce a piecework system that has the effect of lowering wages by 25 percent. Energy sector not producing enough electricity? Decree a "militarized work regime" in the electrical generating industry whereby directors would share responsibility with military officers for "the strict observance of technological exploitation and maintenance norms." Production falling in the coal mines? Decree twenty-four-hour, seven-day-a-week work schedules. Workers will have two days off for the May day parades? Order that they have to make it up in overtime. Food supplies dwindling? Direct all users of private plots to supply the state with at least one cow, one pig, sixty chickens, ten rabbits, one swarm of bees, and four kilograms of silkworm cocoons a year on threat of losing their plots.[95] And what about the food shortages, the lines, the brownouts, and the rusted-out buses that were hauling Romania back into the nineteenth century? Nonsense. The official statistics showed that the consumption of agricultural goods was growing every year "in accordance with the needs of the population." And what if the statistics did not show this in reality? Make them up. In October 1989 Ceaușescu announced that grain production that year had reached sixty million tons. In fact, figures released after the revolution showed it had been fewer than seventeen million tons.[96]

The oppressive conditions in Romania made it very difficult for a democratic opposition to arise there. This was not because of lack of discontent, even outbursts of rage. In 1977, for example, massive strikes broke out in the Jiu mining region, but heavy-handed repression and some wage increases restored order. The leaders of the strike simply disappeared. In 1979 some two thousand persons across the country created the Free Trade Union of the Working People of Romania, but it lasted only two weeks before it was savagely repressed. Eight years later an announcement of a wage cut infuriated workers in the Red Truck factory in Brașov. Even though the Red Truck factory was one of the most favored manufacturing plants in Romania in which almost half the workers were affiliated with the Communist youth league, the meat ration for a worker there in 1987 was fewer than twenty pounds for the entire year.[97] On November 15, 1987, several thousand frustrated workers marched to the center of the city singing a patriotic Romanian song from the revolution of 1848, and proceeded to sack the local party headquarters. Once again vigorous repression put the outbreak down, and the leaders disappeared. The Romanian press made no mention of the incident or of other reported riots and demonstrations in other cities.

In 1983 Ceauşescu ordered that all typewriters be registered with the police, who were to keep a sample page typed from each machine on file in order to be able to trace samizdat publications, of which, therefore, there were very few.[98] Abroad the Securitate apparently murdered regime opponents, and three consecutive heads of the Romanian section of Radio Free Europe died under mysterious circumstances.[99] Whereas in Czechoslovakia and Bulgaria Gorbachev's accession to power obliged regimes at least to mouth the principles of perestroika and glasnost, Ceauşescu made it perfectly clear there would be no such nonsense in Romania. Gorbachev received a markedly cool reception on his visit in 1987, at which time Ceauşescu stressed that each socialist country had the right to "decide its own development, path and forms."[100]

The most notable sign of Ceauşescu's megalomania was his penchant for massive construction projects. In one of these, he tore down one of the largest monasteries in southeastern Europe, a decorated eighteenth-century structure, in order to build a huge complex called the Center of the National Councils of Workers' Democracy. Its main feature was innumerable meeting halls, the largest of which would hold twelve thousand persons and would have a dome three times as large as St. Peter's in Rome, had it been completed. Outside Bucharest he reinstated the Bucharest/Danube Canal project abandoned after Stalin's death, running a local river completely dry in the process and killing all marine life in it. His most massive project he planted smack in the middle of Bucharest: the House of the Republic, an almost inconceivably large palace that his epigones compared to Nero's palace in Rome. To do so, he summarily evicted thousands of persons from their homes and razed eighteen churches, including five historic structures, as well as scores of historically significant houses and buildings. Today the gigantic building, which covers several city blocks, stands completed in outside structure but not on the inside, a grandiloquent monument to Ceauşescu's utter lack of feeling for the human dimension of life and his desperate need for contrived and unassailable grandeur.

Consistent with his dismissal of human needs and with his simplistic concept of proletarian modernity, in the mid-1980s Ceauşescu undertook the reconstruction of the centers of Romanian towns as part of a moribund plan from the early 1970s for "systematizing" the Romanian countryside. Dinu Giurescu writes that in the 1980s the centers of twenty-nine towns, including many sizable ones, were 85 to 90 percent razed. In place of the varied and often charming structures characteristic of Balkan towns, box-like apartment buildings filled with small apartments assigned strictly on the basis of family size were built.[101] In the space of about a decade, Ceauşescu indelibly changed the basic character of Romanian towns.

In the countryside the analogous plan was to bring the city to the country by consolidating the thirteen thousand Romanian villages, in which just under 50 percent of the population still lived, into about seven thousand villages grouped around five or six hundred administrative centers.[102] "Old-fashioned" and "inefficient" individual peasant homes would be bulldozed and replaced by "modern" and "efficient" two- and three-story cement apartment houses, thus bringing all Romanians together, Ceauşescu rhapsodized, into one harmonious class of working people, a truly socialist society.

By the time Ceauşescu was removed from power, only a few village resettlements had taken place, but the international backlash against this brutal plan was substantial. The focus of much of the attention was the allegation by Hungary that the resettlement plan was designed to destroy the Hungarian nationality in Transylvania. This was an exaggeration, since as far as is known the only villages actually bulldozed were Romanian and the suffering that could be anticipated from the plan would be spread throughout the entire country. But the Hungarians were quite right that Ceauşescu had every intention of denationalizing the Hungarian minority in Transylvania and had been engaged in that project for many years.

For the first ten years or so after World War II the Hungarian minority in Transylvania, which numbers more than two million persons, received fairly good treatment, and ethnic relations in Transylvania were not particularly strained.[103] The Hungarian Autonomous Region, founded in 1952, was not really autonomous and did not include all the Hungarians, but it did at least recognize Hungarians as a separate people and Hungarians were permitted their cultural and even political organizations. Because of these benefits, Gheorghiu-Dej declared the nationality problem in Romania solved as of January 1953.[104] But after the Hungarian Revolution of 1956 Romanian-Hungarian relations deteriorated. In 1959 Georghiu-Dej merged the Hungarian-language university of Cluj (Bolyai University) with its Romanian counterpart (Babeş University) and began chipping away at the Hungarian Autonomous Region. It was finally abolished in 1968.

During the 1970s criticism of Romania because of its assimilationist pressure on the Hungarian minority in Transylvania grew, not only because of increasing complaints from Hungary, but also because of the growth of international interest in human rights touched off by the Helsinki accords and by President Jimmy Carter's emphasis on the subject. Ceauşescu, always thin-skinned and committed to an elaborate historical myth of constant Romanian presence in the Carpathian basin since Roman times, fought the growing international criticisms with those weapons at his disposal—propaganda, denunciations, and disinformation.[105] Using as his justification the nationalist argument that Hungarians were foreigners aiming to destabilize Romania, he narrowed the scope of Hungarian-language education, limited the number of bilingual signs, intensified pressure on Hungarian churches, and periodically announced that the nationality problem in Transylvania was solved, but to no avail. By 1988 numerous international organizations, ranging from Amnesty International and the Conference on Security and Cooperation in Europe (CSCE) to the United States Department of State, had cited Romania for civil rights abuses. In that year Ceaușescu renounced Romania's right to most favored nation trade treatment by the United States to avoid a full-scale investigation of his regime by Congress, even though this cost his export-oriented economy more than $250 million in trade. Early in 1989 Romania refused to sign a CSCE agreement on human rights, and later in the year Ceaușescu placed Romania's representative to the United Nations Commission on Human Rights under house arrest because in Geneva he released a devastating report on abuses in Romania.

Overt dissent appeared in 1989. Most courageous were the defiant letters of Doina Cornea, a specialist in French literature who had long since lost her position at the university in Cluj.[106] Echoing the antipolitical themes of the 1970s, Cornea's open letter to Ceaușescu accused him of crushing "people's innermost being, humiliating their aspirations and their legitimate claims, humiliating their conscience, [and] compelling them, under pressure of terror, to accept the lie as truth and the truth as a lie." Mircea Dinescu, a poet who came under suspicion when he praised perestroika and glasnost in a visit to the Soviet Union in 1988, lost his editorial position and publicly complained. The poet Anna Blandiana also raised her voice in protest. Three editors from *România Liberă* (Free Romania), Romania's second most important official newspaper after the party's *Scinteia* (Spark), were sentenced to death when they tried to publish an anti-Ceaușescu edition of their paper in the spring of 1989 (the revolution intervened to prevent the sentence from being carried out).[107] Most striking, six former senior officials in the Romanian Communist party, including a founding member of the party, ninety-four-year-old Constantin Pirvulescu, wrote Ceaușescu an open letter enumerating his enormous failures, from his building projects through the resettlement plans to the destruction of agriculture and the forcible reduction of living standards.[108]

But nothing moved Ceaușescu. Isolated internationally, his economy reeling, with letters from impressive dissenters beaming back into Romania from Radio Free Europe, he showed no signs of wavering. Late in November 1989, after the Berlin Wall had fallen, after Zhivkov had resigned, and after street demonstrations had begun in Prague, the Romanian Communist party held its Fourteenth Party Congress. Ceaușescu gave the traditional six-hour speech interrupted by "stormy applause," criticized his neighbors for not taking a socialist approach to their problems, and accepted another unanimous election as president. With the dissidents under house arrest, the country kept quiet by the ubiquitous and brutal Securitate, and Ceaușescu apparently steady on course, it seemed unlikely that Romania would experience the same kind of unrest that had swept regimes out elsewhere.

But it did. Even more brittle than its neighbors, hollow at its center, and out of touch with reality, the Ceaușescu regime disintegrated overnight when the moment of truth came. The incident that began the explosion was a decision taken in May 1989 to transfer Hungarian Reformed minister László Tőkés from his church in Timişoara to a remote village.[109] Tőkés had aroused the wrath of the authorities by criticizing the resettlement plan, correctly arguing that it was an effort to destroy the peasantry, and by pointing out violations of civil liberties and calling for ethnic solidarity. For many months he had successfully resisted the order to leave Timişoara, using the argument that according to the rules of the Hungarian Reformed church only his congregation could dismiss him.[110] On December 10 he notified his congregation he had received the final order to move by the fifteenth, whereupon the parishioners set up a nightly vigil at the church. When by the fifteenth the crowd had grown to about a thousand persons, including many Romanians and Serbs who live in the ethnically mixed city, the authorities were unable to evict Tőkés forcibly. The next day crowds, particularly students and young people, gathered in the streets of Timişoara, until by early evening five thousand persons surrounded, but did not enter, party headquarters. No shots were fired. Early on the seventeenth the army, having deployed its forces but still not attacking the people, sent military bands to march in the street in an effort to calm the situation. During the day several skirmishes took place, including the setting on fire of at least one tank.

On that same day, December 17, Ceauşescu, meeting with his chief advisors in Bucharest, severely criticized his commanders for not acting decisively, repeatedly demanding that the demonstrators be mowed down à la Tiananmen Square.[111] He sent the secretary of the central committee in charge of the army to Timişoara to take charge. About 5:00 P.M. that afternoon the shooting began. During the night of December 17–18 the army conducted a massacre in Timişoara. At the time it was said that four thousand persons were killed, perhaps even ten thousand. Although the number was actually far smaller—the official count announced in June 1990 by the new government was ninety-seven—the discovery of hastily dug graves containing mutilated bodies a few days later gave revolting evidence that a serious bloodletting had occurred.[112] Reassured, Ceauşescu left on December 18 for a scheduled two-day visit to Iran.

But the demonstrations did not stop. In Timişoara a general strike completely shut down the city on December 19. By the end of that day the army began to withdraw. The professional officer corps in Romania was none too happy with Ceauşescu, who did not trust them. Naively confident in the superior socialist morality of proletarians, Ceauşescu had instituted a program early in the 1980s of rapidly training reliable workers from factories to be officers and immediately placing them in command of units. He thought this would make their loyalty more certain. What it did, of course, was to alienate the professional officers. The army was poorly equipped, especially in comparison with the Securitate, and its troops often were used for demeaning nonmilitary uses, such as bringing in crops or even working in factories. In mid-1989, for no announced reason, promotions for that year were canceled, leaving many of the most able officers in a highly irritated state. The army may have decided as early as December 19 that it did not want to continue to shoot Romanians in support of Ceauşescu. On the evening of December 21 it had become quite clear that the army had abandoned the royal family. On December 22 a Democratic Front Committee assumed power in Timişoara. The army had completely withdrawn.

While Ceauşescu was in Iran, demonstrations and strikes spread to other cities. On December 20 demonstrations began in Arad, for example.[113] The only information that appeared in the Romanian media concerning these events was the vague admonition to reject the "offensive by reactionary and imperialist circles." By the time Ceauşescu returned and went on television to praise the army for carrying out "to the full its duty to the country, the people, and the gains of socialism," the crisis had become extremely serious.

Ceauşescu apparently was beginning to grasp the danger. He undertook to salvage the situation through repression, by playing the nationalist card, and by rallying the working class, in which he continued to believe he had real support. In his December 20 speech Ceauşescu announced that any further outbursts would meet with bloody retribution, for which he would take full responsibility. By December 21 demonstrators in other parts of the country, such as Cluj, were being fired upon. To rally anti-Hungarian feeling, Ceauşescu claimed that "hooligans" and "fascists" from abroad had instigated the demonstrations. One report claims that government organizers quickly put together two trainloads of workers from Craiova and sent them to Timişoara to provide a show of proletarian opposition to the insurgents. When the Timişoara committee received the workers with bread and salt (the traditional peasant gesture of welcome) and told them that everything was under control and that Timişoara opposed Ceauşescu, they went back to Craiova.[114]

Ceauşescu ordered party units in factories around the country to condemn the Timişoara "bandits," although thus far, with the exception of his own speech, Romanian news media had not actually described what was happening there. This strategy did not work everywhere. In Cluj, for example, young workers from the industrial area behind the railroad station marched toward the center of the city on December 21 shouting "Down with Ceauşescu." But when many factories did comply in the routine manner to which Ceauşescu was accustomed, he decided—perhaps encouraged by men around him who saw a chance to get rid of him—to show his control of the situation by conducting a mass meeting in the center of Bucharest on December 21.

A mass meeting of this kind in Romania was a highly staged event. The first ten rows or so of "citizens" facing the tribune would be members of the Securitate in civilian clothes, unarmed in case they got any strange ideas. Workers were recruited by organizers in factories, given special admission cards, assembled in designated spots, and otherwise given the day off. Security forces surrounded all the entrances to the meeting place and admitted only those with cards. In this way sometimes fifty thousand or more "enthusiastic" Ceaușescu supporters could be rallied, as they had been only a month before on the occasion of the Fourteenth Party Congress. But this time, perhaps in the confusion of a last-minute event that was canceled once and then scheduled again, perhaps because plotters deliberately arranged it, perhaps because student protesters created a disturbance, or perhaps because of spontaneous combustion, during Ceaușescu's speech first some whistling, then shouts of "Ceaușescu dictator" unaccountably broke out at the periphery of the crowd. Some say that firecrackers were set off. Astonished television watchers across the country saw pictures of the crowd raising fists, then Ceaușescu looking up startled, then an ineffectual gesture of quieting the crowd, then Elena saying, "Be calm! Be calm!" then a blank screen. In about two minutes the picture came on again, now showing Ceaușescu alone, but the damage had been done. Romanians all over the country, some of whom had begun to demonstrate in their own cities, saw the "genius of the Carpathians" waver, and they smelled blood.

The events of the next three days were then and remain today enormously confusing.[115] Fundamentally what happened is that the army decided to side with the people in the streets, probably in cooperation with a group of plotters who quickly arranged to form the National Salvation Front (Frontul Salvării Naționale—FSN). Serious fighting seemed to break out in the center of Bucharest on December 22, the day the self-selected leaders of the FSN appeared on television to proclaim themselves the new provisional government. This fighting, which produced an enormous expenditure of small arms ammunition and led to the accidental burning to the ground of the university library, was ostensibly between the army, now loyal to the nation, and the Securitate forces, still loyal to Ceaușescu. The latter allegedly were bolstered by teams of highly trained Arab and other terrorists. Throughout the country, towns armed themselves to fend off these terrorists.[116] But none ever appeared. Since then observers have wondered why, if there was a real struggle against opponents of the new regime going on, the only building on Palace Square not marked with bullet holes was precisely the one containing the FSN leaders; or why the television tower that permitted the provisional government to get its message to the world was not disabled by a presumably well-trained Securitate; or why, over the next two years, Securitate people seemed to end up in high governmental positions.

By the evening of December 22 crowds were threatening the central committee building in Palace Square. Ceaușescu, still somehow believing in his powers to command the masses, tried to speak to the people, but the microphone did not work, and it became apparent that the crowds were entering the building. Along with Elena, Ceaușescu managed to flee by helicopter only a few steps ahead of the angry insurgents. The Ceaușescus had several options at this point—to fly to a prepared military location and fight back, to escape abroad, or, apparently as Nicolae himself preferred, to fly to an area like his native Oltenia, where he felt the workers supported him.[117] Instead, the helicopter that was supposedly taking them to safety landed before reaching whatever was to be its destination. After a farcical commandeering of a passing truck the Ceauşescus fell into the hands of the new government. Three days later, on December 25, after a kangaroo trial that lasted nine hours, Nicolae and Elena Ceauşescu were found guilty of genocide and shot to death by a firing squad.[118]

The full story of the events of the Romanian revolution has yet to emerge. At the two extremes are the plot theory and the elemental emanation of popular will theory.[119] Some believe that the entire operation, from the demonstrations in Timişoara to Ceauşescu's death, were the work of a plot put in train some time before by the eventual leaders of the FSN. In its extreme form, such as the view that the Hungarians were behind this plot, this type of explanation is more a reflection of the propensity for plot theories among some elements of Balkan society than it is a likely scenario. But less extreme forms of the plot theory are not at all implausible. It does seem likely that some measure of previous planning, or at least laying out of scenarios and possible options if an opportune moment should arrive, did occur. The other extreme is the myth assiduously maintained by the FSN that the revolution was a spontaneous outburst of the heroic Romanian people, who granted the FSN the heavy responsibility to introduce democracy to Romania. Given the utility of such a theory for government and the fact that almost the entire leadership of the new regime were Communists who ran their new country with a heavy hand, one may also doubt the accuracy of that claim.

Wherever the truth lies, it would be a mistake to concentrate on conscious actions put into effect by plotters. The Romanian revolution was accomplished by the spontaneous and self-activating actions of hundreds of thousands of people across Romania who acted courageously at a time when it was not at all clear that several decades of serious repression was about to end. Some of these people paid with their lives, the only people to do so in East Europe's miraculous year. Their sacrifice suggests that Romanians wanted to overcome the humiliation of the dark years with at least as much passion as did the Czechs, the East Germans, or any of the other peoples of the region. Perhaps the summary view of the Romanian experience that is closest to the mark was the perceptive observation of Nicu Ceauşescu, the ne'er-do-well son of the deposed rulers who by mid-1991 was the only member of the family or its entourage still in prison. He characterized the events in Romania as a "coup d'état that took place against the background of a revolution, or a popular revolt."[120]

Nicu Ceauşescu, for all his faults, understood the essence of the revolutions of 1989. Whatever specific events happened in the various countries involved, all of them were made possible by people throwing off forty years of passivity. The popular revolutions of 1989 produced many potent visual images of the people in action: dancers on the Berlin Wall; thousands of people in Sofia maintaining candle-lit vigils; a Romanian demonstrator in Cluj baring his chest to armed soldiers, who subsequently shot him to death. Other memorable images included the somber and impressive face of Tadeusz Mazowiecki as he took office as the first non-Communist premier in almost forty years, Ceauşescu's surprisingly ineffectual hand gestures when the crowd began jeering, and the gruesome pictures of his bloody remains.

Symbolically the most powerful of them all was the picture of Alexander Dubček, the living relic of failed socialism, and Václav Havel, the embodiment of the impossible hope, waving together to hundreds of thousands of Czechoslovaks gathered below them in Wenceslas Square: two bookends to twenty years of economic futility and moral failure cheered by the primal force of a liberated people. Dubček was the symbol of resistance to an unwanted imposition and Havel the symbol of hope in a much wanted future, but it was the people cheering them that turned the processes unleashed by Gorbachev and nurtured by Polish and Hungarian reformers into revolution. Their leaders wavered, the people caught a whiff of freedom in the air, and they reacted. "This is the time," the Czechs chanted, tired of not just the dreariness they lived in, although they were tired of it, but humiliated by the thousands of petty restraints the authoritarian regimes imposed on their lives. Yes, they wanted sausages and bananas and fresh air in the literal sense, but more than that they wanted to step into what they dreamed would be the fresh air of freedom. Chanting words like "Freedom," "Democracy," and "Solidarity," 1989's equivalent to the "Liberty, Equality, and Fraternity" of 1789, hundreds of thousands of ordinary citizens, rarely mobilized before or since, toppled the rotted Communist regimes of East Germany, Czechoslovakia, and Romania, and to a certain extent Bulgaria too. Cheering Dubček and Havel, for one magnificent moment hundreds of thousands of Czechs merged with millions of people throughout Eastern Europe in two ecstatic if short-lived sentiments—joy that the old regime was on its way out and hope that a better future was on its way in.

6

1990 and 1991: The First Two Years of a Long Time

On December 25, 1991, two years to the day after the shooting of the Ceaușescus completed the dramatic events of 1989 in Eastern Europe, Mikhail Gorbachev resigned as president of the Soviet Union in order to permit its constituent parts to come together under the loose umbrella of a newly created Commonwealth of Independent States. After forty years of being the bête noire of the international system, the Soviet Union simply disappeared. It is far too early to know what will be the outcome of this momentous collapse of the original home of the hyperrationalist experiment, but it is absolutely certain that troubled times will be the fate of those trying to create new social structures in the former Soviet Union and that the entire international system faces an uncertain and potentially dangerous period. Still, it is difficult not to agree with Gorbachev's own assessment of his accomplishment:[1]

> Fate had it that when I found myself at the head of the state it was already clear that all was not well in the country. . . . The society was suffocating in the vise of the command-bureaucratic system, doomed to serve ideology and bear the terrible burden of the arms race. It had reached the limit of its possibility. . . . We could not go on living like that. . . . [R]enovating the country turned out to be far more complicated than could be expected. However, what has been done ought to be given its due. This society acquired freedom, [and] liberated itself politically and spiritually. . . . The totalitarian system has been eliminated. . . . The movement to a diverse economy has started. . . . We opened ourselves to the world.

Gorbachev had his limitations. He did not realize that the party was unreformable; he neither understood nor approved of the market; he did not grasp the visceral power of ethnic feeling; and he was unwilling to push his own reforms beyond a certain point. But these limitations do not dim his accomplishment. He cleared away the superstructure of the totalitarian system so that new societies might be built on their ruins. We do not yet know the shape of these new societies. The frenetic modern world, where communications across continents take microseconds, has a yearning for quick results and instant analysis. Societal change on the scale facing Eastern Europe and the Soviet Union, however, takes time. Many years will pass before we have a firm grasp of what processes the revolutions of 1989 and 1991 have unleashed, and some of the initial efforts that seemed so important when they occurred will prove to have been false starts. But in the two years between Ceauşescu's death and Gorbachev's resignation, East Europeans entered into the process of pluralism with enthusiasm and panache. Indeed, they had no choice: with both the antirational and the hyperrational experiments at an end, pluralism was the only option that remained.

In Western societies, however controversial the issues and however bitter the debate, public contestation takes place within a structure and using a discourse that all sides take for granted. In Eastern Europe after 1989, however, all the issues came onto the agenda at once, including the discourse and the structure. For that reason, the first two years of the entry of Eastern Europe into the pluralist world were confusing and difficult. The feeling that important structural decisions were being made lent an urgency to public life that contrasted starkly with the deadness of public life only months or years before. It is impossible in the compass of this chapter to discuss all the issues of the initial post-1989 period. They will take their own book. Instead this chapter concentrates on three issues perceived during those two years as being the most important ones in creating the new pluralism in Eastern Europe: the creation of a functioning democratic polity; transformation of the economy from centralized planning to market mechanisms; and ethnopolitics.

Elections

The new pluralism began in Eastern Europe with elections. Whatever demands opposition groups had before 1989, each agreed that one reform came before all others: free and open elections. These were seen as good in their own right, but even more, they were considered the essential first step leading toward economic reform. If only the Communist party's domination could be eliminated through democratic elections, the opposition thought, the new governments, unhindered by the obsolete ideologies and dreams of the totalitarian past, would be able to restore vitality to the economy. The belief that only a freely elected government could command the loyalty needed to introduce painful economic reforms was perhaps naive, since democratically elected governments are not always able to take difficult but necessary economic steps. But after forty years of government without popular mandate, only bona fide democratic elections held any hope of restoring the shattered legitimacy of state apparatuses that had ceased to command any respect. One of the first things every new government in Eastern Europe did, therefore, was to organize elections.

With the exception of Poland, the formerly Communist regimes of Eastern Europe, along with the Yugoslav republics of Croatia and Slovenia, all conducted their first freely contested parliamentary elections in more than a generation during the three-month period between March 25 and June 17, 1990.[2] In Hungary the distinct personalities of the main opposition organizations and their division into two main camps had already created a party structure by the end of 1989. Widespread acceptance of the new constitutional arrangements created by the roundtable and modified by the referendum of November lent an initial normalcy to Hungarian politics. Elsewhere the suddenness of the events, the short time available for preparation, and the lack of existing electoral rules or traditions made these first free elections in forty years hectic and confusing events.

Parties bloomed in incredible profusion—pluralism with a vengeance. Observers from the Commission for Security and Cooperation in Europe counted eighty-two parties in Romania and over forty in Bulgaria. In every country all parties, without exception, favored the introduction of democratic norms, and almost all, including Communists, advocated marketizing economic changes as well. In their other characteristics, however, the parties broke down into five types. First were the Communists, their reformed successors, usually called the Socialist party, and their satellite parties. Second were the unified representatives of civil society, which were of two subtypes: those who saw themselves as a movement rather than a political party, such as Solidarity and Civic Forum/Public Against Violence, and those that were coalitions of a number of newly emerging parties, such as the Demos in Slovenia or the Union of Democratic Forces in Bulgaria. Third were the democratic parties of the center, such as the Hungarian Democratic Forum or the Croatian Democratic Union, which called upon older visions of national glory, tended toward populist rhetoric, and tapped Catholic allegiances. Fourth were a number of new parties emerging out of the pre-1989 democratic opposition that favored Western individualism and neoconservative forms of marketization but that at the same time emphasized social issues. Prominent among these were the Alliance of Free Democrats and FIDESz in Hungary as well as the Slovenian Liberal party. Fifth, many prewar parties, like the Social Democrats or the Christian Democrats, even the Smallholders party in Hungary and the National Peasant party in Romania, reappeared on the scene. Of lesser significance were the large number of small special interest parties. Besides the various green parties, which had real claims to public attention, the most piquant of these tiny parties was the Party of the Friends of Beer in Czechoslovakia.

The amount of time these parties had to organize themselves, define their programs, and find plausible candidates was very short. The most sophisticated campaigns were probably those run in Hungary, but everywhere enthusiasm replaced the stultifying pro forma character of elections in the Communist era. In every country newspapers began to appear in profusion, particularly in Romania, where within six months over one thousand new papers and magazines sprouted. Television, on the other hand, remained in the hands of the authorities, whether they were former oppositionists like the Civic Forum in Prague or recycled Communists like the National Salvation Front in Bucharest. State television gave the main electoral contestants air time, but usually not with entire fairness. Newspapers that did not back the government party often found it difficult to get newsprint, a problem that papers backing the National Salvation Front in Romania or the Bulgarian Socialist party in Bulgaria did not seem to face. Still, with the exception of Romania, international observers found the elections fairly conducted.[3]

The public took heartily to the new phenomenon. With the exception of Hungary, where turnout was disappointing, over 80 percent of the electorate voted. The revived prewar parties and the Communist satellite parties did poorly everywhere, as did the splinter groups. The Hungarian Smallholders party, which campaigned on a single issue—return to peasants of land seized forty years earlier—had the best showing among the old parties, getting 11 percent of the vote in Hungary. Christian Democrats did best in Slovakia, where they got 15 to 20 percent. Christian Democrats got only 5 percent of the vote in Hungary but that gave them twenty-one seats in the national assembly, just enough to permit them, in the time-honored way of strategically positioned small European parties, to exercise an influence out of all proportion to their size by entering into the governing coalition. The Greens, who brought horrific environmental problems to the public's attention and whom many believed would do well, fared poorly.

The most intriguing aspect of the elections was how closely their results mapped the imperial boundaries many had thought destroyed by World War I. One of the conceits of the early Bolsheviks, as well as of the enthusiastic postwar Stalinists in Eastern Europe, was that by destroying private property and seizing control of public discourse they could create a truly new person, a new Soviet man who would cast aside the political culture of the past. Even in the West the possibility of reforming human character through scientifically designed propaganda techniques was taken seriously, as the popularity of the term *brainwashing* suggests. It had long been clear that these efforts had failed. But not many realized that East European societies constituted a palimpsest containing long-lasting and semipermanent impressions of a dimly remembered past. The outcome of the first free elections in more than fifty years suggested that patterns of political culture are far more enduring than kinetic and impatient moderns have wanted to believe.

In southeastern Europe, the former Ottoman lands in which Orthodoxy survived as the dominant national faith—Romania, Bulgaria, and Serbia (to be discussed in Chapter 7)—the victors were the old Communist parties, reformed in name and perhaps in the Bulgarian case in practice but still projecting a community-oriented, paternalistic style reminiscent of an Orthodox Christian past. In the former Habsburg lands the results divided along the old division between Austrian and Hungarian dominions. In the former, which included Slovenia, the Czech lands, and parts of Poland, movements representing civil society were most successful. Solidarity won of course in Poland, while in the Czech lands Civic Forum won, as did the Demos in Slovenia. But in the formerly Hungarian land of Croatia and in Hungary itself, where the aristocratic parties of the Hungarian nobility had dominated in the nineteenth and early twentieth centuries, the parties that won obtained a good deal of their support from their emphasis on the oligarchic national past. Slovakia, which was part of Hungary before World War I and, like Croatia, had a fascist government during World War II, had an interesting mixture of results. Public Against Violence, the Slovak version of Civic Forum, won the election, but it received only about half the percentage of votes that the Civic Forum got in Bohemia and Moravia. The more conservative, nationally oriented parties, the Christian Democratic Movement and the Slovak National party, together outnumbered the Public Against Violence in the Slovak National Council.

Communist Retreads Set Up Shop in Romania

Within days of the installation of the National Salvation Front (FSN) in Romania, observers began to complain that it looked a lot like the old Communist party without Ceauşescu.[4] The two main figures of the FSN, Ion Iliescu and Petre Român, came from impeccable Communist backgrounds. Iliescu had been one of the stars of the party in the 1960s, and in the 1970s he rose as high as candidate member of the politburo. Inside the party Iliescu was identified with reform, although he never made any public statement to that effect, so he never achieved the highest rank. On the other hand, neither did he fall into disgrace. During the 1980s he remained in limbo as director of the State Technical Publishing House, considered by insiders to be a person capable of running the country if an opportunity arose. Român was the son of a lifelong Communist and Spanish Civil War veteran. After living a privileged youth he became an engineering professor, which he was at the time of the revolution. Young, handsome, and aggressive, Român liked to be surrounded by technocrats and saw himself as mediating technical solutions with the West.

An organized democratic opposition had not existed in Romania prior to the revolution—it had to create itself afterward. On the formal side, many of the old parties of interwar Romania re-established themselves, including the National Peasant party, the National Liberal party, and the Social Democratic party. The Hungarian minority in Transylvania formed the Hungarian Democratic Union, and dozens of smaller groups put together their own minuscule organizations. But these parties of the past, the most important of which were headed by quite old men who returned from emigration to pick up where they and their predecessors had left off forty years earlier, were not the source of democratic innovation in Romania.

A few days after the revolution a few sociologists and other intellectuals in Bucharest began the Romanian pluralization process by creating the Group for Social Dialogue. The express purpose of the group was to create a civil society, something completely lacking under Ceauşescu's tyranny. The group began publishing *22*, a weekly journal that quickly became Romania's leading critical voice, held public forums offering divergent viewpoints, conducted public opinion surveys, and published its own independent reports on current events. Within a few months, however, newspapers supporting the FSN began attacking the group's members, claiming they were elitist intellectuals who spread lies about Romania abroad, and this helped to chill the group's ardor for presenting dissenting viewpoints. As time went on, many members of the group came to believe that the antipolitical methods of creating pluralism were too indirect for the new circumstances. After the group's powerful initial impact, by 1992 its influence declined as many members entered more directly into party politics.[5]

Timişoara, the home of the revolution, was a second center of democratic opposition. One of the better democratic weeklies, *Orizont* (Horizon), was established there, and in the spring of 1990 activists published a program they hoped would restore "the ideals of the Timişoara revolution," which included tolerance, the right to free expression, and a ban on all former Communist activists in political life.[6] Within weeks hundreds of organizations around Romania adopted the proclamation.

A third, very visible center of democratic (and sometimes not so democratic) opposition were the students of Bucharest University, who created what they called a "Communist-free zone" in University Square, which is in full view of foreign reporters staying at the Intercontinental Hotel. Starting April 22, 1990, a variety of demonstrators, hunger strikers, and students gathered daily in the square to protest the government's quasi-Communist character, pass out antigovernment leaflets, and listen to political speeches.[7]

All of this oppositional activity had very little impact on the outcome of Romania's first post-Ceauşescu election. The National Salvation Front played two cards astutely, if crudely, in the election campaign. The first was to create a self-serving mythology of the revolution itself. The Front presented itself as consisting of the brave men who had answered the call of an aroused people, had eliminated the evil Ceauşescus, and who were now poised to lead the rejuvenated Romania to a better future in partnership with Europe. An important aspect of this strategy was to decree that the president would be elected by popular vote (there was no referendum on this question in Romania). This not only would produce a strong president, a style familiar to Romanians, but would give the National Salvation Front the opportunity to take advantage of the popularity of their leader, Ion Iliescu. The Front also successfully mobilized the government bureaucracy, which remained in place to conduct the election. In other countries the fear that a well-organized party bureaucracy would overmatch the disorganized opposition did not prove warranted, but in Romania it did.

Equally powerful was the FSN's second card: anti-Hungarian nationalism. Romanians have a strong sense that they are "a martyrized nation."[8] This is not an uncommon feeling in Eastern Europe. Here is Misha Glenny's description of Croatian émigrés returning to help out in Franjo Tudjman's election campaign: "All of them had the 'look.'. . . Translated, the 'look' means: 'We are the most oppressed nation in Eastern Europe, but the time has now come to display our superior cultural values. By the way, we know you are a subversive Western liberal determined to slander us with accusations of anti-Semitism and neo-Fascism.'"[9] Romanians immersed in fantasies such as this see Romania as beleaguered by a hostile Western press, unappreciated by the international community, and undermined by widespread conspiracies, particularly from Hungary.

The most outrageous attempts to play upon these sentiments came from a new weekly entitled *România Mare* (Great Romania), which quickly achieved a circulation of about six hundred thousand.[10] Editor-in-chief Corneliu Vadim Tudor described himself as "the only living Romanian writer ready to admit he had loved Ceauşescu," and his paper was full of turgid and argumentative diatribes against "Hungarian fascism" and the Jewish threat.[11] Narrow, xenophobic, and sycophantic, Tudor and his two main colleagues—Eugen Barbu, an equally fervent Ceauşescu supporter, and Mircea Muşat, a Stalinist historian—argued that Nicolae Ceauşescu was a patriot who defended Romanian sovereignty in Timişoara against "outside forces," such as Hungarians and Jews, that wanted to betray Romania and to keep it out of Europe.[12]

The FSN also took advantage of these sentiments. In the Transylvanian town of Tirgu Mureş/Maros Vásárhely, Hungarians had been demanding greater use of the Hungarian language in education and in street signs. When in March 1990 they conducted a public demonstration to press their demands, an ugly crowd of Romanians attacked them, setting off two days of Hungarian-Romanian rioting that killed at least five people (three Romanians and two Hungarians). The participation of the quasi-fascist organization *Vatră Românească* (Romanian Hearth) made the riots particularly nasty.[13]

Rather than condemning the event as the nationalist excess it was, Ion Iliescu blamed only the Hungarians, whom he characterized as "hooligans," while his foreign minister declared, "It is not the FSN that has alienated the Hungarian minority. The Hungarian minority has decided to alienate itself from the FSN."[14] Investigation of the tragedy went nowhere.[15] Six months later Iliescu said, "As far as the minorities are concerned, I think . . . that there are no insufficiencies in any sphere."[16] With Iliescu and Român continuing to wink broadly at the violently anti-Hungarian and even anti-Semitic tone of *România Mare,* the new leaders of Romania seemed to have few compunctions about calling upon the worst elements of Romanian society to cement their power.

The FSN's strategy worked very well. Iliescu took 85 percent of the popular vote for president and the National Salvation Front took two-thirds of the votes for the two houses of parliament.[17] The weakness of the traditional parties made the Hungarian Democratic Union, with only about 7 percent of the vote, the largest opposition party in the new parliament.

Western observers who doubted the fairness of the elections, which CSCE observers certainly did, had their suspicions confirmed about the new Romanian democracy about one month later. On June 13, 1990, with the elections behind it and the foreign observers mostly departed, the government decided to clear University Square of its by now semipermanent demonstrators. After the police swept the area early in the day, protesters raided state television offices and burned a building belonging to the state security police, the Securitate. In the mêlée four persons died and almost one hundred where shot. At this point President Iliescu announced that the government was threatened with a coup by a "legionary rebellion."[18] Within hours some ten thousand miners from the Jiu Valley armed with wooden clubs and iron bars descended on Bucharest in special trains and proceeded over the course of three violent days to wreck the headquarters and presses of the National Liberal party and the National Peasant party—both close to University Square, beat student protesters inside university buildings, attack opposition party leaders, and confront anyone who continued to protest the government's illiberal makeup. Several people died in these confrontations, and many were seriously injured. Foreign reporters observed that the miners, who had come to the capital twice previously to enforce their views and who were to come again in September 1991, seemed suspiciously well prepared with lists of people to attack and with the addresses of offices of opposition parties and newspapers to smash. With the National Salvation Front legitimated by faulty elections and apparently ready to use the crudest type of violence against its opponents, Romania was off to a rocky start on its road back to Europe.

Bulgarian Communists Turn toward Democracy

A renamed Communist party won the first election in Bulgaria too, but under quite different conditions and with a more positive result.[19] The new Communist leadership brought in by the November coup was more oriented toward reform than were the leaders of the National Salvation Front and less inclined to use crude force against demonstrators. Within two months of replacing Todor Zhivkov, new party leader Petŭr Mladenov advocated renouncing the party's leading role in society, legalized demonstrations, permitted the registration of Ecoglasnost, abolished a number of legal measures that had been used against dissidents, abandoned the hydroelectric plant planned for the scenic Rila Valley, restored to the Turks the right to choose their own names, authorized the formation of political groups, and promised elections.

The opposition showed its maturity as well. By December 7, 1989, less than one month after Zhivkov's removal, the main elements in the opposition, including the trade union Podkrepa, Ecoglasnost, the Independent Association for the Defense of Human Rights, the Sofia discussion clubs, and the newly created Social Democratic party, among others, came together to form the Union of Democratic Forces, (Sŭyuz demokratichnite sile—SDS, abbreviated henceforth UDF), headed by Zhelyu Zhelev.[20] Unlike the Civic Forum in the Czech lands, which considered itself a movement representing all of civil society, the UDF was an explicitly political coalition. Within a week it was able to bring tens of thousands of people onto city streets around the country in support of reform. In Czechoslovakia people power toppled the old regime. In Bulgaria people power provided steady postrevolutionary pressure, constantly pushing the former Communists in the direction of political responsibility and pluralism.

The Bulgarian roundtable discussions, which began on January 16, 1990, were the stormiest in Eastern Europe. Several times the UDF walked out, the first time only two days after the talks opened over the question of whether the proceedings would be broadcast (eventually they were). Many times UDF leaders brought crowds of up to 200,000 people onto the streets to push their points. In February the UDF started its own newspaper, *Demokratsiya* (Democracy), which soon began a wrenching series of exposes of the inhumane Bulgarian prison camps from the 1950s, not only a previously taboo subject but one about which most Bulgarians knew little or nothing. The Communists reacted in January by adopting (unanimously!) a "Manifesto on Democratic Socialism" that advocated a "socially oriented market economy" and transformation into a "new type of modern Marxist party" committed to "human and democratic socialism," and in April it changed its name to the Bulgarian Socialist party (Bŭlgarska socialisticheska partiya—BSP), proclaiming that it had made a complete break with its Stalinist and Zhivkovist past.[21]

Finally, on March 30, after a series of nerve-wracking postponements and mass demonstrations, agreement in the roundtable discussions was reached. The most important point was that a new legislature would be elected and sit not as an ordinary national assembly but as a "Grand National Assembly" that would have the authority to write a new constitution and be charged to do so within eighteen months. The former Communists agreed to accept this condition in return for the UDF's agreement to an early—and therefore advantageous for the Communists—election. The question of how a president should be selected was as contentious in Bulgaria as it was in Hungary, but it was resolved without a referendum. Petŭr Mladenov was to be elected president by the old (Communist) assembly before it adjourned, but he would serve only until the new constitution was written. On April 3 the national assembly adopted the roundtable agreements, elected Mladenov president, and dissolved itself.

The weeks leading up to the election in June were generally peaceful, although several oppositionists were killed.[22] The UDF conducted a vigorous campaign, but one that proved perhaps a bit too vigorous. In advocating "the complete dismantling of the existing totalitarian system in Bulgaria" the party's leader, Zhelyu Zhelev, may have alienated Bulgaria's rural voters.[23] To these voters the Socialists came on as the steady ones, the ones who retained the directive prestige of a paternalistic society and who continued to run the patronage systems that were basic to peasant survival. The Socialists did not go to great lengths to publicize their reform rhetoric in the countryside, and they kept their rural party organization intact. No reform movement from below, like the Horizontalists in Poland or the Reform Circles in Hungary, pressured the party leadership in Bulgaria.

In the election itself the UDF did well in the cities, taking 24 out of 26 seats in Sofia, for example, but by rallying the countryside the Socialists ended up with 52 percent of the national vote and a clear majority in the Grand National Assembly. The UDF received 36 percent, and two other parties, the Movement for Rights and Freedoms, which represented the Turkish minority, and the old satellite party, the Bulgarian Agrarian National Union, split the remainder.

Some foreign observers lamented the victory of the Socialists and rashly concluded that Bulgaria was going the way of Romania. Nothing could have been further from the truth. In fact, the Bulgarian political situation had moved significantly in the direction of pluralism and change. The Union of Democratic Forces secured a strong voice in the Grand National Assembly and began to play the role of a loyal—at least not overtly traitorous—opposition. It refused an offer of coalition from Prime Minister Andrei Lukhanov, who had taken office in February and who was reconfirmed after the election, and it continued to bring people into the streets. The "City of Truth," an encampment of protesters in central Sofia similar to the one in University Square in Bucharest, became an open-air debating society through the summer of 1990. In contrast to Romania, the Bulgarian Socialists tolerated this oppositional pluralism and did not call in their toughs.

Within a month of the election the UDF was presented with an unprecedented opportunity. During a Sofia demonstration on December 14, 1989, a television camera had caught President Mladenov saying, in reference to the demonstrators, "The best thing to do is bring in the tanks." On June 14 the UDF began playing this tape during its allotted television time. On July 6 Mladenov, apparently making a personal decision without even discussing it with Prime Minister Lukhanov, resigned,

forcing the recently elected Grand National Assembly to name a successor.[24] After four ballots and two weeks of controversy the delegates finally
decided on a compromise candidate who had not even been among the
original names mentioned, Zhelyu Zhelev, president of the UDF, with
whom Lukhanov mistakenly thought he could work. Despite their defeat
in the elections, therefore, the UDF broke through at the highest level. A
modest and personally honest man, although initially limited in his political
experience, Zhelev continued to live in his two-room Sofia apartment and
to dismiss his security guard at 5:00 P.M. Although he did not remain free
of accusations of helping his former associates in the hallowed Balkan tradition, on balance Zhelev has provided Bulgaria with the type of ethical
leadership more usually associated with central Europe than with southeast
Europe.

Multiparty Democracy in Hungary

In Hungary, two main political factions replaced the Communists as the
dominant political forces, a centrist, populist, Christian tendency, and a
liberal, urban, and Western tendency. The Hungarian Democratic Forum
(MDF) was the main party of the first of these. The MDF contained two
wings, the third-road populists and the centrist moderates. The former
believed that a third way, a special Hungarian social arrangement between
communism and capitalism, could be found. The idea of a third way was
common in Europe in the 1930s. It was used, for example, by the Nazis
to justify their system as a new order between East and West.[25] In Hungary
third-road ideologues drew on a tradition of populism from the 1930s and
from the immediate postwar period, which opened them to criticism from
the left that they were anachronistic, insensitive to the principles of liberal
government, and even fascist. They stressed the special character of the
Hungarian past, advocated an egalitarian socioeconomic program in which
small entrepreneurs produced for the world market in specialized niches,
and opposed quick economic fixes that would bring multinational corporations into Hungary and the "selling out" of Hungarian national assets
to foreigners.[26] The dominant wing of the MDF, however, was in the
tradition of center right European parties. It favored a full transition to a
market economy, but in a staged, coherent, and continuous way. It spoke
of repossessing the national tradition, called for renewed reliance on religion and the family, and claimed to speak for all Hungarians everywhere.

The Democratic Forum's main opponent, the Alliance of Free Democrats (SzDSz), were the urbanists—the intellectual dissidents, the human
rights advocates, and the environmental activists who had centered their
activities in Budapest during the 1980s. These westernized Europeanists
sought a total dismantling of the Communist political and economic systems and favored a radical economic program that would trade austerity
in the short term for fiscal and economic soundness in the long term. Some

of them were Thatcherites, liberals in the European sense of the term, but the main tenor of their thought was social democratic. They feared the MDF's small town mentality, as they thought of it, and the negative implications of the third road for individual freedoms. The main ally of the SzDSz was the Young Democrats (FIDESz). The programs of the two parties differed in nuance, but their main difference was that the leaders of the Free Democrats tended to be seasoned Budapest intellectuals, whereas the leaders of FIDESz tended to be very young intellectuals from the provinces.

In Hungary the electoral campaign was open, professional, free, and bitter.[27] The Free Democrats and FIDESz concentrated their initial energies on discrediting the former Communists, and succeeded in uncovering several juicy scandals, such as the transfer of a vacation resort to party insiders under the guise of privatization and the continued surveillance of political parties by the security services. The really bitter campaigning was between the radical spokespersons of the Democratic Forum, who accused the Free Democrats and FIDESz of being filled with pampered Jewish sons of Communists, and Free Democrats and their allies, who attacked the MDF's anti-Semitism, parochialism, and incompetence.

The victors were the parties of the center and the right. The Democratic Forum won 44 percent of the vote, while their two rightwing allies, the Smallholders and the Christian Democrats, won 12 percent and 6 percent respectively. On the other side the Free Democrats won 23 percent and FIDESz 6 percent. The Communists, with 8 percent, ended up out in the cold, their plans of being the first Communist party to legitimate itself at the ballot box shattered. Lacking a clear majority, the Democratic Forum formed a coalition government with the other two parties of the right. By the end of May the new legislature approved historian József Antall, head of the Democratic Forum, as prime minister of a coalition government.

At this point, the two main opposing parties, the MDF and the SzDSz, undertook an important move of reconciliation that helped put Hungary on a reasonably stable path toward pluralism. The ruling coalition had a solid majority in the legislature of 61 percent, but this fell short of the two-thirds needed to pass "measures of national importance," which in the period of transition would be practically everything. The surprise solution was for the Free Democrats and FIDESz to agree to a constitutional change that would permit most measures to pass with a simple majority, all except those dealing with civil liberties, in return for which the president would be a Free Democrat. Having displayed righteous indignation at the Democratic Forum for its putative deal with the Communists in September 1989, the Free Democrats made their own deal with the Forum in April 1990. Instead of reform Communist Imre Poszgay becoming president, which is what the democratic opposition feared in the fall, Árpád Göncz, a historian of limited political experience but excellent oppositionist credentials (he had served six years of a life sentence for participating in the revolution of 1956), assumed that office in the spring. One could hardly imagine a more fitting conclusion to Hungary's negotiated revolution.

Civic Forum Takes Charge in Czechoslovakia

After the enormous psychological high of going from domination by men like Miloš Jakeš and Jan Fojtik in November 1989 to rule by men like Václav Havel and Jiří Dienstbier in January 1990, almost anything would have been anticlimactic for the Czechs and Slovaks. The brief but decisive struggle of Civic Forum and Public Against Violence against the Communist regime gave these movements enormous momentum in the early months of 1990, a momentum they turned into victory in the June elections. Not really political parties, these broad and inchoate representations of a not yet fully formed civil society included points of view ranging across the entire political spectrum. They ran on the basis of respect for human rights, marketizing reforms, and democratic reforms, none of which were particularly controversial in the spring of 1990. With one major exception, therefore, the pathway to the first Czechoslovak election was relatively smooth.

The dispute that arose early in 1990 seemed in itself minor or even silly but it foreshadowed the dispute that led to the breakup of the Czechoslovak state on January 1, 1993. It concerned the name of the new state. The federal assembly found what it considered a reasonable compromise between the Czech delegates, who favored the name "Czechoslovak Federative Republic," and the Slovak delegates, who favored "Czecho-Slovak Federative Republic," when it voted to use both names, the former in the Czech lands, the latter in Slovakia, with the proviso that the hyphenated version be spelled "Czecho-slovak," that is, with Slovak not capitalized. Many Slovaks found this solution unacceptable, and demonstrations followed in Bratislava and elsewhere. After a month of sometimes emotional national debate, the name "The Czech and Slovak Federal Republic" was finally adopted.

President Havel correctly noted that the dispute was not a trivial matter concerning minor orthographic conventions but was rather a symptom of fundamentally differing social patterns, economic structures, and outlook between the two peoples. More Catholic, more conservative, more rural, and at the same time more economically concentrated in large defense industries, Slovakia had not experienced the same history as the Czech lands. Whereas Bohemia and Moravia had been a medieval state, had traditionally looked toward Vienna, and had industrialized in the nineteenth century, Slovakia had never been a state, had been dominated by a Hungarian nobility that looked toward Budapest, and had remained primarily a peasant economy in the nineteenth century. In addition, the Czechs had developed a reputation for democracy while dominating Czechoslovakia after World War I, whereas Slovakia had become a satellite collaborator of Nazi Germany during World War II.

In January 1990 the inexperienced and idealistic new leadership of Czechoslovakia confirmed the worst fears of some Slovaks when Foreign Minister Jiří Dienstbier announced that he intended to stop all international arms shipments from Czechoslovakia. Since most of the industries that supplied these arms were in Slovakia, many Slovaks concluded that the federal government, which seemed intent on creating a liberal secular state on the basis of the ideas of Prague intellectuals, was unsympathetic to their special problems. Slovak nationalists also feared that former Charter 77 activists would limit their ability to deal freely with the Hungarian minority in Slovakia. The hyphen fight was about these issues as much as it was about the name of the country, and in the end they proved insoluble within the framework of a single state.

In the election itself the Civic Forum/Public Against Violence parties won easily over approximately twenty other entries, capturing 56 percent of the seats in the federal assembly. But significant differences divided the Czech and the Slovak lands. In the former, the liberal, Western-oriented Civic Forum took about two-thirds of the vote, but in the latter Public Against Violence took only between 30 and 40 percent of the vote. The Slovak National party, which favored an independent Slovakia, did not do as well as some had feared, achieving only 15 percent of the seats in the Slovak National Council, but together with the conservative and nationalistic Christian Democratic Movement it held a plurality over Public Against Violence in the Slovak National Council. Nationally, the Communist party, which unlike its fraternal parties elsewhere refused to change its name, ended up with 47 seats out of 300 and became the second largest party in the federal assembly.

German Unification

The 1990 election in Czechoslovakia went smoothly, but the hyphen fight actually presaged the breakup of the country. In East Germany the political vector ran in the opposite direction, chaotic politics leading toward unification with West Germany. The fall of the Berlin Wall on the night of November 9–10, 1989, came at a moment of complete confusion for the Communist leaders of East Germany. Two days earlier the government headed by Willy Stoph had resigned, and on November 8 the entire politburo resigned. A special session of the central committee was underway when the Wall fell. When the session broke up on November 10 the departing committee members were well aware that "a revolutionary movement has set in motion a process of serious upheaval," as their statement put it, but at this point they still hoped to be able to regenerate themselves through an "action program" that included provision for increased democratization and the creation of a "socialist planned economy guided by market conditions."[28] The party's most prominent reform figure, Hans Modrow, took office as the new prime minister.

It quickly became apparent that the time for proposals that would have been considered daring in 1985 had passed. Within weeks newspapers were publishing pictures of the comfortable homes party leaders had built for themselves in their private suburb of Wandlitz. Not luxurious by Western standards, these homes, with their special stores, large rooms, and swimming pools, scandalized an East German public that lived in tiny high-rise apartments far from decent stores and with doubtful plumbing facilities. Newspaper articles exposed a trade union chief who had set aside five thousand acres of a national forest for his own hunting grounds, where he was alleged to have shot as many as one hundred elk a year. By mid-January not only had a number of party figures been forced to resign over stories such as these but dozens of formerly high party members were under indictment for corruption. Even Erich Honecker had been indicted for ordering border guards to shoot to kill.

The most direct target of public hatred was the Stasi, the *Staatssicherheitsdienst* (State Security Service). The extent to which the Stasi had corrupted East German society with its surveillance is truly remarkable. When its files were opened to public perusal in 1992, it was revealed that in a country of seventeen million people the Stasi had maintained files on six million persons, amassing 125 shelf miles of information, most of it amazingly trivial. Here, for example, is part of a surveillance report from the files: "Rathenow then crossed the street and ordered a sausage at the sausage stand. The following conversation took place: Rathenow: 'A sausage please.' Sausage seller: 'With or without roll?' Rathenow: 'With, please.' Sausage seller: 'And mustard?' Rathenow: 'Yes, with mustard.' Further exchange of words did not take place."[29] In mid-January 1990, when Modrow did not appear to be moving rapidly enough to disband the security police, crowds in East Berlin invaded Stasi offices, seized some documents, and strewed the streets with others. Similar events in other cities finally convinced Modrow, and by the end of January the Stasi was finished.

Continued gatherings of hundreds of thousands of people in Leipzig, outbursts of violence by skinhead toughs, and continued emigration at the rate of two thousand persons a day caused David Binder of the *New York Times* to remark, "There is a smell of anarchy in the air."[30] But there was the smell of something else in the air too: unification. Despite the denials of both party leader Egon Krenz and Prime Minister Modrow that unification was on the agenda, everyone knew that it was.[31] West German chancellor Helmut Kohl was cautious at first. On November 28, 1989, he outlined a relatively moderate plan of confederation that would establish a number of common agencies. "Nobody knows how a reunified Germany will look. But I am sure that unity will come," he said, "if it is wanted by the German nation."[32] In Leipzig crowds expressed their view with banners saying "One Fatherland, One Nation, One State." Forced to consider the new situation, the ambassadors of the four powers that still technically occupied Berlin (the United States, the Soviet Union, the United Kingdom, and France) met to consider the future of the city and, by extension, of Germany. For the first time since the 1940s the international community began seriously to contemplate the unification it was on record as favoring but that it had long avoided and feared. The ice flow had cracked and begun to move.

The Communists were simply unable to cope with events of this magnitude. Within two weeks of the fall of the Berlin Wall they entered into roundtable talks with the opposition to find a way out. But what opposition? The New Forum, which hoped to be the equivalent in East Germany of the Civic Forum in Czechoslovakia, had only formed in September and had no leader of the stature of Lech Wałesa or Václav Havel. Many other candidates for the mantle of people's representative competed with them. By the time of the second roundtable meeting in mid-December eleven opposition groups joined three churches and five parties from the former National Front in their discussions with the Communist party, now renamed the Party of Democratic Socialism. In less than two months these heterogeneous negotiations led to the creation, on February 5, 1990, of a government of national responsibility that could with some justice be considered representative of the new situation. Eight new ministers without portfolio joined their Communist colleagues and began the demeaning but increasingly inevitable task of dissolving their country.

Many diplomatic issues complicated the unification process. By the Single Europe Act of 1985, which went into effect in 1987, the members of the European Community had pledged themselves to accept approximately 240 new laws and regulations that would turn the Community into a truly single market by the end of 1992. The slogan "1992" had become one of the watchwords of European economic politics. Would German unification derail this process? No one knew, but the specter of an enlarged and enriched Germany was not greeted with enthusiasm by Europeans who felt Germany's economic strength already made it too formidable a partner.

For the Soviets the main issue of unification revolved around their security arrangements. The core Soviet military alliance in Eastern Europe was the Warsaw Pact, which was less a mutual defense system than a series of bilateral arrangements between the Soviet Union and each of the Warsaw Pact members in support of Soviet security objectives. The linchpin of the system was East Germany, where some 370,000 Soviet troops and their families had been stationed for many years. If a united Germany remained part of NATO not only would that eliminate the long-standing first line of Soviet defense against West German revanchism, as the Soviets liked to call it, but NATO would be strengthened perhaps beyond the ability of the Soviets to check. And what would Gorbachev do with the troops if he brought them home, where there were neither barracks nor missions for them?

Others had concerns as well. The most strongly felt was Poland's fear that unification of Germany would call into question the Helsinki Accords that guaranteed its post-World War II border. Helmut Kohl was not prepared to reassure them because he faced a general election late in 1990, and the Social Democrats had been making gains in by-elections, raising their proportion of the vote by more than 5 percent in the Saarland election of January 28, 1990, for example. To hold his party and its coalition together and win the forthcoming election, Kohl had to make sure he did not alienate any of his electoral allies, among which were perhaps two million conservative Silesian Germans who had fled their farms and towns in 1945 and whose lands were now part of Poland. Therefore, whereas Kohl spoke increasingly warmly of the need for unification after the beginning of 1990, he refused to give a categorical guarantee of the Polish borders.

In the confusing early days of 1990, Hans Modrow attempted to seize the initiative. On February 1, after returning from Moscow, he proposed a German unification plan on the basis of a neutral Germany. Kohl instantly and resolutely rejected this retread of a plan offered by Stalin in 1952, but the presence of an offer on the table sent other chanceries to work. Less than two weeks later the two Germanies and the four occupying powers from World War II took advantage of a previously scheduled meeting in Ottawa concerning a different subject to announce that they had agreed on a formula for working out the details of unification, the so-called "two plus four" plan. Proposed and sold to the participants by the United States and closely connected to other negotiations underway over troop reductions, this plan permitted the two Germanies to work out their unification scheme first, whereupon the four occupying powers would, presumably, approve it. The other NATO powers were not brought in, but after Poland protested it was invited to those sessions at which border questions were discussed.

The conditions under which the East German elections were held on March 18, therefore, were unique. In the few months available to them, the East Germans created more than twenty political parties. By early February the most important of them had coalesced into five main parties, which among them represented two general directions, a left and a right. From the beginning, however, the main contest was not among these groupings but between the two main West German parties, the Christian Democratic Union and the Social Democrats. These West German parties stepped into the East German campaign with ample funds and highly sophisticated organizations. Willy Brandt of the Social Democrats and Helmut Kohl of the Christian Democrats gave numerous campaign talks in the East, with Kohl in particular drawing hundreds of thousands of enthusiastic listeners. By this time Kohl had moved into high gear toward unification, which he made the center point of the Christian Democratic campaign. The Social Democrats, on the other hand, under the leadership of the weaker and less appealing Oskar Lafontaine, adopted a critical attitude toward unification, arguing that delay would be the best policy.[33] The election in effect became a referendum on unification.

When the Christian Democratic grouping won over 48 percent of the vote in comparison with only 22 percent for the Social Democrats, the die for unification was cast. The Communists got a respectable 16 percent, but the great losers were the former oppositionists, who proved to be too late and too unrepresentative to have any impact on East German politics.[34] The other East European countries could develop their own style of political pluralism because the democratic opposition emerged more or less in their own national vacuum, even if, as in the case of Bulgaria, it was weak and late. In East Germany, however, the unprepared and inexperienced democratic opposition, burdened with its socialist leanings at a time when the public was rejecting socialism, was no match for its powerful West German political neighbors, who unceremoniously moved in and imposed their West German party organizations on East Germany.

Initially the defeated Social Democrats refused to join in a grand coalition with the victorious Alliance for Germany to lead their country toward unification, but after a month of negotiations they finally consented to enter Lothar de Maiziére's five-party coalition. The new government, representing 75 percent of the voters of East Germany, set as its goal "to achieve the unity of Germany swiftly and responsibly for the whole of the German Democratic Republic . . . on the basis of Article 23 of the Basic Law."[35]

This last referred to the device that would permit the unification to proceed quickly without the necessity of writing a peace treaty or resorting to some other cumbersome device. Strictly speaking, West Germany did not operate under a constitution but under the *Grundgesetz* (Basic Law) of 1949. Article 23 of this law permitted new *Länder*, or German regional states, to fall under the jurisdiction of the Basic Law after accession to the Federal Republic. The Saarland, which was not included in the original West German state at the end of World War II, had joined West Germany as the tenth *Land* in 1956 using this provision.[36]

Political unification was one thing—increasingly uncontroversial, relatively cheap, and comparatively easy, now that the European powers accepted its inevitability. Economic unification was something else. The East German economy was already reeling under the impact of the revolutions in Eastern Europe and the economic decline of the Soviet Union. When West Germans had a chance to take a firsthand look, they were appalled at the waste, inefficiency, pollution, and disorganization of East German industry. The cost of unification would be great on both sides. West Germany would have to provide substantial unemployment benefits and other social guarantees, as well as enormous investment funds, while the East Germans would suffer the uncertainty and humiliation of unemployment and massive structural redistribution.

The first great question to be solved was monetary union. In March 1990 the Bundesbank completed a study suggesting that the East German mark be exchanged at the rate of two East German marks for one West German mark, which was an economically reasonable proposal—indeed, given the near worthlessness of the East German mark, a generous one. But as soon as the proposal leaked out one hundred thousand East Germans gathered in Berlin to protest. Eventually, against the better judgment of the head of the Bundesbank, Kohl's government agreed to exchange the East German mark on a one-for-one basis for wages, pensions, and savings up to six thousand East German marks, depending on the age of the person holding the savings. In other areas the exchange basis would be two-to-one. This meant that on the average, when the exchange took place on July 1, 1990, one West German mark was exchanged for one and one-half East German marks.[37] At that moment East Germany lost its independence in monetary and trade matters, economically becoming part of West Germany.

Uncertainty over the cost of incorporating the German Democratic Republic into West Germany became a potentially serious problem for Helmut Kohl in the spring of 1990, especially after the elections in East Germany. The more West German economists looked at the decrepit East German industries, the more pessimistic became their estimates of what would be needed to set things right. Already resenting the large number of what they considered undisciplined and incompetent East Germans who had flooded westward, some West Germans began wondering if unification was such a good idea. The Social Democrats, who seemed to be picking up strength in by-elections in West Germany, sought to take advantage of the unease by calling for further negotiations rather than simply annexing the East by means of Article 23. These feelings were not assuaged when Hans Modrow complained that the $4.1 billion West Germany had pledged in outright aid in February 1990 was not even half enough.

To forestall the unease on both sides of the border, in May Kohl announced the "German Unity Fund" in what seemed at the time to be the stupendous amount of almost $70 billion, which would finance the reconstruction of East Germany, he claimed, without any additional income taxes.[38] Actually, the cost turned out to be much higher and Kohl did raise taxes (but only in 1991, after the election). During 1990 alone, social security compensation and a variety of other payments by many agencies pushed the amount of transfers to East Germany to almost $29 billion, a formidable amount that was nonetheless only the down payment on the hundreds of billions to follow.[39] But by producing a specific plan, mentioning a definite amount for the Germany Unity Fund, and promising no tax increase, Kohl adroitly deflected the investment issue.

While the financial steps were being taken, the two-plus-four process was grinding away. The main issue among the Great Powers was whether the united Germany would remain in NATO. For a long time Gorbachev resisted this outcome, but after a personal discussion with Kohl in Stavropol just before the third two-plus-four meeting, Gorbachev agreed that the new Germany could remain in NATO. By mid-July the way was cleared among the great powers.

Several contentious issues still remained to be resolved. West German electoral rules were adopted for the national election coming up late in

1990, with the exception that for that election alone the 5 percent threshold for representation in the Bundestag would apply separately in East and West Germany, thus giving some smaller East German parties a chance. Abortion was another major issue. East Germany allowed abortion on demand, whereas it was severely restricted in West Germany. The compromise was to permit the East Germans to retain their law for two years, during which time the Bundestag would write a new law for the united Germany.[40] And then there was the technical problem that East Germany was not organized into the five traditional *Länder* that the Basic Law required but into seventeen *Bezirke,* or counties. The East German Volkskammer (legislature) solved that problem in July by abolishing the *Bezirke* and restoring the *Länder.*

Jews throughout the world were understandably nervous about the unification. Their fears could never be completely allayed, but the Volkskammer did what it could. Shortly after convening in April it unanimously adopted as one of its first orders of business a resolution accepting what the German Democratic Republic had never accepted before: guilt for what it termed the "immeasurable sorrow" of "nationalism and racial delusion [that] led to genocide, in particular of Jews from all European countries, of the people of the Soviet Union, of the Polish people, and of the Romanies and Sintis. This guilt should never be forgotten."[41]

Polish fears that a united Germany would start claiming its old territories in the east were put to rest when both German parliaments adopted resolutions renouncing any such claims and when the two-plus-four treaty made the post-World War II borders definitive. Finally, in order to permit the Soviets to withdraw their 370,000 troops plus dependents by the end of 1994, West Germany agreed to pay the Soviets $7.6 billion for their costs of withdrawal and to assist them in constructing new bases in which to house the soldiers once they returned to the Soviet Union. In addition, the West Germans gave the Soviets a $1.9 billion interest-free loan to help them defray the costs of maintaining their troops during the interim period.

With these and many other ducks in line, on September 12, 1990, the six concerned states signed the two-plus-four treaty and on October 3 the two Germanies became one. What one year earlier no one had imagined possible had become a reality. On December 2, when Germany held its first all-German elections since 1932, Helmut Kohl and his ruling coalition reaped the rewards of his handling of the unification by taking 55 percent of the vote in both east and west. The Free Democratic party of Hans-Dietrich Genscher, the foreign minister who had been saying since 1987 that Gorbachev really meant it, made impressive gains. The Social Democrats, who campaigned on a platform stressing the costs of unification and emphasizing social and environmental issues and who early in 1990 had realistic hopes of winning this election, took only 33 percent of the vote, their lowest figure since 1957. Because of the special rules for 1990,

Alliance 90 got one seat in the Bundestag and the former East German Communists two, but they enjoyed few prospects of maintaining even that minuscule position in the future.[42] East Germany passed into history.

The Next Step: Economic Change

Within little more than six months of the revolutions of 1989 the political changes the democratic opposition had dreamed of for years had been made. Parties had formed, elections had been held, and new, non-Communist governments were in power. Now, it seemed, the way was clear for economic reform. But what reform? Everyone agreed that prices should be accurate, that there should be a large and active private sector, that currency should be stable, that there should be a commercial banking system, and that workers should be protected during the transition. But every detail of how to achieve these things was a matter of intense political controversy. Bitter arguments swirled around broad questions that even in theoretical terms were not resolvable—What should be the pace of marketization? What should be the sequence of reform measures? What level and form of taxation would encourage entry of new firms and at the same time produce enough revenue for the state? Should inflation be controlled at the cost of higher unemployment? Should property be restored to owners from which it had been confiscated years before? What should be done with state farms and cooperatives?—and many, many other questions.

Each country had to face these issues with an inexperienced political elite that was struggling to define itself while trying to create new political forms and devise economic reforms. Worse, no country's economic fate was entirely in its own hands. Links with the Soviet Union and CMEA built up over forty years made Soviet economic problems the problems of all, while world economic conditions, particularly those in the European Community, significantly shaped the situation.

Perestroika may have been good medicine for the Soviet economy, but unfortunately it killed the patient. In the two years between Ceauşescu's death and Gorbachev's resignation, the Soviet Union undertook a number of large and small reforms that destroyed traditional Soviet ways of doing business but did not create adequate new ones. In 1990 the Soviet economy declined about 4 percent, and in 1991, when the center collapsed completely, it declined an additional 15 percent. This economic free-fall put enormous pressure on Eastern Europe, which had conducted at least one-third of its trade with the Soviet Union.[43] Problems in the Soviet oil industry were particularly harmful. In 1990 Soviet exports of crude oil to Eastern Europe dropped approximately 30 percent just at the moment when the Gulf crisis provoked by Iraq's invasion of Kuwait forced East Europeans to forego imports from Iraq and caused the price of oil to spike.[44] As if that were not enough, in 1991 Soviet republics began to arrogate to themselves many economic functions. The sheer difficulty of finding a partner authorized to make a deal in this confused situation was not the least of the impediments to trade.

As Soviet economic conditions worsened, CMEA trading mechanisms collapsed. CMEA members conducted trade among themselves in transferable rubles, a fictitious trading currency used in clearing arrangements. In June 1990 the Soviet Union announced that after December 31, 1990, all its foreign trade would be conducted at world prices in dollar equivalents. Whereas this was certainly an admirable long-term goal, the small amount of hard currency available to most Soviet and East European firms, the lack of convertibility of their own currencies, the sclerotic nature of the Soviet banking system, and the low level of competitiveness of the goods involved provoked an unprecedented trading crisis among the CMEA partners. During 1990 trade among the East European economies declined "perhaps as much as one fifth in volume," while between Eastern Europe and the Soviet Union it declined about 15 percent. Romania suffered the worst, with its exports dropping 46 percent in 1990, having already fallen 11 percent in 1989.[45]

Hungary and Poland built up huge credits with the Soviet Union as they both continued to manufacture and ship goods even though their Soviet counterparts were not paying and could not obtain letters of credit. Eventually the size of the credits became insupportable and the East Europeans had to stop shipments, leaving many of their Soviet-oriented production lines producing unsalable goods for an already overstocked inventory. In desperation, trading partners began to return to barter arrangements analogous to those conducted under the old system of material balances. For example, in September 1991 Poland agreed to ship the Soviet Union six hundred thousand tons of potatoes and several thousand tons of apples and onions in exchange for one and one-half billion cubic meters of natural gas.[46] If Russia, Belarus, and Ukraine can stabilize their economies, they will be natural trading partners for Eastern Europe. But in 1990 and 1991 the earlier overdependency on Soviet markets created serious difficulties in Eastern Europe.

The economic situation in Western Europe and America was much better than in the Soviet Union, but by their own standards the Western economies were in a cyclical downturn.[47] Still, confronted with a new situation with the end of the cold war, the West began to react. The Americans, who had been running huge budget deficits for years and who were in a recession, established a two-year SEED program (Support for East European Democracy) in 1989 in the modest amount of $1 billion, but bureaucratic infighting delayed the actual expenditure of funds, which in any case were to go mostly for studies and similar soft aid—a "hand-up rather than a hand-out," as the State Department put it. This compared with approximately $4 billion the United States provided to Israel in 1990.

Potentially the most important institution created to assist Eastern Europe was the European Bank for Reconstruction and Development (EBRD), which thirty-nine industrial nations, including the United States, established with an initial capital of $12.4 billion in April 1991.[48] The World Bank raised the amount of loans it committed to Eastern Europe in its 1991 fiscal year by $1 billion, but this still only made a total of $2.9 billion committed to Eastern Europe, or less than 5 percent of its total lending potential. Of this amount, $1.4 billion went to Poland, leaving substantially smaller amounts for the other countries. Europeans found other constructive yet inexpensive ways to help. In March 1990 the Organisation for Economic Cooperation and Development, a research and statistical organization that grew out of the Marshall Plan, created a Centre for Co-operation with European Economies in Transition, which began to bring a wide range of international expertise to bear on specific problems that the East European economies faced, such as poor statistical techniques. Significant emergency humanitarian aid was provided as well, particularly to Romania and Bulgaria.

Poland received a special kind of aid that other countries envied but could not obtain—forgiveness of half of its debt to foreign governments. Polish debt stayed fairly stable from 1980 through 1985, but in 1986 it began rising again until it reached almost $50 billion by the end of 1990. At this point debt servicing was taking 91 percent of Polish foreign currency earnings. When the Solidarity government came to power in September 1989, Poland had already stopped servicing its debt. After lengthy negotiations, in March 1991 the Paris Club of seventeen creditor nations agreed to cut Poland's debt held by foreign governments, which amounted to $33 billion, by 50 percent over a four-year period. This unique arrangement, combined with several supplementary agreements, reduced interest payments 80 percent for three years and gave Poland helpful breathing space. None of the other East European countries received such a concession, although Bulgaria was able to reschedule its debt on relatively favorable terms.

Despite these steps, in the first two years after the revolutions, the new democracies in Eastern Europe felt they were being punished for lax Western lending policies toward their economically inefficient totalitarian predecessors. Whereas risky loans and guarantees had seemed easy for their Communist predecessors to obtain, support for the new democracies seemed a lot harder to pry loose. All we want, said the president of the National Bank of Hungary, is for "the West not to treat the new democratically elected countries worse than they treated the old Communist regimes."[49] But in comparison to the normal speed of international interactions, the Europeans and the Americans reacted quite rapidly to the radically new situation in Eastern Europe. And estimates of the total need were frightening. EBRD estimated the East Europeans could absorb about $2.5 trillion over a twenty-year period (that is, $125 billion a year), whereas the Centre for Economic Policy Research estimated that the amount required could range between $103 and $226 billion a year for at least ten years.[50]

Strategies of Economic Change

In the first months after the revolutions of 1989 many in the West assumed that with the extinction of the Leninist regimes East European countries would enter directly into a stage of transition to a market economy. Countless academic conferences were held on the subject under the assumption that it was well known, at least in broad outline, how the process would go. First, the East Europeans would stabilize their currencies through restrictive macroeconomic policies, which meant controlling inflation at the cost of creating unemployment. Then they would reorganize their state-owned enterprises into corporate form and put them under private ownership; write a body of law protecting property rights and regulating business; create a commercial banking system and a capital market; and teach workers, managers, lawyers, judges, and bureaucrats unfamiliar with market mechanisms new ways of doing business.[51] The difficult question seemed to be not what needed to be done but what the pace of the changes would be.

The dominant school of thought in 1990 argued that this pace should be rapid. Since all aspects of an economy are interrelated, these economists argued, it would not be possible to reform one or two areas gradually. A general reform must attack everything at once and put the elements of a liberal capitalist economy in place as quickly as possible. This would produce temporary and perhaps serious hardship, but as soon as the "shock therapy" took hold prices would become accurate, currency would stabilize, foreign trade would pick up, and competition among rationally organized private enterprises would create efficiency. From the political point of view, these analysts argued, shock therapy was desirable as well, because unless reforms were introduced very rapidly at the time when the public was thirsting for change, opposition to the painful medicine would have time to mobilize and thus to prevent the necessary improvements.

In an important sense the strategists of shock therapy were utopian, because they looked upon East European societies as blank slates on which the planners could write the prescriptions for creating the desired end product, a functioning capitalist economy. They believed that the existing structures had little or no value and had to be replaced as soon as possible on behalf of an idealized future goal, and sometimes they sounded not a little like their predecessors. "We want to construct an ideological turnpike," said Václav Klaus, Czechoslovak finance minister, "not travel the winding roads from one system to another. We want to enter an ideological turnpike and proceed as fast as possible toward a market economy."[52]

Over time, a more conservative school of thinking arose, one that recognized that structural differences existed among the East European economies and believed that no East European society was a blank slate. This school argued that incremental reform built on the knowledge that already existed in society, coupled with simultaneous encouragement to new enterprises, would produce a more deeply rooted reform. János Kornai, one of the first alternative voices to shock therapy, argued that the privatization of socially owned assets should be achieved by "an organic process of development and social change," and Peter Murrell pointed out that no reform that considered workers and managers as obstacles rather than clients or beneficiaries was likely to succeed in the long run.[53] In the first flush of post-1989 enthusiasm, however, grand plans for rapid change were the order of the day, at least in East Germany and Poland.

Germanizing the East German Economy

When economic and then political union eliminated the German Democratic Republic, many of the most difficult problems facing other East European countries were automatically solved. Stable currency arrived backed by a strong government and an independent Bundesbank; property rights came under the protection of firmly established West German law; and eastern Germany entered directly into the European Community. Legal ownership of all the more than eight thousand East German enterprises was turned over to *Treuhandanstalt* (Treuhand), a new organization established in March 1990 solely for the purpose of privatizing them.[54] Treuhand quickly established supervisory boards for each company, worked out reasonable balance sheets, and began selling or closing firms at the rate of ten to fifteen a day. East Germans not only fell under the generous West German social security system but often continued to work in factories kept open by subsidies paid by the federal government during the transition period. Marvin Jackson counted twenty-seven separate "adjustment and integration assistance measures for the new states of eastern Germany" undertaken by the Federal Republic in 1990. More than half the industrial firms in West Germany said early in 1991 that they intended to invest in East Germany eventually.[55] No other country in Eastern Europe began its transformation with such advantages.

On the other hand, no other East European country suffered such an instantaneous and total collapse. When the West German deutschmark became the legal currency of East Germany and wages were raised to compensate for the unfreezing of rents and other price changes, many East German enterprises immediately went bankrupt. East German firms, now able to buy and sell on the European market in hard currency, had little interest in importing inferior goods from their former partners or in exporting goods to them for inferior money. Many firms simply canceled their contracts with former CMEA partners. Since the German Democratic Republic had been the second most important trade partner for every country in Eastern Europe, the disruption of its trade patterns reverberated throughout the region. CMEA had not worked well, but at least it worked. When the Soviet Union began having troubles making good on its credits and East Germany became a hard currency country, the entire system collapsed, leaving enterprises that had once interacted adequately with each other orphaned. In East Germany production in the sector that Communists had most prized, heavy industry, fell approximately 60 percent during 1990 and 1991.

East German collapse accelerated the differentiation of German society into haves and have nots, with a large proportion of the latter in eastern Germany. Even after the wage hikes that followed unification, nominal incomes in eastern Germany remained 50 percent of those in the West. By the end of 1991 about 1.2 million persons were without work and 2 million more were on reduced work hours, which sometimes meant receiving one's pay, or partial pay, for doing no work at all. East Germans reacted to the realization that salvation was not right around the corner much as they had reacted against communism a year earlier. In the first six months of 1990, 238,000 persons emigrated from East to West, leaving some areas populated mainly by the unskilled, the middle-aged, and the old. When Helmut Kohl visited Erfurt in April 1990, instead of cheering him, as they had before the election, demonstrators threw eggs and tomatoes at him.

But unlike 1989, the walls did not come tumbling down. Having taken over the East German economy, the West Germans continued systematically to reorganize it according to their own standards. Treuhand received some criticism for going too slowly but in comparison to the rest of Eastern Europe, as well as in comparison to that great privatizer Margaret Thatcher, who took eleven years to sell off less than 5 percent of the British economy, it moved with lightning speed. By mid-1991, despite the assassination of its first director by a terrorist group, Treuhand had completed the Herculean task of evaluating the eight thousand enterprises under its control using Western accounting principles, closed more than four hundred losing companies, and sold off more than three thousand others. The privatization of all small-scale enterprises was essentially complete by mid-1991, and administrators hoped that they could finish the privatization process in all five *Länder* by 1994.

More significant, the West Germans were pouring tens of billions of marks into the eastern part of the country. In 1991 it is estimated that the net transfer amounted to $86 billion, while in 1992 the figure rose to over $100 billion.[56] Much of this money was in the form of unemployment payments, subsidies, and other efforts to keep consumption up, but a large proportion went into infrastructure—building modern roads, installing new communications networks, and rebuilding bridges. In only one of these projects, the West Germans undertook a $30 billion renovation of the East German telephone system that anticipated raising the number of telephones from 1.8 million in 1989 to 7.1 million by 1997, installing ten million miles of fiber-optic and copper cables, and building two thousand digital telephone exchanges.[57] Already by July 1991 a long distance network of thirty-four thousand lines replaced the primitive East German equipment that had provided only two hundred outgoing long distance lines.[58] Progress such as this gave credence to the prediction of Birgit Breuel, head of Treuhand, that by the end of the century eastern Germany would leapfrog the rest of Europe in the modernity of its infrastructure.

Despite the accurate feelings of many East Germans that the "Wessies" were manipulating them and treating them condescendingly, despite the understandable depression many felt as their sense of worth collapsed in unemployment, despite the trauma produced by the opening of the Stasi files, and despite the not unfounded fears that pockets of permanent poverty were being created in eastern Germany—if the remarkable rate of investment could be sustained, eastern Germany stood every chance of being substantially reintegrated economically with the West by the year 2000.

Poland's Shock Therapy

East Germany suffered the most dramatic shock after its revolution of 1989, but the country that got the most attention for its "shock therapy" was Poland. Poland's moribund economy suffered under the multiple difficulties of being overly centralized, committed to large heavy industrial enterprises, wracked by hyperinflation, heavily in debt, and overcome with environmental pollution. When the Mazowiecki government came to power in September 1989, it turned its attention to these problems with amazing rapidity. Pushed by a new minister of finance, the young economist Leszek Balcerowicz, the new regime produced a comprehensive plan for economic reform only a month after taking office.[59]

Balcerowicz, who had been trained in the United States, agreed with the advice offered him by Jeffrey Sachs, a Harvard economist who became the most vigorous and prominent advocate of shock therapy in Eastern Europe.[60] He decided on a two-stage strategy, the first stage of which involved measures to stabilize the currency and stop inflation, open Poland to the world economy, free most prices, and ease entry into business by small entrepreneurs. Once monetary problems were in hand and world prices were disciplining Polish enterprises, Balcerowicz intended to follow with a rapid privatization of state-held enterprises. On December 29, two and one-half months after the government proposed Balcerowicz's radical plan, a reluctant Sejm, which contained a large number of Communists, adopted the program. Western governments, to whom Balcerowicz's daring manuever constituted proof of Poland's commitment to transition, reacted favorably with new loans, grants, and guarantees.

One of the biggest surprises of the reform, as well as the most immediate proof of the correctness of at least part of it, was the almost instantaneous flourishing of small retail trade and services, something that happened throughout Eastern Europe the moment prices were freed. Within a month enterprising Poles had found ways to fill shops with goods of all kinds, from toilet paper to kiwis. An army of informal operators, many of them from as far away as Russia, began selling an enormous variety of merchandise on the streets. The most piquant sign of the new entrepreneurial energy was the transformation of the square surrounding the former Palace of Culture—the gingerbread symbol of Stalinism that dominates part of downtown Warsaw—into a bustling center of small-scale street capitalism.[61]

Instead of complaining about standing in lines, now Poles complained that whereas the shops were full they could not afford to buy anything. Official statistics, which showed a drop in real wages of 30 percent over the course of 1990, seemed to support this complaint. But someone was buying, because the shops and informal sellers not only stayed open, they began expanding, leasing space, and finding new products to sell. In fact, since most Poles had participated heavily in the second economy before the reform, a phenomenon not captured in official statistics, many found that they could survive quite well in the new circumstances. A precipitous drop in inflation helped. From a figure of over 50 percent per month in October 1989, it fell to almost zero in April 1990, before rising to an average of 5 or 6 percent per month through the end of 1990. What is more, the złoty remained stable. Since it was initially undervalued, Polish exporters prospered in 1990. For the first time since Gomułka, Poland experienced a trade surplus and its state budget even managed a small surplus.

Not all the entrepreneurial activity that enlivened Poland was undertaken in the spirit of hard work and frugal investment. Many trimmers found ways to enrich themselves that skirted or even broke the law. Bank scandals were particularly flagrant. Two exceptionally enterprising swindlers took advantage of Poland's primitive banking system with a check kiting scheme that netted them more than $300 million in only a few months before they escaped abroad with their loot.[62] Within two years the craving for conspicuous consumption among newly wealthy Poles supported a Mercedes dealership in Warsaw and dozens of chic shops along Novi Świat and other central Warsaw streets.

In the long run, the accumulation of private capital this display of wealth represented is what will marketize the Polish economy, assuming that the Polish government is clever enough to encourage successful entrepreneurs to reinvest their profits in Poland rather than sending them to Switzerland. But in the short run the contrast between the conspicuous consumption of sometimes shady operators and the difficulties faced by peasants and ordinary workers spelled trouble for Balcerowicz's austere wage and price policy. The trade and current account surplus of the reform's first year proved to be an artifact of temporary financial relations rather than a permanent phenomenon; in 1991 both the trade balance and the state budget slipped back into deficit. By the end of that year unemployment was over 10 percent and rising rapidly, while gross domestic product had declined another 9 percent from its 11.6 percent drop in 1990. Despite the debt relief granted by creditors that reduced servicing by 80 percent, the Polish government could not put together investment in its infrastructure equaling even one-tenth of Treuhand's initial $23 billion budget in eastern Germany.

Large Privatization in Poland

Small privatization occurred quickly in most East European countries, with the exception of Romania. In Poland by the end of 1991, 57 percent of the small-scale trading firms and 45 percent of the building industry were in private hands. More than 1.2 million private Polish companies registered for business in 1990 and 1991.[63] Large privatization, however, was a different story. In Poland, Balcerowicz was not able to get the second phase of his shock therapy, the reorganization of thousands of socialist enterprises, off the ground. According to public statements of many leaders, the weaning of these firms from their government subsidies could best be accomplished by rapidly selling them off. The trouble was that no one wanted them. Employing hundreds or even thousands of unnecessary workers, sometimes producing a product so inefficiently that it was worth less than the materials that had gone into making it (the so-called value-subtractor firm), and usually saddled with enormous environmental deficits, the metal-eaters were unattractive candidates for any kind of investment. Certainly foreigners hesitated to put money into these companies, while inside Poland private sources for such investments were minimal. Janusz Lewandowski, who was head of the Ministry of Ownership Transformation during 1991, succinctly summed up the problem he faced: "Privatization is when someone who doesn't know who the real owner is and doesn't know what it's really worth sells something to someone who doesn't have any money."[64]

Privatization of one kind had started in Poland as early as 1987, when some farsighted members of the nomenklatura began to find legal ways of gaining control of the assets of the enterprises they administered. Sweetheart leasing deals and spinoffs to newly organized private firms were among the arrangements that became known as "nomenklatura capitalism."[65] During the confused summer of 1989 the large number of these "spontaneous privatizations" favoring the bureaucracy produced a storm of public revulsion. The new government took ten months to put together its plan, which was not unreasonable considering the necessity to devise a plan that would counter the sense that only Communists and crooks were benefiting from privatization. On August 1, 1990, the newly formed Ministry of Ownership Transformation began the process it claimed would privatize the Polish economy in three years.

The first device the privatizers tried, late in 1990, was to offer five of the soundest state enterprises for sale to the public at prices established by Western experts under rules that favored the small investor.[66] The auction was not encouraging, since the shares could be sold only after extending the deadline for bids. Using this method, by the end of 1991 the government had sold a total of only twenty-seven firms.

Paradoxically, the very vigor of civil society that had made 1989 possible in Poland inhibited large privatization. Unlike eastern Germany, where the West Germans went about reorganizing eastern Germany whether the East Germans liked it or not, the Polish government had to take Polish workers into account. During the period of martial law, workers' councils, which had been created at the time of legal Solidarity and which continued on a pro forma basis from that time on, were able to survive in many industrial enterprises. When the Communist party collapsed, these councils asserted their right to participate in management. In March 1990 Mazowiecki's government, under political pressure, found it expedient to give these councils the right to approve any decision to privatize their own firms.

This move suggested that no privatization plan would work in Poland that did not face up to the problem of distributive justice. Therefore, the next step the government took was to announce a voucher plan. Under this scheme, proposed by Janusz Lewandowski even before 1989, each citizen would receive—free of charge and as a matter of right—a voucher permitting him or her to invest in one of several holding companies managed by Western firms. These in turn would invest in Polish enterprises.[67] Citizens would benefit, presumably, when the management firms paid dividends based on their success in turning the enterprises they had purchased to profitability. A certain portion of the vouchers were set aside specifically for workers in each enterprise. By giving a little stake in the process of privatization to every citizen, albeit indirectly, and by particularly favoring workers, Lewandowski hoped to make the distribution of socially owned assets as politically palatable as possible. Before this plan could be implemented, however, it became bogged down in the political crises of 1990 and 1991, which are discussed later in this chapter. A plan based on Lewandowski's idea of mass privatization involving Western-managed investment funds passed only in April 1993.

Czechoslovakia's Voucher Plan

Czechoslovakia adopted a privatization plan for its large industries based on vouchers as well, but with differences that corresponded to the differences between Polish and Czechoslovak society. Less pressured by a mobilized public than in Poland, or perhaps pressured in a different way, the Czechoslovak government did not set aside any vouchers specifically for workers. Neither did Czechs and Slovaks get their vouchers for free. Czechoslovak citizens had to register their vouchers, which were worth one thousand investment points, for a fee of 1,035 crowns, which was a little less than half an average worker's monthly wage. They could keep their vouchers for personal investment or they could entrust them to an investment firm, but they could not sell them immediately. Czechoslovak vouchers were not supposed to be a gift based on the principle of distributive justice, although that factor was not absent from the plan, but required their owners to make a cost/benefit analysis and undertake a certain amount of risk.

The privatization of many large firms in Czechoslovakia took place through a contrived auction. First, each enterprise submitted a plan to the government showing how much of its assets it wished to offer to the public. For example, the famous Plzen brewery offered 40 percent of its shares to the public through vouchers, 20 percent to investment funds, and 40 percent to investors through banks, of which 5 percent was set aside for employees. The East Slovak Ironworks, on the other hand, decided to offer all of its available shares to the public through vouchers.[68] To begin the process the government placed an arbitrary value on the shares—100 points for three shares. Bidders selected their companies and sent in their choices at one of the hundreds of offices set up around the country for the purpose. In cases where the demand exceeded or fell substantially short of the number of shares offered, a pricing committee of three persons reset the price upward or downward as the case might be, and a second round was held. After that round and succeeding rounds, the process was repeated until all or most of the shares had been assigned. All the bidding was covered fully in the newspapers, and each bidder received a computer printout of the situation from a central office at each stage. It took five rounds to complete this "first wave" of privatization, which included about fifteen hundred firms. The fifth iteration took place in December 1992 and early in 1993 the shares were to be distributed.[69]

The Polish voucher plan did not contemplate permitting individuals to "buy" shares of individual firms. Instead they had to go through state-certified asset managers. The idea, in part, was to guard against unwise use of the vouchers by an uninformed citizenry. In Czechoslovakia, however, the point of the process was to establish an equities market where none had existed before, not to protect citizens. The Czechoslovak innovators wanted citizens to use their vouchers as they saw fit because they believed that when confronted with real choices about risk and profit, Czechs and Slovaks would make decisions no less rational than people anywhere. Since in actuality many people make quite irrational decisions about their money, this meant that some would be swindled out of their vouchers, others would spend them foolishly, and others would speculate profitably. But this happens in every economy, and the Czechoslovak planners believed that positive results of a learn-by-doing privatization would far outweigh these certain but not fundamental failings.

In the early 1990s it remained unclear what the economic results of the Czechoslovak voucher plan would be, but from the psychological point of view the scheme was a real success. At first most Czechs and Slovaks were not too interested in the plan. A survey taken early in 1991 indicated that only 15 percent of the people had any interest in a voucher program.[70] The government hoped that out of a population of fifteen million people about four million would register their vouchers, but by November 1991 registrations were moving slowly. At that moment a company called (in Czech) Harvard Capital & Consulting (HC&C) began advertising that it would guarantee to return 10,350 crowns (that is, ten times the original investment) to any investor within one year if the investor was disappointed in how his or her vouchers were doing with HC&C.[71] Suddenly lines of citizens appeared at post offices around the country registering their vouchers. Eventually more than four hundred investment firms popped up, some promising even higher returns than HC&C, and by the end of the registration period in January 1992, 8.7 million Czechs and Slovaks had registered their vouchers.

The contrast in public attitudes between Poland and Czechoslovakia was palpable. In Poland privatization was perceived as something to be resisted, a threat imposed by Warsaw intellectuals. Many Poles associated private enterprise with shifty operators at the top and Ukrainian peasants selling underwear from a camping cot on the streets at the bottom. In Czechoslovakia the feeling was very different. Almost every active citizen was involved in the privatization process, figuring what to do with his or her vouchers. Even those who condescendingly spoke of the plan as a sort of lottery out of which they expected nothing were also discussing the tip their brother-in-law had given them about company X or the rumor they had heard about investment firm Y. The risk for the government in all of this, of course, was enormous, because the possibilities for disenchantment were great. But at the very least in Czechoslovakia privatization had everyone's attention.

The confidence and drive behind this daring plan came from Václav Klaus, Czechoslovakia's vigorous minister of finance.[72] Klaus first read Friedrich von Hayek's critique of Marxist economics, *The Road to Serfdom*, in the 1960s, when he was a student in North America, and it convinced him that "socialism not only does not work but cannot work."[73] Klaus became a Friedmanite economist, and during the normalization period he was banished to the Czechoslovak State Bank. In 1987 he became assistant director of the Institute for Economic Forecasting, where a small staff of like-minded economists had managed to hide themselves working on econometrics and other highly technical studies.[74] An active participant in the creation of Civic Forum at the Magic Lantern but not a signer of Charter 77, Klaus became minister of finance in the coalition government of December 1989. His neoconservative fiscal policies achieved a balanced budget and contained inflation.

During 1990 and 1991 Klaus emerged as the dominant figure in the federal government by defeating two rivals, Valtr Komárek and Václav Havel. Komárek had been a relatively liberal Communist under Husák and had been the director of the Institute for Economic Forecasting. As deputy premier in the government that took office late in 1989 he favored decentralization and demonopolization but remained in favor of retaining significant state control over enterprises. Klaus, on the other hand, favored full liberalization of prices, internal convertibility of the crown, and the voucher plan. Other former Communists, such as Ota Šik, who had returned from exile, advocated a slower rate of transition. But after the election of June 1990 Komárek was dropped from the council of ministers. Klaus remained minister of finance, supported by two allies heading the ministry of the economy and the ministry for economic reform. In September 1990 the government adopted its official reform document, the Scenario for Economic Reform, incorporating most of Klaus's ideas.[75]

Havel's concern about Klaus's economic policies was that the human cost of too radical a plan might be high. Havel also disagreed with Klaus over the role and function of Civic Forum. Many of the old Charter 77 antipoliticians, now in positions of power, valued Civic Forum's nationwide character as a democratic movement on behalf of civil society. Klaus, on the other hand, did not believe the broad, antipolitical ethic was appropriate for the post-1989 situation. He wanted to turn Civic Forum into a disciplined liberal party in the European sense (that is, a neoconservative party). His election as chairman of Civic Forum in October 1990 led early in 1991 to splitting the movement into two elements, the majority supporting Klaus and the minority, mostly old Charter 77 activists, supporting the broader and looser style of the old Civic Forum.

When Civic Forum split, Klaus did not lose the political support of the coalition of forces that had won the June 1990 election, and so he was able to implement the Scenario for Economic Reform. During little more than one year, the Czechs and Slovaks permitted full foreign ownership of firms; passed two comprehensive laws on restitution to those who had lost property under the Communist regime; balanced the budget; passed laws on the privatization of small industry, large industry, and land; introduced a new tax system on a Western model; adopted a comprehensive social security system that significantly decentralized welfare administration; and maintained Czechoslovak competitiveness by several currency devaluations.

During 1990 Czechoslovakia enjoyed the best economic performance of any country in Eastern Europe, although it was quite bad by world standards. Net material product declined only 3.1 percent, exports to developed market economies actually increased (although overall trade declined), and inflation was a relatively manageable 10 percent.[76] This good performance could be attributed not only to Klaus's management, but also in part to the few modernizing risks the Husák and Jakeš governments had taken in the 1980s. At the end of 1989, Czechoslovakia's foreign debt stood at only $7.9 billion, and during 1990 it went up only another $200 million.

Slow but Steady in Hungary

In Hungary, marketization proceeded at a different pace and from a different base. Whereas the Czechoslovak economy had countenanced few alternative forms of ownership over the years, Hungary's much more varied economic structure, especially as the changes of the 1980s took effect, placed it in the most advantageous position in Eastern Europe to turn toward world markets. When József Antall's government took office in mid-1990, Hungary already allowed private businesses of up to five hundred employees, permitted foreign owners to repatriate their profits in convertible currency, and levied an income tax. Hungary joined the International Monetary Fund (IMF) and World Bank in 1982 and achieved most-favored nation trade status with the United States initially in 1978, so it had long since begun its integration into Western mechanisms. Its gross foreign debt per capita was the highest in Eastern Europe, but the determination of all major parties not to reschedule or to default convinced Europeans that Hungary was a stable place for investment.

Foreign firms wasted no time in jumping into the Hungarian arena. During 1990 the number of joint ventures more than tripled, until by the middle of 1991 over 10 percent of all sizable Hungarian firms had a joint venture agreement with some foreign investor. Admittedly, over half of the joint ventures were small, involving less than $160,000 each, and the total investment was far less than Hungarian specialists calculated would be ideal, but Hungary got off to a much better start than either Poland or Czechoslovakia. Foreign investment reached $1.2 billion by mid-1991 and had more than doubled that by the end of 1992. When the government of Prime Minister Antall invited foreign investment firms to evaluate candidates for large privatization, an alarming number of Western accounting and law firms crowded into Budapest to overhaul Hungarian accounting methods, to supervise the foreign investments, and to bid on the privatization plan.[77] Trade with former CMEA members took a disastrous downturn, but trade with the West picked up 18 percent in 1991 and hard currency bank accounts held by Hungarians doubled to $1.5 billion.[78] By March 1992 one knowledgeable observer could suggest that the Hungarian economy was "over the hump."[79]

The impressive early developments in Hungary lent at least temporary support to the argument of the gradualists. There was no shock therapy in Hungary. Whereas in both Poland and Czechoslovakia advocates of rapid reform were able to assert themselves in the new governments, in Hungary the moderate philosophy of the Democratic Forum (MDF), which was reinforced by the necessity to enter into a coalition with the Smallholders and the Christian Democrats, forced a slower pace of privatization. The Hungarians had a second advantage, which was political stability. In Poland divisive political debates over how to replace Jaruzelski and how to elect a new Sejm dominated politics during 1990 and 1991, and in Czechoslovakia the government elected in mid-1990 had only a two-year mandate. But in Hungary the next election was not scheduled until 1994. Václav Klaus had to hurry to get his economic reforms in place before the uncertainty of the 1992 election but József Antall had time to pursue a more measured policy.

Because privatization had gotten underway in Hungary during the Communist regime, sometimes in the form of nomenklatura capitalism and sometimes in the form of ill-advised sales of public assets, Antall's government actually had to centralize the privatization process to prevent the situation from becoming chaotic. The strategy of the State Property

Agency (SPA), which was created in the spring of 1990, was to evaluate the firms being privatized before selling or otherwise disposing of them. When the SPA put its first twenty firms up for sale in 1990, it did not actually ask for purchase bids but rather for tenders from international consulting firms willing to manage the restructuring of a firm for a fee or for a percentage of the eventual sale price. The consulting firms began the restructuring, but one year after the beginning of the process, all twenty firms remained unsold.

While the government was painstakingly evaluating enterprises, a significant portion of the Hungarian economy was being transformed by a completely different device, the creation of what sociologist David Stark calls "enterprise limited liability companies."[80] Hungarian law did not permit state enterprises to privatize themselves, but the law did permit the creation of brand new limited liability companies. A very large number of state enterprises, therefore, reorganized themselves by creating "new" corporations that "purchased" or otherwise acquired assets of the old enterprise. The stock of these new businesses was owned by other "new" enterprises, by banks, or by state enterprises. According to sociologist József Böröz, from the end of 1988 to August 1991 the number of joint stock companies in Hungary rose from 116 to 777 and the number of limited liability corporations from 451 to 26,827. Almost all of these were enterprise limited liability companies that represented little new investment.[81]

The rapidly growing number of Hungarian corporations was not necessarily a sign that private ownership was booming in Hungary but rather a sign that Hungarian managers had found a way to insulate themselves from state interventions and other difficulties. In this complex of new organizational forms, cross-ownership, interlocking directorates, and managerial networks were the underlying reality. Some, like David Stark, were critical of this operation, since it appeared simply to replicate old networks without bringing any new ideas into play. Others, like Peter Murrell, considered the development a positive one, since the process of creating these new interlocking firms was incremental, it built on rather than destroyed the practical knowledge that is essential for the functioning of an economy, it created space for innovation, and it did not depend on a super blueprint of the economy that informed all decisions.

Early in 1993 initial enthusiasm for Hungarian gradualism waned somewhat. Just as some advocates of the "third way" had feared, foreign investors had picked off the most profitable firms, leaving the State Property Agency with the huge, outdated enterprises. In June 1992 the Hungarian government recognized that 30 to 40 percent of the least productive parts of the economy would remain in its hands and created the State Assets Handling Company to manage those firms. Neither was the Hungarian legislature able to keep its budget deficit within bounds. In January 1993 the International Monetary Fund held up access to a $500 million loan for just that reason. Unlike Poland, where industrial production took a turn up in 1992, Hungarian industrial production continued its decline, although at a slowing pace.[82] Poland's improving performance and Hungary's slip left up in the air the question of which policy was best—shock therapy or gradualism.

The Third Shoe: Ethnic Relations

In the euphoric first six months of 1990, when people throughout Eastern Europe were still celebrating their unexpected extraction from a failed communism with hope and enthusiasm, it seemed to many that two main tasks lay ahead. These were to create democracy and to marketize the economy. In the two years that followed the revolutions of 1989, however, a third task of equal, perhaps in some cases greater, importance arose: finding the mechanisms that would permit different ethnic groups to live together peacefully. The most atrocious case of ethnic conflict is the Yugoslav civil war, the sources of which are discussed in Chapter 7, but the ethnic geography of the entire East European region, coupled with the high value placed on ethnic identity in contemporary politics, created volatile situations in a number of specific hot spots.

The question of why nationalism or ethnicity is such a central political issue in the twentieth century has not been answered satisfactorily. In an age of decolonialization, broad media access, and open elections, political figures use nationalist appeals to mobilize populations or to legitimate their policies. The power of nationalist justifications is related to the notion of equity introduced by the French and American revolutions. During the overwhelming majority of human history, societies have organized their social relations around the obvious fact that human beings are not born equal in personal endowments, social position, gender, or wealth. Ideologies, both political and spiritual, were in significant measure devices for mythologizing that fact. In the twentieth century, however, the idea has become widespread that, whatever the inequalities of the real world, one of society's main purposes should be to conduct its affairs fairly. This by now almost universal view, often practiced in the breach, provides the fundamental moral justification for modern social movements, from unionism to feminism to nationalism.

Nationalists argue that equity in politics is impossible unless "their" people or region is "ruled" by co-nationals. This is palpably not true, since it is quite possible for minority groups to be treated fairly in national states and for national leaders to treat their own co-nationals monstrously. But the argument strikes a very deep chord in those who respond to it, which is, of course, the reason that politicians so often play the nationalist card. This makes the difficult analytical problem less a historical one than a psychological one. Why do so many people respond so enthusiastically to the politicization of their estrangement from the other?

In its extreme forms ethnic politics is a device for avoiding responsibility. "Strangers are guilty—that is the conviction of a nationalist," wrote Adam Michnik.[83] This is one of the reasons that the most vigorous nationalists in the new Eastern Europe were former Communists. They, along with millions who collaborated in large or small ways, were united in what Jiřina Šiklová calls the "solidarity of the culpable."[84] In Romania it was the sycophantic admirers of Nicolae Ceauşescu who published the xeno-phobic *România Mare*. In Serbia Slobodan Milošević, an unreconstructed Communist apparatchik, avoided economic and social issues by mounting attacks on Albanians and Croats. In Bulgaria the former Communists fomented Turkish-Bulgarian confrontations; in Slovakia former security police provided the manpower for ugly nationalist incidents, such as throwing eggs at Václav Havel in the fall of 1991; in Poland the core of the anti-Semitic supporters of Stanisław Tymiński, the enigmatic presiden-tial candidate of 1990, and of his "Party X" were former Communist security police. Adam Michnik's comment about Polish anti-Semitism holds true for ethnic politics throughout the region: "When anti-Semitic opinions are expressed in Poland, Jews are not the issue, whatever the authors of the opinions themselves may think. The question is whether there will or will not be a Polish democracy."[85]

Eastern Europe is considerably less ethnically diverse in the 1990s than it was in the 1930s. There are three main reasons for this, none of which would be chosen by any rational person. First, the overwhelming majority of East European Jews were killed in World War II, and most of the sur-vivors eventually emigrated. Second, the very large German communities throughout Eastern Europe were forcibly removed to Germany, with many Germans dying in the process. The bloody expulsion of almost six million Germans from what is today western Poland made an ethnically homogeneous Poland possible. The harsh but fully understandable removal of the 3.2 million Germans living in the Sudetenland between 1945 and 1948 greatly simplified the ethnic picture in Bohemia, just as the emigration of most of the Saxon Germans from Transylvania and of the Germans living in the Vojvodina simplified those historically diverse areas.[86] Third, border changes increased homogeneity. The accession of the sub-Carpathian Ukraine to the Soviet Union removed most of the Ruthenians (Ukrainians) from Czechoslovakia, and the shifting of Polish borders about 150 kilometers to the west rid Poland of most of its Ukrai-nian and White Russian minorities.

These wrenching changes left all the countries of Eastern Europe rel-atively ethnically homogeneous, with the exceptions of Yugoslavia, dis-cussed later, and Czechoslovakia, which became roughly two-thirds Czech and one-third Slovak. In Czechoslovakia politics between the election of mid-1990 and the election of mid-1992 became bogged down in the ques-tion of what Slovakia's relationship would be to the federation. One of the main assignments of the Czechoslovak federal assembly elected in 1990 was to write a federal constitution, which it planned to do by the end of 1991. From the start, however, the negotiations went slowly. Slovak pol-iticians wanted to make sure that Slovakia would be able to organize in its own way without first having to accept a constitution written in Prague.

Therefore they proposed that before a constitution be written a state treaty be signed. The Czechs hesitated because in international law state treaties are signed only between sovereign states, so that such a treaty would implicitly recognize Slovak sovereignty. As discussions over this issue in 1991 wore on, it became clear that no agreement that the Czechs would be willing to sign would be satisfactory to the Slovaks, and vice versa. Constitutional negotiations became gridlocked. In exasperation, late in 1991 President Havel proposed a number of measures to push the process forward, such as a referendum and giving the president special powers until the 1992 elections, but the Slovak members of the federal assembly, in league with former Communists, were able to prevent any of these initiatives from being adopted.

The most powerful political movement in Slovakia immediately after the velvet revolution, Public Against Violence (VPN), was an antipolitical movement like Civic Forum, and it suffered the same fate. In March 1991 its more nationalistic wing, led by Slovak prime minister and former Communist Vladimír Mečiar, left the movement and formed its own party. Mečiar had two complaints: first, the leadership of VPN did not take Slovak national issues sufficiently into account; and second, VPN too strongly supported the economic reforms coming out of Prague. These, he argued, were damaging the Slovak economy, which was both more rural and more concentrated in rust-belt defense industries than the Czech economy. Mečiar attracted the support of nationalists, who liked his nationalism, and former Communists, who were opposed to marketizing reforms. His own past was a question mark, since he was accused of links with the security police, of using security files to damage his political enemies, and of protecting former security agents; but he always succeeded in shrugging these accusations off with the argument that they were part of a plot hatched against him by the Czechs. Since all of Mečiar's characteristics were antithetical to the leaders of VPN, they withdrew their support of him as prime minister, and in May 1991 he had to step down in favor of Jan Čarnogursky, head of the Christian Democratic Movement.

In June, 1992, however, a scheduled election brought Mečiar back to power in Slovakia. Public opinion polls indicated that most Slovaks wanted to keep the federal republic of Czechoslovakia, but the paradoxical result of this election was to put a man in power who was dedicated to independence for Slovakia. Very quickly the die was cast when Slovak representatives in the federal parliament prevented the reelection of Václav Havel as president of the federal republic. On July 17, the same day that the Slovak National Council declared that Slovakia was a sovereign country, Havel resigned. The election also had confirmed Václav Klaus's power in the Czech lands. Fairly quickly he decided that if Mečiar and his party wanted to separate, the Czechs would be better off to let them go. Klaus and Mečiar entered into negotiations that, while not cordial, were at least productive. After overcoming some constitutional difficulties agreement was reached, and on January 1, 1993, Czechoslovakia, a country that had not existed before 1918, went back out of existence, replaced by the Czech Republic and the Slovak Republic. The split was peaceful—some called it the velvet divorce—but the aggressive nationalism and authoritarian style of the new Slovak leadership led some to wonder if independence for Slovakia had not created more problems for central Europe than it had solved.

Two other types of ethnic diversities characterized post-1989 Eastern Europe.[87] The first concerned long-standing indigenous populations such as the Jews, the Gypsies, and the Bulgarian Turks. The second concerned ethnic islands that could not be drawn into the borders of the postwar national states, primarily Hungarians living in Slovakia, Transylvania, and to a lesser extent, in the Vojvodina.

The Holocaust acutely sensitized West Europeans and North Americans to anti-Semitism in Eastern Europe, and they have had little trouble in finding it, even after 1989.[88] Controversy over the possibility of opening a Carmelite chapel at Auschwitz, the comment by Lech Wałęsa during his electoral campaign that he was "one hundred percent Polish," and anti-Semitic overtones in the electoral campaign of the Hungarian Democratic Forum have all brought Western criticisms. The most openly expressed anti-Semitism can be found in Romania, despite the existence there of fewer than twenty thousand Jews, most of them quite old.[89]

What these well-publicized criticisms have missed is that the situation in Eastern Europe regarding Jews is vastly different today than it was before World War II. East Europeans are acutely aware that they will be quickly and sharply criticized by the international community for public expressions of anti-Semitism, and many leaders and intellectuals have taken steps to indicate that they do not endorse anti-Semitic outbursts. Immediately after his election Lech Wałęsa became the first Polish president to visit Israel, and in January 1991 the Polish episcopate published a pastoral letter reiterating the Catholic church's dogma that Jews did not murder Jesus and telling its followers that anti-Semitism was wrong.[90] In East Germany, one of the first things the newly elected parliament did early in 1990 was to take on the guilt of the Holocaust. In Hungary, Western criticism of anti-Semitic intimations in the Hungarian elections of April 1990 brought investigations and clear statements from President Árpád Göncz that anti-Semitism had no place in Hungarian politics. The Hungarian government also made itself a major transit point for Soviet Jews en route to Israel. Between mid-1989 and mid-1991 more than 125,000 Jews from the Soviet Union emigrated to Israel via Budapest.[91] For a long time the National Salvation Front in Romania did almost nothing to repudiate public expressions of anti-Semitism in Romania. But in September 1991 President Iliescu did visit Israel, and at the same time Prime Minister Petre Român called *România Mare* a "racist, chauvinist" publication that should be banned.[92]

In Poland a strong movement to reconceptualize the relations between Poles and Jews has been under way since the mid-1980s. The Jaruzelski government developed good relations with Jewish cultural organizations abroad, sponsored the restoration of cemeteries and synagogues, and encouraged the publication of a flood of books about Polish-Jewish relations.[93] Since 1989, both in scholarship and in public discussions, Poles have moved beyond stereotyped thinking and begun to grapple seriously with the issue of anti-Semitism. No parties or individuals espousing anti-Semitism were elected to national office in Poland either in 1989 or in 1991.

In Hungary, which was the only Communist country in Eastern Europe during the 1970s and 1980s where public anti-Semitism was considered in bad taste, Mária Kovács finds that the increase in anti-Semitism since 1989 is "restricted almost exclusively to symbolic politics." This does not mean that symbolic politics are not painful. In August 1992 the reactionary poet István Csurka, vice-president of the Democratic Forum (MDF), created a firestorm of controversy by blaming "non-Magyar deeds" fomented by an international Jewish conspiracy as the main problem facing Hungary. His views strike a chord with a certain segment of Hungarian society. But Kovács writes that anti-Semitic appeals in Hungary have led neither to any obvious electoral successes nor "to any evidence of discrimination by private or public businesses, public agencies, the state bureaucracy, or the police. . . . Majority attitudes toward the Jews have remained polite and tolerant."[94]

One cannot say that Eastern Europe is free of anti-Semitism, but are there societies that can make that claim? Anti-Semitism is widely recognized in Eastern Europe today as unacceptable and actual discrimination does not exist. Scholars and creative artists are even beginning to confront the historical record. When anti-Semitic graffiti appear on an East European wall, they are the product of fringe elements no longer able to secure broad public support, just as in the West.

A similar report cannot be given on the condition of the Gypsies, who have replaced the Jews at the bottom of the East European status ladder. Perpetual outsiders, traditionally linked with petty thievery, and always involved in small trading, the Roma, as they call themselves, have become the most persecuted and despised people in Eastern Europe.[95] During World War II the Roma suffered their own holocaust (*Porajmos* in Romany), losing as much as 70 percent of their European population. Unlike the Jews, however, Romany survivors did not receive any apologies or compensation, nor do they have a new homeland.

Most of the postwar Communist regimes attempted to "solve" the Romany problem through integration. The rate of Romany literacy and infant survival increased substantially in every country under communism, although it still remained significantly below that of the majority population. On the other hand, the Roma experienced, and continue to experience, considerably fewer opportunities than other citizens. In Communist Czechoslovakia, for example, Romany children who did not speak the local language—and most of them did not—were sometimes packed off to special schools for the mentally retarded. In Romania a significant portion of the children abandoned under Ceauşescu's natalist policies were Romas, and in Hungary only about 1.5 percent of Romany workers rose to the category of "skilled worker." These and many other data reflect the contempt in which the majority cultures in Eastern Europe hold Romas. The fact that Romas are disproportionately involved in crime has not improved the situation. Since the revolutions of 1989, racist attacks on Romas have greatly increased, but on the other hand the increased openness of society has permitted Romany activists to make their case and to assert their rights with greater vigor. With no homeland, Romas are without foreign protectors. Therefore their situation is not one that is likely to threaten the peace of the region. But in ethical terms the question of how Romas interact with the majority cultures in which they live will continue to be one of the important litmus tests of ethnic relations in Eastern Europe.

The Turkish issue in Bulgaria is quite different from the issues surrounding the Jews and the Roma. Despite Todor Zhivkov's vigorous anti-Turkish campaigns of 1984–1985 and 1989, Turks and Bulgarians have lived together fairly peacefully since World War II, in part because the Turks themselves have shown remarkable restraint. The Movement for Rights and Freedoms, founded early in 1990 and led by one of Bulgaria's most able politicians, Ahmed Dogan, became a principled defender of the rights of minorities in Bulgaria. Turks, who constitute approximately 10 percent of the Bulgarian population, took to Dogan and his party with enthusiasm, making it by the end of 1991 the third most important party in Bulgaria. The Union of Democratic Forces maintained a positive program toward the Turkish minority, forcing a revocation of Zhivkov's assimilation decrees almost immediately after the revolution and supporting the integration of Turks into Bulgarian society.

An unexpected aspect of the improvement in the position of the Turkish minority in Bulgaria was that at the governmental level relations between Bulgaria and Turkey improved remarkably. During the Communist era, Turkey, which is a member of NATO, maintained strong military forces close to the southern border of Bulgaria as part of the West's policy of containment. Turkey presented itself as defending the southeastern flank of the European continent against possible Communist encroachments. The Bulgarians, on the other hand, considered the concentration of Turkish troops on its border a threat to Bulgarian sovereignty and an unwelcome pressure on behalf of the Bulgarian Turkish minority. With the demise of communism, however, the NATO strategy of containment became obsolete and in 1990 Turkey and Bulgaria began negotiations on several levels, including the military. These negotiations proved remarkably successful. Late in 1991 Turkey promised to reduce its force levels on the Bulgarian border and exchanges of high level military delegations lessened Bulgaro-Turkish tensions. Many educated Bulgarians favor a positive policy toward Turkey because they believe that Turkey is the country most likely to invest in Bulgaria and to provide regional economic leadership. A few Bulgarians are even enthusiastic about the Turkish-sponsored idea for a Black Sea economic zone, which came to an initial stage of fruition in the summer of 1992, when nine countries signed a "Declaration on Black Sea Economic Cooperation."[96]

A second general type of ethnic problem in Eastern Europe concerns the remnants of populations living in countries that are not their national state. The most numerous of these are Hungarians. Approximately ten million Hungarians live in Hungary, but about two million live across the border in Transylvania (Romania), another six hundred thousand in Slovakia, and another five hundred thousand in the Vojvodina (Yugoslavia/Serbia). The exact historical circumstances of each of these enclaves differs, but they all ended up in their present countries as a result of the Treaty of Trianon that the defeated Hungary had to sign at the end of World War I. During the interwar period the basic aim of Hungarian foreign policy was to revise Trianon. One of the several reasons Hungary entered into an alliance with Hitler's Germany was that it received the ethnically Hungarian portions of Transylvania (Romania), Slovakia, and Yugoslavia as rewards. When the prewar borders were re-established in 1945, the Soviets prevented Hungary from raising any of the old Trianon claims. In 1975 Hungary signed the Helsinki accords, thus formally renouncing any revisionist border claims.

It was a shock, therefore, when on June 2, 1990, József Antall, recently installed as prime minister of Hungary, declared in a speech to the Hungarian Democratic Forum that whereas he was legally the president of the ten million Hungarians living in Hungary, he considered himself spiritually the prime minister of all the fifteen million Hungarians in the world. Antall explicitly stated that Hungary, as a signatory of the Helsinki accords, rejected changing borders through violence (he did not reject changes by other means), but he went on to say that "historically" he had to condemn a treaty (Trianon) in which Hungary lost two-thirds of its territory. When this statement raised considerable fuss, Antall did not help by reiterating that he believed his government had "a moral and spiritual duty to be responsible for every member of the fifteen million Hungarian community."[97] Later statements by other MDF officials confirmed that this remained that party's position.

Transylvania remains the main bone of contention. Romanians contend that they have a historic right to Transylvania because they have lived in the Carpathian region since before the time of Christ, that they were oppressed by Hungarians until Transylvania became part of Romania and even afterwards during World War II, and that they continue to face machinations from Budapest to regain the area. Hungarians contend that when they arrived in the region in the ninth century, no Romanians were there so Hungarians have the valid prior claim, that Transylvania was a part of Hungary for centuries, and that the Hungarian population there suffers from continuing pressure for Romanization.

Anyone who has ever witnessed a confrontation between Hungarians and Romanians over Transylvania, or between any two of the other contesting national groups in Eastern Europe, for that matter, will recognize that neither side is prepared to make the one admission that is the beginning of wisdom in interethnic relations: that on at least one occasion, just once, perhaps in the distant past, my side was, just slightly to be sure, wrong. Sooner or later both sides in these arguments will have to summon the moral strength to say, yes, in the past we have not always been entirely fair with you—now let us get on with the business of creating structures that will permit us to live together in the future. Discussions with Hungarian and Romanian politicians and intellectuals suggest, however, that time will be long in coming. The belief among Hungarians that Romania is a dark and primitive country is just as widespread as the belief among Romanians that the Hungarians are engaged in a campaign, supported by a wealthy and influential Hungarian emigration, to retrieve "their" part of Transylvania.

The best example Eastern Europe offers of how admission of past errors can soothe ethnic hatreds are the agreements that Germany reached with Poland and to a lesser extent with Czechoslovakia, Bulgaria, and Hungary. As Norman Naimark has observed, the Nazis pursued a qualitatively different kind of oppression of Poles than any experienced previously in the long relationship between Germany and Poland.[98] Before the eighteenth and nineteenth centuries Germans and Poles lived together quite well. Even in the age of nationalism German domination was at least civil and legalized. But during World War II the Nazis, operating on the principle that the Poles were not quite human, went far beyond any previous style of domination, killing three million Poles and purposefully degrading the survivors. When the Red Army gave the Poles the chance to retaliate in 1944 and 1945, they wreaked terrible vengeance against the Germans. Gomułka's policy in 1945 explicitly was to get rid of them all, and he almost succeeded. About 5.5 million Germans fled Poland, leaving perhaps 1.7 million dead. Today the German minority in Poland numbers about sixty thousand.

The wounds created by the viciousness of the German-Polish bloodletting still exist. Skinhead attacks on Poles crossing into eastern Germany in 1991 were only the most dramatic evidence. But the civil war in Yugoslavia proved the danger of permitting feelings of this sort to become the common currency of daily politics, and the Poles and the Germans did not take the Serbian and Croatian route. Even before the two Germanies were united, Helmut Kohl, despite the temporarily equivocal position he took on Poland's western border, repeatedly stated that his policy toward Poland was one of reconciliation on the model of Konrad Adenauer's policy toward France at the end of World War II. Adenauer had realized that stability in Europe demanded rapprochement between the bitter enemies of the previous hundred years, and Kohl (or perhaps it was Genscher) recognized that stability for Germany in the post-1989 world demanded rapprochement with Poland. The Poles too recognized that their ability to create a stable democracy and to restore economic prosperity demanded

good relations with their neighbors, not just with Germany but with Lith-
uania, Belorus, Russia, and Ukraine as well. Accordingly, Poland has been
in the forefront of countries seeking and attaining good relations with the
new states of the former Soviet Union and in reaching agreement with
Germany.

Poland's first success in this process was inserting itself into the two-
plus-four process. Insisting on participation in discussions of its western
border, Poland was able to conclude an Oder/Neisse treaty with Germany
on November 14, 1990. The second treaty of German–Polish cooperation
was the mutual friendship treaty of June 17, 1991.[99] Both treaties contained language of regret and of mutual responsibility for suffering. In
these treaties Poland and Germany both publicly and officially state that
they seriously wronged the other party in countless ways, they are sorry
for it, and they intend to do better in the future.

Specifically, the treaties call for a variety of confidence-building contacts between the two countries, including investment in infrastructure in
the regions on both sides of the common border, which in each case are
underdeveloped. More significant, they also facilitate the transfer of
administrative practices characteristic of the German "social market economy" to Poland. The Germans favor this kind of cooperation because it
pulls Poland into the German orbit and because they want to prevent a
Polish collapse. The Poles favor it because it offers them something they
greatly lack: proven methods of conducting a capitalist economy.

Perhaps the most striking feature of the treaties was the full Polish
recognition of German nationality rights—schools, language, cemeteries,
and monuments. Silesian patriotic organizations in Germany and some
nationalistically oriented German groups in Poland continued to raise
questions about the German minority, the justice of the border, and similar
contentious issues. But the leaderships in both states remained committed
to achieving friendship rather than hostility. As the French/German case
proved, this did not mean that there would never be differences of views
between Poland and Germany, but, as the same case also demonstrated,
the possibilities for fruitful and peaceful relations, even when enclave
minorities are involved, are unlimited if the leaderships of both countries
continue seriously to seek them.

The Second Round of Elections

In the future each East European country will conduct its elections, its
changes of government, its political struggles with the same modest glare
of North American attention evoked by similar processes in Belgium or
Portugal. All in all, this will be a healthy development. But during the first
few years of Eastern Europe's new pluralism, each new milestone was an
important one because it introduced political habits that could have a
forming effect on the shape of the emerging political culture. In the two

years between Ceaușescu's death and Gorbachev's resignation, only two East European countries conducted a second round of elections. Poland held two such elections, first one for president and then one for the national assembly, while Bulgaria conducted an election for its national assembly first and then held one for president.

With the coming to power of Tadeusz Mazowiecki in September 1989, the governance of Poland passed into the hands of an elite group of Polish intellectuals who were intelligent, dedicated to public service, and committed to transformation. In a very short time they put together an economic program they believed would save Poland and began implementing it. At first they were able to count on the enthusiasm generated by Solidarity's dramatic electoral victory in mid-1989, but within six months their position began to weaken. The unexpected but almost complete elimination of the Communists as a political factor meant that as time went on the composition of the Sejm, the position of Jaruzelski as president, and the fact that Communist generals Kiszczak and Siwicki remained ministers of internal affairs and of war respectively came to seem more and more anachronistic. Social groups not taken into account by the Balcerowicz plan became restive. Farmers, who suffered almost instantaneous losses by being thrown onto the market without at the same time being offered credit facilities, protested that the regime was antifarmer, and by September 1990 the United Peasants' party withdrew its support from Mazowiecki's government. Workers' councils from the large enterprises that would be hurt by cutting off subsidies protested the government's lack of consideration of their needs, as did government employees and others.

Early in 1990 Lech Wałęsa, always sensitive to the direction of the political winds, began to indicate that he too was not satisfied with the pace of reform. He suggested that the Citizens Committees, the political arm of Solidarity founded late in 1988, become directly involved in politics by supporting specific parties, and he began insisting on an "acceleration" of reform. The Mazowiecki camp, including Bronisław Geremek, head of the Solidarity parliamentary faction; Henryk Wujec, secretary of the main Citizens Committee; and Adam Michnik, editor of *Gazeta Wyborcza*, believed that Solidarity should not change into a partisan political party but should retain its character as a movement based on what they called "the Solidarity ethos." The issue was not dissimilar to the one in Czechoslovakia, where many of the Charter 77 intelligentsia wanted to maintain the movement quality of Civic Forum while Václav Klaus wanted to turn it into a political party.

When Wałęsa found himself facing opposition from his old comrades, he purposely destroyed the unity of Solidarity by firing Wujec as secretary of the Citizens Committee, withdrawing the Solidarity logo from *Gazeta Wyborcza*, and forming his own political arm, the Center Alliance. The irritated Mazowiecki forces countered with their own organization, Civic Movement-Democratic Action. They tried to appease farmers and workers' councils with concessions and to deflect criticism by firing generals

Kiszczak and Siwicki, but Wałęsa's motto of "acceleration" touched a chord with the Polish public. Despite the vigorous efforts of such respected figures as Adam Michnik, who called Wałęsa unpredictable, irresponsible, incompetent, and incapable of reform, the antipolitical faction of Solidarity that once stood for civil society against the rule of martial law was not able to counter Wałęsa's criticism that it constituted a closed elite of intellectuals who wanted to run the country in their own way.[100] "Poland's future cannot be built on [the basis of] one political orientation only," Wałęsa said.[101]

Jaruzelski, realizing his day was over, agreed to resign from the presidency, and in September the Sejm called for an election. Several candidates came forward to oppose Wałęsa, including Mazowiecki, who decided that he had to run in order to allow the people to pass judgment on his vision of a stable democracy. By the time the election was held on November 25, the Wałęsa forces were in the ascendancy, Geremek having been forced out as head of the Solidarity parliamentary caucus; but to everyone's surprise Wałęsa did not win a majority on the first ballot, taking only 40 percent of the vote. Even more surprising, Mazowiecki did not come in second. Stanisław Tymiński, a mysterious eccentric who claimed to have made a fortune in Canada and Peru, took 23 percent of the vote to Mazowiecki's 18 percent. Tymiński's success was based on strong support in small towns and in areas such as Katowice, in which the Balcerowicz plan threatened workers with unemployment. In the runoff Wałęsa won by a three-to-one margin, but the fact that one-quarter of the voters preferred the bizarre Tymiński suggested an unexpected depth of social alienation in Poland. Nevertheless, when Wałęsa took office at the end of 1990 and installed a new cabinet—the Mazowiecki government resigned immediately after the election—he kept Balcerowicz as minister of finance and vowed to accelerate the transformation process.

If the main political struggle of 1990 was how to rid Poland of one of the institutions contracted by the roundtable agreements—General Jaruzelski—the great political struggle of 1991 was how to get rid of the other—a Sejm in which 65 percent of the seats had been allotted to Communists and their allies. This time the battle was not between Solidarity factions but between the new president Wałęsa and the Sejm over the form of the election law they both agreed was needed. It was a complex and petty fight that began over principle and ended as a pure power struggle. The principle at issue was whether the method of election would be highly proportional, thus favoring small parties, or mostly winner-take-all single-member districts, which would favor large parties and coalitions. The Sejm favored the former and Wałęsa the latter, but by the time the issue was fully joined in the late spring and summer of 1991 both sides had become enmeshed in a sea of spiteful recriminations and arcane differentiations in which the principles became swallowed up in a struggle over who would win. Eventually the Sejm prevailed. The complex law governing the elections to the new Sejm was so highly proportional that parties receiving as little as 5 percent of the vote in some districts could win a seat.

Over sixty parties participated in the October 27, 1991, election, and twenty-nine of them placed members in the Sejm.[102] The largest party, Mazowiecki's Democratic Union, received only 12 percent of the popular vote. So little cohesion existed in the Sejm that it would take at least five parties to achieve a majority, but of course the largest parties were not allies. Six of the nine largest parties were descended from Solidarity but bore significant wounds from the struggle over the presidency, two were descendants of the Communists, and one was the Confederation for an Independent Poland, the nationalist party founded underground in 1982. This great dispersion of power was not entirely the result of the election law. If a 4 percent cutoff had been used to eliminate the small parties, the nine largest parties all still would have entered the Sejm.

Solidarity suffered from the same historical burden as Civic Forum, only to a greater degree. When great differences of opinion could be brought under the Solidarity umbrella during the restrictive conditions of Communist rule, the illusion was created that a general spirit of constructive democracy infused the Solidarity movement. The Geremek-Michnik-Mazowiecki forces valued that spirit and believed it could sustain Poland in its period of transformation. But under conditions of pluralism that ethos was doomed to failure. The bitter struggles over the presidency in 1990 and the electoral law in 1991 consumed, at least temporarily, whatever goodwill the contesting factions might have had toward one another, so that when the dust settled a coalition government proved very difficult to put together. In a sense, this was the negative political price Poland paid in the early 1990s for the positive virtues of the Solidarity movement of the 1980s.

After a nine month crisis, however, a seven-party coalition was finally achieved, bringing Hanna Suchocka, Eastern Europe's first female head of government, to office as prime minister. Suchocka proved to be a strong personality. Facing a series of widespread strikes, none-too-supportive leadership from President Wałęsa, and a nervous Sejm, within ninety days she put together a coherent governmental program and set about systematically putting it into effect. She skillfully negotiated a so-called "Pact on Enterprises" with the labor unions that would premit privatization to move ahead and then found ways to blunt the strikes called by competing union interests. She impressed foreign governments with her economic program and kept her coalition in line despite an increasingly contentious political climate. By the beginning of 1993 Polish economists were reporting that industrial production had stopped its decline and had actually begun to rise again.

Bulgaria held an election for its national assembly on October 13, 1991, just two weeks before the Polish election. In this election the Union of Democratic Forces (UDF) achieved a working majority, an outcome that contrasts sharply with the Polish experience. The UDF was not a national movement in the same sense as Solidarity or Civic Forum but an explicitly political coalition constructed for the purpose of winning elections. The main political issue of Bulgarian politics in 1991, the equivalent of Poland's struggle over electoral rules, was the new constitution. The Grand National Assembly had been elected primarily to write a constitution, but because the Bulgarian Socialist party (BSP—the former Communists) held a majority by virtue of its electoral victory in 1990, the opposition feared that any constitution coming from it would be unacceptable. For that reason, the UDF adopted the position that the constitutional draft that was working its way through the legislature in 1991 should be voted on only after new elections to the national assembly. The BSP did not agree, holding, quite naturally, that the Grand National Assembly in which they held a majority from the 1990 election was fully competent to confirm a new constitution.

Two of the main parties in the UDF—Bulgarian Agrarian National Union-Nikola Petkov (BANU-Nikola Petkov) and the Bulgarian Social Democratic party (BSDP)—decided to side with the Socialists on this issue and therefore were forced to leave the United Democratic Forces. The remaining members of the UDF continued their vigorous opposition to the constitution. At one point thirty-nine UDF members of the assembly walked out in an effort to prevent passage, and in the days before the final vote twenty members staged a hunger strike. But on July 12, 1991, more than three hundred out of the four hundred members of the assembly signed the new constitution, and it became law. Despite the concerns of the UDF, outside observers, and even some inside observers, considered it a sound constitution and a signal accomplishment for the Bulgarian political process.[103]

The election rules for the Bulgarian parliamentary election of October 1991 did not favor small parties, as the Polish law did. As a result, the groups that had broken off from the UDF to vote for passage of the constitution, as well as other splinter factions, fell below the 4 percent cutoff and placed no deputies in the national assembly. Only three parties jumped the 4 percent hurdle: the mainstream UDF obtained 110 seats out of the 240 available; the Socialists took 104 seats; and the Movement for Rights and Freedom, or the Turkish party, took 24 seats. The UDF did not have a majority in the new legislature, but there was no question that the Movement for Rights and Freedom would support the UDF, since it was the Socialists who spearheaded the nationalist rhetoric against the Turks. On the other hand, it would have been difficult both internally (inviting nationalist criticisms) and externally (harming relations with Greece) to appoint Turks to cabinet positions, which in a normal parliamentary system would have been the reward given to the swing party. Ahmed Dogan, the Turkish leader, solved this problem in a statesmanlike way by announcing that the Movement for Rights and Freedom supported the government but had no expectation of receiving any cabinet portfolios.

Bulgaria's presidential election was not as divisive as Poland's election, although Bulgaria did have its own Tymiński. He was Georgi Ganchev, a former fencing champion and basketball player who got almost 17 percent of the vote in the first round. The main contest was between Zhelyu Zhelev, president since mid-1990, and Velko Volkanov, who was supported by the BSP. The campaign was heated, especially since all the candidates except Zhelev were more or less nationalist. The BSP in particular ran a populist campaign, blaming the UDF for Bulgaria's poor condition, even though it had been in power only two months, and accusing it of being the Turkish party. They went so far as to portray Zhelev wearing a fez. Zhelev, and his vice-presidential candidate Blaga Dimitrova, one of Bulgaria's most honored poets, ran a much more measured campaign, not particularly nationalistic, and consistent with the integrity that Zhelev had brought to the president's office. In a close runoff election held in January 1992, Zhelev took almost 53 percent. Foreign observers breathed a sigh of relief, since many thought that it was "thanks to Zhelev's mediatory skills that Bulgaria, unlike Romania and Yugoslavia . . . witnessed neither conflict between extremist forces nor large-scale social upheavals."[104]

On balance the record of the first two years of the new pluralism was not bad. Each country had restored electoral politics and was in the process of constructing democracy, although that path was far from smooth. Centralized planning had been abandoned, and if the industrialized dinosaurs of the old regime had not yet been domesticated, at least small privatization had been successful and governments were trying to face up to the task of rationalizing heavy industry. Even in the sphere of ethnic relations the success of Poland in dealing with its neighbors and in facing its history of anti-Semitism provided a balance to the breakup of Czechoslovakia and the issue of the Hungarian enclaves. These were, of course, far from the only problems and issues that confronted Eastern Europe. What to do about the environment? How to deal with the Communists from the old regime? How to get into the European Community? What to do about military production? How to restore property seized by the Communist regimes? How to create a commercial banking system? What to do about refugees? What should the tax structure look like?

But under the surface of the bitter and highly visible confrontations over these issues that filled the headlines, millions of individuals began to undertake the autonomous acts of self-activization that constitute the underlying strength of pluralist societies. In the newspaper business, for example, the formerly official paper in almost every country professionalized itself and came under competitive pressure from privately financed papers. *Cotideanul* (The Daily) in Bucharest, *24 Chasa* (Twenty-four Hours) in Sofia, and *Vreme* (Time) in Belgrade were only the best of a new breed of information services that were at the same time making a profit (or at least hoping to). The Rotary Club returned to Poland; private undergraduate faculties charging tuition opened in Bursa and Varna; Czech speculators sent Prague real estate prices skyrocketing; an alternative elementary school came to Brno; fresh paint began appearing on shops in small Polish towns; the Budapest school system converted from a unitary system to one with twenty-four districts; a Romanian entrepreneur began building motels; local governments planned new parks and recreation centers.

In Czechoslovakia after 1968 and in Poland under martial law the Communist regimes spoke of "normalization," which in fact meant reimposition of an abnormal and false public life. The first two or three years of the post-Communist period are the beginning of the real "normalization" process in Eastern Europe, the fulfillment of the desire so many of its citizens expressed after 1989 to become "a normal country." This will mean that bad things will happen, but so will good things. There will be failures and there will be successes. For the second time in the twentieth century the peoples of Eastern Europe have embarked on an effort to create functioning pluralist societies. Let us hope that this second try comes closer to what they want in the long run than the first one did.

7

The Devil's Finger:
The Disintegration of
Yugoslavia

Yugoslavia had neither a velvet revolution nor a velvet divorce. Midway through 1991 two of its six constituent republics, Slovenia and Croatia, declared their independence, provoking a vicious civil war that spread in 1992 to Bosnia and Herzegovina. Ethnic emotions run deep throughout Eastern Europe, but nowhere did they reach the level of bestiality as they did in Yugoslavia. As one observer put it, the devil must have pointed his finger at this country.[1] Grotesque atrocities, ethnic cleansing, bombardment of priceless cultural artifacts, hundreds of thousands of refugees, cities destroyed, obsessive propaganda and disinformation—these were the realities in many parts of Yugoslavia at a time when other East European countries were holding elections, negotiating with the European Community, writing constitutions, privatizing industry, and otherwise trying to find their way back to Europe. What happened? How did Yugoslavia, the first Communist state to break with the Soviet Union and the most open Communist state in the world in the 1960s, come to this depressing impasse?

The answer is not simple, but it revolves around the inherent weakness of Yugoslavism itself. The concept emerged first in the nineteenth century, when Slavic peoples in Russia and Eastern Europe were beginning to understand that they spoke related languages.[2] In a day of powerful empires, Panslavism suggested that the Slavs might form the basis of a powerful empire of their own some day. Among the Yugoslavs (the term means "South Slavs"), the idea came to expression in the 1840s in the work of Ljudevit Gaj, a Croat who argued in his journal *Danica* (Morning

Star) that all the south Slavic peoples were branches of the same Illyrian tribe. In the 1860s Illyrianism gave way to the Yugoslavism of the Catholic bishop of Croatia, Josip Juraj Strossmayer, who also believed in the cultural unity of the South Slavs. When he founded an Academy of Arts and Sciences in Zagreb in 1867, he did not name it the Croatian Academy but rather the Yugoslav Academy. Serbs in the 1860s also had a program for uniting the South Slavs in a single state, the ideal of a Balkan federation propagated by Prince Michael Obrenović. But Prince Michael, despite some desultory negotiations with Bishop Strossmayer, believed unification should take place under Serbian leadership. From the earliest days of the idea of Yugoslavism, therefore, the orientation of Serbian and Croatian Yugoslavists differed, the latter thinking in broad cultural terms and the former thinking in practical terms of a state under Serbian leadership.

Serbs and Croats living in the Austrian half of the Habsburg Empire found ways to cooperate politically prior to World War I, and a number of Croatian and Serbian intellectuals in Zagreb and Belgrade, especially students, were enthusiastic about Yugoslavism in the years before World War I. But it could not be said that the idea had struck very deep roots by 1914. Much stronger was the idea of nationalism. This is the issue over which World War I began. Austria-Hungary attacked Serbia not for any clear-cut economic or strategic aims but because of the belief that the independent state of Serbia represented the national principle of governance, which, if accepted, would destroy the Habsburg state. Since medieval times *Kaisertreue,* or "loyalty to the emperor," had been the principle that held the varied Habsburg lands together. If all the peoples of that multinational empire were to adopt the notion championed by Serbia—that each ethnic group had the right to its own sovereign state—the empire was doomed.

From the beginning of the war many South Slavs were thinking about what the postwar arrangements would be. As early as September 4, 1914, Nikola Pašić, prime minister of Serbia, informed the Allied Powers (Russia, France, and Great Britain) that the best way to assure the containment of Germany would be to create a strong national state in the Balkans that would consist of all Serbs, Croats, and Slovenes.[3] In December 1914 the Serbian government officially adopted a set of war aims calling for "the liberation and unification of all our unliberated brothers: Serbs, Croats, and Slovenes." The non-Serbs in this state were not to be partners exactly, but in victory the Serbs intended to grant them equal rights as Serbs or as associated peoples.

On the Slovenian and Croatian side, some Dalmatian and other Croatian émigrés created the Yugoslav Committee, which lobbied in London for the recognition of a new postwar state, much in the way that Tomaš Masaryk did in America on behalf of Czechoslovakia. In 1917 leaders of the Yugoslav Committee and of the Serbian government met on the island of Corfu and agreed to establish a democratic, constitutional Kingdom of Serbs, Croats, and Slovenes under the Serbian dynasty. The cultural and religious rights of all three peoples were be preserved in this new state, although Albanians, Bosnians, Macedonians, and other minorities were not mentioned. But the Corfu Agreement left one major question unsettled: Would Yugoslavia be a centralized state as the Serbs wanted (and still wanted in 1991) or a federation of equal and sovereign peoples as the Croats wanted (and still wanted in 1991)?

The actual founding of the new state took place just after the last days of the war in conditions of utmost confusion: The Austro-Hungarian state collapsed; an allied army, which included a significant number of Serbian divisions, pushed into the Balkans from Salonica and spread out toward the Adriatic, where it encountered a hostile Italy; and demobilized soldiers returning from Russia created "green armies," quasi-revolutionary movements whose members often were little better than bandits.[4] Independent committees and councils arose in many South Slavic areas, but the only realistic option they had was to gravitate toward Serbia, which was the only entity among them (except tiny Montenegro) that European powers already accepted as a sovereign state.[5] Representatives of the Montenegrins, the Bosnians, and the Hungarians and Serbs from the Vojvodina all decided to link up with Serbia in a new Balkan state.[6] In Zagreb, the National Council of Slovenes, Croats, and Serbs, newly formed by politicians who until shortly before had been more or less loyal to the Habsburgs, decided to follow suit on behalf of the Croats and Slovenes. The council had little choice, since the alternative was to create an independent country, which would have faced powerful Italian claims, a victorious Serbian army, and none-too-sympathetic great powers. Only one member of the Council, Stjepan Radić, leader of the Croatian Peasant party, favored independence, and even he acquiesced temporarily in the decision to join with the others.[7] Late in November delegates from the various councils gathered in Belgrade, and on December 1, 1918, King Aleksandar of Serbia announced the formation of the Kingdom of Serbs, Croats, and Slovenes.[8]

Even though the constituent peoples voluntarily entered into the new state, which Woodrow Wilson and the other wartime leaders blessed in Paris in 1919, the question left unsettled at Corfu immediately provoked bitter political controversy. The Serbs, having fought heroically in the Balkan Wars of 1912–1913, having suffered greatly during World War I, and having won in 1918, quite naturally expected that the new state would be an extension of the old Serbia. The Croats, noting the overbearing way in which the Serbs had incorporated Macedonia in 1913 and anticipating that the Orthodox Serbs would not be sympathetic to their Catholic World War I adversaries, feared a centralized state with its capitol in Belgrade. Unfortunately, rather than fight this fundamental issue out in the constituent assembly elected for that purpose, the Croatian Peasant party, which under Radić held the loyalty of the overwhelming majority of the Croatian peasantry, chose to boycott the constitution-writing process. The constitution promulgated in 1921, therefore, was essentially a Serbian document that could never be satisfactory to the Croats, although the Serbs did find ways to placate Slovenian and Bosnian political figures. From the very beginning, the actualization of the never-too-widely-accepted idea of a single South Slavic state, a Yugoslavia, was seriously, probably fatally, flawed.

Politics during the 1920s in the Kingdom of the Serbs, Croats, and Slovenes were extremely volatile, to the extent that in 1928 a disgruntled Montenegrin member of Parliament shot five Croatian representatives on the floor of the assembly itself, killing three of them, including Stjepan Radić. In 1929 King Aleksandar, fed up with the constant squabbling, seized power on his own, suspended the legislature and the constitution, reorganized the country into provinces based on river valleys, and changed the name of the state to Yugoslavia.

Aleksandar did his best to turn his diverse collection of peoples into a nation, but his efforts to impose Yugoslavism by force only discredited the idea. Yugoslavism became associated in the minds of non-Serbs with Serbian oppression, and in the minds of the many leftist Serbs Aleksandar sent to prison, simply with oppression. After Aleksandar's assassination in 1934 by a Macedonian terrorist, the Croats were able to distance themselves from Yugoslavia by extracting an agreement from Belgrade in August 1939 that granted Croatia autonomous status. The agreement also granted the Croats territorial gains around Mostar in Herzegovina and in northeast Bosnia that closely approximated the territories the Croats seized in 1992. But the agreement came far too late to permit Yugoslavia to prepare for Hitler's onslaught. When the Wehrmacht took less than two weeks to crush Yugoslavia in April 1941, the first experiment in creating a multi-national Yugoslav state came to an ignominious and, for some, unlamented end.

The second Yugoslav experiment began in the depths of World War II. From the beginning, the Communist resistance under Josip Broz Tito, fighting for its life in the vastness of Bosnia and Herzegovina, intended to create a revolutionary Marxist state, but at the same time Tito understood that a new Yugoslavia would have to be based on a more evenhanded treatment of the various Yugoslav nationalities. From the first meeting in 1942 of the Anti-Fascist Council for the National Liberation of Yugoslavia, as the precursor to the postwar government was called, the Communists advocated a Yugoslavia that would be "a voluntary union of separate peoples" and began using the slogan "Brotherhood and Unity." When they recreated Yugoslavia in 1945, it was as a federal state consisting of six equal republics and two autonomous regions within the Republic of Serbia. The new republics were Slovenia, a relatively prosperous South Slavic people in the northwest; Croatia, a Catholic people living along the Adriatic coast as well as along the Sava River; Bosnia and Herzegovina, an ethnically mixed republic with a strong Muslim tradition; Montenegro, a small mountainous entity of Serbs with a proud tradition as mountaineer fighters; Macedonia, an entirely new entity that set about creating a Macedonian language and national culture; and Serbia, Orthodox Christians who were the largest group in Yugoslavia, but not a majority.[9] Serbia also contained two autonomous provinces: Vojvodina to the north with a significant Hungarian minority, and *Kosovë* to the south, which ethnically was predominantly Albanian.[10] This new federal republic of equal peoples was probably as good a solution as the inextricably mixed ethnic character of the region permitted.

The Yugoslav Communists were brutal in imposing their revolutionary programs, but their position on ethnic equality shone in sparkling contrast to the bestiality of the Independent State of Croatia. During World War II the fanatical band of fascist enthusiasts, called Ustasha, who ran that state were so ardent in their massacres and forced removals of Serbs, Communists, Jews, Gypsies, Muslims, and others they defined as non-Croatians that even the Germans were shocked.[11] To many, the Communist program of brotherhood and unity also offered a superior choice to the one offered by the Chetniks, the official resistance force of the Yugoslav government in exile under the leadership of Draža Mihailović, which also committed atrocities during the war and whose Serbian orientation was obvious.

The Partisans, as the Communists called themselves, had one other advantage: They won the three-cornered civil war (Chetnik, Ustasha, Partisan—Serb, Croat, Communist) that went on simultaneously with Yugoslav resistance to fascism. This gave them the power to impose their vision of a Communist Yugoslavia by force. In 1945 they rid themselves of the Ustasha problem by killing tens of thousands of Croats, not all of them guilty of crimes, and in 1946 they captured and executed Mihailović. They also cleared the field of thousands of other potential political opponents by the less dramatic but no less effective means of arrest, imprisonment, and intimidation.

These traditional methods were eminently successful in creating a Communist state in Yugoslavia, but they had a serious long-term negative effect, especially in Croatia. The wartime experience in Croatia was as far beyond the ordinary experience of Croats as the Holocaust experience was beyond the ordinary experience of Germans. And yet it happened. In Germany the question of responsibility for the Nazi period has been debated, discussed, refined, and talked about for forty years. As a result, most adult Germans are sensitive to their historical experience and determined that it should not happen again. A real democracy has become established in Germany in good measure because Germans have faced their unpleasant past squarely.

In Croatia, by contrast, and in fact throughout Yugoslavia, the wartime horrors were never openly confronted. Hundreds, perhaps thousands, of researchers investigated every aspect of the partisan struggle, but basic questions about the relationship between the Independent State of Croatia and Croatian culture and history, or between the Chetniks and Serbian history, were never asked. Every society, perhaps every person, contains a dark element that, in the right circumstances, can burst through the normal crust of civility in an explosion of murder and plunder. But Serbs and Croats were not permitted to face that experience in their own past, to atone for it, to understand it, and to commit themselves to not repeating it. Instead of permitting the Yugoslavs to face this unpleasant past, the Communists simply condemned the horrors of the wartime experience as an extreme outburst of bourgeois society and proclaimed that such things could not happen in the new order. Any effort to confront the issues directly was forbidden. This failure to provide for remembrance and reconciliation, not only in Croatia but in other parts of Yugoslavia as well, was one of the most significant negative aspects of the imposition of Communist rule in Yugoslavia. The wounds of World War II were covered over, but they never healed.

The Yugoslav Communists possessed three unifying elements that lifted their effort to build a multinational Yugoslavia above earlier ethnic conflicts, at least potentially. These were their Marxism, which provided an ideology of internationalism; their partisan experience, which bonded the leadership together with powerful feelings of purpose and commitment; and their leader, Josip Broz Tito, whose authority was unquestioned during his lifetime. These advantages did not mean that no ethnic controversies erupted in the second Yugoslavia. Ivo Banac has shown how pervasive and divisive these struggles were even in the early postwar days.[12] But in contrast to their predecessors in the first Yugoslavia, the main Communist leaders had a vision of a socialist Yugoslavia in which nationality problems would wither away if they were suppressed long enough. Tito himself hoped that someday a sense of Yugoslavism would supplant the sense of individual nations, and the party platform of 1958 spoke of a "Yugoslav socialist consciousness." But the linkage of "Yugoslav" and "socialist" contained a critical weakness that Tito and his colleagues could never have imagined. As long as the Communist movement remained strong, Yugoslavism was not in danger. If nationalism reared its head the party could and did push it back under the surface. If the League of Communists of Yugoslavia should disintegrate, however, then the Yugoslavism it championed would disintegrate too.

And the party did disintegrate, not in the sudden and dramatic way that the parties of Hungary and Czechoslovakia did, but over a long period of time through an incremental process of decentralization. The most original innovation of the Yugoslav Communists was their attempt to structure their economy, and eventually their entire public life, on the principle of self-administration (also called self-management). At first the idea was simply that workers should manage the socially owned factories in which they worked. But self-administration is inherently disaggregating. If each enterprise should manage itself, why not each republic, each city, or each village? If self-management was good for factory workers, why not for hospital workers, university employees, or even government employees? Indeed, why not for the party itself?

Yugoslav experimentation with market mechanisms reinforced the decentralizing character of self-management. The market is by definition decentralized. In its search for economic mechanisms more viable than the Stalinist ones it had installed from 1945 to 1948, the Belgrade regime began to dismantle its absolute economic authority as early as 1954 by giving enterprises some leeway in making business decisions and by devolving a small but significant amount of power over enterprises to local governments. Once begun, the process of devolution continued for thirty-five years, until in 1991 the center lost control completely.

Both economic and political disagreements drove the decentralization process, with the ethnic factor always lurking close beneath the surface. By the 1960s the republics of the northwest, because of their advantageous location on the Adriatic coast, were earning considerable foreign exchange from tourists. How much of that should they keep and how much should go to the federation for countrywide use? Croatia and Slovenia argued that the center took too much, while the other republics complained that Croatia and Slovenia kept too much. A similar controversy raged over the allocation of investment resources. Was it better to invest funds in the developed republics, which once again were Slovenia and Croatia, where one reasonably could hope the monies would be used effectively to increase productivity, or in the poorest parts of Yugoslavia, which desperately needed development but where a good portion of the funding probably would be wasted?

These tough economic issues would have been difficult to arbitrate even in an ethnically homogeneous environment. But Yugoslavia was far from homogeneous. All sides perceived controversies over economic efficiency, investment allocation, and convertible currency rules in ethnic terms. Therefore the arguments were always more intense than they otherwise might have been. Constant efforts by the Communist leadership at the center could control the debates and downplay their ethnic elements, but they could not solve the basic conflicts of interest.

The economic debates of the 1960s and 1970s were not as disruptive as they might have been because Yugoslavia prospered during those decades. The modest marketizing reforms the Yugoslavs undertook in the 1960s led to significant growth that not only benefited industry but trickled down to ordinary people as well. Dennison Rusinow summed up the results with the comment that in the mid-1960s Belgrade was "the only Communist capital with a parking problem."[13] This palpable economic improvement convinced Tito, always the final arbiter in any controversy in which he took an interest, to side with those who favored a more open economy. In 1965 the economic reform known as the "New Measures" revalued the currency, opened up foreign trade regulations, and gave enterprises more autonomy. With Tito's blessing, Yugoslavia became the most open Communist state in the world. Its citizens could freely travel— over a million of them were working as guest workers in Germany by the end of the 1960s—and they could even emigrate. Despite contemporary reports about how badly the Yugoslav economy worked and despite continual tinkering, the influx of foreign loans during the 1970s made that decade the most prosperous time ordinary Yugoslavs have ever known.

The Politics of Decentralization, 1966–1976

The political concomitant to the economic reforms was decentralization of the party and of the federal political processes.[14] Two tendencies characterized the party during its early years in power: a centralizing one associated with the Serbian head of the federal security services, Aleksandar Ranković, and a decentralizing one associated with the Slovenian theorist of self-management, Edvard Kardelj. The struggle reached its climax in 1966 with the removal of Ranković, considered at that time second only to Tito himself, for "factional activity." Although Ranković's downfall was always discussed publicly in terms of the deformation of self-management and similar acceptable rubrics, popularly his demise was seen as a defeat for the Serbs. Such a simplified interpretation overlooked the diversity of opinion within each ethnic group and undervalued the views and influence of the smaller republics, but it was widely held nonetheless.[15] Revelations of Ranković's brutal policies against the Albanians in *Kosovë* and the Hungarians in the Vojvodina provided grist for the mill of those who saw in Ranković a rebirth of Serbian hegemonism.

The defeat of the centralizing Ranković led to an assertion of authority by party organs in each republic and the confirmation by the Ninth Party Congress of March 1969 that the League of Communists of Yugoslavia comprised eight constituent bodies, one each for the republics and one each for the two autonomous provinces. As Steven Burg puts it, the Ninth Party Congress "institutionalized the existence of eight distinct blocs in the Yugoslav political system. . . . Conflict between the blocs became dominated by the national cleavages that divided them."[16] The Yugoslav Communists had no intention of dissolving their party in the late 1960s, but the actual decentralization put in train by Ranković's fall began the process anyway.

Decentralization came to formal government structures at the same time. The passage in 1971 of twenty-three constitutional amendments led to the adoption in 1974 of a new constitution and in 1976 to a new "Law on Associated Labor," all suffused with the spirit of self-administration. The amendments of 1971 and the constitution of 1974 established a complex system of delegates and consultations at all levels of government, while the law on associated labor divided all economic enterprises, even hospitals and charitable organizations, into what the Yugoslavs called "Basic Organizations of Associated Labor," which were to be the fundamental negotiating units in each self-managing enterprise. Edvard Kardelj, the architect of the 1974 constitution, characterized the complex new system as a "pluralism of self-managing interests." This sounded good, but in practice the new laws made it almost impossible for the federal government to pursue a coherent economic program, since each republic now held a suspensive veto of federal legislation, and very difficult for enterprises to run them-selves efficiently, since each Basic Organization of Associated Labor held what amounted to its own mini-veto of enterprise operations.

The most important political provision of the new constitution was the raising of the autonomous regions of *Kosovë* and Vojvodina to a status equivalent to that of the republics by giving them a voice equal to the republics in the newly created nine-person presidency and by giving them an equal ability to hamstring federal legislation. Only after a lengthy series of steps could the federal government override the objections of a republic or an autonomous region to a particular piece of legislation, and then only when it was declared vital to the interest of the entire federation.

Giving the autonomous regions equal status with the republics was particularly repugnant to some Serbs. They looked back to Serbia's history as an independent state; its victories in both the Balkan wars and World War I; its domination in the interwar years of Macedonia and *Kosovë*, which were then integral parts of Serbia; and the inclusion of Vojvodina after 1945. After World War II Macedonia became one of the six constituent republics, and after 1974 *Kosovë* and Vojvodina became almost equal to the republics. Was this the fruit of all their struggles—to win the wars and lose the peace?

The more radical of the critics went further, pointing out that many Serbs lived outside the Republic of Serbia and hinting that border changes in Croatia and Bosnia were needed to create a Greater Serbia. In one particularly interesting complaint, which rehearsed the arguments Slo-bodan Milošević used in 1991 to justify his war on Croatia, Mihailo Djurić argued in 1971 that Serbia was[17]

> already in an unequal position with respect to the other nations in Yugoslavia, such that the proposed constitutional changes, in the final analysis, are directed against its deepest vital interests. The final consequence of the change will be its complete disintegration. It is obvious that the borders of the present Social-ist Republic of Serbia are neither the national nor the historical borders of the Serb nation. As is well known, outside the borders of Serbia the Serbian nation lives in four of the five other republics, but not in one of these republics can it live its own life. . . . The Serbian nation must turn to its own devices, it must begin to fight for its dangerously threatened national identity and integrity.

The main stream of Serbian communism in 1971 harshly condemned Djurić's arguments, and he spent time in prison for voicing them. More moderate Serbian Communists found another, less ethnically charged way to criticize the decentralizing thrust of the constitutional changes. These critics argued that it was not possible to have a united state without effi-cient, independent, and strong central governmental organs. In particular they argued that it was absolutely crucial to Yugoslav economic well-being that the center control banking, fiscal matters such as the currency, and international trade rules.

Croatian leaders dismissed these not unreasonable arguments as camouflage for the real Serbian desires. Savka Dabčević-Kučar, a leading advocate of the Croatian position, suggested that behind the economic arguments for a strong center lurked Mihailo Djurić's pleas for a Greater Serbia. Calls for unity at the federal level, in Dabčević-Kučar's view, were only "a mask behind which [Serbian] hegemonism hides its face." She considered even Yugoslavism an "unacceptable phenomenon" denoting "some superior supranational phenomenon."[18]

In the most important area, the adoption of the new constitution in 1974, the Croats essentially sustained their position. Federal powers were weakened and republican powers strengthened, both in the party and in government, and Vojvodina and *Kosovë* received greater authority, thus reining in the Serbs. But Croats could not savor their victory because of a controversy over Croatian nationalism in 1971. After the fall of Ranković it became easier, although not officially condoned, to express nationalist viewpoints throughout Yugoslavia. In Zagreb, late in the 1960s, *Matica hrvatska* (Croatian Home), a Croatian cultural society dating from the 1840s, came into the hands of nationalists, including the future president of Croatia, Franjo Tudjman.[19] Undertaking an aggressive publicity campaign to create local clubs on the basis of a nationalist program, Matica raised its membership from about two thousand to just over forty thousand by the end of 1971.

Meanwhile, a trio of Croatian party leaders (Mika Tripalo, Pero Pirker, and Savka Dabčević-Kučar) were pressing Tito for a radical reform of the Yugoslav currency system that would give Croatia more control over its foreign currency assets. During 1970 the Croatian party split between the old hands, who wanted to clamp down on nationalism, and this trio of younger leaders who began using nationalist arguments. Tripalo and his colleagues rejected complaints from other republics that nationalism was starting to get out of hand in Croatia with the remarkable argument that in Croatia nation and class had become identical, so that pursuit of Croatian national aims was the same thing as pursuing the interests of the working class. As the year wore on, the political climate in Zagreb became heated, both inside the party and among the supporters of Matica hrvatska. This Croatian group now openly pursued what Dennison Rusinow reluctantly characterized as the policies of a "nineteenth-century National-Liberal party . . . with roots deep in the intellectual and political history of the Habsburg Monarchy." The result, as Rusinow tortuously put it, "is something that belongs in that part of a typology of political and ideological systems which is loosely and sometimes misleadingly called fascist."[20]

In November 1971 the nationalist newspaper *Hrvatski tjednik* (Croatian Weekly) brought things to a head by publishing a proposal from Matica hrvatska for a new Croatian constitution. It provided that Croatia was "the sovereign national state of the Croatian nation," that it had the right to secession, that Croatian would be the sole official language, that Croatian authorities would have full control of all tax revenues collected in Croatia, and that there would be a Croatian territorial army.[21] The suggestion was even made that Croatia should have its own representative at the United Nations. These proposals, which Franjo Tudjman's Croatian Democratic Union successfully put forward again twenty years later (in 1992 Croatia became a member of the United Nations), were completely unacceptable to the rest of Yugoslavia, so radical at the time as to be beyond discussion.

The climax to this volatile situation came late in November, when students at Zagreb University went on strike over the foreign currency issue. Dennison Rusinow suggests that the strikers may have "reckoned that if even just a few factories joined them, the triumvirate and their Party following would have to [join them also], facing Tito with a civil war if he called in the army."[22] But that calculation was twenty years too early. In 1971 the population at large did not join in.

When Tito finally realized the seriousness of the situation, it was he who stepped in, bringing all the important party leaders to his hunting lodge at Karadjordjevo near Belgrade, where he imposed a solution. Matica hrvatska was closed and its leaders, including Tudjman, imprisoned; many student activists were arrested; the Croatian triumvirate resigned; and the party itself was "cleansed." To be evenhanded, in 1972 Tito purged the Serbian party too, so that by the time the constitution of 1974 was adopted he and his center of old partisan leaders had reasserted their dominance.

The restructurings from 1966 through 1976 and the nationalist confrontations of the same period satisfied no one. The Serbs felt aggrieved because they had lost the battle to prevent decentralization and resented Tito's sacking of their relatively moderate leaders. The Croats were frustrated that the center had crushed what they considered their legitimate ambitions for national identity. Tito had reasserted the center's authority explicitly on the basis of revolutionary power, but at the same time he had permitted the creation of a decentralized constitutional arrangement that made it very difficult for that center to conduct ordinary business. Order had been restored by the special intervention of the only person in Yugoslavia with authority commensurate to the task, Tito himself. But in the day-to-day life of the federation impasse and controversy became endemic.

The Economy Turns Down

In 1980 Tito performed his last service to Yugoslavia—he took a long time dying. He entered the hospital early in January for a blood clot and had his leg amputated; after declining physically over the next four months, he died. When somber martial music interrupted the normal television programming on the afternoon of May 4, 1980, the Yugoslavs, who had been a bit panicky in January and February, were more or less prepared, at least for the short run. Tito's death was not just the end of the personal rule of a pleasure-loving but not unloved dictator. It also marked the end of the entire postwar generation whose commitment to Marxism, to the partisan experience, and to Tito himself had provided the glue that kept Yugoslavia together. Persons aged forty and under, as well as many older people, found the endless celebrations of the partisan movement, which was in fact a thrilling and inspirational struggle against terrible odds, simply boring. And self-management proved to be a fraud. Workers had almost no say in how their enterprises were run, despite spending sometimes as much as 30 percent of their time in meetings of their Basic Organizations of Associated Labor. In many of the less successful firms networks of party officials maintained their control through local party connections, republican governments, and the Socialist Alliance. By the time of Tito's death many Yugoslavs had come to the same conclusion about socialism as had the citizens of the other East European states: it was a sham.

To make matters worse, just before Tito's death the economy took a downward turn. During the 1950s rapid Yugoslav growth had been fueled by American aid.[23] In the 1970s, much as in Poland and elsewhere, growth was fueled by foreign loans. But, as in Poland, instead of igniting export-driven growth, the loans of the 1970s either ended up in the pockets of the workers in the form of increased consumption and a higher standard of living or were wasted in inefficient investments undertaken for political reasons. Efficiency did not increase, but debt grew rapidly. In 1979, when the second oil crisis hit and the loans slowed down, the Yugoslav miracle was over. As an editorial in Socialist Alliance's newspaper *Borba* (Struggle) put it, "The present hardships are in great measure due to rising domestic consumption being fostered on the basis of foreign loans."[24]

Economic difficulties were also due to the same soft budget constraints and political interference that characterized every socialist economy.[25] Despite Yugoslavia's favorable reputation in the 1970s as a hybrid of both the planned and the market economy, Yugoslav Communists were just as enamored of metal-eating industries as Communists anywhere. Instances of incredible waste were perhaps even more commonplace in Yugoslavia than in the other socialist economies, since eight political entities all felt they had to have their own "modern" industries, however irrational their operation might be. For example, the giant iron ore processing plant at Kavadarci in Macedonia, started in the 1960s, gobbled up almost one-half billion dollars in convertible currency loans and an equivalent amount of domestic investment before being scrapped in the 1980s because the available local ore was too deficient in iron to make the plant feasible, a fact known before the project was begun. In Serbia the steel plant at Smederevo on the Danube, started in 1963 and not yet finished in 1987, cost $1.5 billion in hard currency plus the equivalent of $1 billion in dinars. It was losing so much money in 1987 that all enterprises in Serbia were forced to contribute an amount equivalent to one-half of one percent of their production to keep it going, since, after all, it employed eleven thousand workers.[26]

Heavily in debt, hamstrung at the center, and with a dispirited workforce, in the 1980s the Yugoslavia economy declined precipitously. Almost every measure went into reverse—social product dipped, efficiency dropped, real income went down, and investment declined. One of the few indicators that went up was inflation, making ordinary citizens acutely aware that their standard of living was falling. Yugoslav governments spent most of the 1980s stumbling from austerity programs to currency devaluations to restructuring plans to price and wage freezes to bridging loans in a fruitless search for stabilization. One author counted twenty price freezes implemented and dropped between 1965 and 1985.[27] Constant stop-and-go stabilization programs produced the worst of both worlds, a result known elsewhere in the 1980s as stagflation. On the one hand, real wages and the standard of living dropped—the price of the reforms that were tried—but on the other hand, efficiency did not improve, inflation worsened, and growth rates stayed low. Under these unstable conditions the very term *stabilization,* introduced in the reforms of 1979 and used throughout the 1980s, became so devalued that its mere mention brought wry smiles to Yugoslav faces.

Serbia and Kosovë

The significant political activity of the 1980s did not take place at the federal level, which was the focus of most foreign attention. During the 1980s the future of Yugoslavia was being decided in the republics, particularly in Serbia and Slovenia, but also to a certain extent in Croatia. The road to civil war began in March 1981 when Albanian students took their demands for better conditions at the University of Prishtinë to the streets in the time-honored tradition of students everywhere. Their demonstration touched a nerve of Albanian patriotic feeling, and over the next month anti-Serbian demonstrations demanding that *Kosovë* become a Yugoslav republic became so massive that the federal government sent in troops.[28]

Serbs have been hostile to Albanians at least since the nineteenth century. This hostility is in part a function of the Serbian origin myth created in the nineteenth century and available since then to nationalist demagogues. Because the medieval Serbian empire was located in what is today *Kosovë,* many of the most important Serbian cultural monuments can be found there, including the patriarchate of Peć, the center of Serbian Orthodoxy during the Ottoman period, and many Serbian Orthodox monasteries and churches containing late Byzantine frescoes of exceptional quality. The Serbian national mythology holds that the Orthodox church preserved Serbian national consciousness over the centuries of Ottoman domination, endowing these monuments with highly charged emotional significance. *Kosovo polje* (The Field of Blackbirds), not far from Prishtinë, was the site of the Serbs' epochal battle with the Ottomans on June 28, 1389.[29] The cycles of oral poetry that preserved the story of that battle (and of Serbian medieval experiences), along with the Byzantine frescoes, are the most important Serbian contributions to European culture.

The importance of the Kosovo myth to Serbian politics lies not in these actual historical qualities but in its selection by the nationalists as the appropriate symbolic universe of Serbianness. It provides a vocabulary of experiences outside of time, so to speak. For example, the contrast between the mythically heroic battle fought by the brave Serbian warriors at Kosovo and the final outcome, which was Ottoman domination, can be understood as the "normal fate of Serbs"—to die for freedom in war and yet to be denied the fruit of victory, that is, to win World War I and yet "lose" in 1945 and 1974. To refer to a rival as a modern Vuk Branković, who in the epics is understood to be a traitor, is to smear that rival with a morally devastating accusation that is beyond appeal. Slogans attractive to the ear can be written in the decasyllabic style of the folk poetry and Slobodan Milošević can be described in terms reminiscent of the folk epics.[30]

This style of discourse isolated only one strand of the Serbian experience, the religio-romantic strand, and shut out others, such as the liberal strand. At Serbian political rallies in 1988 one saw many pictures of Vuk Karadžić, the nineteenth-century gatherer of the folk epics, and of Petar Petrović Njegoš, the great epic poet of the same period, but few of Dositej Obradović, the early nineteenth-century advocate of Enlightenment rationalism. One of the accomplishments of the Serbian nationalists has been to fill the public space with the Kosovo strand of Serbian history that suits their mobilizational strategies and to downplay the rationalist strand that stands in mute criticism of those strategies. "In comparison to myth," said one critic, "history is fatiguing."[31]

Many Serbs feel emotional about *Kosovë*, but few Serbs actually live there. The proportion of Serbs living in *Kosovë* dropped from 24 percent in 1953 to less than 10 percent in 1990.[32] This does not bother the most extreme nationalists, who claim that *Kosovë* remains Serbian even if not a single Serb lives there.[33] The more common nationalist argument is that the Serbian population has declined precipitously because of harassment by lawless, irredentist, racist Albanians. More likely reasons are the high birth rate of the Albanians (more than thirty-two per thousand) and the poor economic prospects in the region (unemployment was about 25 percent in 1980), which has led to Albanian as well as Serbian emigration.

Kosovë is poor, but not for lack of resources devoted to its economic development. Up to 1980, about half of the federal monies allocated for underdeveloped Yugoslav regions went to *Kosovë*. But these funds tended to go into loss-producing capital-intensive industries, such as mining and power generation, rather than into labor-intensive industries like consumer production, so they did not alleviate unemployment. Worse, a significant amount of the money ended up increasing the number of administrators in the social sector, so that instead of improving efficiency, the investment funds probably decreased it. Whereas in 1954 per capita income in *Kosovë* was 48 percent of the Yugoslav average, in 1980 it had dropped to only 28 percent of the national average.[34] Prishtinë University was one institution that received investment funds. Nonexistent in 1960, by 1980 it had thirty-five thousand students. The idea was noble: provide *Kosovë* with the human capital it would need to develop. But with few suitable jobs available, Prishtinë University was not preparing a new class of managers so much as it was producing thousands of educated, unemployed, and very frustrated young men, an almost perfect formula for unrest.

When the unrest came in 1981 the Serbs and the federal government both denied that they bore any fault for the serious problems the region faced, calling the outbreak a counterrevolution led by outside agitators who were trying to unite *Kosovë* with Albania. There was a certain superficial plausibility to this argument, since in the 1960s *Kosovë* had adopted the literary language used in Albania rather than one based on its own dialect, and at least half of the books used in Prishtinë University originated in Albania. But from the initial riots in 1968, through the second wave of demonstrations in 1981, right up to the civil war of 1991, the leaders of every major Albanian movement in *Kosovë* stoutly denied any interest in joining Albania and demanded only that *Kosovë* become a republic in Yugoslavia.

The battle lines were clearly set. On the one side Albanians, who constituted 90 percent of the population of *Kosovë* and wanted to have their own republic in the Yugoslav confederation; on the other side Serbs, to whom Kosovo was an emotional homeland that they wanted to control more fully than the 1974 constitution permitted them. With such incompatible aims, the level of agitation and conflict grew through the 1980s. The Serbian media blamed all problems on the Albanians, refusing to recognize that Serbian repressive acts had any relationship to the problems. Between 1981 and 1985 the predominantly Serbian police arrested over three thousand Albanians and killed more than one hundred Albanian protesters. On their side, the Albanians firebombed the ancient patriarchate at Peć and harassed Serbs into leaving the province (although the many stories of Albanian rapes of Serbian women seem to have been manufactured by the Serbs).

Slobodan Milošević

After Tito's death it took several years for Serbian resentments over *Kosovë* to reach a public level of expression. In the late 1970s Serbian president Dragoslav Marković produced a confidential "Blue Book" criticizing the constitutional arrangements of 1974, but it never was publicly discussed. During the early 1980s Serbian historians, novelists, and poets found it not only increasingly easy to publish works with explicitly Serbian national themes but they found that these works sold very well. Taking cognizance of the increased interest in Serbian patriotism, in May 1985 the Serbian Academy of Sciences undertook to produce a memorandum on the Yugoslav condition. When in September 1986 a version of the document was leaked to the press, it created a sensation. The SANU Memorandum, as it became known, criticized Tito and his successors for discriminating against the Serbs.[35] Serbia's poor economic condition, the academicians argued, was due to Serbia's inability to control its own destiny. By raising the autonomous regions to almost republican level in 1974, non-Serbian Communists such as Tito and Kardelj had denied Serbs the right to their own state. Not only were Serbs suffering "physical, political, legal, and cultural genocide" in *Kosovë,* but many Serbs in other republics were threatened by the same fate.[36] "The economic subjugation of Serbia," the memorandum concluded, "can be understood only if one understands its political inferiority."[37]

The SANU Memorandum became public not long after Slobodan Milošević became head of the Serbian League of Communists.[38] Slobodan Milošević is not an attractive man. He is reclusive, stubborn, vindictive, narrow-minded, and covetous of absolute power. Born just after the start of World War II (in August 1941) of an activist Communist mother and a Montenegrin Orthodox priest, both of whom later committed suicide, Milošević was a good law student at Belgrade University but a narrow and driven one not given to extracurricular activities. Hitching his star to his university friend Ivan Stambolić, the nephew of an important partisan leader, he rose along with Stambolić. Until 1986 little distinguished Milošević from other successful apparatchiks. His enthusiasm for Marxism seemed perhaps excessive, but otherwise he was simply one of hundreds of Yugoslav careerists who had made their way through the system because it was the system in which they found themselves. When Stambolić moved up to the Serbian presidency in May 1986 and Milošević took his place as head of the party, no one in the West, except a handful of specialists, took particular notice.

Milošević's breakthrough came on April 24, 1987. On that day an excited crowd of ten thousand agitated Serbs and Montenegrins had gathered in front of a building in Kosovo polje, where a meeting to discuss their complaints against the Albanian pressures was underway. When the crowd became unruly, police used rubber truncheons to force them back. Milošević, who was attending the meeting, heard the ruckus and stepped outside to calm the crowd. "I want to tell you," he said, "that you should stay here. Here is your land, here are your houses, your fields and gardens, your memories. . . . [By leaving] you would betray your ancestors and disappoint your descendants. But I do not propose that in staying you continue to endure a situation with which you are not satisfied. On the contrary. We have to change it. . . . Don't tell me that you can't do it alone. Of course you can't do it alone. We will change it together, we in Serbia and everyone in Yugoslavia."[39] Various versions exist of the key phrase he uttered in the heat of this moment, such as "No one will ever beat a Serb again" or "No one has the right to beat the people!" Whatever his exact words, ordinary people throughout Serbia responded to the image of Milošević "standing up for Serbs." When he returned to Belgrade, a friend reported, "he was like a heated stove. He was full of emotions. He could not control his feelings. He could not calm down."[40] Milošević had discovered he possessed the heady power to move people.

The more liberal party leadership headed by Milošević's old friend and mentor, Ivan Stambolić, had been a calming influence in the tensions between Serbs and Albanians over control of *Kosovë*. Stambolić believed that Serbs were treated unfairly in the 1974 constitution, but he argued that Serbia's relations with *Kosovë* were a Yugoslav problem, not a narrowly Serbian one. He had been negotiating in a relatively patient way with the other republics to change the constitution to bring *Kosovë* into closer alignment with Serbia. In contrast to Milošević, Stambolić believed that the party should allow differences of opinions, and he brought along younger persons with an engaging openness.

Milošević, on the other hand, believed in the Stalinist party model—abject loyalty to every aspect of the leader's position. He thought *Kosovë* was a Serbian problem, not a Yugoslav one, and he was not a patient man. Rallying support among former Ranković supporters, academicians at Belgrade University, and mid-ranking party functionaries who found the idea of a strong leader appealing in the post-Tito vacuum, Milošević promised that the *Kosovë* problem could be solved quickly and unilaterally, by force if necessary.

At the key eighth session of the Serbian central committee held in September 1987, a surprised Stambolić, who had heard warnings about his old friend's intentions but chose to ignore them, found himself confronting a solid phalanx of local party delegates prepared with speeches calling for a new and more aggressive leadership. Defeated, Stambolić soon was recalled from the presidency and replaced by an old partisan general.

Stambolić's sudden defeat marked the beginning of a new order for Serbia. In the next three months, in a process he termed "differentiation," Milošević purged the Serbian party of those who would not give prompt assurances of total loyalty. From their new positions in control of the state television station and of what was once Serbia's best newspaper, *Politika* (Politics), Milošević's cronies attacked anyone who would not abjectly support him, branding them as opposed to party unity and, worse, as anti-Serb. In *Kosovë* itself Milošević thoroughly purged party members too lenient toward what the Serbs now routinely but inaccurately called Albanian irredentism.[41] By early 1988 Milošević had become the most dynamic, visible, and frightening politician in Yugoslavia.

Milošević thinks in nineteenth-century terms. He is completely insensitive to other ethnic groups and knows nothing of the give-and-take of democratic politics. He simply wants to make the Serbs the strongest and most united people in his part of the world, at whatever cost. Initially he probably thought that he could achieve control of the Yugoslav federal system through taking command of the League of Yugoslav Communists. When the party disintegrated, he tried to get control of the federal government, particularly the presidency and the army. Finally, when the federation collapsed, he turned to a more direct method of achieving his nationalist aims: the creation of a Greater Serbia dominating the center of the Balkans by armed force.

His first step was to rewrite the constitutional arrangements of 1974.

By accusing everyone who opposed him of being involved in an unprincipled alliance against Serbia, Milošević bullied the other republics into accepting Serbia's right to change its constitution and thereby to limit the rights of *Kosovë* and the Vojvodina. He packed the *Kosovë* assembly, found a way to replace the leadership of the province of Vojvodina with his own people, and pushed his amendments through.

His most powerful tool in achieving this goal was mass rallies. In the rest of Eastern Europe people power, as it was called after huge popular demonstrations brought Corazon Aquino to power in the Philippines in 1986, was a force for democracy and pluralism. In Serbia, however, Milošević mobilized people power to destroy Yugoslavia and to create the conditions for civil war. In September and October 1988 thirty thousand, fifty thousand, one hundred thousand, even one million people gathered in Serbian cities to shout their approval of Milošević's effort to subdue *Kosovë*. When Albanians tried rallies of their own or conducted strikes in the important mining industry, as they did in November 1988, Milošević sent in the riot police and arrested their leaders. In February 1989 the most dramatic protest broke out when Albanian miners barricaded themselves underground and went on hunger strikes. Milošević eventually tricked the miners into coming up, whereupon he arrested their leaders for "counterrevolutionary activities." In the rest of Eastern Europe people power toppled the old Communist regimes in the name of democracy. In Serbia, Milošević manipulated the same force by racist appeals in order to legitimate his transformation of the League of Communists of Serbia into a nationalist party organized on neo-Stalinist principles.

The Serbian Assembly, along with the assemblies of *Kosovë* and Vojvodina that Milošević now dominated, approved the new constitutional arrangements, putting the autonomous regions firmly under the control of the Serbian central government in March 1989. Acceptance of the constitutional provisions produced six days of rioting in *Kosovë*, which Milošević subdued with substantial loss of life (estimates ranged from 20 to 140), but many Serbs rejoiced over the restoration of Serbian unity, as they thought of it. "Sovereignty returned to Serbia," crowed the headline in *Politika*. "What was more natural, more humane, more democratic, for the Serbian people," said Borisav Jović, Serbian representative to the federal presidency, "than, in accordance with their peace-loving traditions, to again enter upon the stage of history and make a demand in the form of the simplest, the most noble formula of justice and equality. . . . [Serbs are] the people who in the modern history of the Balkans made the greatest sacrifices and demonstrated the greatest scope and evidence of its love for freedom and democracy. . . . Serbia is equal now."[42]

But Milošević's successful subjugation of *Kosovë* was a disaster for Yugoslavia and, perhaps, in the long run, for Serbia too. By running roughshod over the democratic elements in both Serbia and *Kosovë*, Milošević confirmed the worst fears of the other members of the Yugoslav federation, especially the Slovenes and the Croats. The likelihood that they would sympathize with any future Serbian calls for Yugoslav unity dropped nearly to zero.

Slovenia and Croatia React

Slovenes, as close neighbors of Italy and Austria, had long considered themselves somewhat removed from the passions of Balkan politics. They also took pride in being the most prosperous Yugoslav republic.[43] More open economic policies and considerable experience with Western business practices permitted Slovenes to produce roughly 20 percent of Yugoslavia's domestic product and 25 percent of the country's hard currency exports while constituting only 8 percent of the Yugoslav population. Slovenia did not suffer much repression in the fallout from the 1971 crisis in Croatia, and during the 1970s Slovenian intellectuals adopted an antipolitical stance. When Tito died Slovenia boasted perhaps the most independently minded intelligentsia in Yugoslavia. By the mid-1980s its capital city Ljubljana could boast of an influential student press, a strong group of intellectuals surrounding the avant-garde journal *Nova revija* (New Review), and the first stirrings of alternative movements of feminists, gays, peace activists, and environmentalists.[44]

These modest beginnings sprang to public life in the spring of 1988, when the journal of the Socialist Youth League, *Mladina* (Youth), published an article claiming that the army was planning a lightning arrest of important Slovene political figures in order to stop the growing Slovenian nationalism. *Mladina* had already annoyed the army by calling the Yugoslav chief of staff a "merchant of death" for selling arms to Ethiopia, and it followed with an article showing how Yugoslavia had conspired with Sweden to ship arms to Libya. Angry army officials hauled three journalists and one noncommissioned officer into military court and convicted them of revealing military secrets. The enormous hostility against the army this event and its outcome evoked was not only a sign of antimilitarism among Slovenian youth, although it was that. It signified also a rejection of Communist Yugoslavia as typified by the partisan generation and a rejection of Serbian centralism, because Slovenes perceived the army to be dominated by predominantly Serbian generals.

The *Mladina* trial galvanized the Slovenian democratic opposition. Supporters of the accused formed a defense committee, which they quickly turned into a Committee for the Defense of Human Rights that demanded and got an investigation of the army. In the fall of 1988 members of this committee went on to create four political parties, technically under the mantle of the Socialist Alliance but actually new formations.[45] In May 1989 these parties, along with the Slovenian Writers Union, produced a political program advocating political pluralism and expressing the desire "to live in a sovereign state of the Slovene people."[46] Shortly thereafter they proposed making the next election, scheduled long before for spring 1990, open and multiparty. In the meanwhile, a group of leftist intellectuals, students, workers, and even some party members formed the Social Democratic Alliance of Slovenia, which advocated a Western-style democratic socialism, while a group of nonsocialists created the Slovenian Democratic Alliance, dedicated to the establishment of parliamentary democracy.[47] By February 1989 Radio Free Europe analyst Milan Andrejevich could report that about one hundred grass roots organizations and ten independent political groups were active in Slovenia.[48]

Far from condemning these pluralist endeavors, Slovenian Communists found ways to accommodate themselves to them, first by suggesting that the new movements remain part of the Socialist Alliance and then by moving in the direction of pluralism themselves. Early in 1989 Milan Kučan, the head of the League of Communists of Slovenia, welcomed what he called "the opening up of political space." "There is no real democracy without political pluralism," he said.[49] In April 1989 the Communists ran a direct, secret, and contested election, the first of its kind in Yugoslavia, to elect the Slovene representative to the federal presidency. And in September of the same year, using the precedent set by Milošević's successful effort to change Serbia's constitution, the party pushed constitutional changes through the Slovenian assembly that declared Slovenia a "sovereign and independent state." The assembly asserted Slovenia's right to secede, claimed the authority to veto the use of armed force in its territory, and deleted the provision that the League of Communists should play the leading role in society.

Creeping pluralization in Slovenia outraged Slobodan Milošević. He accused the Slovenes of endangering Yugoslavia by threatening secession, which invited civil war. The Slovenes did not look upon it this way. Their strategy, which evolved in the doing rather than in any programmatic statement, was to put a clear choice before Milošević: Negotiate with us for a viable kind of federated Yugoslavia or we will leave. The Slovenes denied they were advocating the breakup of Yugoslavia. "This is not secession," the speaker of the Slovene assembly said blandly. "We want to remain part of Yugoslavia."[50] We want a third Yugoslavia, the Slovenes were saying, not one dominated by Serbia and one organized by Communists, but one based on truly voluntary association.

The Slovenes were Milošević's most active critics in Yugoslavia, particularly of Serbian actions in *Kosovë*. In March 1989, for example, one million persons out of a total population of only about two million signed a declaration protesting the Serbian treatment of Albanian miners and criticizing the longstanding state of emergency in *Kosovë*. Milošević, always on the attack, criticized the Slovenes for their "fascist hatred" of Serbia and accused them of an "unscrupulous coalition" with the Croats to denigrate Serbs. Slovene leaders responded by characterizing the Serbs as "irrational" and "arrogant." In December 1989 Milošević attempted to take his version of people power to Ljubljana by organizing a mass meeting there of Serbs similar to the successful rallies he had held in Serbian towns and cities in 1988. When the Slovenian authorities forbade the meeting, an angered Milošević asked Serbs to boycott Slovenian goods. It became distinctly unpleasant to ask for a Slovenian product in a Belgrade store. In retribution for the boycott, which affected about 7 percent of its trade, Slovenia began to hold back its payments to the federal fund for the undeveloped regions, which lessened the monies Serbia would have available for *Kosovë*. Convinced that Milošević was a nationalist tyrant and increasingly certain that each Yugoslav republic would have to make its own political arrangements, in December 1989 the Slovenian legislature agreed to hold open, multiparty elections, which it set for April 1990.

Croatia was not as open intellectually or politically as Slovenia, and, while its economy was in better condition than those of the southern republics, its prosperity was not uniform. Some regions, such as the one northwest of Zagreb where Tito had been born or the mountainous regions inland from the Adriatic and heavily populated by Serbs, were very poor. Others, such as the beautiful and popular Dalmatian Coast or the industrial region around Zagreb, were quite prosperous. Croatia's main problem, however, was not economic. It was ethnic. About 12 percent of the population of Croatia were Serbs, a significant portion of whom were concentrated in the poor Karst region of southwest Croatia. In that area bitter fighting between Serbs and Croats had taken place during World War II, and in 1971 some of the most active nationalists on both sides had re-emerged there.

In the increasingly tense situation provoked by Milošević and by the general crisis of communism, the nationalists could not be silenced, although the Communist regime tried to do so. For example, it imprisoned opposition leader Franjo Tudjman in the early 1980s and upon his release forbade him to speak in public. But in January 1989 Tudjman read a draft program for a political party he proposed founding at a meeting of the Croatian Writers' Union, and in June 1989, after a request for a public meeting had been denied, he and a few others gathered in what they called a "non-public place" to create the Croatian Democratic Union (Hrvatska demokratska zajednica—HDZ). By the end of the year some sixteen independent groups had formed in Croatia and the reform Communists, who were now in the ascendancy in the party, agreed that Croatia too would have to strike out in its own direction. Early in February 1990 the Croatian assembly passed a broad political reform that scheduled open, multiparty elections for April and May 1990.

The Collapse of the Center

With political decisions made at the republican level pushing Yugoslavia in two different directions, a centralizing Serbian one and a pluralizing Croatian/Slovenian one, the federal government found itself hamstrung by political impasse and economic decline. During the 1980s no Yugoslav government proved able to work the complex Yugoslav system of delegations and consultations effectively. Overall debt did not increase, because of a series of last-minute reprieves from the international banking community based on unfulfilled promises of reform, but inflation began to run at 100 percent per year and more. The climax came in December 1988 when, for the first time in socialist Yugoslavia, a government lost a vote of confidence in the federal assembly and resigned. The political crisis this unprecedented resignation touched off gave Yugoslavia one final chance for survival, because the man who emerged as prime minister in March 1989, Ante Marković, proved able to take control of the federal mechanisms and to push through a substantial economic reform.

Marković's strategy was to outflank the republics and the party. Former prime minister Branko Mikulić had put forward five reform plans, but all failed because they had to be vetted by the republican presidencies and party leaders. Marković minimized these negotiating steps and went straight to the legislature. He promised that his new ministers, whom he appointed by ability and not primarily by party connections, would henceforth be responsible to the federal assembly, and he used the assembly's committee structure to promote his plans. In parliamentary countries this is the normal way governments pursue their legislative programs, but in Yugoslavia Marković's maneuvering was a daring—and difficult—innovation. It took the new prime minister most of 1989 to get approval for his plans, but in December of that year the federal parliament passed the most comprehensive and hopeful economic reform Yugoslavia had ever seen.

Marković was a market-oriented Communist who stressed deregulation, elimination of laws that hindered entry into the market, privatization of small businesses, and creation of capital markets. But in order to put these ideas into effect, Marković, just like Balcerowicz and Klaus, first had to get control of the macroeconomic situation, primarily by stopping inflation. Despite a succession of austerity measures, price freezes, and currency manipulations throughout the 1980s, when Marković took office in March 1989 the rate of inflation was several hundred percent a year and climbing. By the end of 1989 it reached over two hundred percent a month.

Marković's reform, which went into effect on January 1, 1990, wrote off all the contaminated debts produced by the worthless promissory notes that Yugoslav firms had been giving each other, thus taking a long step toward getting control of the money supply.[51] Marković made the new "heavy" dinar convertible at seven to the deutschmark, introduced a balanced budget, inaugurated restrictive monetary policies, froze wages for six months, and freed all prices except about 20 percent of the retail prices and 25 percent of industrial production. The results of this shock therapy were spectacular. Inflation dropped precipitously, reaching close to zero after a few months, foreign exchange reserves rose dramatically, and foreign debt declined. Encouraged, foreign investors flocked to Yugoslavia. During 1990 and the first few months of 1991 almost three thousand foreign firms initialed agreements calling for about $1.2 billion of investment in the Yugoslav economy (although little of the money had actually arrived by the time the civil war began).[52]

From the foreign point of view, Marković was a miracle man, clearly the hope of the future for Yugoslavia. As Yugoslavia began to pull apart late in 1990 and early in 1991, almost every foreign leader from George Bush through Mikhail Gorbachev to Pope John Paul II indicated his support for Marković's government. As late as June 21, 1991, only a few days before civil war broke out, United States Secretary of State James Baker visited Belgrade to encourage Marković and to advocate the maintenance of federal Yugoslavia in its old form.

Inside Yugoslavia, however, Marković was increasingly unpopular. Non-Serbs saw him as a centrist Communist trying to impose rules from Belgrade, whereas Milošević's supporters reviled him with populist slogans as a man undermining socialism and ruining Yugoslavia on behalf of foreign bankers. Borislav Jović, a member of the federal presidency and a close ally of Milošević, called Marković "a foreign agent" who advocated the "uncontrolled transfer of social ownership into private hands" and the "sale of property to foreigners for next to nothing." Joze Pučnik, head of the oppositional DEMOS alliance in Slovenia, understood that Marković would never be able to get the feuding republics to agree. He called Marković "one of the biggest bluffers that ever managed to obtain Europe's support."[53]

Despite the apparent initial success of his economic reforms, Marković's fatal disability was the same as that of every other federal leader in post-Tito Yugoslavia. He showed great skill in conceiving his program and in finding a way to get it approved, but no amount of skill was adequate to overcome the unwillingness of some, even all, of the constituent republics to continue an economic program that required restraint. As soon as the six-month freeze on wages expired, workers everywhere demanded increases—and got them. The federal bank's inability to keep track of the money supply reached its climax in December 1990, when Milošević found a way to divert $1.8 billion, which was half of the entire amount available for the increase in money supply scheduled for 1991, to Serbia's use. He simply passed this enormous amount out in bonuses, wage increases, subsidies, and interest-free loans in a classic vote-buying spree during the month before Serbia's elections in December 1990.

Many observers in the West believed that, despite the political skirmishing, economic rationality eventually would bring Yugoslavs to their senses. After all, the World Bank and the IMF were prepared to release funds that would free up over $4 billion in investment resources for Yugoslavia, and foreign investors were prepared to add more if Yugoslavia remained stable. With Milošević and the other republics raiding the federal treasury (both Slovenia and Croatia also siphoned off significant amounts late in 1990) and with inflation starting up again, early in 1991 the IMF and the World Bank told the Yugoslavs they would release the funds scheduled for that year only if the republics agreed to implement economic discipline. But the confidence that Yugoslavs would respond to economic stimuli proved to be misplaced. By early 1990 emotions in Yugoslavia had reached the point at which economic arguments ceased to have an impact. Marković failed not for economic reasons but for political and emotional ones. His country was collapsing.

The glue that had held Yugoslavia together, the League of Yugoslav Communists, led the way toward this collapse by disintegrating early in 1990.[54] Yugoslav Communists were not immune to the forces for change sweeping Eastern Europe, as the changes in Slovenia and Croatia testify. Yet, understandably, many party members could not bring themselves to turn their backs entirely on the past. Thus the draft resolution placed before the special party congress that convened at Milošević's insistence on January 20, 1990, was a muddled document unsuited to the needs of the day. It supported Marković's economic reforms but called only for a mixed economy, not for the creation of a market system. It proposed that the League of Communists of Yugoslavia (LCY) achieve political legitimacy in the future through free elections, but it did not mention multiparty elections. And it confirmed the Serbian constitutional changes of 1989. These proposals were far too cautious for the Slovenes. They proposed a substitute motion that explicitly advocated a multiparty system, secret ballots, "asymmetric federalism," and a federal League of Communists made up of separate, independent parties. To make it precisely clear where the Slovenes stood, their proposal pointedly called for the introduction of democracy in *Kosovë* and the abolition of "democratic centralism," the code word for Milošević's neo-Stalinist methods.

Milošević rejected the Slovenian amendments out of hand, calling them an invitation to "internecine warfare in the party and the country," and on the same day the congress voted them down by a wide margin.[55] Frustrated and sensing the futility of participating in a party unable to resist Milošević, the Slovenes walked out. Two weeks later in Ljubljana they announced the formation of an independent party based on the principles of social democracy (the Party of Democratic Renewal) and withdrew from the LCY.

Milošević tried to turn the walkout to his advantage by proposing the congress continue without the Slovenes, but the delegations from Croatia, Macedonia, and Bosnia-Herzegovina refused, so the congress suspended its meeting without even electing a new leadership. *Borba* correctly analyzed the significance of these events in its headline the next morning: "The League of Communists no Longer Exists."[56] Ante Marković bravely maintained that "Yugoslavia continues to function with or without the League of Communists," but he was wrong. The League of Communists had been what held Yugoslavia together. When it disappeared Yugoslavia could not be far behind.

Free Elections in the Republics

Slovenia and Croatia were prepared for the disappearance of the League of Yugoslav Communists because they had already scheduled elections to create new governments. These first free parliamentary elections in Yugoslavia since before World War II took place at the same time elections were going on in the rest of Eastern Europe—April and May 1990. The details are complex, since each country has a tricameral legislature and the presidents were elected differently, but the results in each place were clear. In Slovenia the parties that grew out of the *Mladina* controversy of 1988 had banded together with several others, such as the Greens and the Tradesman's party, to form the oppositional alliance called DEMOS (Demokratska opozicija Slovenije—Democratic Opposition of Slovenia). Their main opponent was the Party of Democratic Renewal (Stranka demokratične prenove—SDP), or old Communists. Both parties had superficially similar platforms, which included marketizing reforms and more independence of action for Slovenia in Yugoslavia, but the Party of Democratic Renewal was slightly less insistent on these planks and had the sizable disadvantage of having been in power for forty years. Accordingly, the DEMOS took a clear majority of seats in two of the three houses of the legislature and the largest block of seats in the third house. Lojze Peterle, head of the Slovene Croatian Democrats, the party that obtained the largest number of votes among those parties that made up the DEMOS coalition, became prime minister on May 16, 1990.

In the direct elections for president, however, the former leader of the Communist party, Milan Kučan, took the runoff with almost 60 percent of the vote. Most observers did not perceive this as a victory for the Communists but rather as a personal victory for Kučan, whose popularity had peaked after his confrontation with Milošević at the special party congress in January. All in all, it seemed that the Slovenian voters picked the most democratic-sounding of the available choices without completely rejecting the progressive Communist leadership that had been defending Slovenia's separate path for the past several years. The new government contained a mix of radical nationalists, moderate nationalists, and liberal economic reformers, most of them politically unseasoned intellectuals.

The outcome in Croatia was quite different. There the Croatian Democratic Union, led by Franjo Tudjman, waged an overtly nationalistic campaign against the Communist party, now renamed the Party of Democratic Changes (Stranka demokratska promjena—SDP), that for many years had opposed Tudjman's brand of xenophobia as dangerous and destructive. It was no contest. Praising the Independent State of Croatia, the degenerate fascist state of World War II, as an "expression of the historical aspirations of the Croatian nation for its independent state," Tudjman called for a Croatia within its "historic and natural boundaries," advocated the "economic, spiritual and cultural union of Croatia and Bosnia-Herzegovina, which form a natural, indivisible political unit and are historically destined to be together," and asserted, in a manner reminiscent of Todor Zhivkov's claim about Turks in Bulgaria, that many of Bosnia's Muslims were in fact ethnic Croats. At the same time he was staking out these claims to a Greater Croatia, Tudjman railed against "Great Serbian hegemonistic desires" and promised to rectify what he called the overrepresentation by Serbs in the government, the police, and the media.[57]

The Party of Democratic Changes, on the other hand, supported pluralism ("We are serious" was its slogan), backed Marković's painful economic reforms, and campaigned against nationalism and for the maintenance of Yugoslavia. One of its candidates, Dravko Tomac, put it this way: "Yugoslavia has to be a federation because 2.2 million Serbs live outside Serbia in other Yugoslav republics. About 1.1 million Croats live outside Croatia. This means that the national question cannot be settled within a single republic, but within Yugoslavia as a federation." Creation of anything other than a true federation, Tomac said, would mean civil war.[58] Rejecting Tomac's accurate prediction, Croatian voters gave the Croatian Democratic Union 60 percent of the vote, and at the end of May 1990 Franjo Tudjman became president of Croatia. In his first few weeks in office Tudjman distanced himself from his more radical colleagues, but few doubted that he intended to conduct his regime with little sympathy for non-Croats.

The other four republics in Yugoslavia joined the electoral bandwagon six months later. In Serbia, Milošević had conducted a suddenly called election late in 1989 in which he permitted only his own candidates to run. The quality of this election may be indicated by the fact that just after the polls closed one Belgrade district reported that 102 percent of the registered voters had voted, 92 percent of them for Milošević.[59] Still, the genuineness of Milošević's popularity, especially in the countryside, could scarcely be doubted. Some thought that the elections to the Serbian National Assembly one year later—they took place in December 1990— might provide an opportunity for an opposition to form and conceivably even to challenge Milošević's Communists. The main opposition late in 1990 came from the Serbian Renewal Movement (Srpski pokret obnove— SPO), led by an eccentric writer named Vuk Drašković, who affected a full beard reminiscent of the Chetniks of World War II, flourished a dramatic cape, and tried to be more nationalistic than Milošević. At the last minute, ten democratic opposition parties formed a United Serbian Opposition, attempting to do for Serbia what the DEMOS did for Slovenia, but it was too little, too late. Whereas both the DEMOS and the Croatian Democratic Union profited from their nationalism, in Serbia, Milošević had already appropriated that sphere beyond recall. Many educated young people ridiculed and ignored the election and Milošević's Socialist party did poorly in Belgrade and some other urban areas; but in the country at large the socialists took 77 percent of the vote while Milošević himself swept into the presidency again with 65 percent.

Elections took place in the other three republics in December 1990 also. In Montenegro the League of Communists of Montenegro took 66 percent of the vote and its leader, Momir Bulatović, became president. Bulatović was a young and potentially reform-minded Communist, but for the time being he threw Montenegro's weight fully behind Milošević. In

Bosnia-Herzegovina, on the other hand, the three parties representing the three main ethnic groups received a number of votes and a number of seats roughly comparable to their population size. This meant that the Bosnian Muslim party (Party for Democratic Action) got 32 percent of the seats (lower than their approximately 44 percent of the population but still a plurality), the Serbian Democratic party got 26 percent, and the Croatian Democratic Community got 15 percent. The Communists trailed badly with 10 percent and evaporated as a force in Bosnian politics. Despite serious tensions and divisions, the new Bosnian parliament selected Ilija Izetbegòvić, a Muslim moderate, as president.[60]

In Macedonia the victor was the Democratic party of Macedonian National Unity/IMRO. The addition of "IMRO" sent a chill through the Balkans, since it was the acronym of the Internal Macedonian Revolutionary Organization, an ultranationalist, terrorist organization active in the first half of the twentieth century. In the first round of the Macedonian elections, IMRO had not fared as well as the Albanian party of Democratic Prosperity, which eventually ended up with 21 percent of the seats in the Macedonian legislature. Whereas most of the attention on Albanians in Yugoslavia justifiably centered on *Kosovë*, a large Albanian minority lives in a compact area of northwestern Macedonia, where they suffered repression at the hands of the Macedonians in the 1980s analogous to that suffered by the Albanians at the hands of Serbs in *Kosovë*. Their good performance on the first round of elections generated a sudden interest among Macedonian voters in the IMRO, which ended up with 31 percent of the seats after the second electoral round. The League of Communists of Macedonia, now the Party for Democratic Transformation, took second place, gathering 26 percent of the seats. The new assembly elected Kiro Gligorov, a reform Communist, as the president of Macedonia.

By the end of 1990, therefore, all of the six Yugoslav republics had elected, in more or less free elections, new legislatures and new presidents. Ironically, all of the presidents were former Communists, including even Franjo Tudjman, but only two of them, Milošević and Bulatović, continued to rule in the manner of their predecessors. The only important figures in the country who had not been elected were at the federal level. There the federal assembly, the presidency, and of course Ante Marković himself had all come to office on the basis of the constitution of 1974. Their inability to claim the legitimacy of popular election was a fatal liability in the post-1989 world.

The Road to Civil War

From the first free elections in the spring of 1990 it took a little more than a year for war to begin. Three events that took place in July 1990 hinted at the direction in which Yugoslavia was headed. In Serbia, Milošević remained unsatisfied with the constitutional changes he had rammed through in 1989. Even though his security forces occupied *Kosovë*, forty thousand Albanians still demonstrated in Prishtinë in January 1990 for free elections, and in February the army had to be sent in to quell riots. Milošević's response was to propose a completely rewritten constitution. This one would permit multiparty elections, which he correctly believed he would win, thus outflanking the new but weak democratic opposition, and would tie the autonomous regions, *Kosovë* and Vojvodina, more firmly to the Belgrade center. His first step in this strategy was to call a referendum on two weeks' notice asking for popular approval to write a new constitution before the December elections.

In reality, Milošević was asking for approval to crush *Kosovë* and to pursue his nationalist arguments with Slovenia and Croatia. Just before the vote, he forcibly disbanded the *Kosovë* legislature, which still contained a majority of ethnically Albanian members, ostensibly in response to strikes and other disturbances but actually to inflame the electorate. On July 2, 1990, the overwhelming majority of Serbs approved Milošević's strategy. On the same day 114 members of the *Kosovë* legislature—all the Albanian representatives who had been locked out of their offices—met and declared that *Kosovë* was now fully independent of Serbia and should be considered a constituent republic of Yugoslavia. Within days the Serbian assembly not only rejected the *Kosovë* declaration of independence but "permanently" abolished the *Kosovë* legislature and transferred all its functions to the Serbian assembly in Belgrade. Not to be outdone, the fugitive Albanian legislators convened secretly in September and produced a Constitution of the Republic of *Kosovë*, which, while remaining a dead letter under the new Serbian laws, remained the basis for the continued assertion by Albanian activists that the will of *Kosovë* was to be a republic like the other republics of Yugoslavia. The situation in *Kosovë* remained at an impasse: a small minority of self-righteous Serbs fully in control by force of arms, the large majority of frustrated Albanians dispossessed and hostile.

On the same day the Serbian voters approved Milošević's xenophobic policies, the Slovenian Assembly in Ljubljana formally declared Slovenia to be fully sovereign, thus taking the measures already adopted in September 1989 one step further. Slovenia now asserted that its laws took precedence over those of the federation, that it could control the armed forces on its soil, and that it intended to conduct its own foreign and trade policy. At this point, these actions by the Slovenes remained assertions rather than actualities, but they could now be understood as part of a systematic Slovenian strategy of incremental and orderly dissociation from Yugoslavia.

The third group of July events surrounded constitutional changes approved by the Tudjman government in Croatia on July 25, 1990. Since his electoral victory in May, Tudjman, instead of finding ways to calm the fears of the large Serbian minority in Croatia, had done just the opposite. He proved unwilling to talk seriously with their representatives while at the same time purging police forces of Serbian members and provoking confrontations by disarming police forces in predominantly Serbian towns.

He adopted the ancient Croatian red-and-white checkerboard shield, which had also been the emblem of the Ustasha regime. His response to the shock felt by Serbs and other non-Croats who remembered the genocide practiced by that regime was to say that if they did not like the new shield they could leave Croatia. Tudjman's legislature ignored the demands of the non-Croats to define Croatia as "a state of free peoples," defining it instead as "the national state of the Croatian nation."[61] Insensitive measures such as these led the more excitable members of the Serbian minority in Croatia to conclude that Tudjman was preparing the same kind of genocide against Serbs that the Ustasha regime had practiced.[62] The Belgrade media, controlled by Milošević, encouraged and abetted this overreaction, greatly inflaming the situation.

It was one thing for Slovenia to declare its sovereignty, since it has no coherent ethnic minorities and has a well-defined border with its neighbors. It was another thing for Croatia to do the same without taking special precautions to mollify its Serbian minority. The Serbs of Croatia are not a compact group, although a few local government units contain a majority of Serbs. Nevertheless, with the encouragement of Milošević and Vuk Drašković in Belgrade, not to mention some even more extreme fanatics like Vojislav Šešelj, who styled himself a Chetnik, arrayed himself in bandoleers, and talked about killing Croats, the leaders of the Serbian minority that lived in the poor mountainous regions of Croatia now began systematically to prepare for secession. By the end of July 1990 they created the Serbian National Council as their representative body, and in August they undertook a clandestine referendum allegedly showing that almost 100 percent of the Serbs in southwestern Croatia favored autonomy. Less biased observers noted that the area the Serbs sought to control, which they called Krajina, was only about two-thirds Serbian, the rest being Croats and other nationalities, and that an autonomous Krajina would contain only about one-quarter of the Serbs living in Croatia. Nevertheless, on October 1, 1990, the Serbian National Council declared the Krajina autonomous, and in February 1991 it formally announced its secession from Croatia as the Independent Republic of Krajina and expressed its desire to unite with Serbia.

Had this process of Serbian dissociation from Croatia been as peaceful as the previous paragraph makes it sound, Yugoslavia might have survived in some form. But it was far from peaceful. From April 1990, when Serbian irregulars killed a dozen Croatian policemen in the village of Borovo Selo, violence between Croats and Serbs in Croatia escalated. In August 1990, when Croatian police in the town of Benkovac tried to disarm some Serbian reservists, armed Serbs barricaded roads and patrolled the streets. From that point on irregular Serb paramilitary forces began to arm themselves, to disrupt communications by downing trees across roads, and to destroy Croatia's tourist industry with slashed tires, brawls, and worse. The number of incidents multiplied, as did the outlandishness of the rumors and the virulence of the hostility. Tudjman called the Serbian actions "an armed uprising," while in Belgrade Vuk Drašković called for a "declaration of war" to prevent another Croatian genocide against the Serbs. In November 1990 Milošević's government began imposing a tariff on goods imported from Croatia and Slovenia, to which the Croats responded by instituting a confiscatory tax on all properties held in Croatia by Serbs from Serbia, which included a large number of summer homes on the Adriatic Coast.

Meanwhile, the Slovenes continued to put pressure on federal authorities either to reach a reasonable agreement or to resign themselves to losing Slovenia. On December 23, 1990, a large majority of Slovene voters approved a referendum in which they vowed to declare their independence in six months if a satisfactory arrangement could not be reached. In February 1991 the Slovenian assembly began passing enabling laws that would permit them to become independent, the government made plans to print Slovenian money and open missions abroad, and border guards entered training. In March 1991 the assembly advised Slovenian youths that they could choose to serve in Slovenian territorial defense units or police instead of answering their conscription calls to the Yugoslav National Army, and in May it announced that Slovenia would secede from Yugoslavia on June 26, just six months after the referendum of December. The Croats announced they would follow suit.

In the end, Milošević proved willing to let Slovenia go, but not Croatia. In June 1990, while discussing the new constitution he wanted to install, he said that Serbia "links its present administrative borders exclusively to a Yugoslavia constituted as a federation. . . . If one does not want a federal state, the question of Serbian borders is an open political question."[63] By this formulation Milošević presented the Croats with an impossible choice: either they had to accept a federation dominated by Milošević or face a Serbian attempt to add one-third of Croatian territory, and possibly regions of Bosnia and Herzegovina as well, to a Greater Serbia. If he could control the Yugoslav army (Jugoslovenska narodna armija—JNA), either through the federal presidency or indirectly through Serbian generals, Milošević would have an overwhelming force at his disposal to put that policy into effect. With no really good options but unwilling to knuckle under to Milošević's threats, Croatia began, like Slovenia before it, to prepare for what increasingly seemed inevitable—secession.

The unknown quantity in this volatile situation was the JNA. The army was the only remaining Yugoslav institution that seemed to be functioning adequately on a federal basis at the end of 1990, but since about 70 percent of its officers were Serbs or Montenegrins and since its leadership consisted of old partisan warriors who refused to acknowledge that communism was dying in Eastern Europe, many feared that it would either throw its weight behind Milošević or that it would seize power in a coup of its own.[64] A bizarre document leaked early in 1991 suggested that many army officers believed that socialism was the greatest accomplishment of the twentieth century, that the CIA had worked with Gorbachev to destroy the Warsaw

Pact, that the LCY was the most progressive force still in Yugoslavia, and that the Slovenian and Croatian leaders were essentially traitors.[65]

The final humiliation of the federal government came in May 1991, when, by the normal rotation agreement, Borislav Jović was to step down as chairman of the presidency and the Croatian member was to succeed him. That Croatian member was Stipe Mesić, a critic of Serbian policy in *Kosovë*. Once in office, he promised, he intended to visit *Kosovë* to report on the conditions of oppression there. The Serbs used their four votes (Serbia, Vojvodina, *Kosovë*, and Montenegro) to deadlock the eight member presidency so that Mesić could not achieve the majority needed to take office. In protest the Croatian and Slovenian delegates to the federal assembly walked out. With only one month to go before the promised Slovenian declaration of independence, Yugoslavia found itself with a rump federal legislature and no executive authority.

Hope for a rebirth of a new Yugoslavia now rested with the republics. It seemed a good sign, therefore, that in March 1991 the presidents of the six republics began face-to-face weekly meetings at a number of Tito's old personal retreats in an effort to stop what everyone conceded was a freight train running out of control. At these meetings the presidents of Macedonia, Kiro Gligorov, and of Bosnia-Herzegovina, Ilija Izetbegović, acted as mediators between the two basic positions that had divided Serbs and Croats from the time of Bishop Strossmayer and Prince Michael. The first position, supported by Croatia and Slovenia, was that Yugoslavia should be a voluntary association of sovereign republics. The second, supported by Serbia and Montenegro, was that Yugoslavia be a united state in which the federation exercised control over banks, foreign affairs, security, and similar matters. The conferees at first thought they could conduct a federation-wide referendum to resolve this question, but this proved impossible. Gligorov and Izetbegović proposed what they called an "asymmetric federation," a murky idea that was nevertheless the only potentially viable proposal made in the months leading up to civil war. But neither Serbia, which insisted on maintaining the old Yugoslavia and held that the Croats were mistreating Serbs (they never mentioned *Kosovë*), nor Croatia, which complained the Serbs were in armed rebellion with Milošević's encouragement and rejected any plan for meaningful autonomy for its Serbs, would even discuss the proposal.

As June 26 approached, violence in the Serbian parts of Croatia continued to increase. Late in February and early in March an effort by Serbs to disarm Croats in their newly proclaimed Republic of Krajina led for the first time to the intervention of the Yugoslav army.[66] In April, Serbian terrorists attacked Croatian settlements in the unique ecological area around Plitvice Lakes, and in April the army mobilized and took up positions throughout the Serbian parts of Croatia. By May sporadic but bloody fighting was taking place in a number of Croatian towns, but it was difficult to say just which side started shooting first and what role the army was playing.

By this time public opinion in both Serbia and Croatia had been completely inflamed by vigorous campaigns of disinformation and propaganda. Each side ran hours of television stories showing mass graves from World War II being dug up and describing the bestial atrocities committed, always by the other side of course, in gruesome detail.[67] One observer commented that Yugoslavia seemed to be turning into a country of necrophiliacs.

On June 25, 1991, one day before planned, the Slovenes declared themselves independent and the Croats quickly followed suit. When previously trained Slovene guards moved to take over border posts, the Yugoslav National Army decided to intervene. Miscalculating completely the nature of their opponent, the army apparently believed it could send a few armored columns to the Slovenian border posts and simply occupy them. But the crafty Slovenes expertly blockaded the highways, cutting off the columns, while at the same time surrounding and seizing many caches of arms stored around the country. The Yugoslav military doctrine in case of foreign invasion had been to retreat to the hills and to fight a guerrilla war along the lines of the partisan effort. Toward this end, the army had stored large amounts of arms in isolated places throughout the country. When the Slovenes seized many of these caches in the first three or four days of the army's operations, they suddenly went from being a weakly armed militia to being a force reasonably well equipped with antitank and armor-piercing weapons. With its columns stalled along the Slovenian highways and the Slovenes able to destroy a significant amount of their armor, the army now thought better of its intervention. Within three weeks it had retreated back to Croatia. From that time on Slovenia continued an accelerating process of turning itself into an independent country. Early in 1992 it achieved formal diplomatic recognition from the European Community.

Croatia, however, was another story. There the situation in 1991 went from bad to worse to appalling. The armed confrontations of the first half of 1991 now turned into active efforts by an aroused and well-organized variety of Serbian paramilitary forces, including volunteers from within Serbia itself, to seize as much of Croatia as it could, while the disorganized and poorly armed Croats, aided by mercenaries from abroad, tried to resist.[68] At first the Yugoslav National Army seemed to be acting to keep the two sides apart, but with the collapse of the federal government it soon became apparent that the army had entered the war on the side of the Serbs. With no clear front, atrocities and virulent propaganda on both sides, incompatible aims, and murky lines of authority, the Yugoslav civil war became bloody and mean-spirited. Bitter hatred born of friends killing lifelong friends, of mutilations, of wanton destruction, of complete economic ruin for hundreds of thousands of refugees so contaminated all the parties that it is hard to imagine Serbs and Croats living peacefully together for at least a generation.

The European Community reacted with shock at the outbreak of civil war almost in its midst but found it very difficult to find an effective response. The Conference on Security and Cooperation in Europe proved to be useless in the face of this level of conflict, as did the West European Union. The European Community attempted to bring the warring sides together in a series of meetings in The Hague, but when truce after truce was immediately broken, it had to admit defeat, although desultory negotiations continued. Finally, a United Nations negotiating team, headed by former United States secretary of state Cyrus Vance, was able to achieve a break in the fighting, and in the spring of 1992 blue-helmeted United Nations troops, operating under a mandate from the Security Council, took up positions in Croatia. By the time of arrival of the United Nations force, Serbs had been able to seize about one third of Croatia's territory, which, under the truce arrangements, they continued to occupy.

At about the time the UN forces arrived in Croatia, a new arena of conflict heated up. Bosnia and Herzegovina (called simply Bosnia below) was the most ethnically mixed of the Yugoslav republics. The largest group, about 43 percent of the population, consisted of Muslims, or Bosnians as they are also known. These descendants of people who either converted or immigrated centuries earlier during the Ottoman era speak Serbo-Croatian but, because of their religion and culture, they consider themselves a separate people. Serbs constituted about 34 percent of the population of Bosnia and Herzegovina, Croats about 17 percent. None of these three groups lived in ethnically compact regions that could be encompassed by any rational border. President Izetbegović likened Bosnia to the skin of a leopard, with each spot a different group.

Serbian and Croatian nationalists both have claimed that Bosnia should be theirs, but in 1992 it was the Serbs who provoked the Bosnian war. Influenced by Serbian nationalistic enthusiasms of the late 1980s, Bosnian Serbs, under the unbalanced leadership of Radovan Karadžić and with the encouragement of Slobodan Milošević, began a propaganda campaign against Izetbegović, whom they falsely accused of being a Muslim fundamentalist. By raising the issue in this way they brought back primitive memories of the Ottoman period, which Serbian tradition characterizes as one of bloody oppression of Serbs. Serbian activists started establishing local units of government, creating militia to "protect" themselves, and proclaiming their desire to become part of Milošević's Serbia.

As the war progressed in Croatia, the situation in Bosnia became more and more tense. The issue that set the mix on fire was diplomatic recognition in the spring of 1992. The European Community had not immediately recognized either Slovenia or Croatia when they declared their independence in 1991. The United States in particular did not believe it would be fruitful to do so while Serbian aggression was going on and a civil war was in progress. But Germany insisted, perhaps because of historical ties to Slovenia and Croatia, and in December 1991 the European Community agreed to recognize those former Yugoslav states that met certain requirements, including the protection of human rights. This was more or less a subterfuge, since Germany said it would recognize Slovenia and Croatia on January 15, 1992, regardless. The commission examining the documentation found that only Slovenia and Macedonia met the requirements for recognition, but because of the German demarche, on January 15, 1992, the European Community formally recognized Slovenia and Croatia. Since this action substituted a partial solution for the all-Yugoslav solution the negotiators at the Hague had advocated, it almost certainly contributed to a worsening of the situation.[69]

In the case of Bosnia, the European Community suggested that a referendum on the question of independence would be appropriate. When the overwhelming majority of those voting in the election of March 1, 1992, approved, the Western powers recognized Bosnia's independence. But this move galvanized the already agitated Serbs, who had boycotted the election. Within days armed Serbian detachments were seizing territory in Bosnia and Serbian troops began a seige of Sarajevo, Bosnia's capital. By the summer Bosnia had degenerated into a chaotic and brutal three-sided civil war. Franjo Tudjman's government sided with the Bosnians, but at the same time managed to carve out some of Herzegovina for itself, and of course Milošević supported the Serbian rebels. Milošević ordered the Yugoslav National Army to withdraw from Bosnia, but when it did so it left its enormous supply of arms in the hands of Serbian irregulars, so that whereas the Serbian military forces in Bosnia were mainly local free-booters out of the control of any centralized command, they were very well armed. These Serbian forces quickly occupied two thirds of Bosnia and terrorized the Muslim Bosnians into the greatest flight of human refugees Europe had seen since World War II. The Serbs conducted a policy of "ethnic cleansing," by which they meant killing or causing to flee all the non-Serb population of the areas they held. By utilizing the most primitive and brutal methods imaginable, including the purposeful mass rape of Muslim women with the dual goal of making them unacceptable to their men and forcing them to bear Serbian children, the Serbs turned themselves into the pariahs of Europe. Western leaders began calling the Serbian leaders war criminals and making plans to convene a war crimes tribunal to deal with the terrible atrocities committed on all sides. Peace negotiations conducted in Geneva by United Nations and European Community negotiators produced plausible plans, but by 1993 the old multi-ethnic Bosnia, which Nobel Prize–winning Yugoslav novelist Ivo Andrić had described with such power in his novel *Bridge on the Drina*, was gone, perhaps forever.[70]

One other republic of the former Yugoslavia (the country that calls itself "Yugoslavia" today consists of Serbia and Montenegro, but it is no longer internationally recognized) remained in limbo during this period: Macedonia. Originally Macedonia was a geographical term, but early in the twentieth century, when the Ottomans were pushed out of the Balkan peninsula, Macedonia was divided among Greece, which received a little over half of the area; Bulgaria, which received about 15 percent; and Serbia, later Yugoslavia, which received the rest. The Macedonians speak their own Slavic language, are Orthodox Christians, and have their own national consciousness, although 20 to 40 percent of the population, depending on who does the counting, are Muslim Albanians. In 1945 the Communists created the Republic of Macedonia (it had been part of Serbia in the interwar years), and in 1991 this entity sought international recognition. Macedonia fulfilled the European Community's requirements, and by the end of 1992 it had Eastern Europe's only multi-ethnic cabinet (five Albanians, one Turk, the rest Macedonians). But recognition was prevented by the Greeks, who alleged that the term "Macedonia" was exclusively a Greek term and hid aggressive aspirations of the Macedonians to the northern part of Greece. It was not until early in 1993 that Macedonia was finally admitted to the United Nations under the name "The Former Republic of Macedonia," and one by one the European states began to extend formal recognition. Macedonia's future, however, remained gravely in doubt.

And finally there was *Kosovë*, the initial focal point. Amazingly, leaders of the Albanians in *Kosovë* still continued to maintain at the end of 1991 that their hope was to enter a renewed confederation of sovereign and equal republics. But as that prospect grew less and less feasible, in the spring of 1992 the Kosovars declared their independence. The only country to recognize them was Albania. The Albanians in *Kosovë* have been remarkably restrained in the face of extreme provocations by the Serbs, perhaps because they are poorly armed and know that the Serbs will not hesitate to massacre them. But with unemployment in the 40 percent range, with education at a standstill, and with no governmental functions reserved for them, it remained in doubt how long could they maintain their moderate stance. Together with their conationals in Albania and other parts of Yugoslavia, the Albanians constituted a population of about five and one-half million, more than the Croats and almost three times as numerous as the Slovenians. How long could it be before they attempted to assert that position in the Balkans to which ethnic politics seemed to entitle them?

8

Epilogue and Prologue:
The New Pluralism

In the twentieth century East European nations have found it difficult to follow paths of their own choosing. Apparently released from the grasp of ancient empires by World War I, all the new countries of Eastern Europe soon became participants, willing or unwilling, in Adolf Hitler's disastrous experiment in antirationalism. Escaping that monster bleeding and gravely injured, they turned only to find themselves caught in the jaws of a second beast, Joseph Stalin's equally disastrous foray into hyperrationalism. Because of its unfortunate geographical location between Russia and Germany, Eastern Europe became the primary field on which the two immense twentieth-century experiments were conducted. In the very long run, a hundred years from now, say, these interludes will be seen as relatively short-lived aberrations from the general trend of European development, which is the elaboration of pluralism; but for those who lived through them they were difficult, even horrible, times. Those experiments are now over, their failed wreckage strewn over the fields and cities of Eastern Europe.[1] For the first time East Europeans have a relatively unrestricted opportunity to enter into the mainstream of European development.

Unlike in 1918 and in 1945, they start with a positive model to emulate, the European Community. Whatever problems beset the Community, it is unquestionably more prosperous, more democratic, and more generous than the divided Europe of 1918 or the defeated and crushed Europe of 1945. Pressure from Russia is also temporarily displaced, as that great land tries to find a way out from under the rubble of the last seventy years. East Europeans today are experiencing what is likely to be a relatively

253

short period of freedom to create their own styles of governance, since it is highly likely that in time Russia and Ukraine will be restored to strength, with unforeseeable geopolitical consequences. In attempting to take advantage of this lull in the negative external pressures that shaped their history in the twentieth century, the East European countries do not start from a blank tablet. At least three common experiences shape the way they are reacting to their new opportunities.

The first is the fact that the entire region is, and has been for a long time, European in political aspiration, economic ambition, and cultural orientation. Historical memories in east central Europe go back to the great empires, in some cases even to independent and powerful medieval states, not just to the relatively short-lived twentieth-century experiences as independent states. In the sixteenth century, Poland/Lithuania was the largest commonwealth in Europe; Hungary was recognized as a kingdom by the pope in the year 1000; the first German university was founded in Prague in 1348. No one in the eighteenth century would have considered Bohemia, Hungary, or Poland not part of Europe, insofar as the concept was contemplated at the time. Even in southeastern Europe, which was under Ottoman control for hundreds of years, the nineteenth century saw a full turn from a southward orientation to a northward one in which the Balkan countries adopted European political and cultural norms. By World War I Balkan countries were just as "European" as, say, Ireland, Portugal, or southern Italy were at the time. Nazism and Stalinism temporarily cut off the East European nations from their natural course of development as European states. The experience of Greece, the only East European state to remain outside of communism and yet one whose conversion to Western norms from Ottoman standards is relatively recent, suggests what a more natural direction of development might have been. All political and economic policies in Eastern Europe today begin from the unshakable and accurate perception that these countries are and should be European.

A second basic ingredient of East European politics is more difficult to pinpoint, even to name, but it might be called the political culture of smallness. Today every country, even the largest and most powerful, has come to realize that it operates in an interdependent world in which decisions made elsewhere have an impact on it. But the largest and strongest countries know that they have considerable power in their own right to affect the direction of world affairs. Small countries do not have that confidence. Traditionally they have had to conduct their affairs in the knowledge that they have little control over the great forces of international politics or economics. In the nineteenth century the great powers took over the administration of several of the most important assets of the Balkan states in order to pay off Western bondholders; today the International Monetary Fund and World Bank tell East Europeans how to run their economies in order to satisfy their Western creditors. The European Community has provided a workable solution for its small members by enrolling them in a voluntary and mutually beneficial association with their powerful neighbors, and this, in part, is why the East Europeans want to enter that association. Until they do, knowledge of their relative inability to influence affairs will continue to encourage defensive policies designed to compensate for a sense of exclusion rather than positive policies based on a sense of inclusion. In countries like Slovakia, Romania, and Serbia, the fear that Germany has taken aim at them pushes their nationalist governments toward destructive policies that have the self-confirming effect of further alienating them from the Europeans they wish to join.

The third constant is that every country of Eastern Europe, having accepted the general principles of political democracy and market economics, has committed itself to a pluralist future. Because of their differing historical memories, the manner in which they extracted themselves from communism, the initial decisions they made, and the varying quality of their leaderships, each country is implementing these principles in a slightly different way. Indeed, this variety of response is one of the strengths of the process underway in Eastern Europe. The initial hope that shock therapy would bring a rapid transformation to a smoothly functioning market economy throughout the region had a utopian quality to it that was not consistent with the introduction of pluralism. The very term "transition," used constantly in 1990 and 1991, suggested a well-defined and clear-cut goal that could be achieved in a relatively limited timespan and that could be recognized when one had achieved it. But in fact pluralism is a state of permanent transition. There is no final resting point at which one can say the process is complete. What the East European countries were doing in 1991, what they are doing today, and what they will be doing in years to come are simply living the process. They are already engaged in the pluralist project of defining themselves.

Sometimes the self-definition already has been successful; more often it has not been; but in each case the process seems comparable to European experience. Poland has created small- and medium-size businesses and turned foreign trade toward the West, but it also suffered severe political crises (Poles might take heart from the example of Italy, however). The voucher plan in Czechoslovakia is unique, but the Czechs and the Slovaks have split apart (the historical experiences of Belgium and the Netherlands might be instructive for the Czechs and Slovaks, however). The creation of thousands of interlocking directorates in Hungary is creating an economy with a specific characteristic, but Hungary appears to be dividing economically into a rich western region—urban, educated, bordering on Europe—and a poor eastern region—rural, poor, bordering on Ukraine (Hungarians might find the example of England, with its historically rich south and poor north, encouraging). In Romania and Bulgaria land restitution is proceeding apace, but privatization is going slowly, and in Romania, at least, political change seems to be going slowly as well (here the development of Spain and Portugal might be an appropriate analog). The comparative historical examples adduced in these parenthetical remarks are far from precise, but they do suggest that the new East European states all have committed themselves to the pluralist process of creating democratic norms and market relationships that are similar, in broadest outline at least, to those experienced elsewhere in Europe.

It is easy to be pessimistic about how well the process is going. For one thing, democracy is proving to be less beguiling up close than it was at a distance. The antipolitical strategy of living in truth and creating a civil society has proven less useful under the fluid and open conditions of postcommunism than it was under the rigid old regimes. The writings of Václav Havel and Adam Michnik were inspiring to read in the 1970s and 1980s, and they are inspiring to read today. But the notion of maintaining solidarity against a totalitarian enemy was in its way a positive reflection of the hyperrationalist assumption that the people are one, that a single group or organization can adequately represent the general will. The antipoliticians sought to create an independent society in which self-activated individuals voluntarily associated themselves for their various purposes, but at the same time they understood themselves to be the leaders of that civil society, the ones who spoke for society at large against the usurpers. Neither Solidarity nor Civic Forum could sustain that pretense when the totalitarian state disappeared. In order to do so, its leaders would have had to turn from the democrats they really were to totalitarian activists—to build their own Bastilles, as Michnik put it. In the place of the antipolitical leaders have come dozens of professional politicians of all stripes, many considerably less attractive than the historians, philosophers, and musicians that the velvet revolutions brought forth. Their cacophony is disorienting to those who believed that democracy would be a political paradise and discouraging to those who hoped for simple, clear solutions.

For most East Europeans—those out of the range of Western television—democracy and the market were empty concepts, representations of a better life, perhaps, but without content. They were the positive symbols of what was good about the West in the way that Yalta was a negative symbol of what was bad about the postwar division of Europe. Many people were dismayed, therefore, when their new democracies turned out to be characterized by pettiness, obstructionism, raw ambition, and all the other less attractive aspects of parliamentary democracy that exist in the West but are hidden under a façade of civility that has evolved over time.

East Europeans entered into the democratic era without experience in compromise, in fact with considerable distaste for it, and this has not helped their initial efforts to find solutions. East European intellectuals in general have been nurtured in a rationalist tradition in which they see themselves as the natural leaders of society. Confronted with the confusion of the post-1989 world they tend to react with comments such as "the people do not understand the issues," or "we need a generation to educate the population to democratic values," or "perhaps for now a strong hand is needed." But what many observers of the initial post-Communist period have forgotten is that the Western democracies did not come to a politics of accommodation through a process of calm deliberation. The situation of the East European intellectuals is not different in kind from the one faced by the American revolutionaries, who saw the state legislatures filling with "specious men" after 1776 and who realized that they would have to build their new constitution around the distasteful but unavoidable fact of human contentiousness. The pluralist governments that have emerged since that time have always been marked by posturing, venality, "specious men," and wrong turns, as they still are. And yet, after all the threats of the twentieth century, they continue to function.

The Western tendency to criticize East European politics in terms of an idealized version of democracy rather than in terms of its actualities is repeated in the economic sphere. Apologists of capitalism like to characterize it in terms of Max Weber's Protestant ethic. The successful capitalist worked hard, saved money, honored contracts, and exercised stewardship. This positive picture of the capitalist is true as far as it goes, but there is another side of the coin, less stressed but also true. Capitalists, especially those who went outside of Europe to find their fortunes, were also often pirates, slavetraders, and speculators who had little compunction about working other human beings to death, subjugating the weak, and cheating the public. The remarkable thing is not that such people exist—they still do and they always will—but that stable pluralist societies were constructed in spite of them. To find freebooters in Eastern Europe today is no surprise. The surprise would be if they prevented the emergence of a pluralist society there.

Another cause for discouragement, even for fear that a restored Europe will be less stable than was a divided Europe, is the virulence of the nationalist emotions that came almost immediately to the surface after 1989. In the nineteenth century nationalism could be understood as mostly a liberal phenomenon, an effort on the part of East Europeans to translate the French revolutionary promise of fairness and equity into a language appropriate for shaking off the ancient empires. When nationalists came to power in the twentieth century, however, they proved to be far less liberal, using ethnic arguments to identify and push aside "enemies," such as Jews or other "foreigners," in their midst and to justify the demand for adding territories deemed part of the national heritage. This style of irridentist nationalism continues to exert its baleful influence, but it is not impossible that the twenty-first century style of nationalism will be less disruptive and more protective of the status quo. The international agreements of the last half of the twentieth century have produced standards of minority treatment and of border inviolability that could, when backed by an international structure analogous to the European Community, reduce twenty-first century nationalism to a form of patriotism not inconsistent with political stability. In the European Community today, for example, it is possible for a Florentine to be a city booster, a Tuscan patriot, an Italian citizen, and an advocate of European unity all at the same time, or at least at different times as the situation demands.

Given the disaster in Yugoslavia, it is important to note that at least some East European countries seem to understand that raw nationalism has serious negative consequences. Yugoslavia collapsed because it was not a truly voluntary federation and it was not based on pluralist principles. The concepts for creating a third Yugoslavia existed—protection of minority rights, inviolable borders, voluntary accession to the community—but the utter lack of leadership in Croatia and Serbia made certain that they would not be used. In Croatia, a leader absorbed in an outmoded idea of an integral Croatian nation failed to realize the consequences of not accommodating the minorities in his land, and in Serbia a leader still thinking in early twentieth-century terms of creating his people's regional hegemony by force—an idea that the European Community was founded to repudiate—brought the latent fears of his people to the surface in a most vicious way. These approaches contrasted starkly with that of Ilija Izetbegović, president of Bosnia and Herzegovina, whose skillful, although in the end unsuccessful, leadership constantly held out the possibility of compromise and accommodation.

The destructive narrowness of the policies of Tudjman and Milošević may be contrasted with the constructive breadth of the steps taken in Poland, where religious, secular, and cultural leaders have rejected anti-Semitism and initiated treaties of friendship with their neighbors. The Poles seem to have grasped that the essence of wisdom in ethnic politics is to accept responsibility for the past. This must not be a shameful admission but simply recognition of historical fact. As Adam Michnik put it, "If—being German—I feel proud because of Goethe, Heine, and Thomas Mann, even though it wasn't I who wrote their books, I also have to feel shame because of Hitler, Himmler, and Goebbels, even though I never had any sympathy for that ensemble. That is what responsibility consists of."[2] As German president Richard von Weizsacker said in 1985, "We must understand that there can be no reconciliation without remembrance."[3] The secret of the Polish treaties with Germany was that both sides expressed regret for their actions in the past and only then went on to establish cooperative programs for the future. In Yugoslavia the main rhetorical contacts among the many sides of its civil war were accusations of the other side's guilt. Nothing lasting can be built on that basis, and it seems likely that it will be a long time before a genuine agreement can be reached among the Yugoslav peoples on the basis of responsibility, remembrance, and reconciliation.[4]

Another structural element that is disrupting the smooth flow of East European public life is the continuing legacy of communism. The huge industrial combines that sometimes constitute the only employer in a city or a region continue to exist. The old elites have not disappeared. Their members now sometimes serve as directors of banks or private enterprises of various kinds and may still be dominant in the security forces or in new nationalist parties. Furthermore, a social ethic that is antithetical to capitalism remains widespread. There is also the wrenching problem of how, even if, to punish those who brought the country to its low point. These problems exacerbate tensions in every country of Eastern Europe, as already contentious issues are discussed in an atmosphere of recriminations, accusations, and humiliations.

Is it possible to be optimistic when one observes the difficulties, the chaos, the squabbling, the ineptitudes, the vanities that characterize daily politics throughout Eastern Europe? With the exception of Yugoslavia, I think it is, especially if one takes a longer view. The difference between Eastern Europe today and Eastern Europe twenty years ago is that its problems are there for all to see. Totalitarian states hide their weaknesses and present a surface of unity, efficiency, and strength. Pluralist societies hide their strengths and present a surface of disarray, confusion, and weakness. In pluralist societies all problems are fair game for public debate, whereas in totalitarian societies no public debate concerns real issues. For that reason, nothing ever gets solved in totalitarian states. All the problems continue to fester, causing their structural damage but without hope of repair. Pluralist societies, whatever their difficulties, do in fact change, albeit slowly. Once they solve, or at least ameliorate, a problem, the formerly highly visible dysfunction disappears and the solution becomes an invisible structural strength.

The East Europeans have brought all of their problems to the surface at once, and they are severe. There is no hope that the new regimes will solve them all right away or even ever. But at least they are now available for solution. Each country in its own way will solve something here, something there, and when it does, the new arrangements will enter into the structural strength of that society, creating a new political culture and a new style of economic behavior. These will not look just like any of the Western models that analysts tried to suggest for Eastern Europe in the first days after 1989 (the French model, the Swedish model, and so forth). They will be their own models, not a third way between capitalism and communism, but a tenth, eleventh, or thirtieth way. It is highly likely that some seriously bad choices will be made, and not at all beyond possibility that political figures advocating neofascist or neocommunist solutions will achieve power, as happened in Greece in 1967. But these regimes will not be able to sustain themselves in the way that they might have earlier in the century. Even if they do they will only sentence their countries to another stay in the wilderness such as they experienced in the last forty years.

My East European friends often accuse me of being a typical example of that well-known phenomenon, the naive American. I simply do not understand the deep-seated problems, the hatreds, the personalities, and disasters that are the daily currency of East European politics. Perhaps they are right. They certainly know more than I about the details of their own situation, and it is not at all difficult to paint a dark picture of the problems facing each East European country. But I am a historian, not a politician. In history every end is also a beginning. But beginnings, especially when they involve important sociopolitical reorientations, are only that. Experience with other significant historical innovations suggests that it is impossible to predict how and when we will understand just what the specificities of Eastern Europe's restoration to the European tradition are.

The British invented the principles of liberal government, the politics of accommodation that insists that the opposition play a central role in governance. Traditionally, the events that ushered in that innovation have been considered to be the Puritan Revolution of the 1640s and the Glorious Revolution of 1688. In fact, however, the term *loyal opposition* did not come into use for the first time in Britain until 1826 (even then it was a heavily ironic term used in derision), and many British historians argue that the principles today associated with liberal government did not receive their first practical form in parliament until the Great Reform Act of 1832. Americans celebrate 1776 as the date of the American Revolution, but two of the most important issues raised by that revolution, slavery in a land where "all men are created equal" and the rights of states in a federal system, were not solved until half a million men died in a huge civil war almost ninety years later. François Furet, the dean of historians of the French Revolution, entitles his most important book on that seminal event *La Révolution: de Turgot á Jules Ferry, 1770–1880* because he believes that not until the creation of the Third Republic in 1875 were the principles of the French Revolution firmly established in French political structures, once again almost ninety years after the initial events.

It is not likely that it will take ninety years for the nations of Eastern Europe to work out the implications of the initial steps they took toward pluralism in 1989. Theirs was not a revolution of total innovation, like the great classic revolutions, but rather the shucking off of a failed experiment in favor of an already existing model, pluralist democracy. But the creation of viable East European variants of pluralism will be a difficult and confusing task. Given the very nature of pluralism, there will never come a point at which the architects of the changes will be able to stand back and admire their completed work. New developments and forces will constantly challenge East European countries to adapt, renew, and change. This is good, because it will push this part of Europe to innovate, perhaps even to find new meanings in democracy and in the market economy, thus making its contribution to the pluralist tradition, as each European country in the West has done. But the pathway is crooked, and we do not have a map. Over time, all the East European countries, including even the former Soviet Union, will eventually create viable pluralist systems, but the details of how each individual country will accomplish this—whether it will encompass a neofascist detour, whether it will lead fairly rapidly to integration into the European Community, or whether entirely unanticipated solutions will be found—remain to be seen.

Notes

Introduction

1. In June 1990 in Prague, an exhibit of documents and videos from the years preceding the velvet revolution produced as its main reaction laughter (*New York Times,* June 6, 1990). In January a show in Sofia of cartoons done clandestinely by Todor Tsonov over a thirty-five-year period satirizing Todor Zhivkov, deposed Bulgarian leader, led viewers "to gape, chuckle, even laugh out loud" (*New York Times,* January 22, 1990). In East Berlin in April 1990 banners from the great mass gatherings of 1989 were juxtaposed to a museum exhibit celebrating the fortieth anniversary of the Communist seizure of power. East Germans streamed through the exhibit, "looking hard and laughing harder" (Robert Darnton, *Berlin Journal, 1989–1990* [New York: W. W. Norton, 1991], 330).

2. Quoted by Karl Dietrich Bracher, *The German Dictatorship: The Origins, Structure, and Effects of National Socialism* (New York: Praeger, 1970), 10. I would like to thank Richard Wolin for this citation.

3. Isaiah Berlin, "The Counter-Enlightenment," in his *Against the Current,* ed. Henry Hardy (New York: Penguin Books, 1982), 19.

4. René Déscartes, "Discourse on the Method of Rightly Conducting the Reason," *The Philosophical Works of Descartes,* trans. and ed. Elizabeth S. Haldane and G.R.T. Ross (N.p.: Dover Publications, 1955), 1: 119.

5. Pascal provides a good epigraph for these failures: "Two excesses: to exclude reason, to admit nothing but reason" (Blaise Pascal, *Pensées* [New York: Viking Penguin, 1966], 85).

6. John M. Montias, *Central Planning in Poland* (New Haven, Conn.: Yale University Press, 1962), 50. See also Martin R. Myant, *Poland: A Crisis for Socialism* (London: Lawrence & Wishart, 1982), 33.

7. For a graphic discussion of the poverty in rural Croatia, where, for example, almost no households owned a bed, see Rudolf Bićanić, *How the People Live: Life in the Passive Regions (Peasant Life in Southwestern Croatia, Bosnia and Hercegovina; Yugoslavia in 1935)*, trans. Stephen Clissold, rev. Marian Despalatović, ed. Joel M. Halpern and Elinor Murray Despalatović (Amherst, Mass.: University of Massachusetts Department of Anthropology, Research Report no. 21, 1981).

8. Charles Gati, *Hungary and the Soviet Bloc* (Durham, N.C.: Duke University Press, 1986), 69; see also Neal Ascherson, *The Polish August: The Self-Limiting Revolution* (New York: Viking, 1982), 35–36.

9. Martin R. Myant, *The Czechoslovak Economy 1948–1988: The Battle for Economic Reform* (Cambridge: Cambridge University Press, 1989), 4–8. "The atmosphere in Czechoslovakia at the time was favorable for [nationalisation] because the desire for greater equality had deep historical roots in . . . broad segments of society" (Alice Teichova, *The Czechoslovak Economy 1918–1980* [London: Routledge, 1988], 101).

10. John R. Lampe, *The Bulgarian Economy in the Twentieth Century* (London: Croom Helm, 1986), 124.

11. G. M. Tamás, "Farewell to the Left," *Eastern European Politics and Societies* 5 (1991): 92.

12. Oskar Lange and Fred M. Taylor, *On the Economic Theory of Socialism* (Minneapolis: University of Minnesota Press, 1938), 89. Lange's formulations were better than most, but they still contained the problem of average rather than marginal cost and an inability, without private ownership, to determine accurate pricing. When Hayek pointed this out, Lange responded in a personal letter saying: "I do not propose price fixing by a real central planning board as a practical solution. It was used in my paper only as a methodological device" (quoted by Gabriel Tempkin, "On Economic Reforms in Socialist Countries: The Debate on Economic Calculation under Socialism Revisited," *Communist Economies* 1 [1989]: 38). Lange did not make this damaging admission public, however.

13. Note, however, that the socialist argument is based on the same underlying goal as neoclassical economics: efficiency in resource allocation. For a persuasive argument that this assumption has led to a serious misunderstanding of socialist economies, see Peter Murrell, *The Nature of Socialist Economies: Lessons from Eastern European Foreign Trade* (Princeton, N.J.: Princeton University Press, 1990), the thesis of which is more fundamental than its subtitle suggests.

14. Abram Bergson, "Socialist Economics," in *A Survey of Contemporary Economics,* ed. Howard S. Ellis (Philadelphia: The Blakiston Company, for the American Economic Association, 1948), 412.

15. Joseph Rothschild, *Return to Diversity: A Political History of East Central Europe Since World War II* (New York: Oxford University Press, 1989), 145.

16. Myant, *Czechoslovak Economy,* 91.

17. Iván Berend, *The Hungarian Economic Reforms, 1953–1988* (Cambridge: Cambridge University Press, 1988), 147.

18. David S. Mason, *Revolution in East-Central Europe: The Rise and Fall of Communism and the Cold War* (Boulder, Colo.: Westview Press, 1992), 20–21. By the mid-1970s growth rates started to decline.

19. See László Szamuely, "The First Wave of the Economic Mechanism Debate and the 1968 Reform in Hungary (1954–1957)," *Acta Oeconomica* 29/1–2 (1982): 1–23; and idem; "The Second Wave of the Economic Mechanism Debate and the 1968 Reform in Hungary," *Acta Oeconomica* 33/1–2 (1984): 43–67.

20. On Hungarian reform see Xavier Richet, *The Hungarian Model: Markets and Planning in a Socialist Economy* (Cambridge: Cambridge University Press, 1989).

21. Myant gives a telling example of how improper it was for low-ranking party members to raise serious economic questions. When the party organization in the main Tatra factory in Kopřivnice inquired why Czechoslovakia stressed heavy industry when it lacked the necessary raw materials, they were accused of being an "anti-state group" and eleven party members were disciplined (Myant, *The Czechoslovak Economy,* 111).

22. Ota Šik, *Plan and Market under Socialism* (White Plains, N.Y.: International Arts and Sciences Press Inc., 1967). Among Šik's many other works, see especially *For a Humane Economic Democracy,* trans. Fred Eidlin and William Graf (New York: Praeger, 1985).

23. Teichova, *The Czechoslovak Economy,* 152.

Chapter 1

1. Leszek Kołakowski and Stuart Hampshire, eds., *The Socialist Idea: A Reappraisal* (New York: Basic Books, 1974), 1–2.

2. Václav Havel, *Open Letters: Selected Writings, 1965–1990,* ed. Paul Wilson (New York: Vintage, 1992), 9.

3. A more sophisticated but far less well-known critique of the new bureaucratic elite (the new class) in the Soviet Union is Claude Lefort, "Totalitarianism without Stalin," in his *The Political Forms of Modern Society: Bureaucracy, Democracy, Totalitarianism,* ed. John B. Thompson (Cambridge, Mass.: The MIT Press, 1986), 52–88. The article was first published in 1956.

4. Milovan Djilas, *The New Class* (New York: Praeger, 1967, 22d printing as corrected), 69.

5. Peter Raina, *Political Opposition in Poland* (London: Poets & Painters Press, 1978), 82–95. The complete text of the *Open Letter* may be found in *Revolutionary Marxist Students in Poland Speak Out,* ed. George Lavan Weissman, trans. Gerald Paul (New York: Merit Press, 1968).

6. See Gerson Sher, *Praxis: Marxist Criticism and Dissent in Socialist Yugoslavia* (Bloomington: Indiana University Press, 1977).

7. Mihailo Marković, "Marxist Philosophy in Yugoslavia: The Praxis Group," in Mihailo Marković and Robert S. Cohen, *Yugoslavia: The Rise and Fall of Socialist Humanism* (London: Bertrand Russell Peace Foundation, 1975), 37.

8. For a useful discussion of the *Praxis* philosophers, see Aleksandar Pavković, "Two Thaws in Yugoslav Philosophy," in *Glasnost in Context,* ed. M. Pavlyshyn (London: Berg, 1990), 69–82.

9. Gale Stokes, ed., *From Stalinism to Pluralism* (New York: Oxford University Press, 1991), 153.

10. Pavel Tigrid, "Czechoslovakia: A Post-Mortem," *Survey* 73 (Autumn 1969): 133–64.

11. Party leader Antonín Novotný had gone to some trouble to insult the Slovaks earlier in the year by returning a gala gift from Matica Slovenska, the Slovak cultural organization, as "unacceptable" (William Shawcross, *Dubček: Dubček and Czechoslovakia, 1968–1990* [London: Hogarth Press, 1990], 154).

12. Václav Havel, *Disturbing the Peace: A Conversation with Karel Hvížďala,* trans. Paul Wilson (New York: Alfred A. Knopf, 1990), 98. In his article of April

4, 1968, Havel said, "Therefore I see the only genuinely consequential and effective route to the idea of democratic socialism . . . is a revitalized model of a two-party system, one that corresponds to a socialist social structure" (Havel, *Open Letters,* 30).

13. Dennison Rusinow, "Anatomy of a Student Revolt," American Universities Field Service, *Southeast Europe Series,* vol. 15, nos. 4 and 5; and April Carter, *Democratic Reform in Yugoslavia: The Changing Role of the Party* (Princeton, N.J.: Princeton University Press, 1982), 207–18.

14. Philosophy students and faculty continued a sustained series of protests and confrontations until in 1975 seven professors of philosophy were removed from active teaching.

15. Miodrag Perišić, conversation with author, January 16, 1992.

16. David Ost, *Solidarity and the Politics of Anti-Politics: Opposition and Reform in Poland since 1968* (Philadelphia: Temple University Press, 1990), 46–47. Zygmunt Bauman agrees that the Polish intelligentsia "flirted" with the political leadership (Joanna M. Prebisz, *Polish Dissident Publications: An Annotated Bibliography* [New York: Praeger, 1982], quoting an article by Bauman in *Krytyka* from 1978, 77).

17. See his speech to the court prior to being sentenced to three years in prison in December 1968 (Raina, *Political Opposition in Poland,* 179). Kuroń taught his scouts that a true Communist was "a man who fights for social justice, for freedom and equality, for socialism." Kuroń and Modzelewski, who had been released from jail just in time for the March events, found themselves returned to prison for an additional three and one-half years at the same time Michnik was sentenced, along with many other activists.

18. Raina reports expressions of sympathy from three factories in Wrocław, Warsaw, and Kraków, but in comparison with the outbursts to come in the 1970s and in 1980 they were minor (Raina, *Political Opposition in Poland,* 140).

19. For a detailed discussion of the events of 1970–1971, see Roman Laba, *The Roots of Solidarity* (Princeton, N.J.: Princeton University Press, 1991). See also Lawrence Goodwyn, *Breaking the Barrier: The Rise of Solidarity in Poland* (New York: Oxford University Press, 1991). Goodwyn's book expands Laba's insights into a full-scale social interpretation of post-World War II Polish history. For critiques of these two books see Michael Bernhard, "Reinterpreting Solidarity," *Studies in Comparative Communism* 24/3 (1991): 313–30; and Timothy Garton Ash, "Poland After Solidarity," *New York Review of Books* (June 13, 1991). Bernhard criticizes some of Laba's interpretations but calls his reconstruction of the strikes of 1970–1971 "the standard account." Goodwyn, Bernhard writes, "will read like a fairy tale to anyone with more than a passing acquaintance with . . . Solidarity" (330).

20. Elements taken from the speech of Józef Cyrankiewicz, December 17, 1970, quoted by Laba, *Roots of Solidarity,* 63. On the same page Laba quotes Cyrankiewicz as saying in 1956, "Every provocateur or madman who dares to lift his hand against the power of People's Poland will have that hand chopped off."

21. These figures come from a party report accepted by the central committee in June 1983 and published in *Nowe Drogi* in October of that year (*Keesing's,* 32,799).

22. Later the myth was spread that Minister of Defense General Jaruzelski had not been a party to the killings and had announced to an emergency session

of the politburo that "Polish soldiers will not fire on Polish workers." Laba convincingly demonstrates this widespread and influential story to be a piece of very successful disinformation. In 1983 Jaruzelski said to a reporter from the *Christian Science Monitor* that "workers who strike are not Polish" (Laba, *Roots of Solidarity,* 88–90 [quotation on p. 90]).

23. Neal Ascherson, *The Polish August: The Self-Limiting Revolution* (New York: Viking Press, 1982), 104.

24. Zbigniew M. Fallenbuchl, "The Strategy of Development and Gierek's Economic Maneuver," in *Gierek's Poland,* ed. Adam Bromke and John W. Strong (New York: Praeger, 1973), 60.

25. "What kind of communist society is it that has no sausage?" Nikita Khrushchev once remarked (quoted in Mark Franklin, *Khrushchev* [London: Pelican, 1966], 148). Goodwyn argues that it was not just the Communists who believed that workers were preoccupied with "stomach issues" but the entire Polish intelligentsia (*Breaking the Barrier,* 98).

26. Robert W. Dean, "Gierek's Three Years: Retrenchment and Reform," *Survey* 20/2–3 (Spring–Summer 1974): 66.

27. Laba, *Roots of Solidarity,* 43; and Kazimierz Poznański, "Economic Adjustment and Political Forces: Poland since 1970," *International Organization,* 40/2 (Spring 1986): 291.

28. Martin R. Myant, *Poland: A Crisis for Socialism* (London: Lawrence & Wishart, 1982), 69.

29. Zbigniew M. Fallenbuchl, "The Polish Economy in the 1970s," in *East European Economies Post-Helsinki* (Washington, D.C.: Joint Economic Committee of the United States Congress, 1977), 835.

30. Poznański, "Economic Adjustment and Political Forces," 281.

31. Myant, *Poland: A Crisis for Socialism,* 108. James R. Thompson reports that by the end of the 1980s only 54 percent of the Perkins engines produced in the Massey-Ferguson production facility left the factory rated "satisfactory" on the first try, and that the mean time to failure of the seventeen different models of tractors Ursus produced ranged from 80 to 150 hours, far below Western standards. To suggest how poor a reputation Ursus had in Poland, Thompson notes that Polish farmers "choose to buy even Russian tractors in preference" ("A Glimpse at the Dark Side of Socialist Industrial Planning," *Sarmatian Review* 12/1 [January 1992]: 104).

32. Mario Nuti, "The Polish Crisis: Economic Factors and Constraints," in *Crisis in the East European Economy: The Spread of the Polish Disease,* ed. Jan Drewnowski (New York: St. Martin's Press, 1982), table 1.2, p. 22; and table 1.1, p. 20.

33. Quoted by Dean, "Gierek's Three Years," 68.

34. Václav Havel, "Letter to Gustav Husák," in his *Living in Truth,* ed. Jan Vladislav (London: Faber & Faber, 1990), 31.

35. Laba, *Roots of Solidarity,* 23, 65, and 68.

36. Adam Michnik, "A New Evolutionism," in *Letters from Prison,* trans. Maya Latynski (Berkeley: University of California Press, 1985), 146.

37. Leszek Kołakowski, "Hope and Hopelessness," *Survey* 17/3 (Summer 1971): 46.

38. Leonid Brezhnev, "Speech to the Fifth Congress of the Polish United Workers' Party (November 12, 1968)," *Current Digest of the Soviet Press* 20/46 (1968): 3–5.

39. This is the title of a Kuroń article from the 1980s (see Ted Kaminski, "Underground Publishing in Poland," *Orbis* 31/3 [Fall 1987]: 328).

40. Mihály Vajdá, *The State and Socialism* (New York: St. Martin's Press, 1981), 2–3. Vajdá's introduction provides a superb sketch of how this student of Lukács lost his faith in Marxism but retained his belief in freedom.

41. Havel, *Living in Truth*, 29.

42. Michnik, *Letters from Prison*, 86.

43. Havel, *Living in Truth*, 90.

44. George Konrád, *Anti-Politics* (New York: Harcourt Brace Jovanovic, 1984), 120.

45. Adam Michnik, *L'Église et la Gauche: Le Dialogue Polonais* (Paris: Éditions du Seuil, 1979), 204.

46. Havel, *Disturbing the Peace*, 181.

47. Havel, *Living in Truth*, 57.

48. Vaculík's speech appears in Dušan Hamšík, *Writers against Rulers* (New York: Random House, 1971), 181–82.

49. Konstanty Gebert, "An Independent Society: Poland under Martial Law," *Alternatives* 15 (1990): 359, quoting his own work originally published in February 1982. "What the dissidents wanted to do was to erect their own ramparts and to live, behind them, a communal life worthy of free individuals" (György Bence, "Social Theory in Transition," *Social Research* 57/2 [Summer 1990]: 252).

50. Norman Manea, *On Clowns: The Dictator and the Artist* (New York: Grove Wiedenfeld, 1992), 104.

51. Havel, *Disturbing the Peace*, 186.

52. Soviet dissidents originated this strategy in the 1960s, but their work had little influence on the development of opposition in Eastern Europe.

53. President Jimmy Carter's policy of supporting human rights, announced in his inaugural address, had an impact too. In the Soviet Union Andrei Sakharov praised Carter for being the first head of state to announce "an unambiguous commitment to the international defense of human rights" (quoted by Michael Scammell, "The Prophet and the Wilderness," *The New Republic*, February 25, 1991, 34).

54. *Conference on Security and Cooperation in Europe: Part II*, Hearings before the Subcommittee on International Political and Military Affairs of the [House] Committee on International Relations (Washington, D.C.: U.S. Government Printing Office, 1975), 123.

55. The twenty-two persons arrested included members of other groups as well. See Timothy W. Ryback, *Rock around the Bloc: A History of Rock Music in Eastern Europe and the Soviet Union* (New York: Oxford University Press, 1990), 141–48. Ryback reports that at the trial, the Plastics' attorney countered the government's charge of vulgarity by reading a 1922 letter of Lenin's in which he said "bureaucracy is shit." Nonetheless, four of the most prominent musicians were convicted. They received sentences of from eight to eighteen months for "disrespect of society" and for being "filthy" and "obscene."

56. Havel, *Disturbing the Peace*, 128.

57. H. Gordon Skilling, *Charter 77 and Human Rights in Czechoslovakia* (London: Allen & Unwin, 1981), 212.

58. See Ost, *Solidarity and the Politics of Anti-Politics*, 64–66. On the concept of civil society see John Keane, *Civil Society and the State* (London: Verso, 1988).

59. Adam Michnik, "A New Evolutionism," in his *Letters from Prison,* 135–48.

60. Jan Józef Lipski, *KOR: A History of the Workers' Defense Committee in Poland, 1976–1978* (Berkeley: University of California Press, 1985), 34.

61. Baranczak reports how he, Michnik, and some friends were present at a Warsaw court when a group of "weeping, wailing, cursing women left the courtroom, . . . each of them stupefied by the fact that as a result of a trial she wouldn't see her husband for the next two, three, five years and that nothing could be done about it. I stood next to Adam at that moment. His eyes were dry but I knew him well enough to see that he had just hit upon one of those ideas of his. . . . KOR was formally founded a few months later. . . . It began not with anyone's political program or ideological statement. It began with a simple impulse of compassion" (Stanisław Baranczak, *Breathing under Water and Other East European Essays* [Cambridge, Mass.: Harvard University Press, 1990], 46).

62. Lipski, *KOR,* 44–45 and 64.

63. Since the acronym for the society thereby became very awkward (KSS "KOR") I will continue to refer to the organization simply as KOR.

64. The Poles have an earthier term for samizdat: *bibuła,* which also means toilet paper.

65. For a brief history of *Petlice* by its founder see Ludvík Vaculík, "A *Padlock* for the Castle," *Index on Censorship* 3/89: 31–33.

66. In 1985 research by the Center for Journalism in Kraków estimated that by 1980 one in every four Poles had read an underground publication and about two hundred thousand persons read *bibuła* regularly (Bernhard, "Reinterpreting Solidarity," 319).

67. The "a" is added to the acronym to turn it into the word *nowa* (pronounced "nova"), or "new."

68. Nuti, "The Polish Crisis," 37.

69. Ted Kaminski, "Underground Publishing in Poland," *Orbis* 31/3 (Fall 1987): 314.

70. Quoted by Keith John Lepak, *Prelude to Solidarity: Poland and the Politics of the Gierek Regime* (New York: Columbia University Press, 1988), 165.

71. The opposition felt the same way. "We took [the searches, the arrests, and the spells in prison] in our stride as occupational hazards, disturbing, yes, but by now commonplace" (Lech Wałęsa, *A Way of Hope* [New York: Henry Holt, 1987], 103).

72. Interview with Damian Kalbarczyk, February 19, 1992.

73. The initial declaration of April 29, 1978, appeared in *Survey* 24/4 (Autumn 1979): 93–98.

74. Michnik, *Letters from Prison,* 144.

75. For the initial programs of these two organizations see Raina, *Political Opposition in Poland,* 468–96.

76. Bernhard has been "able to establish the identity of six hundred or so activists involved in KOR initiatives in twenty localities" ("Reinterpreting Solidarity," 320).

77. E.g., Fiona Tupper-Carey, "The Post-Revolutionary Conflict between the Romanian Uniate Church and the Romanian Orthodox Church," paper presented at the 75th Anniversary Conference of the School of Slavonic and East European Studies, University of London, December 14, 1990.

78. Maryjane Osa, "Pastoral Mobilization and Symbolic Politics: The Cath-

olic Church in Poland, 1918–1966," Ph.D. diss., University of Chicago, 1992, 135. I would like to thank Dr. Osa for permitting me to read her dissertation, particularly Chapter 5, from which the information on the Great Novena is taken.

79. Andrzej Micewski, *Cardinal Wyszyński* (San Diego: Harcourt Brace Jovanovich, 1984), 407.

80. For a useful description of the intellectual confrontation between Marxism and Catholicism in Poland as well as a discussion of the main Catholic groups (*Pax, Znak,* and *Więź*), see Norbert A. Zmijewski, *The Catholic-Marxist Ideological Dialogue in Poland, 1945–1980* (Aldershot, Great Britain: Dartmouth, 1991). Jacek Kuroń, for example, appeared in *Więź* as M. Gajka (88).

81. Raina, *Political Opposition in Poland,* 408.

82. Michnik, *L'Église et la Gauche,* 100.

83. KOR's weekly, *Biuletyn Informacyjny,* published these instructions on April 30, 1979. Quoted by Jan Kubik, "John Paul II's First Visit to Poland and the Collapse of the Official Marxist-Leninist Discourse," Harvard University, Department of Sociology, Center for Research on Politics and Social Organization, Working Paper Series (1989), 8.

84. Kubik, "John Paul II's First Visit," 14.

85. "It is impossible, therefore, to understand and evaluate without reference to Christ the past contribution of the Polish nation to *the advancement of the human person and the person's very humanness,*" *The Pope Speaks* 24/3 (1979): 268.

86. Grzegorz Bakuniak and Krzysztof Nowak, "The Creation of a Collective Identity in a Social Movement: The Case of 'Solidarność' in Poland," *Theory and Society* 16 (1987): 413–16.

87. Goodwyn believes that the pope's visit had little impact in mobilizing Poles, while Garton Ash argues that it was the symbolic beginning point of the events that created 1989 (*Breaking the Barrier,* 177; and Timothy Garton Ash, *The Magic Lantern: The Revolution of '89 Witnessed in Warsaw, Budapest, Berlin, and Prague* [New York: Random House, 1990], 133).

88. Wojciech Roszkowski, interview, February 21, 1992.

89. Havel, *Living in Truth,* 71.

90. Paradoxically, this policy had the unintended effect of insuring that strikes would occur, because only if they went on strike did workers receive the pay raises.

91. "Kuroń's house—which throughout the entire existence of KOR served as a club, a hotel, a press office, and a coordination center—began to resemble a madhouse," recalled Jan Józef Lipski (*KOR,* 425).

92. Timothy Garton Ash, *The Polish Revolution: Solidarity* (New York: Charles Scribner's Sons, 1984), 39. Neal Ascherson, *The Polish August: The Self-Limiting Revolution* (New York: Viking Press, 1982), 147, has the quotation this way: "Remember me? I gave ten years to this shipyard. But you sacked me four years ago!" For an eyewitness account, see Stan Persky's interview with Jerzy Borowczak, "At the Lenin Shipyard," in *The Solidarity Sourcebook,* ed. Stan Persky and Henry Flam (Vancouver: New Star Books, 1982), 73–80.

93. Ascherson, *The Polish August,* 132.

94. For Wałęsa's description of his childhood and early life see his autobiography, *A Way of Hope.*

95. Ascherson, *The Polish August,* 148.

96. For Wałęsa's authorized account, see Wałęsa, *A Way of Hope,* 121–22.

97. Goodwyn shows his propensity for contesting everything previous writers

have written on Solidarity by claiming, on the basis of a photograph taken at the time, that this number should be six hundred (*Breaking the Barrier,* 382).

98. Jerzy Janiszewski, "Solidarnosc [*sic*]: Design for a Logo," in Persky and Flam, *The Solidarity Sourcebook,* 79–80.

99. Laba and Goodwyn hold that this shows it was the workers' experiences in Szczecin in 1970 and 1971 that provided the crucial innovations of 1980, not the work of KOR. Goodwyn repeatedly accuses other historians of not providing details of how ideas are transmitted from intellectuals to workers, but he provides no details of how the 1970–1971 experience in Szczecin was transmitted to Gdańsk. Bronisław Geremek points out that when the delegation from Szczecin arrived in Gdańsk in August 1981 it consisted of three men about twenty-five years of age who came seeking suggestions on how to proceed in Szczecin. Geremek says that the Szczecin experience became known to him only in 1984, at which time the similarities between it and the Solidarity strike "astounded" him. In 1980 no one knew about that experience, he says, and no one talked about it. On the other hand, Geremek believes that Wałęsa "was formed in the *Robotnik* milieu" (interview, February 21, 1992). The direct influence of KOR through *Robotnik Wybrzeża* and through the organizational work of Borusewicz seems clear enough.

100. From a discussion in 1988 quoted by Ost, *Solidarity and the Politics of Anti-Politics,* 77.

101. The five were Bogdan Cywiński, Tadeusz Kowalik, Waldemar Kuczyński, Jadwiga Staniszkis, and Andrzej Wielowiejski.

102. Jadwiga Staniszkis characterizes the first meeting of the negotiators as follows: "a peculiar half-relaxed atmosphere and gentle, ironic tones predominated. One of the reasons was that the experts on both sides . . . were more or less members of the same Warsaw society. . . . We could very easily have changed places (if only our political attitudes were taken into account). This attitude made the negotiations easier" (*Poland's Self-Limiting Revolution,* ed. Jan T. Gross [Princeton, N.J.: Princeton University Press, 1984], 55).

103. For example, one of the controversial issues was what words to use to describe the union: "free" (*wolny*), "self-governing" (*samorządny*), or "independent" (*niepogledły*). The advisory group of intellectuals said "free" would raise problems, since it would suggest the union could join the International Labor Organization, which the Soviets probably would not permit. Therefore they recommended "independent." Wałęsa said why not "free and independent." Finally they replaced "free" with "self-governing," and the government accepted this. Geremek cites this as an example of the collegial give-and-take relationship that existed between the advisory committee of Warsaw intellectuals and the Interfactory Strike Committee of workers (interview, February 21, 1992).

104. The agreement is reprinted in many places, including Leszek Szymanski, *Candle for Poland: 469 Days of Solidarity* (San Bernardino, Calif.: Borgo Press, 1982), 92–99.

105. Ascherson, *The Polish August,* 164.

106. This does not mean the party learned its lesson. In 1984 David S. Mason interviewed Minister for Trade Union Affairs Stanisław Ciosek, who told him: "The interests of the working class are uniform; they all want the same thing—an improvement in the standard of living" ("Poland's New Trade Unions," *Soviet Studies* 39/3 [1987]: 501).

107. Solidarity's Program of October 16, 1981, from *Poland, 1981: Towards Social Renewal,* ed. Peter Raina (London: Allen & Unwin, 1985), 326.

108. Laba, *Roots of Solidarity,* 68, quoting Stewart Steven, *The Poles* (New York: Macmillan, 1982), 176.

109. Gwiazda used the phrase in his open letter to Lech Wałęsa after the Bydgoszcz crisis (Garton Ash, *Solidarity,* 280). On the same page, Garton Ash quotes Father Józef Tischner as follows: "Solidarity is a huge forest planted by awakened consciences. . . . Revolution is an occurrence in the realm of the spirit."

110. Garton Ash, *The Polish Revolution,* 164.

111. See Ryszard Kukliński, "The Suppression of Solidarity," in *Between East and West: Writings from* Kultura, ed. Roberta Kostrzewa (New York: Hill & Wang, 1990), 72–98. This article was originally published in *Kultura,* and in English in *Orbis* 32 (1988): 7–31. Accompanying the latter was an article by Zbigniew Brzezinski, "White House Diary, 1980," 32–38, giving the national security advisor's story of how seriously the United States took the Soviet threat. On December 6, 1980, the CIA reported that the Soviets were going into Poland within forty-eight hours in what it called a "peaceful mode." There was massive evidence of Soviet troop movements comprising twenty-seven divisions. Compare with Ascherson, *The Polish August,* 208–17. From 1970 until the CIA helped him leave Poland in 1981, Kukliński passed over 35,000 pages of documents to the United States containing a vast amount of sensitive Soviet and Warsaw Pact information (*Washington Post,* Sept. 27, 1992, 1).

112. See Werner G. Hahn, *Democracy in a Communist Party: Poland's Experience since 1980* (New York: Columbia University Press, 1987).

113. Hahn, *Democracy in a Communist Party,* 81.

114. About the time Jaruzelski took over party leadership, the Solidarity news agency published a report that special units had been formed to put down Solidarity and that in two months they would be used (Garton Ash, *The Polish Revolution,* 234). Kuklinski confirms that a final decision had been made at least by the end of October (Kuklinski, "Suppression of Solidarity," 91). Apparently East German leader Erick Honecker had suggested martial law to the Soviets as a possible solution as early as May 1981 (RFE/RL Daily Report, Dec. 13, 1991).

115. Zbigniew M. Fallenbuchl, "The Economic Crisis in Poland and Prospects for Recovery," in *East European Economies: Slow Growth in the 1980s* (Washington, D.C.: Joint Economic Committee, Congress of the United States, 1986), 365 (technically the 12 percent drop was in domestic net material product); *Keesing's,* 31,390.

116. Bogdan Borusewicz says: "The campaign that authorities presented as organized and super-efficient was, in reality, a chaotic struggle," but the same can be said for all human endeavors. The rapidity and success of the imposition of the operation speaks for its relative efficiency (Maciej Łopiński, Marcin Moskit, and Mariusz Wilk, *Konspira: Solidarity Underground,* trans. Jane Cave [Berkeley: University of California Press, 1990], 23).

117. Robert Maxwell, ed., *Jaruzelski: Prime Minister of Poland* (Oxford: Pergamon Press, 1985), 28–30.

118. In 1992 three members of the special forces who had been at Wujek were indicted for murder.

119. Władysław Frasyniuk, quoted by Łopiński, Moskit, and Wilk, *Konspira,* 11.

Chapter 2

1. Transylvania, which is now part of Romania, had had strong trade ties with central Europe since medieval times.

2. Yugoslavia, which is also part of southeastern Europe, is an especially complex case and will be discussed separately in Chapter 7.

3. Daniel Chirot points out that in the interwar period even the notorious rural overpopulation of Romania was on the way toward solution, since in the 1930s industrial employment grew at an annual rate of 3 percent per year, whereas annual population growth averaged only 1 percent. See Daniel Chirot, "Social Change in Communist Romania," *Social Forces* 57 (1978): 458–59.

4. A man imprisoned with Ceauşescu during the war says that "although he claimed to be a shoemaker, [Ceauşescu] seemed incapable of learning a trade" (Pavel Campeanu, "The Revolt of the Romanians," *New York Review of Books,* February 1, 1990, 30).

5. Between 1969 and 1972 Bulgaria consolidated 800 existing state and collective farms into 170 agroindustrial complexes. Some controversy exists as to how successful they were. Robert J. McIntyre says they helped improve Bulgarian living standards, while Michael C. Wyzan says, "Far from being a model for other socialist countries, they have come to be emblematic of Zhivkov's penchant for frequent and ill-considered organizational change." See Robert J. McIntyre, "The Small Enterprise and Agricultural Initiatives in Bulgaria," *Soviet Studies* 40 (1988): 602–15; and Michael C. Wyzan, "The Small Enterprise and Agricultural Initiatives in Bulgaria: A comment on Robert J. McIntyre," *Soviet Studies* 41 (1989): 646–53.

6. RFE, Bulgarian SR/1, January 18, 1988.

7. Michael Shafir presents such an explanation for the lack of opposition in Romania: *Romania—Politics, Economics and Society: Political Stagnation and Simulated Change* (Boulder, Colo.: Lynne Rienner Publishers, 1985), 150–58. Some in Bulgaria also believe that the "absence of a legitimate and strong moral agency like the Polish church" accounts for the inability of oppositionists to find each other (Jeffrey Goldfarb, *After the Fall: The Pursuit of Democracy in Central Europe* [New York: Basic Books, 1992], 164).

8. For a good discussion of these points see Maria N. Todorova, "Improbable Maverick or Typical Conformist? Seven Thoughts on the New Bulgaria," in *Eastern Europe in Revolution,* ed. Ivo Banac (Ithaca, N.Y.: Cornell University Press, 1992), 148–67.

9. See the various characterizations gathered in *Current Biography,* 1976, 460–61; and Vladimir Tismaneanu, *Reinventing Politics: Eastern Europe from Stalin to Havel* (New York: The Free Press, 1992), 221.

10. Todorova, "Improbable Maverick," 162.

11. For an English version of this document, see William E. Griffith, *Sino-Soviet Relations, 1964–1965* (Cambridge, Mass.: MIT Press, 1967), 269–96.

12. Chirot, "Social Change in Communist Romania," 482.

13. Mary Ellen Fischer, *Nicolae Ceauşescu: A Study in Political Leadership* (Boulder, Colo.: Lynne Rienner Publishers, 1990), 85–94.

14. A. Ciurchescu, as quoted by Dennis Deletant, "The Past in Contemporary Romania: Some Reflections on Current Romanian Historiography," *Slovo* 1 (1988): 91.

15. Katherine Verdery contrasts the symbolic-ideological strategy with the

use of remunerative mechanisms to maintain social control. After 1971 Ceauşescu used fewer and fewer of the latter and more and more of the former. See Verdery, *National Ideology Under Socialism: Romanian Identity, Intellectuals, and the Politics of Culture* (Berkeley: University of California Press, 1991).

16. For an engaging and amazing description of Elena's nagging and petty character see Edward Behr, *Kiss the Hand You Cannot Bite* (New York: Villard Books, 1991), 169–91.

17. Information from Norman Manea, Romanian author, at the Illinois Summer Workshop in Russian and East European Studies, summer 1990.

18. Mary Ellen Fischer, "Women in Romanian Politics: Elena Ceauşescu, Pronatalism, and the Promotion of Women," in *Woman, State and Party in Eastern Europe*, ed. Sharon L. Wolchik and Alfred G. Meyer (Durham, N.C.: Duke University Press, 1985), 123.

19. Mark Almond, "Worlds on the Brink of Change," *Times Literary Supplement*, January 19–25, 1990, 56.

20. Some authors suggest that in the quasideveloped state of Romania a cult of personality served a logical legitimating function, at least at first. See Mary Ellen Fischer, "Idol or Leader? The Origins and Future of the Ceauşescu Cult," in *Romania in the 1980s*, ed. Daniel N. Nelson (Boulder, Colo.: Westview Press, 1986), 130–33; and Vlad Georgescu, "Politics, History and Nationalism: The Origins of Romania's Socialist Personality Cult," in *The Cult of Power: Dictators in the Twentieth Century*, ed. Joseph Held (Boulder, Colo.: East European Quarterly Press, 1983), 137.

21. Walter M. Bacon, Jr., "The Liturgics of Ceauşescuism," manuscript from the author, 9–10. Brackets in original.

22. Examples culled from the celebrations surrounding Ceauşescu's sixty-fifth birthday (Anneli Maeir, "Ceauşescu's Birthday Extravaganza," RFE, Romanian SR/3, 19 February 1983).

23. Quoted by Paul E. Michelson, "Romania" in *Nationalism in the Balkans: An Annotated Bibliography*, ed. Gale Stokes (New York: Garland Publishing, 1984), 36.

24. Mary Ellen Fischer, *Ceauşescu*, 96.

25. Verdery, *National Ideology Under Socialism*, 132.

26. Discussion at the Illinois Summer Workshop in Soviet and East European Studies, 1990.

27. Shafir, *Romania*, 168–72.

28. Tismaneanu, *Reinventing Politics*, 125.

29. Shafir, *Romania*, 146.

30. Norman Manea, *On Clowns: The Dictator and the Artist* (New York: Grove Weidenfeld, 1992), 20.

31. For East Germany, see Irwin L. Collier, Jr., "GDR Economic Policy during the Honecker Era," *Eastern European Economics* 29 (1990): 12–14.

32. See Robert J. McIntyre, "Pronatalist Programmes in Eastern Europe," *Soviet Studies* 27 (July 1975): 366–80.

33. Henry P. David and Robert J. McIntyre, *Reproductive Behavior: Central and Eastern European Experience* (New York: Springer Publishing Co., 1981), 179.

34. The average number of "legal abortions and women admitted to hospitals for aftercare or the treatment of complications of spontaneous or illegally induced" abortions for the five years 1975 to 1979 was 922 per thousand live births. In Czechoslovakia the number of legal abortions averaged 314 per thousand live

births, in Hungary 501 (although when abortions were unrestricted in 1969–1973 the number was 1,221), in Bulgaria 826, and in Poland 218. See the tables for each country in David and McIntyre, *Reproductive Behavior,* 180, 226, 252, 285, and 128.

35. Dimitru Tepeneag, quoted by Shafir, *Romania,* 150.

36. Charles Gati, *The Bloc that Failed: Soviet-East European Relations in Transition* (Bloomington: Indiana University Press, 1990), 162. The "Gang of Four" were four Chinese political figures close to Mao Tse Tung who implemented the radical reforms of the Cultural Revolution in the late 1960s and were sentenced to long prison terms after Mao's death.

37. David Childs, *The GDR: Moscow's German Ally,* 2d ed. (London: Unwin Hyman, 1988), 64–65.

38. Childs, *The GDR,* 86.

39. Martin McCauley, *The German Democratic Republic since 1945* (New York: St. Martin's Press, 1983), 153; and *Current Biography,* 1972, 228–29.

40. Honecker's biographer reports that Honecker insisted his housekeeper sit at the dinner table with him (Heinz Lippman, *Honecker and the New Politics of Europe,* trans. Helen Sebba [New York: Macmillan, 1972], 236).

41. Jerzy Łisiecki, "Financial and Material Transfers between East and West Germany," *Soviet Studies* 42 (1990): 513–34.

42. Quoted by A. James McAdams, *East Germany and Détente: Building Authority after the Wall* (Cambridge: Cambridge University Press, 1985), 143.

43. The first quotation is from Honecker (McAdams, *East Germany and Détente,* 109) and the second from the party program of 1976 (McCauley, *German Democratic Republic,* 167).

44. Ronald D. Asmus, "The GDR and the German Nation: Sole Heir or Socialist Sibling?" *International Affairs* 60/3 (1984): 409.

45. See, for example, John Starrels, "Nationalism in the German Democratic Republic," *Canadian Review of Studies in Nationalism* 2 (1974): 23–37.

46. Pedro [Sabrina] Ramet, "Disaffection and Dissent in East Germany," *World Politics* 37 (1984): 91.

47. His lectures were published in West Germany under the title *Dialektik ohne Dogma?* (Reinbeck: Rowohlt, 1964). For a brief discussion of the opposition of Havemann and Rudolf Bahro, see Michael J. Sodaro, "Limits to Dissent in the GDR: Fragmentation, Cooptation, and Repression," in *Dissent in Eastern Europe,* ed. Jane Leftwich Curry (New York: Praeger, 1983), 82–116.

48. "Interview with Robert Havemann," *New German Critique* 15 (1978): 45.

49. Rudolf Bahro, *The Alternative in Eastern Europe* (London: New Left Books, 1978).

50. Havemann said that Bahro's critique "emanates from within the palace itself" ("Interview," 46).

51. Quoted by Sodaro, "Limits to Dissent," 99.

52. Andrew Arato and Mihály Vajdá suggested as much in their critique of Bahro and his admirers in "The Limits of the Leninist Opposition: A Reply to David Bathrick," *New German Critique* 19 (1980): 167–75. They were responding to Bathrick's article, "The Politics of Culture: Rudolf Bahro and Opposition in the GDR," *New German Review* 15 (1978): 3–24. See also Bathrick's response, "Rudolf Bahro's 'Neo-Leninism' in Context: Reply to Andrew Arato and Mihály Vajdá," *New German Review* 21 (Fall 1980): 147–53.

53. See Ramet, "Disaffection and Dissent in East Germany," 85–111.

54. This may have been because the Stasi so thoroughly infiltrated the various movements. For example, in 1992 Manfred Stolpe, one of eastern Germany's most popular politicians and a lawyer who defended opposition groups in the 1980s, admitted to having held clandestine meetings with the Stasi, although he also claimed these were only concerning legal matters (*New York Times,* February 5, 1992).

55. Robert F. Goeckel, *The Lutheran Church and the East German State: Political Conflict and Change under Ulbricht and Honecker* (Ithaca, N.Y.: Cornell University Press, 1990), 276.

56. Vladimir Tismaneanu, "Nascent Civil Society in the German Democratic Republic," *Problems of Communism* 38 (March–June 1989): 109.

57. See Norman M. Naimark, "Is it true what they're saying about East Germany?" *Orbis* 23 (1979): 549–77, who argues that none of the positive statistical measures of success during the 1970s in the GDR tapped the fear and resentment of the East German population, which had created widespread apathy and hopelessness. Despite criticism that he had seriously overstated his case, Naimark proved to be correct.

58. Quoted by Hans Renner, *A History of Czechoslovakia since 1945* (London: Routledge, 1989), 87.

59. Vlad Kusin, *From Dubček to Charter 77: A Study of 'Normalisation' in Czechoslovakia, 1968–1978* (Edinburgh: Edinburgh University, 1978), 60.

60. Kusin, *From Dubček to Charter 77,* 136.

61. Kusin, *From Dubček to Charter 77,* 326. Zdeněk Mlynář, on the other hand, considers that Husák "is not, nor ever will be, anything more than a Soviet viceroy in Czechoslovakia" (Zdeněk Mlynář, *Nightfrost in Prague: The End of Humane Socialism* [New York: Karz Publishers, 1980], 227).

62. Milan Šimečka, *The Restoration of Order: The Normalisation of Czechoslovakia, 1969–1984* (London: Verso, 1984).

63. Renner, *History of Czechoslovakia,* 98–101; and Kusin, *From Dubček to Charter 77,* 74–98.

64. Šimečka, *Restoration of Order,* 78.

65. Mark Frankland, *The Patriots' Revolution: How Eastern Europe Toppled Communism and Won Its Freedom* (Chicago: Ivan R. Dee, 1992), 57.

66. Šimečka, *Restoration of Order,* 84.

67. Gary L. Geipel, A. Tomasz Jarmoszko, and Seymour E. Goodman, "The Information Technologies and East European Societies," *East European Politics and Societies* 5 (1991): 394–438.

68. George W. Breslauer, "Evaluating Gorbachev as Leader," in *Milestones in Glasnost and Perestroyka: Politics and People,* ed. Ed A. Hewett and Victor H. Winston (Washington, D.C.: The Brookings Institution, 1991), 402.

69. Robert Kaiser, *Why Gorbachev Happened: His Triumphs and His Failures* (New York: Simon & Schuster, 1991), 78. Kaiser stresses the importance of a programmatic speech of December 1984, when Gorbachev first broached the basics of his program.

70. Pravda, October 5, 1985, as published in the *Current Digest of the Soviet Press* 37 (November 6, 1985).

71. Kaiser, *Why Gorbachev Happened,* 132.

72. Moshe Lewin, *The Gorbachev Phenomenon: A Historical Interpretation* (Berkeley: University of California Press, 1988), 31 and 47.

73. The generational differences outlined here are the work of Soviet anthropologists L. A. Gordon and V. V. Komarovskii, as discussed in Lewin, *The Gorbachev Phenomenon*, 53–55.

74. Jerry F. Hough, "The Generation Gap and the Brezhnev Succession," *Problems of Communism* 28 (July–August 1979): 1–16. Hough published pictures of only four Soviet politicians in this article on the Brezhnev succession: one showing Andropov, Chernenko, and Grishin as representatives of what he called the second generation, and one showing Gorbachev as a representative of the fourth generation. All became general secretary, except Grishin, whom Gorbachev defeated when he became general secretary. Less prescient, although acute in his analysis of generational change, was Seweryn Bialer, *Stalin's Successors: Leadership, Stability, and Change in the Soviet Union* (Cambridge: Cambridge University Press, 1980), who barely mentioned Gorbachev.

75. "Men" is the proper term here. Women had little or no impact at the higher levels of Soviet government.

76. Edward Crankshaw, *Khrushchev's Russia* (Baltimore: Penguin Books, 1959), 90–91 and 130, as quoted by Jerry Hough, *Russia and the West: Gorbachev and the Politics of Reform* (New York: Simon & Schuster, 1988), 20 and 31.

77. Mikhail Gorbachev, *Perestroika: New Thinking for Our Country and the World* (New York: Harper & Row, 1987), 18–24.

78. In 1981 Rezső Nyers, a prominent Hungarian economic reformer and architect of the New Economic Mechanism, noted that the Soviet economy was slowing down and searching "for different types of external cooperation," which meant they were looking at the Hungarian reforms for potential guidance (quoted by Andrew Felkay, *Hungary and the USSR, 1956–1988* [New York: Greenwood Press, 1989], 255).

79. Abram Bergson, "Soviet Economic Slowdown and the 1981–1985 Plan," *Problems of Communism* 30 (May–June 1981), 36. See also Seweryn Bialer, *Stalin's Successors*. Bialer described the economic crisis the Soviet Union faced and predicted younger men would take over and attempt to solve it.

80. On the machinations that lay behind Gorbachev's selection, see Hedrick Smith, *The New Russians* (New York: Random House, 1990), 77; and Kaiser, *Why Gorbachev Happened*, 80–85.

81. Ed A. Hewett, *Reforming the Soviet Economy: Equality versus Efficiency* (Washington, D.C.: The Brookings Institution, 1988), 349–50.

82. In Russian the word *glasnost* "is ambiguous. It conveys the idea of publicity rather than of frankness. The publication of selective reports about the weekly Politburo meeting is an example of *glasnost*, but the very fact that the reports are selective and brief shows the limits of the meaning" (Zhores A. Medvedev, *Gorbachev* [New York: W. W. Norton, 1986], 159).

83. Kaiser, *Why Gorbachev Happened*, 159 and 276.

84. The congress would then elect the actual legislative body, the Supreme Soviet.

85. Kaiser, *Why Gorbachev Happened*, 225.

86. Quoted by Arthur R. Rachwald, *In Search of Poland: The Superpowers' Response to Solidarity, 1980–1989* (Stanford, Calif.: Hoover Institution Press, 1990), 39.

87. FBIS, Soviet Union 3/117, June 18, 1969. In 1976 the assembled parties reconfirmed their rejection of "one leading center" and reaffirmed the theoretical correctness of "national roads" to socialism at a meeting in East Berlin.

88. Compare the 1969 program, which, after asserting that all parties have equal rights, went on to say that "the communist and workers parties, regardless of some difference of opinion, reaffirm their determination to present a united front in the struggle against imperialism" (FBIS, ibid.). Coming less than a year after the proclamation of the Brezhnev Doctrine, the relative importance of "equal rights" and "united front" seemed clear.

89. Mikhail Gorbachev, *Perestroika*, 155–67.

90. FBIS-SOV-81-116, November 24, 1981, G-8.

91. Commenting on the Russo-Hungarian trade agreement of November 12, 1984, finalized in March 1985, Alfred Reisch said: "There can be no doubt that the Soviet Union has succeeded in imposing its will on the much weaker Hungarian regime with a bilateral program that clearly seeks to adjust Hungary's economic development to the long-range objectives of the Soviet economy" (RFE, Hungarian SR/14, 29 November 1984, 3). Writing late in 1985, Vladimir V. Kusin, an astute observer, found Gorbachev's early policy toward Eastern Europe a nuanced continuation of his predecessors' ("Gorbachev and Eastern Europe," *Problems of Communism* 35 [January–February 1986], 39–53).

92. Ilya Zemtsov and John Farrar, *Gorbachev: The Man and the System* (New Brunswick, N.J.: Transaction Publishers, 1989), 217.

93. Both cited from Ted Kaminski, "Underground Publishing in Poland," *Orbis* 32 (Fall 1987): 325. The Warszawski quote is from the underground journal *KOS* of February 8, 1987; the Zaleski sentiment is presumably from the same period but is not specifically documented by Kaminski.

94. Anatoly Dobrynin in *Kommunist* 9 (September 1986), as quoted by Dusko Doder and Louise Branson, *Gorbachev: Heretic in the Kremlin* (New York: Viking, 1990), 205.

95. Zdeněk Mlynář, *Can Gorbachev Change the Soviet Union? The International Dimensions of Political Reform* (Boulder, Colo.: Westview Press, 1990), 123.

96. Western leaders had a pretty good idea that Gorbachev was serious about his reforms, if not about letting Eastern Europe go, by 1987. Robert Kaiser believes that the Reykavík summit of October 1986 and the return of Sakharov in December of that year convinced American policy makers that Gorbachev was serious (*Why Gorbachev Happened*, 140 and 147–49). Gorbachev told Margaret Thatcher in March 1987 that the Brezhnev Doctrine was outdated, and at the Venice summit of Western leaders in June 1987 she argued that Gorbachev was indeed serious, a view strongly supported by German Foreign Minister Hans-Dietrich Genscher from early on (Doder and Branson, *Gorbachev,* 219).

97. *New York Times,* July 6, 1992, A3.

98. See, for example, Joseph L. Nogee and Robert H. Donaldson, *Soviet Foreign Policy,* 3d ed. (New York: Pergamon Press, 1988), 58. I would like to thank William Bishop of Denison University for this reference.

99. Eduard Shevardnadze, *The Future Belongs to Freedom,* trans. Catherine A. Fitzpatrick (London: Sinclair-Stevenson, 1991), 113.

100. Information from Alexei Arbatov, who was in Prague in spring 1989 (conversation, June 25, 1991). Jan Urban agrees that the Soviet embassy was quite isolated. Whereas, for example, the oppositionist Urban was sufficiently friendly with the British deputy chief of mission to be having dinner with him on the night of November 17, 1989, it was not until several days later that the Soviet embassy for the first time sent some of its own people onto the streets to check the assess-

ments it had been receiving from Czechoslovak party and security sources (interview, February 15, 1992).

101. Joseph Rothschild, *Return to Diversity: A political history of East Central Europe since World War II* (New York: Oxford University Press, 1989), 221–22.

102. Norman Stone, "Looking for a Different Sort of Russia," *Sunday Times* [London], November 22, 1987.

Chapter 3

1. Janina Frentzel-Zagorska, "Civil Society in Poland and Hungary," *Soviet Studies* 42 (1990): 765–66.

2. Gábor Révész, *Perestroika in Eastern Europe: Hungary's Economic Transformation, 1945–1988* (Boulder, Colo.: Westview Press, 1990), 99.

3. Paul Marer, "The Political Economy of Soviet Relations with Eastern Europe," in *Soviet Foreign Policy in a Changing World,* ed. Robbin F. Laird and Erik P. Hoffmann (New York: Aldine Publishing Co., 1986), 576.

4. Thomas Vajna, "Problems and Trends in the Development of the Hungarian New Economic Mechanism: A Balance Sheet of the 1970s," in *The East European Economies in the 1970s,* ed. Alec Nove, Hans-Hermann Höhmann and Gertraud Seidenstecher (London: Butterworths, 1982), 185.

5. Paul Marer, "Hungary's Balance of Payments Crisis and Response," in *East European Economies: Slow Growth in the 1980's, Volume 3: Country Studies on Eastern Europe and Yugoslavia* (Washington, D.C.: Joint Economic Committee, 1986), 300.

6. Marer, "Hungary's Balance of Payments Crisis," 301, 320.

7. Iván Berend, *Hungarian Economic Reforms, 1953–1988* (Cambridge: Cambridge University Press, 1990), 241.

8. Quoted by Edward A. Hewett, "The Hungarian Economy: Lessons of the 1970s and Prospects for the 1980s," in *East European Economic Assessment: Part 1—Country Studies, 1980* (Washington, D.C.: Joint Economic Committee, Congress of the United States, 1981), 512–13.

9. Berend, *Hungarian Economic Reform,* 103. Cooperative pay under the Stalinist system was calculated in "workday" equivalents, which one accumulated over the year. If the cooperative made a profit, which was not always the case, it would be split proportionally according to workday credits accumulated. Skilled work, such as tractor driving, received many more credits than ordinary unskilled labor. The new method introduced in the late 1950s paid cooperative members a cash monthly wage at 90 percent of the expected rate and then split any profits at the end of the year.

10. This follows István R. Gábor, "Second Economy and Socialism: The Hungarian experience," in Edgar L. Feige, *The Underground Economies: Tax Evasion and Information Distortion* (Cambridge: Cambridge University Press, 1989), 339–52, but emphasizes the term *informal* rather than *illegal.* Informal economic strategies may be illegal, but they are not antisocial or criminal in intent. For a stimulating discussion of informal strategies see Hernando de Soto, *The Other Path: The Invisible Revolution in the Third World* (New York: Harper & Row, 1989). On the other hand, David Stark argues that "capitalism's informal economy and socialism's second economy are not functional equivalents or structural counterparts" ("Bending the Bars of the Iron Cage: Bureaucratization and Informalization in Capitalism and Socialism," *Sociological Forum* 4 [1989]: 637–64).

11. They did not do this to introduce market mechanisms or private ownership but as part of their view that leases of publicly owned assets in service enterprises would be a socialist way of replacing capitalist ownership. See István Kemény, "The Unregistered Economy in Hungary," *Soviet Studies* 34 (1982): 356–57.

12. Berend, *Hungarian Economic Reforms,* 284.

13. Andrew Felkay, *Hungary and the USSR, 1956–1988* (New York: Greenwood Press, 1989), 252.

14. Kemény, "The Unregistered Economy in Hungary," 358.

15. The following relies on Iván Szelényi, *Socialist Entrepreneurs: Embourgeoisement in Rural Hungary* (Madison: University of Wisconsin Press, 1988).

16. Kemény, "The Unregistered Economy in Hungary," 356.

17. This was a common phenomenon throughout Eastern Europe. See, for example, Andrei Simić, *The Peasant Urbanites: A Study of Rural-Urban Mobility in Serbia* (New York: Seminar Press, 1973).

18. Michael Burawoy and János Lukács, "Mythologies of Work: A Comparison of Firms in State Socialism and Advanced Capitalism," *American Sociological Review* 50 (1985): 733.

19. Susanne Klausen, "First Society, Second Society: Mutual Discontents—An Interview with Elemer Hankiss," *East European Reporter* 3/1 (1988): 63–65.

20. Quoted by Jörg K. Hoensch, *A History of Modern Hungary, 1867–1986,* trans. Kim Traynor (New York: Longman, 1988), 251.

21. Peter A. Toma, *Socialist Authority: The Hungarian Experience* (New York: Praeger, 1988), 56.

22. Elemer Hankiss, "Demobilization, Self-Mobilization and Quasi-Mobilization in Hungary, 1948–1987," *Eastern European Politics and Societies* 3 (1989): 144.

23. Felkay, *Hungary and the USSR,* 252.

24. David Stark, "Coexisting Organizational Forms in Hungary's Emerging Mixed Economy," in *Remaking the Economic Institutions of Socialism: China and Eastern Europe,* ed. Victor Nee and David Stark (Stanford, Calif.: Stanford University Press, 1989), 141.

25. Paul Marer lists thirteen such agencies in "Economic Reform in Hungary: From Central Planning to Regulated Market," *East European Economies: Slow Growth in the 1980s* (Washington, D.C.: Selected papers submitted to the Joint Economic Committee, Congress of the United States, 1986), 293–97.

26. Berend, *Hungarian Economic Reforms,* 284–85.

27. Révész, *Perestroika in Eastern Europe,* 115–16.

28. Stark, "Hungary's Emerging Mixed Economy," 143.

29. Stark, "Hungary's Emerging Mixed Economy," 143, 147.

30. Gábor gives a much higher estimate, calculating that "the second economy must be a source of income of similar importance as the first economy," but I think that is going too far (Gábor, "Second Economy," 356).

31. David Stark, "Work, Worth, and Justice in a Socialist Mixed Economy," Program on Central and Eastern Europe, Working Paper Series no. 5, Minda de Gunzburg Center for European Studies, Harvard University, n.d.

32. Berend, *Hungarian Economic Reform,* 289.

33. Marer, "Hungary's Balance of Payments Crisis," 313.

34. *Keesing's,* 33,679.

35. Using 1978 as 100, by 1984 real wages had dropped to 94.9, whereas real

consumption had risen to 108.3 (Marer, "Hungary's Balance of Payments Crisis," 313–14).

36. The World Health Organization's *Statistics Annual* for 1987 showed Hungarian men to have the shortest life expectancy of any of the thirty-three developed countries covered (84).

37. The eight were György Bence, Ferenc Fehér, András Hegedüs, Ágnes Heller, János Kis, György Márkus and his wife Mária, and Mihály Vajdá. The older ones, Fehér and Heller, who are married, and the two Márkuses, went into exile, while the younger ones stayed in Hungary. Fehér, who Vajdá says was the "politician" among the group and who was on good personal terms with party ideological chief György Aczél, was not among those fired, but he immediately resigned in solidarity with his colleagues (Mihály Vajdá, interview, March 2, 1992).

38. György Konrád and Iván Szelényi, *Intellectuals on the Road to Class Power: A Sociological Study of the Role of the Intelligentsia in Socialism* (New York: Harcourt Brace Jovanovich, 1979).

39. Iván Szelényi, "The Prospects and Limits of the East European New Class Project: An Auto-critical Reflection on *The Intellectuals on the Road to Class Power*," *Politics and Society* 15 (1986–1987): 113.

40. Miklós Haraszti, *A Worker in a Worker's State,* trans. Michael Wright (New York: University Books, 1978). The printing technology of samizdat publications was an important indicator of the stage of the opposition's development. Haraszti was able to prove, for example, that he wrote this book on a manual typewriter rather than an electric, which was a point in his favor. Even a manual typewriter, of course, was an improvement over handwritten texts. In 1980 Gábor Demszky introduced mimeograph, and by 1983 he was printing by offset (Haraszti, interview, February 2, 1992).

41. Mária Kovács, the organizer of these lectures, interview, February 28, 1992. Also Sándor Szilágy, interview, May 17, 1991.

42. Some say the boutique was open every Tuesday evening; others say every Wednesday evening.

43. Interview, February 2, 1992.

44. *Beszélő* (Speaker) was a very clever title. The word also means the visiting period in prison, that relatively brief moment coming at infrequent intervals when one could speak with guarded openness. Among the founders were Gábor Iványi, János Kis, Ferenc Köszeg, Miklós Haraszti, Balint Nagy, György Petri, and Sándor Szilágy. László Rajk was important in distributing the journal, for which elaborate conspiratorial plans were laid. György Bence, Kis's close friend and collaborator, broke with him over the founding of *Beszélő*. Bence favored a broader effort to create an independent society rather than a high-powered journal for intellectuals.

45. See H. Gordon Skilling, *Samizdat and an Independent Society in Central and Eastern Europe* (Columbus: Ohio State University Press, 1989), 181–87.

46. These are Miklós Haraszti's phrases (interview, March 2, 1992).

47. József Bayer, "About Pluralism," an interview in *Mozgó Világ,* JPRS-EER-86-067, 30 April 1986, 54.

48. Two oppositionists, Tamás Bauer and János Tóth, were nominated, and two, Gáspár Miklós Tamás and László Rajk, were kept from nomination by pressure tactics. See Toma, *Socialist Authority,* 48–55; and Barnabas Racz, "Political Participation and Developed Socialism: The Hungarian Elections of 1985," *Soviet Studies* 39 (1987): 40–62.

49. Barnabas Racz, "Political Participation and the Expanding Role of the

Hungarian Legislature," *East European Quarterly* 22 (1989): 459–93. In this detailed examination of the first two years of the new legislature, Racz accurately predicted that by 1989–1990 a "different legislature will have emerged" (482).

50. For a summary of the document, see RFE, Hungarian SR/4, May 18, 1987. It was produced by a commission appointed by Pozsgay.

51. János Kis, Ferenc Köszeg, and Ottilia Solt, "A New Social Contract," in *From Stalinism to Pluralism*, ed. Gale Stokes (New York: Oxford University Press, 1991), 244.

52. For a superb discussion of the process that led from this point to Kádár's resignation one year later, see George Schöpflin, Rudolf Tökés, and Iván Völgyes, "Leadership Change and Crisis in Hungary," *Problems of Communism* 37 (September–October 1988): 23–46, on which the present account relies heavily.

53. For a summary version, see *East European Reporter* 3/2 (March 1988): 49–51.

54. *Keesing's*, 35,593.

55. I use the terms *populist opposition* and *democratic opposition* simply to differentiate two general tendencies, not to suggest that the populist opposition was opposed to democracy, although some critics accused some populists of that failing.

56. Pozsgay later said "We committed ourselves [at Lakitelek] to a multi-party system and an anti-catastrophe [economic] policy" (FBIS-EEU-90-191, October 2, 1990, 19).

57. János Kis, "The End and the Beginning," in his *Politics in Hungary: For a Democratic Alternative*, trans. Gabor J. Follinus (Boulder, Colo. and Highland Lakes, N.J.: Social Sciences Monographs and Atlantic Research and Publications, distributed by Columbia University Press, 1989), 9.

58. Miklós Haraszti, "The Beginnings of Civil Society: The Independent Peace Movement and the Danube Movement in Hungary," in *In Search of Civil Society: Independent Peace Movements in the Soviet Bloc*, ed. Vladimir Tismaneanu (New York and London: Routledge, 1990), 71–87.

59. *Keesing's*, 34,112.

60. Tamás Hofer, "The March 15, 1989, Demonstration in Budapest: A Struggle for Public Memory," typescript in author's possession. I would like to thank Professor Hofer for his help both in Washington and in Budapest.

61. Interview in *New York Times*, July 10, 1988, 1.

62. *Newsweek* [European edition], July 18, 1988, quoted by Schöpflin et al., "Leadership Change and Crisis in Hungary," 42.

63. For a useful list of independent movements in Eastern Europe as of mid-1989, see Jiří Pehe, "An Annotated Survey of Independent Movements in Eastern Europe," RFE/RAD Background Report/100, 13 June 1989. Gábor Demszky also gives brief sketches of most of these organizations in "Initiatives for Hungary," *East European Reporter* 3/3 (Autumn 1988): 49–51, originally published in *Hírmondó*.

64. András Racz, quoted by Gábor Demszky, "Initiatives for Hungary," 51.

65. István Szent-Iványi, an activist throughout the 1980s, says that while Gorbachev's policies had no direct impact on the democratic opposition, the realization that his policies might be consistent with reform in Hungary imperceptibly emerged in the minds of the oppositionists (interview, February 28, 1992).

66. See Hedrick Smith's discussion of Aganbegyan, *New York Times*, April 10, 1988, section 6, p. 36.

67. "East-West Relations and Eastern Europe (An American-Soviet Dialogue)—The Soviet Perspective," *Problems of Communism* 37 (May–August 1988): 60, 62.

68. *Keesing's,* 36,114.

69. *The Current Digest of the Soviet Press* 40/49 (January 4, 1989): 3.

70. Personal communication from László Bruszt. Bruszt and David Stark conducted more than sixty interviews with former leaders of Hungary, including Pozsgay. Bruszt says that in general the more conservative the party leader, the sooner he realized the Soviets were not coming to their aid. The hardliners grasped this in October 1988 when conservative Yegor Ligachev fell in the Soviet Union.

71. *Keesing's,* 36,468.

72. Tamás Hofer, "Dramatugy of the Oppositional Demonstration," talk at the Woodrow Wilson International Center for Scholars, February 13, 1991, provides much of the data for this account.

73. Hofer takes the idea of the cultural tool kit from Ann Swidler, "Culture in Action: Symbols and Strategies," *American Sociological Review* 57 (1986): 273–86.

74. *Keesing's,* 36,746.

Chapter 4

1. "Even in Hungary . . . the brakes look more powerful than the engines," wrote Timothy Garton Ash in December 1988 (*The Uses of Adversity: Essays on the Fate of Central Europe* [New York: Random House, 1989], 298).

2. *Keesing's,* 31,854.

3. David Ost, *Solidarity and the Politics of Anti-Politics: Opposition and Reform in Poland since 1968* (Philadelphia: Temple University Press, 1990), 151.

4. Leszek Lechowicz, "The Mass Media under Martial Law," *Poland Watch* 1 (1982): 41–49.

5. The Association of Journalists continued to meet privately and to seek re-establishment until 1989.

6. Cardinal Wysziński died in 1981. Glemp was elevated to cardinal early in 1983.

7. For a brief but excellent review of the church-related opposition, see Aleksander Smolar, "The Polish Opposition since December 1981," *Occasional Paper 14* (Washington, D.C.: East European Program, European Institute, The Wilson Center, 1988), 31–42. Smolar's short monograph, which is a superb review of its subject, also appears in *Crisis and Reform in Eastern Europe,* ed. Ferenc Fehér and Andrew Arato (New Brunswick, N.J.: Transaction Publishers, 1991), 175–252.

8. Tadeusz Walendowski, "The Polish Church under Martial Law," *Poland Watch* 1 (1982): 54–62; and Tadeusz Walendowski, "Controversy over the Church," *Poland Watch* 2 (1982–1983): 39–44.

9. Mieczysław Rakowski, quoted by Jane Cave, "The Banning of Solidarity," *Poland Watch* 2 (1982–1983): 2. Rakowski went on to add, with the crocodile tears that were his trademark, "Those were our hopes. History has shown how baseless they were."

10. Quoted in Václav Havel, *Open Letters: Selected Writings 1965–1990* (New York: Vintage, 1992), by editor Paul Wilson, 126.

11. Jacek Kuroń, "Theses on what to do in an Impossible Situation," in *Sol-*

idarity under Siege, ed. Andrzej Tymowski (New Haven, Conn.: D. H. Back Press, 1982), 57.

12. The following are taken from Zbigniew Bujak, "Trench Warfare," and Wiktor Kulerski, "A Third Possibility," in *Solidarity under Siege,* 58–63.

13. Macej Łopiński, Marcin Moskit, and Mariusz Wilk, *Konspira: Solidarity Underground,* trans. Jane Cave (Berkeley: University of California Press, 1990), 64. See also the useful remarks by Bujak and Kulerski in Michael T. Kaufman, *Mad Dreams, Saving Graces: Poland, A Nation in Conspiracy* (New York: Random House, 1989), 94–98.

14. Smolar, "The Polish Opposition Since December 1981," 11–30.

15. Bujak estimated the number at 1.2 million (Łopiński et al., *Konspira,* 184).

16. Alfred B. Gruba (pseud.), "Fighting Solidarity," *Uncensored Poland* 1 (January 12, 1984).

17. *KOS,* January 20, 1982, quoted by Smolar, "The Polish Opposition Since December 1981," 12.

18. Sejan (pseud.), "Coming out of the Fog," *Uncensored Poland* 15 (August 2, 1984), 29–42; and John Rensenbrink, *Poland Challenges a Divided World* (Baton Rouge: Louisiana State University Press, 1988), 139–41.

19. Kaufman, *Mad Dreams, Saving Graces,* 48.

20. Leonid Brezhnev died a few hours before Wałęsa's release. David Ost tells the following Warsaw joke: "Jaruzelski says to Brezhnev: 'We must at least release Wałęsa already.' Brezhnev: 'Over my dead body' " (Ost, *Solidarity,* 154).

21. For a thorough discussion of how the principles of martial law were incorporated into the law by the Ministry of Internal Affairs and by amendments to the constitution, the "special regulations during the period of overcoming the socioeconomic crisis," and other regulations, see Jane Cave, "The Legacy of Martial Law," *Poland Watch* 4 (1984): 1–20. For other details see Jane Cave, "The Suspension of Martial Law," *Poland Watch* 2 (1982–1983), 45–52.

22. George Kolankiewicz, "Poland and the Politics of Permissible Pluralism," *Eastern European Politics and Societies* 2 (1988): 169.

23. *Keesing's,* 32,449.

24. "Solidarity Today: A Program Statement Issued by the Interim Coordinating Commission of Solidarity," *Poland Watch* 2 (1982–1983): 127–32.

25. Lech Wałęsa, *A Way of Hope* (New York: Henry Holt, 1987), 257–60.

26. Wałęsa, *A Way of Hope,* 293.

27. *Keesing's,* 33,876.

28. David Ost, "Poland Revisited," *Poland Watch* 7 (1984): 75.

29. Irena Grudzińska-Gross, "Review of the Polish Press: The Politics of Appropriation," *Poland Watch* 4 (1984): 21–25.

30. Solidarity's calls for boycott, along with its analysis of election results, can be found in the appropriate issues of *Uncensored Poland* for 1984 and 1985.

31. J. C. [Jane Cave], "Elections to the People's Councils," *Poland Watch* 6 (1984): 13–21; and *Keesing's,* 34,059.

32. *Keesing's,* 32,448.

33. Quoted by Tadeusz Walendowicz, "The Pope in Poland," *Poland Watch* 3 (1983): 8.

34. This information is from an interview of December 7, 1982, reported by Tadeusz Kaminski, "Poland's Catholic Church and Solidarity: A Parting of the Ways?" *Poland Watch* 6 (1984): 83.

35. Maya Latynski, "The Church: Between State and Society," *Poland Watch*

5 (1984): 21, quoting *O Estado de São Paolo* of March 4, 1984. For a different version of Glemp's speech see *Uncensored Poland* 5 (March 8, 1984): 9–11.

36. Latynski, "The Church: Between State and Society," 22.

37. For example, in the hymn "God, who watches over Poland," he ordered the refrain "O Lord, restore a free Fatherland," which had been written in the nineteenth century, when Poland did not exist as a fully independent state, to become "O Lord, bless our Fatherland" (Kaufman, *Mad Dreams, Saving Graces,* 136).

38. For others see Kaufman, *Mad Dreams, Saving Graces,* 136–37.

39. Kaufman, *Mad Dreams, Saving Graces,* 140–41, quoting a sermon from August 1984.

40. This account relies on Kaufman, *Mad Dreams, Saving Graces;* Jane Cave, "The Murder of Father Popiełuszko," *Poland Watch* 7 (1985): 1–26; and the detailed press reports in *Uncensored Poland.*

41. As of June 1992, the highest officials implicated were generals Władysław Ciaston, deputy minister of internal affairs; and Zenon Płatek, head of church surveillance in the ministry of internal affairs. Both went on trial at that time for being the organizers of the crime (RFE/RL Daily Report, June 16, 1992, 5).

42. Urban had commented, "Even Solidarity activists can get drunk and freeze to death in alleys" (Kaufman, *Mad Dreams, Saving Graces,* 148). Urban also said "everyone knew of cases in which priests had vanished for short periods in order to escape from their vows of chastity." After 1989, Urban, who played a clever but nasty role in the interplay between the government and Solidarity, created one of Poland's most outrageous and most popular periodicals, *Nie* (No).

43. Olszowski's dismissal was occasioned in part by a love affair. Two years later he was in Queens, New York City, living what the *New York Times* called "an anonymous middle-class life" with the woman he loved (*New York Times,* May 20, 1988).

44. Jacek Kuroń, "We Must Not Waste This Opportunity," *East European Reporter,* 2/2 (1986): 26–27. See the same journal, volumes 2 and 3, for several timely analytical articles from the underground press on the confusion surrounding the formation of the Solidarity Provisional Council.

45. The other members were Bogdan Borusewicz, Zbigniew Bujak; Władysław Frasyniuk, Tadeusz Jenynak, Bogdan Lis, Janusz Pałubicki, and Józef Pinior ("Establishment of Solidarity's Provisional Council," *East European Reporter* 2/2 [1986]: 25).

46. Ost, *Solidarity,* 174.

47. Ost, *Solidarity,* 175.

48. Jeri Laber, "Different Strokes in the Eastern Bloc," *New York Times,* November 23, 1987.

49. Apparently Glemp told George Bush's people on the occasion of the vice-president's visit to Poland late in 1987 that he considered Solidarity a closed chapter in Poland's history (John Tagliabue, "Lech! Lech! Lech!" *New York Times Magazine,* October 23, 1988, 41).

50. Quoted by Lawrence Weschler, "Deficit," *The New Yorker,* May 11, 1992, 46.

51. *Keesing's,* 31,390.

52. In 1980 and 1981 in particular Poles showed great interest in the Hungarian reforms. See Zvi Gitelman, "Is Hungary the Future of Poland?" *Eastern European Politics and Societies* 1 (1987): 135–59, esp. 150–58.

53. See Bartłomiej Kamiński, *The Collapse of State Socialism: The Case of Poland* (Princeton, N.J.: Princeton University Press, 1991).

54. Martin R. Myant, "Poland—The Permanent Crisis?" in *Poland: The Economy in the 1980s,* ed. Roger A. Clarke (London: Longman, 1989), 9.

55. Arthur R. Rachwald, *In Search of Poland: The Superpowers' Response to Solidarity, 1980–1989* (Stanford, Calif.: Hoover Institution Press, 1990), 36.

56. Ludwik Krasucki, quoted by Michael T. Kaufman, "Warsaw Learns a New Word: 'Democratization,'" *New York Times,* February 13, 1987.

57. Quoted by John Tagliabue, "At Solidarity, a Quiet Stand on Changes," *New York Times,* October 16, 1987.

58. Statement of December 13, 1987, *East European Reporter,* 3/2 (1988): 34–35.

59. The antipolitical journal *KOS* was important in nurturing this movement.

60. *New York Times,* February 6, 1988.

61. See Jadwiga Staniszkis, "The Obsolescence of Solidarity," *Telos* 80 (Summer 1989): 37–50.

62. Martial law destroyed the actuality of the ten-million strong union, Kulerski said, and May 1988 brought the final realization of this real state of affairs "and helped destroy a myth" ("After May—What Next?": A discussion with several activists, *East European Reporter,* 3/3 [1988]: 39).

63. The comment is by Mieczysław Rakowski, writing in the fall of 1987, as quoted by Garton Ash, *The Uses of Adversity,* 272. David Ost says that preliminary negotiations with some Solidarity representatives started as early as October 1987 (*Solidarity,* 172).

64. Mieczysław F. Rakowski, *Jak to się stało* (Warszawa: Polska Oficyna Wydawnicza "BGW," 1991), 117.

65. Tagliabue, "Lech! Lech! Lech!" 37.

66. This was not a new opinion. In 1967 Leopold Tyrmand wrote a bitter attack on Rakowski that became famous. Among other things, Tyrmand condemned Rakowski as a careerist and *arriviste,* ridiculed his marriage to a concert violinist, and argued that behind his "liberalism" lay "the beautiful and richly illustrated dossier of a totalitarian bully, a Stalinist hireling, a cynical hypocrite, a servile flunky" ("The Hair Styles of Mieczysław Rakowski," in *Between East and West: Writings from* Kultura, ed. Robert Kostrzewa [New York: Hill & Wang, 1990], 111–31). For the "organ grinder" comment see Alina Perth-Grabowska, "Poland in the New Year (or, the Downfall of Communism)," *Studium Papers* 13/1 (January 1989): 5. For a useful corrective to the one-sided views of Solidarity activists about Rakowski, see Richard Spielman, "The Eighteenth Brumaire of General Wojciech Jaruzelski," *World Politics* 37 (1985): 579–82.

67. Maciej Zalewski, "On the Talks That Never Were," *Uncaptive Minds* 1/4 (November–December 1988): 18.

68. Rakowski, *Jak to się stało,* 193. Bronisław Geremek believes the idea emerged earlier in the fall, perhaps as early as late October (interview, February 21, 1992).

69. Interview in *Journal de Genève,* in JPRS-EER-86-006, January 16, 1986, 124.

70. *Uncaptive Minds* 2/2 (March–April 1989): 1.

71. *New York Times,* December 1, 1988: "Many supporters of Solidarity feared the debate," Alina Perth-Grabowska reported. "In general [Wałęsa] fares poorly in debates. He tends to speak incorrectly, with grammatical and stylistic

errors." Rather than hindering him, however, his earthy way of speaking and quick sense of the telling quip totally dominated the ponderous Miodowicz ("Poland in the New Year [or, the Downfall of Communism]," *Studium Papers* 13/1 [January 1989]: 6). For a brief excerpt from the debate see Lech Wałęsa, *The Struggle and the Triumph: An Autobiography* (New York: Arcade Publishing, 1992), 166–71.

72. *New York Times,* January 5, 1989.

73. *New York Times,* January 20, 1989.

74. Geremek, interview, February 21, 1992.

75. Lawrence Weschler, "A Grand Experiment," *The New Yorker,* November 13, 1989, 65.

76. Piotr Stasiński, "Hard Bargains at the Round Table," *Uncaptive Minds* 2/2 (March–April 1989): 4.

77. Weschler, "A Grand Experiment," 64.

78. "'Independence,' Liberal-Democratic Party and Fighting Solidarity," *Uncaptive Minds* 2/2 (March–April 1989): 6; Kornel Morawiecki, "Boycott the Elections," *Uncaptive Minds* 2/3 (May–June–July 1989): 11–12; Leopolita (pseud.), "Why is There So Much Skepticism?" *Uncaptive Minds* 2/3 (May–June–July 1989): 7.

79. Bernard Gwertzman and Michael T. Kaufman, eds., *The Collapse of Communism* (New York: Times Books, 1990), 118.

80. Gwertzman and Kaufman, *The Collapse of Communism,* 120.

81. *New York Times,* July 7, 1989.

82. FBIS-EEU-89-122, June 26, 1989, 66.

83. Rakowski became head of the PUWP on July 19, when Jaruzelski became president. Rakowski resigned as prime minister on August 2 to make way for Kiszczak.

84. For a detailed review of Soviet positions during the crisis, see Michael Shafir, "Soviet Reaction to Polish Developments: Widened Limits of Tolerated Change," RFE, RAD Background Report/179, Eastern Europe, September 20, 1989.

85. See the article by John Tagliabue, *New York Times,* August 18, 1989. Michael Simmons characterized Rakowski as "angry" in the *Manchester Guardian Weekly,* August 27, 1989.

86. Shafir, "Soviet Reaction to Polish Developments," 5.

87. Rakowski, *Jak to się stało,* 243–45. Gorbachev used the term "*Ni hriena*" (literally: "Not horseradish"), which is a rough Russian euphemism that is cruder than "junk" but not as vulgar as "shit." He quickly apologized for using the phrase.

88. Oriana Fallaci, "Even an Angel Can Become a Whore," interview with Rakowski, *Washington Post,* February 21, 1982.

Chapter 5

1. *Keesing's,* 36,664.

2. László Bruszt calls this strategy, typical of hardliners attempting to save regimes as the momentum of reform picked up, "defensive liberalization." See László Bruszt, "Hungary's Negotiated Revolution," *Social Research* 57 (1990): 365–87; and David Stark and László Bruszt, "Remaking the Political Field in Hungary: From the Politics of Confrontation to the Politics of Competition," in *Eastern Europe in Revolution,* ed. Ivo Banac (Ithaca, N.Y.: Cornell University Press, 1992), 13–55.

3. As soon as the roundtable agreement was reached, however, the opposition split again.

4. FBIS-EEU-90-177, September 12, 1990, 23.

5. János Kis, "Not with Them, Not without Us," *Uncaptive Minds* 2/4 (August–September 1989): 33.

6. For Pozsgay's remarks see *Keesing's,* 36,747. Nyers provides the source for the remaining sentiments. See his discussion in FBIS-EEU-89-149, August 4, 1989, 18.

7. This analysis relies on Bruszt and Stark, "Remaking the Political Field in Hungary."

8. For a good discussion of the issues involved, see J. F. Brown, *Surge to Freedom: The End of Communist Rule in Eastern Europe* (Durham, N.C.: Duke University Press, 1991), 115–20.

9. Alfred Reisch, "Cliffhanger Referendum Changes Political Timetable," *Report on Eastern Europe* (RFE), January 12, 1990, 12.

10. Despite the great suspicion of the Left, there was nothing particularly sinister about the suspected alliance, which would be normal in a pluralist society. "I don't think it's necessary to look for a big secret deal," said Miklós Haraszti. "They are allies" (quoted by David Shipler, "Letter from Budapest," *The New Yorker,* November 20, 1989, 97).

11. *Keesing's,* 36,961.

12. The other issues were whether (1) party organs should be removed from work places; (2) the party should give an account of its assets; (3) the Workers Guards should be disbanded, something already accomplished by the legislature before the referendum. All three proposals were approved with 95 percent of the vote (Reisch, "Cliffhanger Referendum," 10).

13. In order for the decision to be legally binding, 50 percent of the registered voters had to vote. This condition was met when 58 percent voted. The difficulty of getting this many out for an election was demonstrated in 1990 when the Communist hardliners got enough signatures to force a second referendum on the same subject and only 15 percent of the registered voters voted. The fact that the November referendum was Hungary's first open election helped.

14. It was unusual to accede to this convention unconditionally. Most countries have added some proviso or condition to their accession. Perhaps at this moment the Hungarians felt they needed action, not quibbling.

15. E.g., Brown, *Surge to Freedom,* 130.

16. See Robert Darnton, "Time and Money," in *Berlin Journal 1989–1990* (New York: W. W. Norton, 1991), 297–309. For the "clueless" quote, see ibid., 199.

17. Irwin L. Collier, Jr., "GDR Economic Policy during the Honecker Era," *Eastern European Economics* 29/1 (Fall 1990): 5–29.

18. Three months after the fall of the Berlin Wall, Erich Honecker admitted the results were fraudulent (*New York Times,* February 16, 1990).

19. Norman Naimark, "'Ich will hier raus': Emigration and the Collapse of the German Democratic Republic," in Banac, *Eastern Europe in Revolution,* 82.

20. *Washington Post,* September 12, 1989.

21. Vladimir Tismaneanu, "Nascent Civil Society in the German Democratic Republic," *Problems of Communism* 38 (March–June 1989): 97.

22. Armin Mitter and Stefan Wille, eds., *"Ich liebe euch doch alle!" Befehle*

und Lageberichte des MfS (Berlin: Basis Druck, 1990), 47. I would like to thank Mary Fulbrook for this reference. See Richard Popplewell, "The Stasi and the East German Revolution of 1989," *Contemporary European History* 1 (1992): 37–63; and Karl-Dieter Opp and Christiane Gern, "Dissident Groups, Personal Networks, and Spontaneous Cooperation: The East German Revolution in 1989," typescript.

23. FBIS-EEU-89-177, September 14, 1989, 29.

24. FBIS-EEU-89-180, September 19, 1989, 25.

25. Michael J. Sodaro, *Moscow, Germany, and the West from Khrushchev to Gorbachev* (Ithaca, N.Y.: Cornell University Press, 1990), 378, quoting an account by Krenz.

26. The figures for the numbers of persons at the Leipzig and other rallies are extremely imprecise and vary from author to author. The numbers presented here are simply those that seem plausible to me and should be considered as indicative of an order of magnitude only.

27. Naimark, " 'Ich will hier raus,' " 89.

28. Ibid., 90.

29. Fred S. Oldenburg, "The October Revolution in the GDR—System, History, and Causes," *Eastern European Economics* 29/2 (Fall 1990): 62.

30. The following is from a report by Marc Fisher, *Washington Post*, November 10, 1990.

31. Sodaro, *Moscow, Germany, and the West*, 379.

32. The full facts on this case may never be known. On June 19, 1992, General Vladimir Todorov, former head of Bulgaria's intelligence service, was sentenced to fourteen months in prison for destroying the files on Markov. Todorov's codefendent, General Stoyan Savov, committed suicide before the trial began (*RFE/RL Daily Report*, June 22, 1992, 5).

33. It was also approximately the time of Brezhnev's death (1982). Zhivkov renamed the huge Kremikovtsi metallurgical combine in honor of the deceased Soviet leader.

34. RFE, Bulgarian SR/7, July 23, 1988, 23–27.

35. Zhivkov had shown his interest in computers by placing one of Bulgaria's premier computer research and manufacturing centers in his home town (RFE, Bulgarian SR/7, July 23, 1988, 23–27).

36. Paraphrased by *Keesing's*, 34,378.

37. The "work of the party" phrase was the title of the main report Zhivkov gave at the special party conference of January 28–29, 1988, and the admonition on glasnost comes from Zhivkov's speech to the central committee plenum of July 28, 1987 (FBIS-EEU-88-018, January 28, 1988, 3; and FBIS-EEU-87, August 5, 1987, B19).

38. For a thorough discussion of the maze of Bulgarian economic reforms and pseudoreforms through 1987, see Richard Crampton, " 'Stumbling and Dusting Off,' or an Attempt to Pick a Path Through the Thicket of Bulgaria's New Economic Mechanism," *Eastern European Politics and Societies* 2 (1988): 333–95.

39. See Stefan Troebst, "Zum Verhältnis von Partei, Staat und türkischer Minderheit in Bulgarien 1956–1986," in *Nationalitätenprobleme in Südosteuropa*, ed. Roland Schönfeld (München: R. Oldenbourg Verlag, 1987), 231–54.

40. Robert R. King, *Minorities under Communism: Nationalities as a Source of Tension among Balkan Communist States* (Cambridge, Mass.: Harvard University Press, 1973), 189.

41. See the statement by Stanko Todorov in *From Stalinism to*

Pluralism: A Documentary History of Eastern Europe since 1945, ed. Gale Stokes (New York: Oxford University Press, 1991), 232–34.

42. Interview, March 14, 1992, with Nikolai Todorov, who reports that Atanasov said this to him in 1985.

43. Ruse itself is no enclave of pure air. Misha Glenny, the BBC correspondent, speaks of "the chemical gas chambers masquerading as cities of Giurgiu and Ruse that glare at each other poisonously from either side of the Danube" (Misha Glenny, *The Rebirth of History: Eastern Europe in the Age of Democracy* [London: Penguin, 1990], 94).

44. This paragraph is based on an interview with Georgi Atanasov (March 17, 1992).

45. Interview with Dragomir Draganov, March 16, 1992.

46. RFE, Bulgarian SR/8, September 1, 1989, 10–11.

47. Information on subsequent developments is drawn from an interview with Nikolai Todorov, March 14, 1992; an interview with Georgi Atanasov, March 17, 1992; and several discussions with Ivan Ilchev while we were both fellows at the Woodrow Wilson Center, 1990–1991.

48. RFE, Bulgarian SR/11, December 15, 1989, 23, quoting Mladenov's letter of resignation of October 27.

49. This information from Ivan Ilchev. Atanasov would not describe the specific arrangements, but he did confirm that Dzhurov took "prudent measures."

50. *Keesing's,* 34,434.

51. Sharon Wolchik, *Czechoslovakia in Transition: Politics, Economics, and Society* (London and New York: Pinter Publishers, 1991), 260. Trade with developed countries declined by the late 1980s to about 15 percent of total trade.

52. Václav Havel, *Letters to Olga, June 1979–September 1982* (New York: Henry Holt, 1989), 190.

53. Václav Havel, *Disturbing the Peace: A Conversation with Karel Hvížďala* (New York: Alfred A. Knopf, 1990), 53.

54. Havel, *Disturbing the Peace,* 8.

55. The regime's total inability to understand a person like Havel is indicated by the criticism it published of him, such as a purported letter from a citizen saying, "Personally, I am not at all surprised that he is a sworn enemy of our socialist society. It prevented him from having a governess, a maid, a gardener and a driver, and from living off unearned profits" (JPRS-EER-89-059, May 18, 1989, 24).

56. H. Gordon Skilling, *Charter 77 and Human Rights in Czechoslovakia* (London: George Allen & Unwin, 1981), 79.

57. *New York Times,* December 8, 1989.

58. Milan Kundera, "A Life Like a Work of Art," *The New Republic,* January 29, 1990, 16–17.

59. London: *Reader's International,* 1987.

60. Jiří Dienstbier was released in May 1982; Václav Havel in March 1983; and Václav Benda and Petr Uhl in May 1983.

61. Miroslav Kusy, "Nationalism, Totalitarianism, and Democracy: An Interview with Miroslav Kusy," in *After the Velvet Revolution,* ed. Tim D. Whipple (New York: Freedom House, 1991), 247.

62. "The Independent East European Information Agency: Interview with Petr Uhl and Jan Urban," *Uncaptive Minds* 2/4 (August–September–October 1989): 45.

63. For Benda's original article and a stimulating discussion of its impact, see

Civic Freedom in Central Europe: Voices from Czechoslovakia, ed. H. Gordon Skilling and Paul Wilson (London: Macmillan, 1991).

64. Pedro Ramet, *Cross and Commissar: The Politics of Religion in Eastern Europe and the USSR* (Bloomington: Indiana University Press, 1987), 78.

65. Timothy Garton Ash, "Prague: Inside the Magic Lantern," in his *The Magic Lantern: The Revolution in '89 Witnessed in Warsaw, Budapest, Berlin and Prague* (New York: Random House, 1990), 96.

66. This was an especially remarkable turnout since approximately one hundred thousand Slovaks were attending a traditional annual pilgrimage at Levoča at the same time (Janice Broun, *Conscience and Captivity: Religion in Eastern Europe* [Washington, D.C.: Ethics and Public Policy Center, 1988], 94).

67. *Keesing's,* 34,433

68. RFE, Czechoslovakian SR/1, January 21, 1988, 45–48. The petition is also reprinted in Broun, *Conscience and Captivity,* 319–21.

69. When Karel Pala, a professor of Slavics at Brno University, asked undergraduates to identify Havel and Kundera on their entrance examinations in the mid-1980s, students reacted quite negatively, considering it not a literary question but a political provocation (interview with Pala, February 10, 1992).

70. Skilling and Wilson, *Civic Freedom in Central Europe,* 135.

71. Havel in JPRS-EER-89-036, April 3, 1989, 1–2; and interview with Jan Urban, February 15, 1992.

72. JPRS-EER-89-036, April 3, 1989, 2.

73. Garton Ash, *The Uses of Adversity,* 238 and 241. Well-informed Czechs and Slovaks at this time also believed the regime would fall in some vague future time like a decade (interviews with Jan Urban [February 15, 1992] and Svetislav Bombík [February 24, 1992]).

74. For a fascinating account of Jan Kavan's post-1989 fate and a brilliant introduction to the Kafkaesque qualities of East European politics, see Lawrence Weschler, "The Velvet Purge: The Trials of Jan Kavan," *The New Yorker,* October 19, 1993, 66–96, and "From Kafka to Dreyfus," *The New Yorker,* November 2, 1993, 62–63.

75. The demonstration on the twentieth anniversary of the Warsaw Pact invasion the previous year had been similarly spontaneous, attracting perhaps ten thousand people. It was leaderless because the activists had been placed in preventive detention.

76. Václav Havel, "A Statement to the Court," *New York Review of Books,* April 27, 1989, 41.

77. On January 2, 1989, Viktor Meier reported in the *Frankfurter Allgemeine Zeitung* that "the prerequisites for democratic renewal in Czechoslovakia over the next few years do not exist," and on March 3 Peter Glotz wrote in *Die Zeit* that "no charismatic leader like Lech Wałęsa is anywhere near the horizon" (JPRS-EER-89-020, March 2, 1989, 4; JPRS-EER-89-054, May 11, 1989, 5).

78. Paraphrase by Allen H. Kassof, *The Chronicle of Higher Education,* January 31, 1990.

79. Information from an interview with Boris Strečanský, February 25, 1992.

80. The document can be found in *Uncaptive Minds* 2/4 (August–September 1989), 35. Its title was designed to recall the important document from 1968 entitled "Two Thousand Words."

81. The phrase "sprang up like mushrooms" is that of Luda Klusáková (interview, February 12, 1992).

82. Interview with Karel Pala, Mirek Čejka, both professors at Brno University, and Aleš Zlámal, librarian, February 10, 1992.

83. For a detailed account of this event and those that followed, see Bernard Wheaton and Zdeněk Kavan, *The Velvet Revolution: Czechoslovakia, 1980–1991* (Boulder Colo.: Westview Press, 1992).

84. According to the November 17 commission created by the federal assembly, which reported early in 1992, a young woman named Drahomíra Dražska is the one who first reported the alleged death. There were many people lying in Narodny Street, with clothing and shoes strewn around, and she thought one of them was dead. When she looked later and saw this person was not there, she thought he had been killed and his body removed. Or she just made it up. In any event, word got to Petr Uhl, and when he uncovered a second similar report he sent the news on to Radio Free Europe (RFE). Another embellishment to this story is the possibility that the police knew the information going to Uhl was incorrect but permitted it to go out hoping to compromise him and his information service. Uhl was in fact arrested a bit later (information provided by Jan Urban).

85. Garton Ash, "Prague: Inside the Magic Lantern," 82.

86. Interview with Svetislav Bombík, organizing member of the Slovak Students Strike Coordination Committee, February 24, 1992.

87. Interview with Boris Strečanský, who participated in the visits to villages in Slovakia, February 25, 1992.

88. Robert G. Kaiser reports that the Soviets summoned Jan Fojtik to Moscow on November 16 to tell him the Soviets were about to repudiate the 1968 invasion of Czechoslovakia and that military officers were hinting to their Czechoslovak associates that the Soviet troops could not be counted on to support any forcible attempt to maintain the government (*Why Gorbachev Happened* [New York: Simon & Schuster, 1991], 306–7). Demonstrators in Brno on Monday, November 20, were surrounded by police called in from southern Bohemia (i.e., not local people), and apparently the decision not to clear the streets by force there was made only at the last minute (interview with Karel Pala, Mirek Čejka, and Aleš Zlámal). The option of using force in Prague after November 17 came only on the next day, when the demonstration was still manageable, but it would have taken a very violent act. After that the crowds were simply too big (and the people's militia too unreliable).

89. Although not, as some Slovaks argued, with an adequate program of autonomy for Slovakia. For Garton Ash's wonderful description of these hectic days see "Prague: Inside the Magic Lantern," 78–130.

90. Everyone I spoke with in Czechoslovakia could remember in detail exactly what they were doing when they heard the news about the events of November 17 and how they reacted in the next few days. Radio Free Europe, getting its information from the East European Information Agency in Prague (i.e., from Petr Uhl and Jan Urban), played an important role in spreading the original news, although some deduced an important event had occurred by reading between the lines of the original internal newscasts. By the middle of the week television was reporting events fairly openly, not only showing Havel but even repeatedly presenting the tape of the police beating the students on November 17.

91. Some miners failed to strike, and in Oštrava three thousand persons conducted a counterdemonstration in support of the government, but the overwhelming majority of Czechs and Slovaks completely stopped work during the two-hour demonstration strike.

92. For how difficult that proved to be, see Václav Havel, "Paradise Lost," *New York Review of Books,* April 9, 1992, 6–8.

93. For an excellent discussion of the hardships of Romanian life in the 1980s, see Anon. [Pavel Campeanu], "Birth and Death in Romania," *New York Review of Books,* October 23, 1986, 10–18.

94. Gail Kligman, "The Politics of Reproduction in Ceauşesca's Romania: A Case Study in Political Culture," *East European Politics and Societies* 6/3 (Fall 1992): 364–418.

95. RFE-Romanian SR/2, January 30, 1984, "Milking private agriculture," 1–4. As was typical of socialist economies, privately cultivated plots, although comprising only 15 percent of Romania's productive area, produced 60 percent of its milk, eggs, and fruit and almost half of its wool, meat, and grapes.

96. For the quotations in this paragraph see *Keesing's,* 33,410, 34,120, and 35,141.

97. See Vladimir Socor's description of this event, RFE/RAD Background Report/231, December 4, 1987. For the meat ration, see William Pfaff, "Romania: Breaking the Silence," *New York Review of Books,* April 27, 1989, 8.

98. The Hungarian minority in Transylvania produced the only known regular samizdat publications in Romania, the short-lived periodical *Ellenpontok* (Counterpoints) and various issues of the Hungarian Press of Transylvania. See Helsinki Watch report submitted to the CSCE May 5, 1987, *Hearing before the Commission on Security and Cooperation in Europe* [CSCE 100-1-16] (Washington, D.C.: Government Printing Office, 1988), 70.

99. One of these, Vlad Georgescu, the brilliant historian and Radio Free Europe analyst, died of cancer at an early age, as did a number of other regime opponents. Friends alleged that when Georgescu had been imprisoned in Romania before leaving the country, the Securitate had flooded his cell with x-ray radiation purposely to give him cancer. Outlandish as this sounds, the Securitate was quite capable of such an act.

100. *Keesing's,* 35,847.

101. Dinu Giurescu, *The Razing of Romania's Past* (New York: World Monuments Fund, 1989), 47.

102. For an excellent discussion see Michael Shafir, "The Historical Background to Rural Resettlement," RFE, Romania SR/10, August 23, 1988, 3–15. See also Per Ronas, "Turning the Romanian Peasant into a New Socialist Man: An Assessment of Rural Development Policy in Romania," *Soviet Studies* 41 (1989): 543–59.

103. A Romanian human rights activist in Tirgu Mureş, Smaranda Enache, recalls good interethnic relations during her schooling in the 1950s and 1960s. "It was a consciously antinationalist time," she recalls (Judith Ingram, "Smaranda Enache: A Transylvanian Life," *Uncaptive Minds* 4/2 [Summer 1991]: 120). Robert R. King writes that "in the first years after the Second World War, Rumania was probably the most generous of the East European states in the treatment of national minorities." No one had many rights in Romania, but all were equal in this regard (*Minorities under Communism: Nationalities as a Source of Tension among Balkan Communist States* [Cambridge, Mass.: Harvard University Press, 1973], 146). For a good summary treatment, see George Schöpflin, *The Hungarians of Rumania* (London: Minority Rights Group Report no. 37, 1978).

104. Raphael Vago, *The Grandchildren of Trianon: Hungary and the Hun-*

garian Minority in the Communist States (Boulder, Colo.: East European Monographs, 1989), 45.

105. The word *myth* here will irritate some Romanians, but the scanty evidence on which the claim is made and the enormous superstructure of justifications and rationalizations that have been built upon that evidence, not to mention the fervor and emotion with which the idea has been propagated, justifies its use.

106. For a good discussion of the situation in Romania in 1989, including the text of Cornea's open letter of April 15, 1989, and other materials, see Dennis Deletant, "Crimes against the spirit," *Index on Censorship,* August 1989, 25–34.

107. Interview with Lazăr Vírgil, longtime correspondent for *România Liberă* in Cluj, March 5, 1992.

108. RFE, Romania SR/3, March 29, 1989; and SR/4, May 4, 1989. On the letter of the six former officials see William Pfaff, "Romania: Breaking the Silence," *New York Review of Books,* April 27, 1989, 8–9, where the letter is reprinted. Pirvulescu was one of the few Communists ever to speak up publicly against Ceauşescu, which he did at the Eleventh Party Congress in 1979. At that time he refused to join in the unanimous vote for Ceauşescu and accused him of creating a personal dictatorship (Vladimir Tismaneanu, *Reinventing Politics: Eastern Europe from Stalin to Havel* [New York: Free Press, 1992], 116).

109. For his authorized version of these events see László Tökés and David Porter, *The Fall of Tyrants: The Incredible Story of One Pastor's Witness, the People of Romania, and the Overthrow of Ceauşescu* (Wheaton, Ill.: Crossway Books, 1991).

110. For an authoritative description of the events in Timoşoara as well as of the rest of the revolution, see Nestor Ratesh, *Romania: The Entangled Revolution* (New York and Washington: Praeger, with the Center for Strategic and International Studies, 1991).

111. See Vladimir Socor, "Pastor Toekes and the Outbreak of the Revolution in Romania," *Report on Eastern Europe,* February 2, 1990, 19–26.

112. Radesh, *Romania: The Tangled Revolution,* 78. The total number of deaths attributable to the revolution given in this report was 1,033.

113. Interview with student from Arad, March 5, 1992.

114. Information from Major Harry Bucur, former party activist in the Ministry of Defense, interview, March 6, 1992.

115. Two excellent articles on these and later events are Matei Calinescu and Vladimir Tismaneanu, "The 1989 Revolution and Romania's Future," *Problems of Communism* 40 (Jan–April 1990): 42–59; and Katherine Verdery and Gail Kligman, "Romania after Ceauşescu: Post-Communist Communism?" in Banac, *Eastern Europe in Revolution,* 117–47. See also Radesh, *Romania: The Entangled Revolution.*

116. A young man from Huneodora reported to me that in that town everyone got down their old hunting rifles and created a kind of civil patrol that defended the town against the terrorists for about five days before they realized no terrorists were coming (interview with Daniel Necşa, March 4, 1992).

117. For a thorough description of the movements of the Ceauşescus during their last three days, see Edward Behr, *Kiss the Hand You Cannot Bite: The Rise and Fall of the Ceauşescus* (New York: Villard Books, 1991), 3–27.

118. Many mysteries surround the trial and execution. For example, whereas rumors claimed that the trial lasted nine hours, only forty-five minutes of heavily edited tape have ever been released. The NSF claimed at the time the executions

were necessary to discourage Securitate terrorists from continuing the fight, but no such terrorists were ever arrested or produced by the regime. Some even suggest that Ceauşescu was killed under torture and then shot before the cameras for effect. The videotape does not show the couple alive prior to being shot nor does it show them bleeding. As for the trial itself, there is little doubt that it was, as one American jurist put it, "a farce" (Alex Kozinski, "The Ceauşescu Show Trial and the Future of Romania," *ABA Journal,* January 1991, 72).

119. For a clear discussion of the various theories see Radesh, *Romania: The Tangled Revolution,* 80–119.

120. Quoted by Calinescu and Tismaneanu, "The 1989 Revolution and Romania's Future," 47.

Chapter 6

1. Gorbachev's resignation speech, *Washington Post,* December 26, 1991, A34.

2. See *Elections in Central and Eastern Europe: A Compendium of Reports on the Elections held from March through June 1990* (Washington, D.C.: Commission on Security and Cooperation in Europe, 1990); and "Elections in Eastern Europe," special issue of *Electoral Studies* 9 (1990). For a summary of the results, except for Croatia and Slovenia, see Vladimir V. Kusin, "The Elections Compared and Assessed," *Report on Eastern Europe,* July 13, 1980, 38–47. For a fascinating map, with extremely useful annotations in English, see "Die Wahlen des Jahres 1990 in Mittel-, Ost- un Südosteuropa," with accompanying text by Werner Weilguni, Arnold Suppan, Valeria Heuberger, and Klaus Koch (Vienna: Österreichisches Ost- und Südosteuropa-Institut, 1991), no. 6.1–G.3 of the institute's *Atlas Ost- und Südosteuropa.*

3. The Commission on Security and Cooperation in Europe report on the Romanian election said that unequal access to media and faulty application of election procedures "cast significant doubt" on the results (*Elections in Central and Eastern Europe,* 97). The commission is the agency created by the U.S. Congress to deal with issues relating to American participation in the Conference on Security and Cooperation in Europe (CSCE) created in Helsinki in 1975.

4. E.g., Matei Calinescu and Nicolas Spulber, "Rumania, an Old Stalinist Charade?" *New York Times,* December 30, 1989, 25.

5. This paragraph is based on an interview with Calin Anastasiu, a founding member of the Group for Social Dialogue, March 7, 1992.

6. "The Timişoara Declaration," *Report on Eastern Europe,* April 6, 1990, 41–45.

7. Chrisula Stefanescu, "Marathon Demonstration in Bucharest's University Square," *Report on Eastern Europe,* June 15, 1990, 41–45.

8. The phrase comes from Vladimir Tismaneanu and Mircea Mihăieş, "Infamy Restored: Nationalism in Romania," *East European Reporter* 5/1 (January–February 1992): 26.

9. Misha Glenny, *The Rebirth of History: Eastern Europe in the Age of Democracy* (New York: Penguin Books, 1990), 128.

10. The extremist *România Mare* has received perhaps too much attention in the West. It is a large weekly, but by 1992 its circulation declined to about two hundred thousand and two other weeklies, *Expres* and *Românul,* were on the verge of passing it.

11. Dan Ionescu, "The Posthumous Ceauşescu Cult and the Its High Priest," *Report on Eastern Europe,* May 31, 1991, 26.

12. For devastating portraits of these "hypnotized dwarves," as he calls them (p. 51), see Norman Manea, *On Clowns: The Dictator and the Artist* (New York: Grove Weidenfeld, 1992), 141–42, and the surrounding discussion.

13. See Dennis Deletant, "The Role of *Vatră Româneascǎ* in Transylvania," *Report on Eastern Europe,* February 1, 1991, 28–37.

14. Glenny, *The Rebirth of History,* 112.

15. FSN supporters claim that the events in Tirgu Mureş were provocations created by Hungarians as part of an ongoing plan by the Hungarian government to destabilize Romania and to establish appropriate conditions for seizing Transylvania. They believe that the anti-Romanian bias of the Western media in this instance was due to the heavy influence of Hungarian émigrés in the West, particularly George Soros (interviews with Adrian Rizea, editor of the nationalist journal *Timpul,* and Col. Dr. Ioan Talpeş, advisor to President Iliescu, March 9, 1992). For a detailed discussion of the government's reaction, which was at the very least equivocal, see Michael Shafir, "The Romanian Authorities' Reactions to the Violence in Tirgu Mureş," *Report on Eastern Europe,* April 13, 1990, 43–47.

16. Interview by Paul Lendvai, FBIS-EEU-90-213, November 2, 1990, 46.

17. For additional details see *The May 1990 Elections in Romania* (Washington, D.C.: National Republican Institute for International Affairs and National Democratic Institute for International Affairs, 1991).

18. Michael Shafir, "Government Encourages Vigilante Violence in Bucharest," *Report on Eastern Europe,* July 6, 1992, 32–39. "Legionary rebellion" refers to the Legion of the Archangel Michael, a prewar fascist organization.

19. Very useful for this discussion were Charles Moser, "Bulgaria: The Road to Democracy," and "The President and the Parliament: Bulgarian Politics 1990–1991," both published in typescript by The Free Congress Foundation, Washington, D.C., 1991.

20. Kjell Engelbrekt, "The Union of Democratic Forces Consolidates before June Elections," *Report on Eastern Europe,* June 1, 1990, 3, presents an excellent descriptive chart of the entities that made up the original UDF compiled by Vera Gavrilov. For a later listing of its membership see Rada Nikolaev, "The UDF's Members and Groups with Observer Status, Spring 1991," *Report on Eastern Europe,* May 17, 1991, 5–8.

21. *Keesing's,* 37,253.

22. *The June 1990 Elections in Bulgaria* (Washington, D.C.: National Republican Institute for International Affairs and National Democratic Institute for International Affairs, 1991), 39. Five deaths of UDF supporters occurred in three separate incidents, but at least three of these were apparently not related to the election.

23. Zhelyu Zhelev, February 12, 1990, quoted by Kjell Engelbrekt, "The Union of Democratic Forces Consolidates before June Elections," *Report on Eastern Europe,* June 1, 1990, 4.

24. This is what Lukhanov told Nikolai Todorov (interview with Todorov, March 14, 1992).

25. "The search for a 'third way,' as an alternative to capitalism or Marxism, occupied much of German thought during the Weimar republic. . . . Everywhere in Europe, fascism was based on the urge toward a third way" (George L. Mosse, *The Crisis of German Ideology: Intellectual Origins of the Third Reich* [New York: Grosset & Dunlap, 1966], 280).

26. For a moderate and cogent version of this view, see Iván Szelényi, "The Third Way," in *From Stalinism to Pluralism: A Documentary History of Eastern Europe,* ed. Gale Stokes (New York: Oxford University Press, 1991), 248–54.

27. For a detailed discussion of the election see Barnabas Racz, "Political Pluralisation in Hungary: The 1990 Elections," *Soviet Studies* 43/1 (1991): 107–36. For the roundtable negotiations concerning the elections and further discussion of the results, see István Kukorelli, "The Birth, Testing and Results of the 1989 Hungarian Electoral Law," *Soviet Studies* 43/1: 137–56. Zoltán D. Barnay and Louisa Vinton, "Breakthrough to Democracy: Elections in Poland and Hungary," *Studies in Comparative Communism* 23/2 (1990): 209–12, provides good comparative comments.

28. *Keesing's,* 37,024.

29. Stephen Kinzer, "East Germans Face their Accusers," *New York Times Magazine,* April 12, 1992, 27.

30. *New York Times,* December 4, 1989, quotation at the end of his article beginning on p. 1.

31. "Now there's no point talking about whether the two Germanys will be reunited," Flora Lewis said in the *New York Times* on December 10, 1989. "The question is when, how, in what context and with what results."

32. *New York Times,* November 29, 1989, 11.

33. Early in February 1990 a poll purported to show that if an election were held in West Germany at that time, the Social Democrats would receive 54 percent of the vote and the Christian Democrats only 11 percent (*New York Times,* February 9, 1990, article beginning on p. 1).

34. In the local elections of May 6, the percentages stayed roughly the same. The Christian Democratic Union dropped from 41 percent to 34 percent but remained the strongest party by a substantial margin. This local vote did not have great significance, since another election took place right after unification.

35. *Keesing's,* 37,379.

36. The Saarland joined West German in 1956 but did not get full rights as a Land until 1959.

37. Economic Commission for Europe of the United Nations, *Economic Survey of Europe in 1990–1991* (New York: Secretariat for the Economic Commission for Europe in Geneva, 1991), 141. For the exact exchange rules and their impact on the money supply, see "The Unification of Germany," *Economic Bulletin for Europe* 42 (1990): 92–93.

38. The amount pledged was 115 billion DM over a four-year period, about 82 percent of the amount to be raised by borrowing amortized over thirty years by both the federal government and the West German Länder (*Economic Bulletin for Europe* 42 [1990]: 95).

39. *Economic Bulletin for Europe* 42 (1990): 94.

40. On June 26, 1992, the Bundestag adopted a new law that permits abortions in the first trimester if the pregnant woman declares she is in a state of distress and undergoes official counseling (*New York Times,* national edition, June 27, 1992, 3.)

41. *Keesing's,* 37,379.

42. Early in 1993 Alliance 90 joined forces with the German Green Party, which did not place any members in the Bundestag in the 1990 election, in hopes of attracting voters growing disenchanted with the regular political parties (*New York Times,* January 20, 1993).

43. For detailed 1990 figures, see *Economic Survey of Europe in 1990–1991*. *RFE/RL Daily Report*, September 19, 1991, 2, gave estimates of four specialists for 1991 Soviet results suggesting a decline of between 9.7 percent and 20 percent.

44. John M. Kramer, "Eastern Europe and the 'Energy Shock' of 1990–91," *Problems of Communism* 40 (May–June 1991): 87. Bulgaria was particularly hard hit by the Gulf War, having to forego more than $1 billion in oil that Iraq owed it. This contributed significantly to the very difficult winter the Bulgarians endured in 1990–1991.

45. *Economic Survey of Europe 1990–1991*, 74, 63.

46. *RFE/RL Daily Report*, September 23, 1991.

47. *Economic Survey of Europe in 1990–1991*, 2.

48. During its first year of operation (ending April 30, 1991), EBRD committed 643 million ECU to twenty-four projects, the largest loan being to Romania's telecommunications company for improving that country's very bad telephone system. Other areas of EBRD operations included food processing, power generation, cellular telephones, and even an equity investment in Burger King franchises in Hungary (*Transition: The Newsletter about Reforming Economies* [World Bank] 3/4 [April 4, 1992], 7).

49. Quoted in *Wall Street Journal*, February 22, 1991.

50. *Keesing's*, 38,155; and John Pinder, *The European Community and Eastern Europe* (New York: Council on Foreign Relations Press for the Royal Institute of International Relations, 1991), 96.

51. For example, see *The Transition to a Market Economy in Central and Eastern Europe* (Paris: Office of Economic Cooperation and Development, 1991). A summary of that publication is Paul Marer, "The Transition to a Market Economy in Central and Eastern Europe," *OECD Observer* 169 (April–May 1991), 4–10.

52. Václav Klaus, "Transition—An Insider's View," *Problems of Communism* 41 (January–April 1992): 73.

53. János Kornai, *The Road to a Free Economy* (New York: W. W. Norton, 1990), 80; Peter Murrell, *The Nature of Socialist Economies: Lessons from Eastern European Foreign Trade* (Princeton, N.J.: Princeton University Press, 1990). See also Murrell, "Evolutionary and Radical Approaches to Economic Reform," and "Evolution in Economics and in the Economic Reform of the Centrally Planned Economies," mimeographs, 1991; and "Conservative Political Philosophy and the Strategy of Economic Transition," *Eastern European Politics and Societies* 6 (1992): 3–16.

54. For a succinct summary of Treuhand's brief, see Martin Schrenk, "Transforming the Ownership System in Eastern Germany," *Transition: The Newsletter about Reforming Economies* 1/9 (December 1990): 1–3.

55. Marvin Jackson, "One Year after German Economic Union: The Impact on the German Economy," *Report on Eastern Europe*, June 28, 1991, 41; and *International Management*, April 1990, 25.

56. *Transition: The Newsletter about Reforming Economies* 3/3 (March 1992): 11.

57. Compare this with Bulgaria's plan, which began in 1992 with release of the first $50 million installment of a $160 million international loan to institute a program that hoped to provide Bulgaria with a new phone system by the year 2006 (*RFE/RL Daily Report*, June 11, 1992, 4).

58. *International Herald-Tribune,* March 12, 1992, 13.

59. For a summary of the statement adopted by the Council of Ministers in October 1989, see *Orbis* 34 (1990): 109–20.

60. For Sach's advice to Poland, see Jeffrey Sachs and David Lipton, "Poland's Economic Reform," *Foreign Affairs* 69/3 (Summer 1990): 47–66. The same authors give a more technical discussion in "Creating a Market Economy in Eastern Europe: The Case of Poland," *Brookings Papers on Economic Activity* (1990): 1.

61. By 1992 much of the huge Palace of Culture itself had been rented out to commercial enterprises, including an upscale department store.

62. David McQuaid, "Art-B and the Pathology of Transition," *Report on Eastern Europe,* September 20, 1991, 15–21; and Lawrence Weschler, "Deficit," *The New Yorker,* May 11, 1992, 66–67.

63. Statement of Janusz Lewandowski, *RFE/RL Daily Report,* October 17, 1991.

64. Quoted by Jan Szomburg, "Poland's Privatization strategy," cited by David Stark, "Privatization Strategies in East Central Europe," Working Papers on Transition from State Socialism, Center for International Studies, Cornell University, 24. I would like especially to thank David Stark for the many papers of his he sent me while I was working on this book. They were of enormous use.

65. Jadwiga Staniszkis, "'Political Capitalism' in Poland," *East European Politics and Societies* 5 (1991): 127–41.

66. See Zbigniew M. Fallenbuchl, "The New Government and Privatization," *Report on Eastern Europe,* March 22, 1991, 11–16.

67. Janusz Lewandowski and Jan Szomburg, "Property Reform as a Basis for Social and Economic Reform," *Communist Economies* 3 (1989): 257–68.

68. *Transition: The Newsletter about Reforming Economies* 3/1 (January 1992): 10.

69. Barry D. Wood, "The Benefits and Perils of Voucher Privatization in the Czech and Slovak Republics," *Meeting Report,* East European Studies, Woodrow Wilson Center, Washington, D.C., January–February 1993.

70. David Bartlett, "Political Economy of Privatization: Property Reform and Democracy in Hungary," *East European Politics and Societies* 6 (1992): 86.

71. HC&C calculated its promise by dividing its estimate of the total worth of the offerings throughout the country by the number of vouchers it estimated would be outstanding. At first this figure came to about seventy thousand crowns, but as the plan picked up momentum the figure dropped to thirty or forty thousand crowns (interview with Karol Dyba, minister of economic policy and development for the Czech lands, February 14, 1992).

72. The plan itself was the work of Dušan Triska, one of Klaus's most trusted associates, based on an idea of Chicago economist Milton Friedman.

73. Klaus interview with Juliana Geran Pilon, *NFF Update* (National Forum Foundation), Winter 1991. Klaus is a blunt and vigorous speaker. Pilon asked the minister of finance what his main challenge was. Klaus answered: "Frankly, one of my main headaches is fighting second-rate American intellectuals who come to Czechoslovakia to lecture and publish all sorts of nonsense telling us how capitalism doesn't work."

74. The Institute for Forecasting was created in 1984 by Valtr Komárek, politburo member, in order to provide better information to the leadership. Its alumni occupy many important positions in post-1989 Czechoslovakia. Karol

Dyba, a former member of the institute, says that among economists it was always possible to speak in terms of one's scholarly convictions, but not in public (interview with Karol Dyba, February 14, 1992).

75. *Economic Survey of Europe in 1990–1991,* 153–54.

76. *Economic Survey of Europe in 1990–1991,* 41, 54.

77. Károly Okolicsanyi, "Joint Ventures Begin to Have a Significant Impact on the Economy," *Report on Eastern Europe,* May 24, 1991, 23–26.

78. Peter Maass, "Flood of Foreign Investment Capitalizes on New Hungary," *Washington Post,* November 10, 1991.

79. Keith Crane, research director of PlanEcon, seminar on the economies of Eastern Europe, Woodrow Wilson Center, March 10, 1992.

80. David Stark, "Path Dependence and Privatization Strategies," *East European Politics and Societies* 6 (1992): 44–45.

81. Figures presented at Junior Scholars Seminar, Wye Woods, August 1991.

82. *Transition: The Newsletter About Reforming Economies* 3/11 (December 1992–January 1993), 14–15, and *RFE/RL Daily Report,* February 8, 1993.

83. Adam Michnik, "Nationalism," *Social Research* 58 (1991): 760.

84. Jiřina Šiklová, "The Solidarity of the Culpable," *Social Research* 58 (1991): 765–74.

85. Quoted by Michael Shafir, "Anti-Semitism without Jews," *Report on Eastern Europe,* June 28, 1991, 30.

86. Perhaps three hundred thousand Saxons remained in Transylvania at the end of World War II out of about eight hundred thousand before the war. The descendents of a community founded in the thirteenth century, they retained some rights during the Ceauşescu regime, such as education in German. Nevertheless, more than one hundred thousand of them emigrated to West Germany in the 1970s and 1980s through a plan whereby the Federal Republic of Germany paid Romania in hard currency for each immigrant. When Ceauşescu finally fell, about half of those remaining left for Germany in the first half of 1990 alone, further weakening the traditional social structures and church communities of that ancient settlement (Dan Ionescu, "Countdown for the German Minority?" *Report on Eastern Europe,* September 12, 1991, 32–41).

87. See *Minority Rights: Problems, Parameters, and Patterns in the CSCE Context* (Washington, D.C.: Commission on Security and Cooperation in Europe, n.d. [1992]).

88. The absence of Jews has little to do with the phenomenon. See Paul Lendvai, *Anti-Semitism without Jews: Communist Eastern Europe* (Garden City, N.Y.: Doubleday, 1971).

89. Michael Shafir, "Anti-Semitism without Jews," *Report on Eastern Europe,* June 28, 1991, 20–32.

90. Anna Sabbat-Swidlicka, "The Bishops Address the Issue of Anti-Semitism in Poland," *Report on Eastern Europe,* February 15, 1991, 17–20.

91. *RFE/RL Daily Report,* December 27, 1991, 5.

92. On March 19, 1992, President Iliescu "condemned the anti-Semitism of right-wing magazines like *Europa* and *România Mare,*" and on March 25 "a government communiqué" said that chauvinist attacks in some periodicals "run counter to the constitution and [counter to] international agreements, and legal bodies should take offenders to court" (*RFE/RL Daily Report,* March 27, 1992, 5). These statements seem designed for foreign consumption, since no action has been brought against *România Mare* by the government. Private citizens, however,

brought more than ninety libel suits against the magazine in its first year of publication (Michael Shafir, "The Greater Romanian Party," *Report on Eastern Europe,* November 15, 1991, 25).

93. Madeline Levine, "Wrestling with Ghosts: Poles and Jews Today," *East European Studies: Occasional Paper* 26 (Washington, D.C.: Woodrow Wilson Center, March 1992), 8.

94. Mária Kovács, "Jews and Hungarians: A View after the Transition," *East European Studies: Occasional Paper* 35 (Washington, D.C.: Woodrow Wilson Center, March 1992), 2.

95. See *The Gypsies of Eastern Europe,* ed. David Crowe and John Kolsti (Armonk, N.Y.: M.E. Sharpe, 1991); Otto Ulč, "Gypsies in Czechoslovakia: A Case of Unfinished Integration," *Eastern European Politics and Societies* 2 (1988): 306–32; David J. Kostelancik, "The Gypsies of Czechoslovakia: Political and Ideological Considerations in the Development of Policy," *Studies in Comparative Communism* 22/4 (1989): 307–23; Nicolae Gheorge, "Roman-Gypsy Ethnicity in Eastern Europe," *Social Research* 58 (1991): 829–44; and Luan Troxel, "Bulgaria's Gypsies: Numerically Strong, Politically Weak," *RFE/RL Research Report,* March 6, 1992, 58–61.

96. The countries were Azerbaijan, Armenia, Bulgaria, Georgia, Moldova, Romania, Russia, Turkey, and Ukraine.

97. FBIS-EEU-90–107, June 4, 1990, 42.

98. The following is based on Norman Naimark, "German-Polish Relations in the New Europe," typescript dated April 2, 1991, which I thank the author for providing.

99. For the treaties and associated speeches see "Das deutsch–polnische Vertragswerk," *Europa–Archiv* 13 (1991): D309–D334.

100. Adam Michnik, "Why I Won't Vote for Lech Wałęsa," *New York Times,* November 23, 1990, oped page. "Lech Wałęsa will not be president of a democratic Poland," Michnik wrote. "Rather, he will become a destabilizing factor, creating chaos and isolating Poland from the rest of the world."

101. Quoted by Louisa Vinton, "Solidarity's Rival Offspring: Center Alliance and Democratic Action," *Report on Eastern Europe,* September 21, 1990, 16.

102. On the entire electoral debate and outcome, see the excellent articles by David McQuaid: "The 'War' Over the Election Law," *Report on Eastern Europe,* August 2, 1991, 11–28; "The Political Landscape before the Elections," *Report on Eastern Europe,* October 18, 1991, 10–17; and "The Parliamentary Elections: A Postmortem," *Report on Eastern Europe,* November 8, 1991, 15–21.

103. Petŭr Beron, for example, former chairman of the UDF, considers the constitution balanced and fully in the tradition of Western constitutions (interview, March 17, 1992).

104. Rada Nikolaev, "The Bulgarian Presidential Elections," *RFE/RL Research Report,* February 7, 1992, 9–14.

Chapter 7

1. Stojan Cerović in *Vreme,* March 4, 1991, from FBIS EEU-91-051, March 15, 1991, 51. John Lampe reported that a friend in Yugoslavia put it this way: "Only the devil's own plan could have designed what we are now doing to ourselves, destroying in a few days what took decades, even centuries to build" ("Yugo-

slavia from Crisis to Tragedy," *East European Studies Newsletter,* Woodrow Wilson Center, Washington, D.C., November–December 1991).

2. The Slavic languages include Russian, Belorussian, Ukrainian, Polish, Czech, Slovak, Serbian, Croatian, Slovenian, Macedonian, and Bulgarian. The major non-Slavic languages of Eastern Europe include Greek, Hungarian, Romanian, and Albanian. The major non-Slavic languages among minorities are Yiddish, Turkish, and Romany. The Baltic languages (Estonian, Latvian, and Lithuanian) are not Slavic languages.

3. Milorad Ekmečić, *Ratni ciljevi Srbije 1914 [Serbian War Aims in 1914]* (Belgrade: Srpska književna zadruga, 1973), 88–89.

4. For an excellent discussion of this period see Ivo Banac, *The National Question in Yugoslavia: Origins, History, Politics* (Ithaca, N.Y.: Cornell University Press, 1984).

5. In Montenegro, the ousting of King Nikola by the unification party led to a revolt and civil war in 1919 and 1920, and to lasting antagonisms in the interwar years.

6. The decision provoked what amounted to a civil war, the echoes of which reverberated through the 1920s and beyond.

7. The Croatian Sabor (legislature) declared Croatia independent and joined forces with the National Council early in November, making Croatia independent for about a month in 1918. This had the effect of legitimizing the council's accession to the new Yugoslav state.

8. At the time of unification Aleksandar was technically prince regent for his father, King Petar, but he had acted as ruler in fact since 1914.

9. Herzegovina is the southwest portion of Bosnia and Herzegovina around the Neretva River. Its name derives from *Herzog,* the German term for "duke," but today simply denotes a geographical region.

10. The Serbian word for the region whose capital city today is Prishtinë (Priština, in Serbia) is *Kosovo,* with the accent on the first syllable. The Albanian word for it is *Kosovë,* with the accent on the second syllable (kos-OV-a). Even though 90 percent of the people who live there today are Albanians who prefer their own usage, I have used Kosovo throughout because it remains the accepted international name.

11. For a brief and balanced discussion of the Ustasha, including good estimates on how many Serbs and other persons died in Yugoslavia during World War II, see Aleksa Djilas, *The Contested Country: Yugoslav Unity and Communist Revolution, 1919–1953* (Cambridge, Mass.: Harvard University Press, 1991), 102–27.

12. Ivo Banac, *With Stalin against Tito: Cominformist Splits in Yugoslav Communism* (Ithaca, N.Y.: Cornell University Press, 1988).

13. Dennison Rusinow, *The Yugoslav Experiment 1948–1974* (Berkeley: University of California Press, 1977), 139.

14. See April Carter, *Democratic Reform in Yugoslavia: The Changing Role of the Party* (Princeton, N.J.: Princeton University Press, 1982); and Steven L. Burg, *Conflict and Cohesion in Socialist Yugoslavia: Political Decision Making since 1966* (Princeton, N.J.: Princeton University Press, 1983).

15. Carter, *Democratic Reform in Yugoslavia,* 19.

16. Burg, *Conflict and Cohesion,* 81.

17. Prof. Dr. Mihailo Djurić, speaking at the law faculty discussion of proposed constitutional amendments in March 1971, quoted by Dušan Bilandžić, *Ideje i praksa društvenog razvoja Jugoslavije* [Ideas and Practice: The Social Development

of Yugoslavia] (Belgrade: Komunist, 1973), 287–88. The 1971 discussion at the Belgrade Law Faculty was so volatile that the journal containing the discussion was banned (it was reprinted in 1990) and some faculty members were removed (Robert M. Hayden, "Recounting the Dead: The Rediscovery and Redefinition of Wartime Massacres in Late- and Post-Communist Yugoslavia," forthcoming in *Secret Histories: Memory and Opposition under State Socialism,* ed. Rubie S. Watson [Santa Fe, N.M.: School of American Research Press, 1993], typescript, 6).

18. Quoted by Burg, *Conflict and Cohesion,* 107.

19. "Matica" is difficult to translate. Literally it means "queen bee," but it has overtones of being the basis of something, of being fundamental. Nationalists might think of "Matica hrvatska" meaning something like "the institutional home of the Croatian national culture and spirit."

20. Dennison Rusinow, "Crisis in Croatia," in four parts, *American University Field Service Fieldstaff Reports, Southeast Europe Series,* 19/1: 15. Rusinow later regretted his use of the inflammatory word *fascist,* which obscured the less prejudicial comparison he had hoped to make.

21. Note that the phrase "the sovereign national state of the Croatian nation" would be offensive to the 600,000 Serbs living in Croatia.

22. Rusinow, *The Yugoslav Experiment,* 306. For this paragraph see Rusinow, 296–306.

23. The Yugoslav growth rate in the 1950s was about 7.5 percent per year, about one-third of which can be accounted for by aid from the United States (Bogdan Denitch, *Limits and Possibilities: The Crisis of Yugoslav Socialism and State Socialist Systems* [Minneapolis: University of Minnesota Press, 1990], 137).

24. Quoted by Desimir Tochitch, "Titoism without Tito," *Survey* 28/3 (Autumn 1984): 16.

25. For a succinct discussion of the Yugoslav economy as "polycentric etatism" with the same problems as other socialist states, see Evan Kraft, "Yugoslavia 1986–88: Transition to Crisis," in *Crisis and Reform in Eastern Europe,* ed. Ferenc Fehér and Andrew Arato (New Brunswick, N.J.: Transaction Publishers, 1991), 455–80.

26. Harold Lydall, *Yugoslavia in Crisis* (Oxford: Clarendon Press, 1989), 83–84. Lydall cites numerous other equally appalling examples.

27. Kraft, "Yugoslavia 1986–88," 471.

28. Estimates of the dead ranged from Senator Jesse Helms's propagandistic estimate of sixteen hundred to the probably too low official figure of nine (Elez Biberaj, "The conflict in Kosovo," *Survey* 28/3 [Autumn 1984]: 50).

29. For a good discussion of the scanty historical sources for this battle, which contemporaries barely knew happened and did not know who won, and of the creation of the legend, see Thomas A. Emmert, *Serbian Golgotha: Kosovo, 1389* (New York: East European Monographs, 1990).

30. This paragraph is based on Ivo Žanić, "Origins of Political Rhetoric Traced," a series of articles in *Polet,* April 21–May 1989, reprinted in JPRS-EER-89-092, August 17, 1989, 28–44. An example of a genuine epic slogan quoted by Žanić is *Oj, Srbijo / što ti lome krila. / Nisu smeli / dok si jaka bila* (Oh Serbia, / Why have they broken your wings? / They didn't dare / while you were strong). Here is a contemporary poetic description of Milošević arriving at Kosovo polje in April 1987: "But the handsome speaker arrives. / The setting sun sets his bristling hair on fire."

31. Žanić, "Origins of Political Rhetoric," 40. Dragisa Pavlović, an opponent

of Milošević's ousted in 1987, is also a severe critic of the Kosovo myth. "Defeat cannot be victory, no matter how great it was," he said. Pavlović sees Serbian salvation only in "a rational critique of the Kosovo myth as the traditional Serbian ideology and of every politics that would take it as its framework" (Dragiša Pavlović, *Olako obećana brzina* [Lightly Promised Speed] [Zagreb: Globus, 1988], 295).

32. For the 1953 figure, see George W. Hoffman and Fred Warner Neal, *Yugoslavia and the New Communism* (New York: Twentieth Century Fund, 1962), 31.

33. Says Serbian writer Milan Komnenić: "Kosovo is Serbia, and that is the way it has to be. If 20 some have fallen, tomorrow 20 times as many and 400 times as many must fall. We have to defend every foot of our territory, every foot of our spirituality. . . . This is the cherished center of our spirituality and our entire identity." Quoted in JPRS-EER-89-112, October 12, 1989, 19.

34. Mark Baskin, "Crisis in Kosovo," *Problems of Communism* 32 (March–April 1983): 65.

35. SANU—*Srpska akademija nauka i umetnosti* (The Serbian Academy of Arts and Sciences).

36. Quoted by Ivo Banac, "Yugoslavia: The Fearful Asymmetry of War," *Daedalus* 121/2 (Spring 1992): 150. See also the same author's "Political Change and National Diversity," *Daedalus* 119/1 (Winter 1990): 141–59; and "Post-Communism as Post-Yugoslavism: The Yugoslav Non-Revolutions of 1989–1990," in *Eastern Europe in Revolution,* ed. Ivo Banac (Ithaca, N.Y.: Cornell University Press, 1992), 168–87. These three articles provide a pungent and authoritative analysis of the Yugoslav situation in the late 1980s.

37. Slobodan Stanković, "The Serbian Academy's Memorandum," RFE, Yugoslav SR/11, November 20, 1986, 11.

38. For an excellent discussion of Milošević's seizure of power see Branka Magaš, "Yugoslavia: The Spectre of Balkanization," *New Left Review* 174 (1989): 3–31.

39. Pavlović, *Olako obećana brzina,* 308–9.

40. This quotation, as well as some biographical details in this paragraph, is taken from an excellent sketch of Milošević and the Serbian situation just before the outbreak of the civil war: Stephen Engelberg, "Carving out a Greater Serbia," *New York Times Magazine,* September 1, 1991. For a description of the April 24 events and an interesting formal talk by Milošević the next day, see FBIS-EEU-87-080, April 27, 1987.

41. Magaš quotes an article by three Milošević supporters, including the former *Praxis* philosopher Mihailo Marković, which claimed that the majority of Albanians were irredentists who wanted to set up an independent "bourgeois society governed by a pro-fascist right wing regime" ("Yugoslavia: The Spectre of Balkanization," 14).

42. Jović to the Serbian Assembly, March 28, 1989, FBIS-EE-89-058, March 28, 1989, 54.

43. See Carole Rogel, "Slovenia's Independence: A Reversal of History," *Problems of Communism* 40 (July–August 1991): 31–40.

44. Miha Kovač, "The Slovene Spring," *New Left Review* 171 (1988): 115–28.

45. For the programs of these parties as well as others, including the Croatian Democratic Union (HDZ), see JPRS-EER-89-077, July 7, 1989, 21–48.

46. They used the title "Majniška deklaracija," invoking by that archaic form

the May Declaration of 1917, in which Slovenian and Croatian deputies to the Austrian assembly called for the creation of a separate South Slavic unit in the Habsburg Empire (FBIS-EEU-89-096, May 19, 1989, 58–60).

47. Milan Andrejevich, "Slovenia's Alternative Political Groups," RFE, Yugoslav SR/12, December 23, 1988, 15–19.

48. Milan Andrejevich, "Slovenia's Alternative Political Groups," RFE, Yugoslav SR/3, February 24, 1989, 23.

49. Milan Andrejevich, "The Spectrum of Political Pluralism in Yugoslavia," RFE, Yugoslav SR/3, February 24, 1989, 4.

50. *Keesing's,* 36,900.

51. The most famous case concerned the failure of Agrokomerc, a huge company in Bosnia that left close to $1 billion of worthless notes behind. On trial for "counterrevolutionary activities," the director of Agrokomerc defended himself by arguing that what he was doing was common Yugoslav business practice.

52. Marković's estimate, FBIS-EEU-91-072, April 15, 1991.

53. For Jović's remark, see FBIS-EEU-91-062, April 1, 1991; for Pučnik's remark, see FBIS-EEU-91-060, March 28, 1991; and for further criticism by Jović, see FBIS-EEU-91-056, March 22, 1991.

54. See Dennison Rusinow, "To be or not to be? Yugoslavia as Hamlet," University Field Staff Report, Europe 1990–1991, no. 18 (June 1991).

55. *Keesing's,* 37,122.

56. The Fourteenth Congress reconvened in May 1990, but without the Slovenian, Croatian, or Macedonian representatives. Its call for a Fifteenth Congress, to meet in September, went unanswered.

57. Quotations from *Elections in Central and Eastern Europe* (Washington, D.C.: Commission on Security and Cooperation in Europe, 1990), 76.

58. CSCE report, *Elections in Central and Eastern Europe,* 74.

59. According to the *East European Newsletter* of March 24, 1990.

60. Serbian nationalists claim that Izetbegović is a Muslim fundamentalist on the basis of a short book he wrote and went to prison for in 1970 entitled *Islamic Declaration.* In this book he says such things as "establishing of an islamic order is . . . the ultimate act of democracy." On the other hand, he also says "islamic order may be implemented only in countries where Muslims represent the majority," which they do not in Bosnia and Herzegovina. Even though this book was republished in 1990, Izetbegović repudiated it and showed by his actions that he was interested in accommodation. I would like to thank Dr. Jelena Milojković-Djurić for the Izetbegović references. See Misha Glenny, "Yugoslavia: The Revenger's Tragedy," *New York Review of Books,* August 13, 1992, 37–43, and the exchange between Nora Beloff and Misha Glenny, *New York Review of Books,* October 8, 1992, 51–52.

61. Robert M. Hayden, "Constitutional Nationalism in the Formerly Yugoslav Republics," *The Slavic Review* 51(1992): 657. Slovenia and Macedonia introduced similar phrases into their constitutions. Serbia did not, but eliminated any provisions for self-rule in *Kosovë* and Vojvodina and in fact ran a strictly Serbian government. For an excellent discussion of the structural weaknesses of Croatian political culture that hindered a pluralistic response in 1990, see Vesna Pusić, "A Country by Any Other Name: Transition and Stability in Croatia and Yugoslavia," *East European Politics and Societies* 6/3 (Fall 1992): 242–59.

62. The term "genocide" has come easily to Serbian lips and pens during the Milošević era. Historians in particular have used it regularly, not just when referring

to the murders perpetrated by the Independent State of Croatia during World War II, where it is justified, but as the appropriate general term describing Croatian relations toward Serbs in Croatia over a hundred-year history. In 1989, when an assistant at Belgrade University was found to have published in 1971 a remark critical of the Serbian minority in Croatia in the nineteenth century, for example, he was fired in order to prevent him from spreading "the ideology of genocide" (FBIS-EER-90-023, February 21, 1990, 15). Dragoljub Živojinović and Dejan Lučić see the criticisms of Serbs by Catholics in Croatia on the occasion of the assassination of Franz Ferdinand in 1914 as "preparations for genocide" (*Varvar-stvo u ime Hristovo* [Barbarism in Christ's Name] [Belgrade: Nova knjiga, 1988], 52–54).

63. Milošević's speech of June 23, 1990, FBIS-EEU-90-123, June 26, 1990, 51.

64. Milan Vego estimated that 103 of the 140 general officers in the Yugoslav National Army and about 9,000 of the 12,100 other officers early in 1991 were Serbs or Montenegrin (talk at the Woodrow Wilson Center, Washington, D.C., April 9, 1991).

65. For some extracts from this document, see Banac, "Post-Communism as Post-Yugoslavism," 183–84.

66. For a balanced discussion of the escalation of violence and the early part of the civil war, see Misha Glenny, "The Massacre of Yugoslavia," *New York Review of Books,* January 30, 1992, 30–35.

67. See Hayden, "Recounting the Dead."

68. Two vigorous accounts of the Yugoslav disaster are Misha Glenny, *The Fall of Yugoslavia: The Third Balkan War* (New York: Penguin, 1992), and Mark Thompson, *A Paper House: The Ending of Yugoslavia* (New York: Pantheon, 1992).

69. For an analysis of U.S. policy see Paula Franklin Lytle, "U.S. Policy Toward the Demise of Yugoslavia: The 'Virus of Nationalism,'" *East European Politics and Societies* 6/3 (Fall 1992): 303–18.

70. Ivo Andrić, *Bridge on the Drina* (Chicago: University of Chicago Press, 1977, orig. pub. 1959).

Chapter 8

1. Here is how Václav Havel describes the differences he notices when coming from Germany into Czechoslovakia: In Germany "there are neat, well-kept fields, pathways, and orchards [in which] you can see . . . evidence of human care, based on respect for the soil. On the other side there are extensive fields with crops lying unharvested on the ground, stockpiles of chemicals, unused land, land crisscrossed with tire tracks, neglected pathways, no rows of trees or woodlots" ("A Dream for Czechoslovakia," *New York Review of Books,* June 25, 1992, 10).

2. Adam Michnik, "Nationalism," *Social Research* 58 (1991): 760.

3. Quoted by Timothy W. Ryback, "Report from Dachau," *The New Yorker,* August 3, 1992, 49.

4. For a fuller treatment of this point, see Gale Stokes, "Nationalism, Responsibility, and the People-as-one," forthcoming in *Studies in East European Thought.*

Index